HOW TO
COLLECT, REFINISH & RESTORE ANTIQUE & COUNTRY FURNITURE

BY H. H. DAMATO

TAB TAB BOOKS Inc.

BLUE RIDGE SUMMIT, PA. 17214

FIRST EDITION

FIRST PRINTING

Library of Congress Cataloging in Publication Data

Damato, H.H.
   How to collect, refinish and restore
antique and country furniture.

   Includes index.
   1. Antiques—Collectors and collecting—
Handbooks, manuals, etc. 2. Antiques—Con-
servation and restoration—Handbooks, manuals,
etc. 3. Country furniture—Collectors and
collecting—Handbooks, manuals, etc.
4. Country furniture—Repairing—Handbooks,
manuals, etc. I. Title.
NK1125.D24   749'.1'028   81-18381
ISBN 0-8306-1401-X (pbk.)   AACR2
ISBN 0-8306-0084-1

Contents

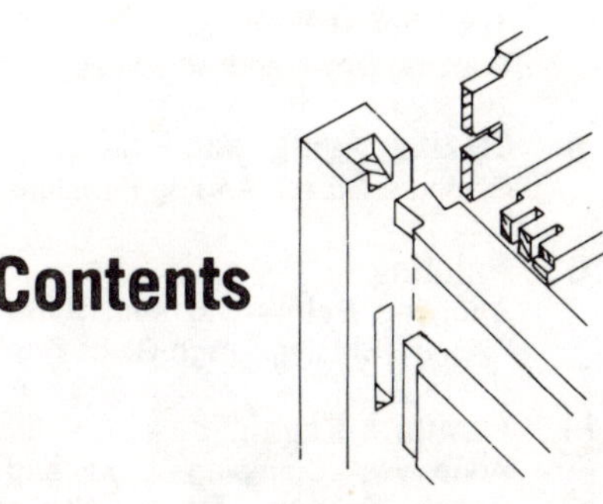

Introduction

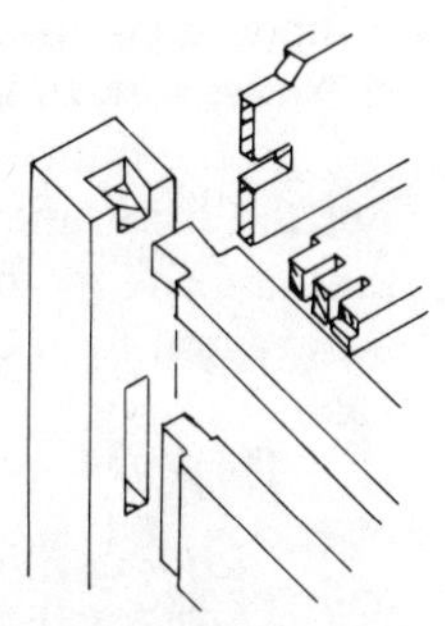

Collecting country antique furniture is romantic, exciting, and economically practical. There is something very special about sitting in a room filled with antique furniture and thinking how many Thanksgivings and Christmases the furniture has seen and what countless numbers of persons have shared moments of joy in its graceful presence. It is intriguing to realize how many others before you have used this furniture, and it is humbling to think how many will see it after you. Notions such as these are romantic; but, antique collectors are romantic—contriving candlelit interiors of gracious furnishings in subtle hues and mellowed patinas.

Collectors are often fascinated by the continuity of antique furnishings that link one time to another. Others appreciate the artistry, handiwork, individuality, and craftsmanship of a bygone era. For the collector, there is excitement in seeking out the treasures of the past. The antiquer dons the cloak of the detective and sifts through mazes of garage sales and rafters of old barns to ferret out the treasures of the past.

Antique furnishings are romantic and exciting, but they are also practical. The person who furnishes with modern, machine-made goods is making a depreciated purchase. The minute the furniture leaves the showroom it is worth less than what was paid. For that matter, it probably never was worth what was paid. Within a few years, the furniture is worth nothing save what it will fetch at a garage sale. Antique furnishings, unlike their modern cousins, will continue to appreciate in value. Most of us do not like to think of our antiques as commodities, but it is nice to know that the investment potential is there.

Not only is country antique furniture a better long-range investment over modern furniture, but it is also often a better initial purchase. An early 19th-century country cupboard can be obtained at a lower cost than a new pine hutch from a department store. Antique ladderback chairs can be purchased for less than their charmless, new, department store relatives.

In the future, country furniture will become more expensive. For the time being it is a good value. If you are willing to expend time and energy to purchase antiques in the rough, and provide your own restoration, then an otherwise good value can become a great value.

This book is directed to novices who are all too frequently overlooked. I have attempted to route the newcomer—in a simple and concise manner—around the painful pitfalls of collecting and restoring.

If you have not attempted a refinishing job prior to the purchase of this book, you might be intimidated by the prospect of possibly destroying an object of value. A little fear is a healthy thing, for it makes us cautious, but by and large there is not need to fear a refinishing job. The techniques presented in this book cover a broad range of activities and they are essentially simple and achievable.

There is, as a rule, someone you know—a friend, a relative or a neighbor—who impresses you with his or her jack-of-all-trades mechanical skills. The only difference between the majority of us and that unlimitedly talented person is courage. The talented person has the courage to try and the courage to accept failure. Courage alone does not lead to success, but it does lead to learning—which eventually leads to success. It is your choice as to whether or not to be this type of person.

If you attempt a project and find that you are in over your head, all is not lost. There is no reason why you cannot take a bag of labeled pieces to a restorer as easily as you can take an entire piece. Chances are that the restorer won't charge a penny more for the job (although there might be a few scolding words). Have confidence. Be the type of person who takes risks, and you will find that life has the potential to be a great deal more interesting.

Books on restoring antiques are not typically read in an evening like a good mystery; nor are they read cover to cover. I surely do not recommend that you read this book in one sitting unless you have some decidedly masochistic tendencies. Nevertheless, I do recommend that you read it from cover to cover prior to beginning your restoration work. By reading the entire book, you will be able to understand the range of your options regarding a particular piece.

The first three chapters deal with how and where to collect, furniture construction, and authentication. If you are only interested in refinishing a piece of furniture, then these chapters can be skipped. If you have any real interest in antiques, they should not be missed. The novice collector should find the first chapter particularly valuable with regard to avoiding dangerous mistakes made in collecting and purchasing. Chapter 2 and 3 contain information on construction methods of antique furniture and the telltale signs of age and wear. Collectively, these two chapters present a basis for authenticating antique furniture on your own. A great deal of factual material is presented. I recommend that you read these sections over a period of time, and that you read them more than once so that the information presented is at your command.

Chapters 4 through 10 deal with the actual methods of refinishing and surface restoration. This is the fun part. A natural tendency is to want to get started. Nevertheless, I urge just a little patience. To accomplish good work, you must avoid being locked into just one method or approach. Read all of the various methods so as to broaden your horizons. Chapter 11 delves into methods of repair. Even if you do not plan to do your own repair work, the information in this chapter will prepare you to intelligently discuss repair work with the restorer of your choice.

As you read this book, you will quickly realize that I am opinionated. There is no feigned attempt at objectivity here. I am sharing with you my knowledge and experience as well as my values regarding antiques. I do not apologize for having strong opinions. I do accept that others have conflicting, but equally valid opinions.

While necessity has forced me to postulate some rules and guidelines, I do recognize both the danger and weakness of all-encompassing rules. If I have made errors, I acknowledge and accept the responsibility. Every attempt has been made to direct the newcomer in a logical and constructive manner. I deeply hope that this goal is fulfilled.

Acknowledgments

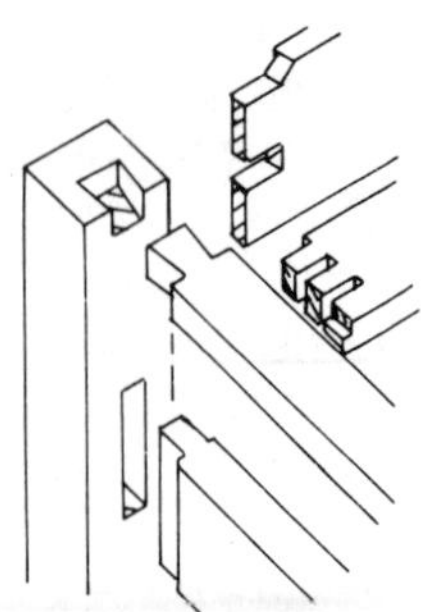

Some time ago, I decided to revise some odds and ends of furniture notes that I had distributed to friends. Through the encouragement of friends and associates, those few pages of notes evolved into this book.

There were many times during the preparation of the manuscript that the faith of others supplanted the faith that I was lacking. I am deeply appreciative of all the kindly people who offered support and listened with good humor to my daily complaints.

I would like to thank the people at TAB BOOKS Inc. for their equanimity in understanding problems related to deadlines.

In particular, I would like to thank Mr. James Conway and Ms. Kim Convicer for their help with the photo work.

More than anyone, I would like to thank G. Halina Damato for the preparation of the manuscript and for the encouragement and faith, without which none of this would have been possible.

Chapter 1
Country
Antique Furniture

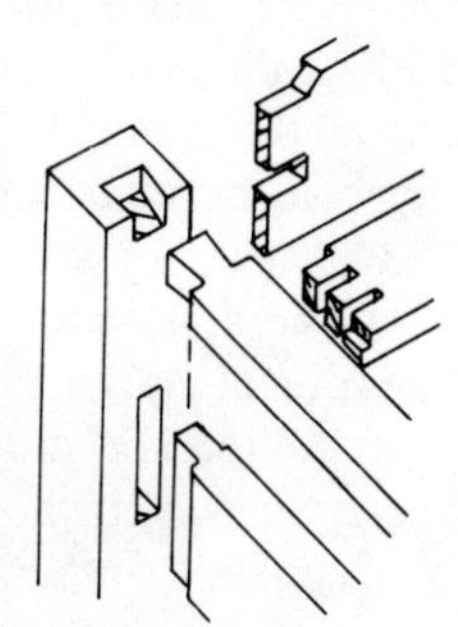

The world of antiques has a marvelous number of debates that tend to confuse the beginner while enticing the advanced collector. The important thing to remember is that these debates deal with opinions and not fact.

Given the title of this chapter, two questions come to mind. What is an *antique*? And what is *country*?

Currently, U.S. Customs Service, for the purpose of importation, considers any item 100 years of age or greater to be an antique. This is a rather simple definition for an antique. Nevertheless, it is one used in numerous antique shops around the country. Most furniture built 100 years ago is antique, but as time passes this definition will be grossly inadequate. It is hard to believe that the vinyl-covered, chrome-plated chairs that stood in a kitchen in 1950 might someday be viewed as valuable antiques. In 1950, these chairs were new junk. In 2050, I suspect they will be old junk!

Prior to the current 100-year ruling, the Customs Service considered an antique any item that was 100 years old as of approximately 1830. The logic of the earlier Customs Service ruling was that, prior to 1830, furniture was handmade by craftsmen. After 1830, it was machine made and mass produced. The earlier Customs Service decision gives us somewhat more to work with in that it suggests that *antique* is not merely a matter of age, but also a statement on the method of production. One problem with this latter definition is the erroneous assumption that 1830 was the year the handwork industry came to an end.

There is a pervasive myth in the antique world. This same myth can be found in many books and in some history texts. The myth has it that, some time in the first quarter of the 19th century, large-scale industrial mechanization was introduced in Britain and the United States. The simple truth of the matter is that the furniture industry did not, by and large, mechanize. It did not convert to mass production techniques until the latter part of the 19th century. If a collector does not dispell this myth, he is going to encounter some real difficulty when dating furniture. A presumption will be made that anything handmade was produced prior to 1830.

The distinction between antique and non-antique is not just a question of mechanization. It is also a matter of what mechanization represents. The difference is one of an old world, pre-industrial society based on hand modes of work versus a new, post-industrial, mechanized, consumer-oriented world. When I speak of antique furniture I am referring to furniture produced in the pre-modern society. The question of age with regard to antiques is not merely how long ago it was made, but rather during what age it was made.

If the criteria of handmade and pre-industrial are used for the purpose of defining antique furniture, there remain a few trifling problems to be conquered. Furniture made in the 20th century is generally not handmade or antique. When you consider the 19th century you run into a few problems. England and the United States had entered the industrial age by 1800 (and both were highly industrialized by 1870). Furniture making remained on a handwork basis for both countries from 1800 to 1850. In 1850, machine utilization accelerated. In the United States the acceleration was major while in England it was minor.

The implication for the antique collector is that if two pieces of furniture made in the same year in the same country are considered, one might be truly antique while the other might not.

For example, you might have a pine and maple washstand with four turned legs and a splashguard made in 1875 by a hand craftsman who had been working in a continuous tradition of handwork. Alongside of this antique washstand you have golden oak, two-door, rectangular washstand with a splashguard made in 1875 in a highly standardized, mechanized factory in Grand Rapids. If you choose the criterion of 100 years of survival, then both pieces are antique. If you choose to see an antique as a statement of hand craftsmanship of a bygone time, then only one item is an antique.

Having drawn out this somewhat elaborate distinction in definition, my preference should be clear. Nevertheless, I do not wish to demean early, mass-produced oak furniture. The oak furniture of the 1870-1920 period is attractive, well-constructed, important, valuable, and considered by many to be antique.

Don't throw away your thinking cap if you have settled upon a definition for antique. There is still the issue of what is and what is not *country*.

One of my greatest aggravations in life is to encounter a customer in an antique shop who, walking amidst a beautifully executed cherry drop-leaf table or a superbly crafted poplar corner cupboard, declares, "Look at all these primitives!" After hearing this comment a few thousand times, only the need to make a living and the law stand between the dealer and imminent hospitalization for the customer. (If the customer is 6 feet, 6 inches tall and 280 pounds, he is allowed greater latitude with his opinion!)

Furniture can be divided into any number of categories that have a logical basis such as large, small, plain, fancy, etc. Categorization is a basic process in communication. Keep in mind that most people agree about the general category while arguing considerably about the specifics. It would be difficult for a Pygmy to convince a New Yorker that anyone over 4 feet, 11 inches is tall.

Furniture can be divided into the following categories: *formal, country,* and *primitive*. Formal furniture consists of 18th- and 19th-century high-style furniture produced in fine cabinet woods such as walnut or mahogany. Formal furniture is presumed to have been made (usually in cities) by the finest craftsmen.

Country furniture draws from the same design influences as formal furniture, but it is designed along less sophisticated lines. In Philadelphia, you could have a fine pembroke table made in mahogany and beautifully banded and inlaid with holly that would be considered formal. You could have another pembroke table, made in western Pennsylvania, of the exact design and skill, made in walnut without inlay, and such a piece would be considered a country piece.

On the other hand, the plain walnut table could have been made in Philadelphia by the same cabinetmaker for a customer of lesser means or simpler taste. In this latter case, the table would still be considered a country piece. In general, *formal* implies city-made and well-made furniture of fashionable wood. The standard formal woods for the 18th and 19th centuries were walnut and mahogany. Pieces of maple and cherry can be high-style formal pieces, but more often than not they are considered country.

Country furniture refers to furniture of less sophisticated design made of local hard woods and soft woods such as maple, cherry, poplar, pine, etc. There is clearly a style distinction between formal furniture and country furniture, but this does not mean one is better than the other. The country cabinetmaker, though less influenced by the most recent fashions, still utilized basic and sound construction techniques. In some cases, the country cabinetmaker was less able to support himself by making furniture than his city counterpart. Consequently, he might also have been the local carpenter, coffin maker, general store proprietor, as well as a seasonal farmer. The many occupations of the country cabinetmaker—in contrast to the highly specialized city cabinetmaker—might have led to design simplicity, but not to inferiority.

Collectors should not rule out that cabinetmaking, like any other occupation in the city or country, had its share of hacks who produced consistently poor furniture. There is more well-made antique furniture around than poorly made furniture because well-made furniture survives. Nonetheless, there is a liberal supply of inadequate furniture still around.

The third category of furniture is called *primitive*. In modern American society, the word primitive tends to evoke some negative connotations. With regard to furniture, some people envision primitive in terms of a half-crazed plainsman, dressed in animal skins cowering in a dimly lit cave, hacking at a log with a dull rock in an attempt to make a bowl. Some 6 to 10 thousand years ago, this *would* have been primitive. This concept of primitive, when applied to the 18th and 19th centuries, is erroneous and dumb.

Primitive, whether applied to furniture or any other endeavor, implies that it is basic. Primitive furniture was the furniture made by the non-professional for his own use and according to his skills. In a contemporary sense, primitive connotes handyman or do-it-yourselfer. Such furniture runs the gamut from simple and functional to over ambitious and pompous. The handyman of the 18th century and early 19th century did not have the option or the money to purchase furniture and utensils from a local retailer. Therefore, he tended to be somewhat less specialized than the modern worker.

In general, primitive furniture tends to be quite simple. Nailed rebate construction and an occasional mortise and tenon are used as opposed to the professional cabinetmaker's work which tends to use dovetailed or mortise and tenon construction throughout. When the lower range of country merges with the upper range of primitive, it is quite impossible to decide which is which. You can take pot luck when deciding which is the work of the talented amateur or untalented professional.

There is a growing tendency on the part of collectors and

dealers to lump country and primitive into the primitive category. I take strong exception to this trend; it is misleading and contradictory.

Another form of categorization, *chronological,* is the distinction between centuries. The concept of a century as a category is just as contrived and debatable as any other category. When speaking chronologically, there is no difficulty. The 18th century is 1700 to 1800 and the 19th century is 1800 to 1900. Historically, the matter becomes somewhat cloudy because historians perceive events not only in their chronological order, but also in the relationship that they have to each other. Some historians consider the 18th century as concluding approximately in 1790 with the French Revolution. Others think it concludes in the vicinity of 1825. We will let the historians have their debate. For our purposes, 1825 makes a better dividing line than 1800 for the 18th and 19th centuries.

In the 18th century, the categories of formal, country, and primitive apply. But there are more specific distinctions or sub-categories based on wood or style. Examples are the Walnut period, the Mahogany period, the Queen Anne period, the Chippendale period, etc. The style periods existed throughout the 18th century and into the first quarter of the 19th century. The Hepplewhite and Sheraton periods marked the end of the rigorously defined and executed styles. Returning to the classifications of formal and country, for period determination the collector will find that country designs are mostly a matter of simplified formal designs.

In the 19th century (after 1825), something very important and different occured. Formal furniture, in what are described as the Empire and Victorian periods, broke radically with the designs of earlier formal furniture. The furniture of these periods became highly ornamented and the look was often confused. In the 1825-1875 period, country furniture ceased to be a simplified reflection of formal furniture. Simplicity of design continued more in accord with the prior century.

Quite simply, when studying 18th-century furniture one studies the formal and in so doing studies country. In the 19th century, the study of formal and country entails basically two different studies. A definition of *country furniture* would read as follows. Country furniture is soundly, professionally made furniture that is functional and aesthetically pleasing. The design of this furniture was influenced by regional considerations as well as by the prevailing urban styles and tastes.

A frequently asked question of the novice collector is, "How should I go about the study of antiques?" There is no set path to this destination. I can, however, make some definite recommendations.

First, purchase a copy of a good antique picture book of traditional 18th-century furniture such as Wallace Nutting's *Furniture Treasury*. There is probably no better source for this purpose than the book by Nutting. Work with this basic antique book until you can distinguish the various style periods. At this point, you should not be worried about what is or is not original nor should you be attempting to tell the difference between regional styles. When somewhat comfortable with the different styles, proceed to the nearest large museum with an American furniture collection so that you can take a look at the real thing. Don't despair if you are not located near a large population center. In most areas of the country, there are community or state historical societies that maintain historical restorations with limited furniture collections. If all else fails, plan your next vacation to an area with a good museum.

The next step is to review books on country furniture. To date, most books on American country furniture are not very comprehensive. Your best bet is to use a library. Ralph and Terry Kovel's *American Country Furniture 1780-1875* is a fine source. Undoubtedly, you will begin to see design relationships between traditional formal furniture and country furniture. In time, these relationships will become clearer.

For your country furniture practicum, you will gain more by traveling to local antique shops than you will by visiting museums. The majority of available country furniture tends to be 19th-century furniture and it is not as yet well represented in museums. Local historical societies and historical restorations, such as Sturbridge Village in Sturbridge, Massachusetts, provide excellent examples of country furniture.

When the study course is completed, the novice collector will be able to tell what an antique piece of furniture looks like. Nevertheless, he might not know whether or not the piece is really antique.

IGNORANCE, ANTIQUES, AND THE CONSUMER

Charles Dickins wrote in *A Tale of Two Cities*, "It was the best of times and the worst of times." What does that have to do with antiques? Well, there are the best of dealers and the worst of dealers. Unfortunately, the latter far outnumber the former. The antique business often depends upon the ignorance of the customer.

There are many honest, expert, and professional dealers who

will not lead the collector astray. There are probably a greater number of dealers who will knowingly and purposely misrepresent their merchandise. The most prolific category of dealers includes those who have little knowledge of the quality or authenticity of their merchandise. This last category is the "looks good" dealer. They most often assess a piece on the basis of "it's got the right look and the right feel." The "looks good" dealer will resist knowledge on the basis that if he doesn't know the truth, then he is not lying to you.

Typical mottoes or philosophies of the shoddy dealer are, "Make up a story," "Tell them what they want to hear," and, "Don't put anything in writing." When questioned about the inconsistencies of a piece, this type of dealer will often respond, "I don't know—that's the way I got it."

There are good dealers and bad dealers. Where does that put the collector? For one thing, you can consider the reputation of a dealer. There are a small number of dealers with a national reputation. If you spend any time at all reading antique periodicals, you will quickly find these dealers mentioned time and time again. With these dealers, you can anticipate honesty and professionalism. Such famous dealers number only a fraction of the total dealers and they offer a range of goods priced beyond the means of the average collector.

It is far more common for a dealer to be known by word of mouth or by the number of advertisements placed in local periodicals. A local reputation can be two-sided. People tend to confuse exclusivity with quality. Likewise, people rarely demean their own decisions once made. Consequently, they might eagerly recommend someone who sells questionable goods. A good local reputation might or might not be accurate. As a rule, however, it is a safer practice to purchase from someone who has a good reputation.

Another factor to be considered in evaluating a dealer is the test of time. There is wisdom in doing business with a dealer who will be there next month and preferably for years to come. The dealer with longevity has a vested interest in his product; dubious sales can haunt the future. Longevity is a good characteristic, but, similar to a good reputation, it can be deceptive. I know of a dealer in 18th-century English furniture who has been in the business for at least 20 years. On successive visits to this shop I have rarely found a piece that has not been tampered with. This dealer proudly proclaims that pieces are made ready for the selling floor in his own workshop upstairs. The reality appears to be that they are created in his workshop!

If this view of the antique world seems bleak, just accept that the best source of protection is personal knowledge and experience. The knowledge required to safely make purchases cannot solely be based on the identification of the proper style or your intuition and personal taste. The wise collector should have a basic concept of historical furniture construction as well as a working knowledge of the impact of wear and age.

PURCHASING COUNTRY ANTIQUES

The novice collector will probably make purchases while still in the early learning stages. Good judgment argues against this action, but we don't always make objective and logical decisions. There are a number of reasons for buying country antique furniture. The most important reason should be that it appeals to you.

Past the point of aesthetic appeal, country furniture is a good buy and a judicious investment. When it comes to price, antiques are a matter of supply and demand. New pieces are constantly being introduced into the marketplace. The history of the antique trade is one of increasing demand. Limited supply with increasing demand invariably means continued increases in prices. This rather simplistic economic formula has resulted in eliminating the collector with an average income from the world of traditional formal antique furniture. In the world of formal furniture, only the mediocre and dubious are found in the modest price range.

The future in formal antiques appears to be dismal. This is not the case with country furniture. Country furniture has only come into vogue during the decade of the '70s. Consquently, supply is larger and demand has yet to peak. The supply of country furniture is not only greater in relative quantity, but also in absolute quantity. The majority of country pieces available was produced in the 1775-1875 period. Not coincidently, the populations of both England and the United States more than doubled in this period. At the minimum, you can presume more than double the furniture was made in the 19th century as opposed to the 18th century. Yet the growth was much greater than that due to the ability of the 19th-century citizen to purchase more than his ancesters could.

Mindful of the law of supply and demand, many a collector—when attempting to sell a recently acquired piece—has been disappointed to find that he is offered less for it than he paid for it. This type of occurrence might appear to be a contradiction, but it is not.

An antique has a wholesale price, a market price, and a retail price. The wholesale price is what a dealer pays for a piece. The market price is, generally, the average price paid for the piece throughout the country. The wholesale price paid by the dealer might be more or less than the market price, but it should not deviate too far from it. The retail price, of course, is the price paid by the consumer.

The important thing to understand is that the real price or value of the antique is not the retail price, but the market price. The antique dealer, not unreasonably, must build into his price the cost of restoration, overhead, and profit on his initial investment.

When an antique is purchased at a retail price, it must appreciate in value an amount equal to the markup before its real value equals the retail price. The process is analgous to a mortgage on a house; the interest must be paid before the principle. When an antique is bought at retail price, it will, under most circumstances, take several years for it to equal the price paid and several years added to that for it to be worth more.

From a purely economic point of view, it is less expensive to go to the source than to buy from a dealer. When a collector goes directly to the source, he assumes the same risks as a dealer. The antique purchased might require more restoration than the collector can provide or, worse, the antique might not be antique. When a dealer makes a mistake, he can distribute the cost among other items. The dealer can also market the mistake as an attractive piece of furniture.

The collector who frequents only dealers should not be criticized. He is merely pursuing a conservative course of action with less involvement and lower risk. Even the more adventurous collector, who competes at the source level, will sooner or later purchase from a dealer if for no other reason than because the dealer has something the collector cannot find elsewhere.

When shopping for antiques, there are some definite do's and don'ts: Don't be timid! Do ask questions! Don't forget that you have common sense! Remember at all times that when spending your money you have a right to accept or reject and that there is no need to impress the seller. I know of a contrary fellow who noticed that his friends put on their Sunday best when they were out to make a major purchase. Thereafter, he put on his grubbies when spending big money. The contrary fellow didn't necessarily make out any better with his purchases, but he sure had a lot of self respect.

Timidity has been the ruin of many a good person, and, to be sure, it will not carry you far in the antique world. A collector should have no reluctance about asking a dealer to review a piece. He should ask him to do so. When a dealer reviews the piece, ask logical questions—not to impress the dealer—to enhance your knowledge. In brief, turn each purchase or potential purchase into a learning experience. If a dealer states something that seems to be in contradiction to what you have learned elsewhere, you must question and challenge in modest fashion. The key to this process is tact. If your manner of questioning suggests that the seller is either disreputable or a misinformed idiot, then you really can't expect a positive response.

When reviewing a piece, do not lose sight of your common sense or reasonable, healthy skepticism. I was recently told that a novice collector, when looking over a wood winder, questioned the dealer as to why there was an incised VIII on the winder. The dealer responded that the maker dated the piece to show that it was made in the 18th century.

Pause a second and consider if that sounds reasonable. Does it seem a little silly? If not, then ask yourself, if someone were going to put a date on a piece, would they not at least put XVIII for 18 and not just VIII for eight? If questioned further, perhaps the dealer would have said that the eight was for the eighth day of the eighth month of the eighth year! No matter how you look at it, this is known as a "snow job."

You don't need specific experience or knowledge of antiques to see the obvious. Given just a bit of knowledge, the task becomes simpler. Very little furniture in the 18th century or 19th century was inscribed with a date. When a date is found, it will almost certainly be in Arabic numerals and not Roman numerals. Craftsmen did not mark their work in the context of centuries. Pieces, when dated, are not dated by century. On the other hand, cabinetmakers often numbered pieces that looked similar, but had to be individually fitted. The rails of beds are often numbered to indicate which bedboard was attached to which. When numbering pieces for assembly, the cabinetmaker would use slash marks or Roman numerals that could easily be made by a chisel.

When questioning a dealer, it is also fair game to assess the attitude of the dealer. When answering questions, is the dealer easy and accommodating or does he become defensive? A dealer can be defensive for a number of reasons. Nevertheless, it isn't a good sign.

In defense of dealers, it is acceptable for them to indicate that they do not know, or at best, that they can offer a highly opinionated and conditional response. The vast quantity of country antiques available has no family histories (or *provenance* as it is known in the trade). Consequently, dealers are working in an area of little certainty. With most pieces, a dealer or a knowledgeable collector can make a series of sound deductions as well as a series of conditional deductions.

When it comes to deductions, the ones made with regard to age are often the weakest. When people shop for antiques they are all too often mystified by the dates: a cupboard made in 1825, a chest made in 1780, etc. Such dates are great, but I can't help but wonder how the dates are determined.

Bascially, there are only two ways to date an antique to a specific year. The first method is when the antique is signed and dated; that is not common and it is often dubious. The second method of specific dating involves having a purchase receipt or a family record that indicates when the piece was made. Records such as these exist only for a fractional percentage of antiques. Therefore, most dating for a specific year is bunk! To be sure, when you encounter a specific date, ask how it was arrived at.

It is far more common to find a piece dated *circa*. Circa literally means approximation. In the trade, it is often assumed to mean plus and minus 20 years. I believe furniture is best dated in terms of quarter century units or thirds of a century. For example, consider a pine chest of drawers that has been handmade with the exception of the drawers (which exhibit early machine-made bullet dovetails). On the early side, you don't tend to find machine-made dovetails prior to 1850. On the far end, the use of pre-modern nails and other items make it unlikely that this hypothetical chest was made after 1875.

Some dealers would choose to date this piece circa 1850. The chest could equally be marked circa 1875. That would have less sales appeal than circa 1850. Applying the 20-year rule to both these dates could be misleading. Even a mid-point dating of circa 1862 could be misleading. If the chest were dated by quarters of a century, then the date would be expressed as "third quarter of the 19th century."

This latter approach would most adequately express the assumptions made regarding the age of the piece. It is more common to find pieces dated in larger units such as the last quarter of the 18th century, the first half of the 19th century (1775-1850), the first three-quarters of the 19th century (1800-1875), or, the first third of the 19th century (1800-1835). A collector should not be dismayed by dating in larger time blocks. They usually represent a realistic approach to dating antique furniture.

Collectors have a discouraging, but understandable tendency, to equate quality with early dating. Good is not a function of age; good is not 1725; good is quite simply good. When purchasing antiques, your first concern should be appeal. Secondly, be concerned with the quality of the piece. If it is an 1875 chest, is it exceptional, good, or mediocre? Is the piece what it represents itself to be? Has the chest been overly restored? Is it a new piece that has been aged or a different piece reworked? The age of a piece is of a lesser concern than these qualitative judgments. Then again, we have a late 17th-century desk that we are just wild about.

To make a reasonable evaluation of a piece of antique furniture, you should examine it to the point of molestation. All antique dealers object to their pieces being manhandled. Most do accept that a piece has to be moved around or turned upside down for examination. If a dealer objects to the examination of a piece, there is little that can be done other than to look for another dealer. Strangely enough, no matter how carefully a piece is examined, the purchaser will find things at home he did not see in the shop. The moral here is that there is no such thing as over examination.

In the process of review with the dealer, the question of repairs should be answered. The collector will have to decide the importance of these repairs. The traditional rule of thumb in the antique business has been that repairs in excess of 10 percent are unacceptable; the piece is no longer considered to be an antique. That rule is accepted by a number of collectors. I think it is patent nonsense.

If you were to find a charming gate-leg table base, the top having been lost in the sands of time, what do you do with it? A purist is likely to say to keep the table base the way it is and appreciate it. If you are the type of collector who uses antiques, you are going to have one heck of a time putting your cup of coffee down.

A realist would say to put a new top on the table and make it functional. You might appreciate furniture as a work of art and as an historical artifact, but you shouldn't forget that it is still furniture. The replacement of the top is not a random process. The restorer should spend some research time to determine what type of top would be historically accurate. The replacement should be made in such a way as not to harm the originality of the base.

The table top would be more than 10 percent of the table; therefore, the table is no longer antique by the 10 percent rule. This is unreasonable. The table base was antique and remains antique. The table base was valuable and remains valuable. And it will most likely have increased its market value with the top replacement. If you have any doubts on this subject, purchase a catalog to an antique furniture sale from one of the fine New York auction houses. In any given Americana sale, you will find pieces with replaced tops and sundry other restorations. The restoration does affect the value of the piece and it should become a negotiating factor with the seller.

The 10 percent rule has some inadequacies. This does not mean that there is no such thing as over restoration or just plain fraud. In the case of a gate-leg table, if at the outset the restorer had two table legs and a few stretchers that he duplicated to complete the base (and subsequently created a new top), then the table would not be an antique. With this example, you have a highly restored table, but not an antique table. The resurrected table will have value as a piece of furniture, perhaps a good piece of furniture, but you should not pay "antique prices" for it. A collector can choose to be snobbish about this type of restoration, but sometimes these pieces have much more character than a new reproduction and they can be used to inexpensively fill out a collection.

There are honest restorations, that should be clearly marked, and then there are attempts at pure fraud. I know of one "antique creator" who takes large antique, dovetailed wood boxes, cuts them into bench seats, and places a nifty price tag on them. There is a shop in Pennsylvania that takes washstands and splits them in two. Each washstand gets two legs and two stretchers; one gets the top and the other gets the splashguard and shelf. Even the drawer parts might be divided up. The missing parts are duplicated and, presto-chango, you have two antique washstands. I could go on at length about this type of dishonesty, but it's too depressing.

There are a number of shoddy restoration or modification practices which, unfortunately, occur on more than a casual basis. There is no pat rule that will help the collector to discover this shoddiness. Only careful observation and personal knowledge can help. For an evening of fantasy detection, look through an antique book and envision what some pieces could be made into.

From time to time, you might encounter the term *marriage*. A marriage is no more than a restoration using antique parts such as by matching odd bottoms with odd tops. Married pieces receive preferential treatment over those restored with new parts. There is, however, no reason in most cases to value them any higher. I have often found that married pieces have proportion problems. When repairing with new parts, the restorer can balance the parts to the general proportion of the piece, but old parts are used "as is" to maintain their integrity. In the past, married pieces were considered disreputable. In recent years, they have unashamedly entered the marketplace and they can be found in the best auctions. Marriages tend to be more in the domain of formal furniture, but they can be found in country furniture. Some marriages can be extremely well executed. Observation is the key word.

Returning to the environs of the antique shop and your intended purchase, you have found a piece that serves a functional need or one that beckons to you with wanton abandon. You have ruthlessly examined the piece and noted all the inconsistencies. Subsequently, you question the dealer about the inconsistencies or doubts. You have judged the response of the dealer as reasonable and learned, uninformed, or bunk. In addition, you have asked the dealer for his considered opinion of the merits of the piece, as well as the national origin of the piece.

The matter of national origin is not one of subtle importance. We have no inhibitions about adding an English or European piece to our collection. If you are intent upon collecting and paying for American pieces, you should not be led astray. For the most part, 19th-century American country furniture is singular enough to prohibit European substitutions, but there is a fair amount of English pine and even some Spanish that could pass for American. Once you get a feel for English furniture, there should be no problem. English pine, which interestingly enough was mostly imported from the Balkans, has a look that is straight grained and even. Discerning the differences in 18th-century furniture, especially in the formal styles, is much harder.

With the other questions answered, there remain two important issues: price and receipt. A good shop has all the pieces tagged with the price. Nevertheless, many shops do not price their items. If a piece is marked, you know if it is in your budget range and you have a base point for negotiation.

Many shops (but not all) build a negotiation factor into the price. There is only one way to find out and that is to ask. Some collectors are embarrased by a haggling process; they really shouldn't be. A dealer is not going to give anything away. If there is a built-in negotiation factor, you will only be getting discounted what the dealer planned for in the first place.

Generally, the dealer has a fixed bottom price that he will not dip below. There will be times when he will be inclined to drop the price even lower. If a collector is buying several pieces, a dealer might negotiate a little more. If a piece has been on the floor for a long while, a dealer might drastically cut the price for turnover. Sometimes, you can save by purchasing at the end of a month. If a dealer has had a poor month, he might negotiate a better price for the cash flow. All businesses suffer seasonal fluctuations. Find out what the cycle is in your area and attempt to purchase in slow months such as January.

A common way to find out if a dealer will negotiate is to say, "Are you prices firm?" Another standard and equally polite phrase is, "Can you do a little better on this?" or, "Is this your best price?" It is acceptable to make a direct offer such as, "Will you take X dollars for this?" If a direct offer is unrealistic or made with arrogance, you can anticipate a similar response. Antique dealers, like most people, will respond to courtesy.

Some dealers might complicate the negotiations a little bit in response to a request for a better price by saying, "Make me an offer." In this event, make a very low offer. The dealer might respond. "I couldn't take less than X dollars." In that case, you have established the base for negotiation. The dealer might also have responded, "No, I've got more money than that tied up in it." In that case, you return the ball to the home court by saying, "What did you have in mind." Once you start playing the negotiation game, it will become easier and easier; it might even become fun. Remember, some dealers will not negotiate and this does not necessarily mean you will be paying more money.

Once a price is agreed upon, the process should be over. But there might still be a pitfall. Do not fail to get a proper receipt. Many shops do not provide a proper receipt. A receipt is not a foolproof method of staving off fraud, but it is one of the few methods available to you. If you find that you have been sold bad goods, you will have no legal recourse without a proper receipt. To accept a purchase without a receipt is to be foolish; to purchase from a dealer who refuses to give a recept is to be a fool.

What is a proper receipt? To start with, the receipt should be on a formal invoice or receipt pad. If this is lacking, a plain piece of paper is acceptable. The receipt should be imprinted with the name of the shop or the dealer. You might be amused by this simplicity, but in recent years the majority of shops I have found issuing receipts fail to have their name on the receipts. If a dealer is using a standard drug store variety receipt pad with no imprint, simply ask him to write in the information. The receipt should be dated and invoiced to you. Once the bill head is completed, proceed to the statement of goods.

The language of the statement will be considered precise. Examine it carefully. The goods should be described in writing just as they were verbally. For example, if a table has been described to you as an 18th-century, country Hepplewhite, drop-leaf table, but the receipt just says "drop-leaf table," then you are in trouble. According to the receipt you have bought a table. It need not be old, antique, or valuable. In all cases, the dealer should state the age of the piece as he described it to you.

When writing a receipt, there are key words like "possibly," "probably," or "in the style of." When a dealer stated "probably" it means just that, *probably*, and you should understand it as such. Realistically, there might be no other course of action than to describe something as probable. Take, for example, a wooden bowl. The bowl is lathe turned, cracked from shrinkage, stained and marred from years of service. It looks like bowls that have been positively identified as 19th century. Without documentation, there is no dealer who can positively identify the age of the piece. In such a case, it is fairly described as "probable 19th-century origin." The use of the word "possible" offers you considerably less certainty. If a desk is listed as "18th century, possible New England origin," what does it mean? What origin is not possible? Generally, when a dealer uses the term "possible" it implies that there is something about the piece that suggest what is possible.

It is not uncommon to find a piece described as "in the style of" Queen Anne, Chippendale, Hepplewhite, etc. These references are to formal style periods and should not deeply concern you when you are considering country furniture. You should be aware of what they mean. Pieces presumed to have been made during the style periods and in accordance with the style are simply described as a Queen Anne lowboy or Hepplewhite secretary. When a piece is described as "in the style of Queen Anne," it means that it was made at some time other than in that style period. The piece could be a valuable 19th-century antique made in the manner of the 18th century, or it could be a relatively worthless 20th-century piece. Whenever a collector encounters this phrase, he should immediately lift his defenses and begin to question.

I cannot emphasize strongly enough the value of a receipt while acknowledging the weaknesses of it. You are paying for the professionalism and expertise of a dealer represented formally in the written receipt. If a dealer refuses to provide a receipt, you must surely question his expertise or motives. If you accept a purchase without a receipt, you are surely defeating your own purposes.

You should also feel free to ask the dealer what his policy is in the event of a dispute over the merchandise. A good shop will give a full refund either in cash or credit in the event of this type of problem. When returning a piece, it is not sufficient to indicate that you don't think it is authentic or that a knowledgeable friend told you so. It will, under most circumstances, take an expert to convince a dealer that he has made a mistake. Even then, it might be difficult if the dispute is one of subtle differences.

A dealer should be easily convinced if it is a matter of outright misrepresentation. Nevertheless, you might have to be prepared to take him to small claims court if you meet with resistance. One obstacle you can anticipate in dealing with matters of misrepresentation is the reticense of other dealers. Few dealers want to aggrevate their neighbors in the trade by disputing their merchandise. A collector will usually do better if he seeks out a reputable appraiser whose livelihood is not dependent upon sales.

It is extremely difficult to discuss, in capsule form, the pitfalls that a novice collector should avoid in an antique shop. There is the possibility of creating the impression that all dealers are green-eyed monsters waiting to devour helpless folk and children. Antique dealers are passionately involved in the entire arena of antiques; they resurrect treasures, stimulate interest and educate. In brief, dealers do many good things and many good people are dealers. For the collector, the task at hand is to learn how to tell the difference between good and bad.

AUCTION ADVENTURES

Antique shops are usually wonderful places that are clean, lit, organized, and staffed with people who can answer questions. Auctions are rarely organized, infrequently clean places where few questions are asked or answered. Why should a collector go to an auction? Auctions are places to save money and compete with dealers for the best merchandise. Auctions are also exciting and fun. It is where you can lose your shirt, socks, shoes and undies!

Country auctions are remarkably the same whether antiques or farm tools are being sold. If you have been to one such auction, you will feel comfortable at another. Your first task is to locate an auction. You can ask a local antique dealer, but they tend to be a little protective about their sources.

The best way to find local auctions is the newspaper. Most auctioneers advertise in major newspapers within the state and several out-of-state newspapers (depending upon how large the state is). Check your newspaper and ask friends and relatives to look in their papers for you. Once you get a process like this started, you will be surprised by the stream of phone calls. Other sources of information include the sundry antique newspapers and trade journals found around the country. Trade papers advertise auctions from coast to coast. Once auctions are located, patrons can request that the auctioneers place them on mailing lists for routine notifications of sales.

Country auctions might or might not be held on a routine basis. Some auctions are weekly or bimonthly; other auctions might be regularly scheduled three, four, or five times a year. Some auctioneers plan a sale after they have acquired enough merchandise. Consequently, they can have no regular schedule and the auctions might be held at different locations throughout the year.

You might encounter an auction house that has a weekly sale featuring assorted household contents and an antique auction once a month. There are numerous auction arrangements, but none are really complicated. You just have to find out which suit your taste.

If you have never been to an auction, start with one featuring household goods. These auctions are known as junk auctions in the trade, but they are good places to get a sense of how an auction works. Junk auctions usually have an auctioneer whose wit is better than the merchandise. This can provide the entire family an evening of inexpensive fun.

Theoretically, all auctions have a *preview*. This is a period of time when all the merchandise is placed out on display for examination. Large or special auctions might schedule a preview for an entire day or two prior to the sale. The average country auction displays merchandise an hour or two prior to the sale. I use the word "theoretically" because of the differences found in the displaying of merchandise.

A really good antique auction has each piece identified with a lot number or inventory number and set out with space on all sides so that examination is possible. The majority of country auctions, however, have the pieces stacked floor to ceiling and three deep to the wall. To see all the merchandise in this type of arrangement would take a dentist mirror, X-ray vision, and the flexibility of Houdini.

Antique shops are clean places; auctions are not. Put on work shoes and grubbies and be prepared to work. Work shoes are not offered as an incidental recommendation. You might well have to climb to examine a piece. Little-known facts about country auctioneering are that it rains during two out of three auctions and that they all have muddy parking lots.

If proper examination are the watchwords for the antique shop, then it is doubly so for an auction—but it is also 10 times as difficult. The volume of articles alone precludes careful examination of everything for either the novice or the professional. You must be selective to be successful. Make a first pass through the auction and identify all the pieces that you might be interested in. Then make a second pass for detailed examination.

Don't be afraid to lift and rearrange to get to something that you are interested in. Auctioneers are far less sensitive than dealers when it comes to the matter of examination. You need not be inhibited; however, no one approves of manhandling. Pedestrian traffic is difficult in these usually tight places. You might be pressured by other collectors to move on or move out of the way. Hold your ground as best you can and exercise good judgment.

The furniture that you encounter at the country auction will, for the most part, be in rough condition as found in the barn, basement, or farm yard. If you give a minute's thought to what kind of furniture is relegated to the basement, you will have some idea of what "rough" means. The furniture you encounter might be falling apart, broken or have pieces missing.

At an auction, you will have to develop a sense for what is repairable by you or a professional. You will also need a rough estimate as to what the cost of repair might be. This estimation of cost must play an important part in the bidding process. For the most part, repair problems are simple glue jobs. For the more advanced home craftsperson, the auction might offer some wonderful buys by way of badly damaged, but worthwhile antiques.

It is not uncommon to find restored and refinished pieces at an auction—but be wary. Refinishing can hide a multitude of sins. Additional attention should be given to these pieces. Over the years, the majority of refinished pieces I have encountered at auctions have been fudged in one way or the other. One of the real advantages of buying at auction is the opportunity to get a piece "as found" before someone has fussed with it.

A piece in the rough offers the best opportunity to ascertain what the piece is, or is not, as well as what has happened to it over the years. Occasionally, you will find a knocked-together piece in the rough put up from old boards with old nails. These aren't terribly common and they are not hard to detect. The real difficulty with buying in the rough is developing the ability to see the proverbial diamond. You must be able to look at a piece of furniture through five coats of paint and several repairs so that your mind's eye visualizes the potential.

This might sound easy, but it is most definitely not. Many a novice collector will pass up a fine piece as well as a fine bargain due to an inability to visualize the final product. There is only one prescribed course of action to develop this technique and that is practice and more practice. If you are an adventurous collector who refinishes and restores your own pieces, the process will be speeded up considerably.

Antique auctions require that you register. If you have never been to an auction before, don't be alarmed. It is a simple process. A registration desk will be signposted. You need merely provide your name and address and some identification. Once you have registered, you will be issued a number that you use for bidding for the remainder of the auction. An account is kept for each number with a running tally. At the end of the auction, you need only present your number to the desk and they will tell you the charge. Because to err is human, you should keep your own tally to make sure that the two agree. You should feel no pressure to purchase just because you have registered. A large number of people at any auction will buy nothing and return their cards unused. The auction house is accustomed to this so there is no ill will.

The stage is set for the auction. You have registered and you have previewed the merchandise to make appropriate choices. All that remains is to buy to your heart's or wallet's content. If you have never been to an antique auction, the wise thing to do is nothing. Attend one or two auctions to get the hang of things before risking your money.

As you become experienced, you will realize a few consistent things about auctions. An example is to never accept the first bid. Some auctioneers like to give a ridiculous first bid, but more often the first price given by the auctioneer represents the full retail value of the item. When the first bid is not accepted, the auctioneer will continue to bid the item lower and lower until someone accepts. Then the process reverses itself and the price is bid up and up— often exceeding the original bid which no one would accept.

Sometimes the auctioneer will refuse to drop the bid beyond a certain point. In such a case he indicates that he will go no lower. When an auctioneer stipulates this, it usually stimulates a good bid offer. If it does not, he merely removes the article from the sale and holds it for a future sale.

To the novice, this might sound like a crazy game. Indeed it is, but don't fight it—play. The thing that makes an auction an auction is the element of chance and the unknown. More often than not, the item will rise to the first bid (but not always). This is why you play the game.

Recently I saw a beautiful salt-glazed, stoneware ovoid crock with cobalt blue decoration that I thought would go for $150 or more. When it was finally offered for bidding late in the evening, at our insistence, we were able to pick it up for $50.

Auctions are often unpredictable but there are some patterns. As a rule, an auctioneer will start with small goods and the least desirable goods while interspersing a good piece here and there. Most people are cautious in the early part of an auction. The auctioneer works on getting the audience involved. If an auction opens with furious and high bidding, it is a sign that it is not going to be a good evening for you. The auctioneer will have a grin from ear to ear.

At some point the auction is going to rise to fever pitch. When this happens, you will know it and feel it. The auctioneer will know it too, and at this point, he will try to move his best goods as fast as possible.

The auction will continue long after the peak has been reached, but it will be subdued. When an auction is at the fever pitch, the bidder should be cautious. It is easy to be carried away. Prior to bidding, you should decide the maximum you are willing to pay. Let the cool logic you had before the auction prevail during the auction and don't go over the maximum (or exceed it only slightly if you do).

Frequently, you will be bidding against dealers at an auction. That is not as bad as you might think. The major advantage that a dealer has is that his volume of purchases allows for a margin of error. If the dealer bids a little too much or the piece turns out to be a clinker, he can disperse the cost among the other pieces he buys.

The collector has one major advantage over the dealer. He can usually outbid the dealer. When a dealer bids on a piece, he must consider profit, overhead, and restoration. Consequently, his bidding is controlled by factors which don't affect the collector at all.

Generally, a collector can outbid a dealer and still rest assured that he is paying less than he would pay retail. Another benefit of bidding against a dealer is that you can usually assume that the piece is worth the price you are paying. There should be no difficulty in identifying the dealers. The style and volume of purchasing should tell you quickly who they are. If a dealer wants a piece for his own collection, he might be willing to bid it far beyond its normal value. Also, he might have a customer who he knows will pay any price. In some unfortunate cases, a dealer might be willing to spend a few extra dollars to teach an ambitious collector a lesson.

How does a collector distinguish himself in some of these sticky situations? Forewarned is forearmed; at an auction, you better know your prices. There are price guides available that are helpful, but a great deal of regional price fluctuations exist. You are best off compiling your own price guide. Pricing isn't complicated. It is simply work. If you were going to purchase a new car, you would go to five or six dealers to generally determine the going price.

The same procedure holds for antiques. With pad and pencil in hand, hit the antique shops in your area and compile a retail price range for the type of items you like. When attending your practice auctions, repeat the same procedure. Before long you will have a working knowledge of prices. You must become conversant with the prices. If you take time to look up a price during a bid, you are going to loose that bid.

Another rule of thumb is that the later you stay at an auction, the better your chance of obtaining a good price. When the auction has passed through the fever pitch, prices will tend to level out modestly. In the later part of the auction, perhaps the last half hour, the auctioneer will slack off on milking the bids in order to rush the merchandise. If there is only one piece that you are interested in, then you have no choice but to bid when it makes its appearance. But if you are interested in a broader range of goods, then you can score in the last minutes of an auction.

Over the years, country auctions have developed a bad name for sundry shady practices. For the most part, I have not found this to be true. But if ever the slogan "Buyer beware" has meaning, it holds for auctions.

On occasion, collectors run into what is known as a dealers' auction. With this type of auction, a group of dealers will decide before the auction what pieces they want. During the course of the bidding, the dealers will work collectively to keep prices down for themselves and to push out other bidders. This practice is technically illegal, but there is no way to stop it. Consortium buying such as this tends to hurt the auctioneers and owners more than the individual collector.

Within the realm of the shoddy, the use of shills is a far more worrisome problem. Some unsavory auctioneers will plant confederates in the gallery to stimulate bidding. The use of shills can make a considerable difference in the tally at the end of an evening. Even if the shill pushes too hard and purchases the piece, it is merely held over for another auction. Remember, the auctioneer works on commission or he might own a large part of the merchandise. His profit is dependent upon getting the best price.

The detection of the shill practice requires a watchful eye and regular auction attendance. If during the course of the auction you notice someone consistently bidding, but dropping out at the final bid, it's time for concern. If there is a little Sherlock Holmes in your character, discretely observe this person when he leaves. Does he have any purchases? Does he take them with him? Does he pay for the goods? Is he driving a car or a van? And so forth. In the following weeks, keep your eyes open to see if this dubious chap returns to the auction, or other auctions for that matter, exhibiting the same unusual buying pattern. If you become a regular at an auction, it is also wise to watch for recurring pieces. Occasionally, there will be a dispute over a piece requiring that it be held over for another auction. If you detect pieces reappearing on a routine basis, it's time to look for another auction.

An auctioneer doesn't have to depend upon shills to push up prices. At a fast auction, the pace of bidding can become brutal. The pace might be such that in addition to the auctioneer there are two or three spotters pointing out the bids. With hands flailing in the air like the crew of the *Titanic* on the way down and spotters yelling, "Here," "There," "Now over here," it is impossible for a bidder to take his eyes off the auctioneer long enough to check the validity of the action. At these moments, it is a simple matter for the auctioneer to see or hear the next bid when it hasn't been made. An auctioneer can be confused by the pace of the bidding, too, and in the process make an honest mistake. Nevertheless, the auctioneer is a professional who should be held to high standards.

Avoid high-paced auctions and let the pro's fight it out. If you find yourself at this type of auction, select a moment when you're not interested in the goods and move to a part of the gallery where you can watch the bidding with a careful eye. If all is well and good, return to the bidding. If you are left with a gnawing in the pit of your stomach, discretely pack it in and head for the nearest ice cream parlor.

When discussing dubious practices of dealers and auctions, there is the danger of catching the lopsided man syndrome. It is necessary to point out these problems, but don't go looking for a bug under every rock. For the most part, these dubious practices in the auction gallery are the exceptions and not the rule.

The major problem confronting a collector at auctions is the limited liability of the auctioneer or gallery. Even at the most respected auction galleries in the country, a guarantee is only extended to the bold faced type in the catalog description. Individual descriptions might make note of restoration or replacement, but the guidelines published for the catalog will have a caveat excepting the gallery from having to list restoration or repair.

The average country auction will have no catalog. Consequently, the guarantee, if there is a guarantee, is extended to only what the auctioneer says and that will be pitifully little. You will not hear the country auctioneer say, "This is a fine late 18th-century splayed-leg tavern table with an original top." You will hear the auctioneer say, "It's a splayed-leg tavern table, a good ol' one."

An auctioneer will use a number of superlatives to describe a piece, but he will rarely make any statement with regard to age and authenticity other than "good," "old," or "good and old." Under the law, in most states, a degree of *puffing* is allowed. Puffing is an advertising concept that implies little white lies or slight exaggerations are allowed.

What this all boils down to is that, at an auction, you are buying what you see—nothing more or less. If what you see is fine and an antique, then well and good. If it is not an antique, it's your option to decline or suffer the consequences. The auction gallery is either the place where you will be hurt or where you will make great purchases; the responsibility is yours.

GARAGE SALES AND OTHER NOOKS AND CRANNIES

Auctions are the primary sources of wholesale antique purchases, but they are not the exclusive source of good buys. For the person who has time and doesn't mind driving, good value can be found at garage and yard sales. The goods represented at these sales will range from good household items to pure, unadulterated junk—with an emphasis on the junk. The average householder doesn't know the difference between an antique and old furniture. Every once in a while a choice piece is found among a stock of used wine bottles or sundry goods.

It is possible to spend an entire day going from sale to sale and not find one antique piece. Surprisingly, I usually find at least one item in every two or three sales.   The lovely part of garage sales is the price of the goods. When you are lucky enough to find a piece at a sale, it is usually dirt cheap. If you are an assertive person, the price might still be negotiated lower. More often than not, I don't attempt to bargain the price down at a yard sale because the items are underpriced at the start. You will have to chart your own course.

Similar to an auction, the risks associated with a yard sale are dependent upon the ability of the purchaser to properly identify and authenticate a piece. The risks aren't nearly as great at a yard sale as at an auction, but hard earned cash can still be launched on the river of no return if foolish mistakes are made.

Not all yard sales are amateur productions. There are persons who hold sales on a regular basis. The enterprising souls who run regular operations scour the countryside to locate pieces for resale. The antiques found at these sales might be modestly less expensive than the local antique store or they might be more expensive. I am not suggesting that there is anything wrong with this type of operation; it is a nice type of hobby/business. The collector should merely be aware of the obvious. Not everything at a garage sale or yard sale is a good value. The collector must be discriminate and aware of prices.

Flea markets represent another alternative to the antique shop. Flea markets are great fun and a grand source of free recreation on a Sunday morning. They are not always the best place for antiques. The merchandise at flea markets should be less expensive than the antique store. The seller's overhead is limited to travel expenses and table rental.

My experience is that the cost of most antiques at flea markets rivals the cost of goods at local shops. If I have a choice of purchasing from an antique store or a flea market when there is only a marginal price difference. I will buy from the antique store. The antique dealer will be at the same location week after week and has a reputation to maintain. The flea market stall might be a one-week proposition. I have seen more bad goods and fudged goods at flea markets than at any other type of source. Like any place else, good buys can be made at flea markets and I don't want to discourage anyone from attending. Nevertheless, do not fall into the trap of presuming that all the merchandise is discounted.

Deals are found at flea markets when you are prepared to exploit regional variations. Simply put, the factors of supply and demand, which control price, vary from one part of the country to another. For example, pantry boxes and seed boxes with lids are a limited and expensive commodity in the mid-Atlantic states while they are a common and modestly priced item at New England flea markets. The collector who is predisposed to travel can do quite well by visiting different parts of the country. Antiquing can be combined nicely with your vacation. If you have already been bitten by the antique bug, you are doing this already.

Alternative sources are not limited to garage sales and flea markets. Antiques are where you find them; that means looking everywhere. Good Will, Salvation Army, Thrift Shops and other such operations selling used furniture and household goods are worth a visit. After you have exhausted the supply of odds-and-ends stores, see if you can get a walking tour of the basements and attics of friends and relatives.

The pursuit of this method must be done with a little care and finesse if you don't want to become the leper of antiques on the block. An amazing number of people have unknown antiques relegated to basements, storage areas, and the like. I am not referring to rare Chippendale mahogany highboys, but you might find pine cottage chests, oak washstands, and other everyday pieces. This approach can be considered getting to the garage sale before the owners decide to have a sale. If this approach seems a little silly to you, don't be decieved. A major source of antiques, new to the market each year, is from persons known as *pickers* who roam the barns and basements of country areas.

Frequently overlooked sources of antiques are furniture strippers. Furniture strippers experience a high default rate on pieces brought in for stripping. After some reasonable period of time determined by local ordinances, the stripper will put the furniture up for sale. The furniture stripper's main concern is to make good the cost of his labor as well as the money lost by having a piece lie around for a year. Consequently, the piece is sold at a modest price. On some occasions, persons will bring a piece to the stripper and ask him to strip and sell it. Regardless of the reason for selling the item, the local furniture stripper might be a good source for modestly priced antiques.

Antique wholesalers are found in various areas of the country. Such wholesalers, for the most part, merchandise container loads of European goods that are picked and packed for them abroad and shipped to the United States.

When the dollar had a great deal more virility than it has had in recent years, these operations were great sources of reasonably priced antiques. In recent times, prices have been escalating and the wholesalers have had to resort to new and less expensive sources of supply such as Spain and Eastern Europe. Nevertheless, good buys are still available.

Antique wholesalers can usually be located through one of the many antique journals or papers. Some of the wholesale operations are open to the general public. Others are available to the trade only and require proper identification to enter. Each of these operations will have a different pricing system such as half the marked price or a standard 20 percent discount. If you are located within reasonable distance of one of the wholesalers available to the public, it will be well worth your time to visit. Even if you don't purchase an antique, there is something exciting about a room as large as a football stadium filled with antiques from end to end.

For the person who is interested in antiques and equally concerned with paying modest to reasonable prices, no source can be left unexplored. With any type of purchase, the quality and value of the antique will be determiend by the ability of the collector to identify, evaluate, and authenticate. Knowledge, confidence, and the willingness to take a risk are the key ingredients of success in the purchase of antiques outside of the confines of the showroom.

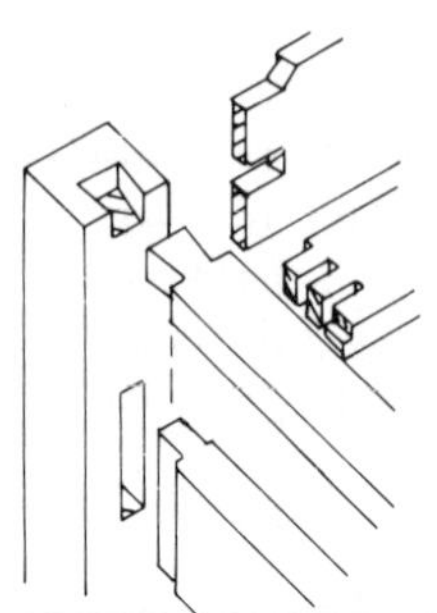

Chapter 2
Antique Furniture Construction

One of the great mysteries in life is the phenomenon of the antique collector who acquires antiques without any knowledge of authenticity. If you choose to purchase by emotion alone, you must be dependent upon the antique shop and the expertise of others. If you are an adventurous and wise collector, you are prepared to make your own decisions and purchase antiques where you find them.

If I were to say that developing the skill to authenticate antique furniture is easy, it would be a lie. There are few persons who can truly call themselves expert, and even those with a lifetime of experience make mistakes. Do not be discouraged; expertise is difficult to obtain in any endeavor. But who said you have to be an expert. It is not difficult to develop a working knowledge of antique furniture, that will allow you to make sound decisions about the authenticity of a piece.

In the following pages, the basics of 18th- and 19th-century furniture construction are discussed. A number of generalized statements are made, but this information should greatly enhance your ability to understand what is and what is not antique.

SAWING

The modern, weekend do-it-yourselfer gives little thought to the convenience of the materials that are available. If a new wood floor is needed, the purchase only requires a simple trip to a store that sells everything from soup to nails. The new pine boards are a perfect 1 inch by 12 inches. In the parlance of modern measurement that means three-fourths of an inch by 10½ inches. It is difficult to appreciate this modern miracle without some understanding of how it was done in the old days.

There are essentially, but not exclusively, two ways to cut wood. The most common method of cutting, both in the past and today, is known as *plain sawing*. With plain sawing, the log is positioned and cut for maximum economy as in Fig. 2-1A. No other method of sawing yields more large boards than this method. When a board sawn in this manner is laid flat and viewed from the edge, the growth rings will be seen arching across the width of the board.

An alternate method of cutting a board is known as quarter sawing. With quarter sawing, the log is cut into four quarters (hence the name) with each quarter being cut into boards. It is obvious, as shown in Figure 2-1B, that the boards will be much smaller and the

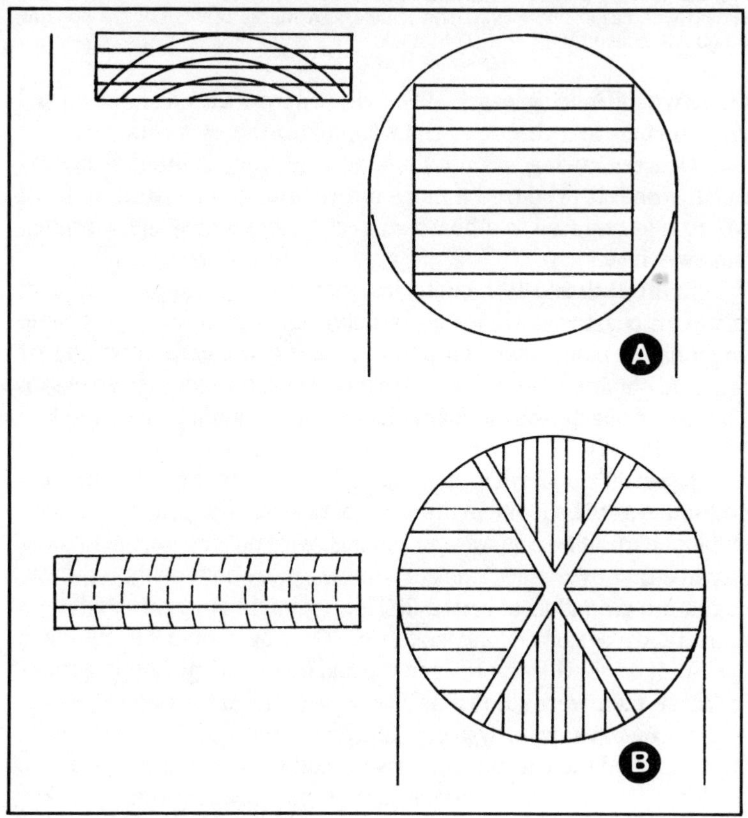

Fig. 2-1. Methods for sawing logs: (A) a plain sawn log, providing maximum board economy; (B) a quarter sawn log providing less board efficiency but greater strength.

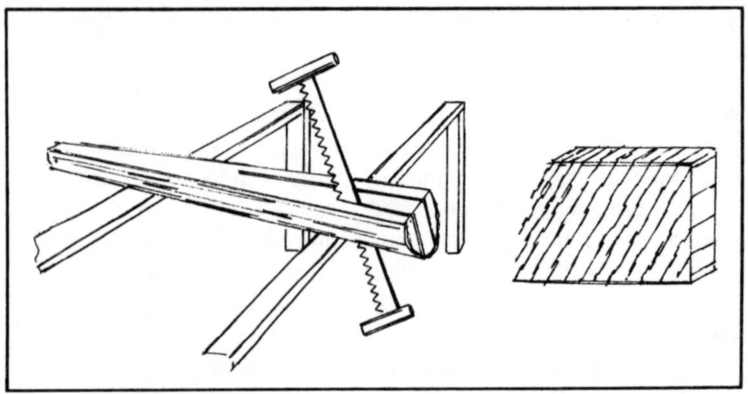

Fig. 2-2. A log is placed over a stanchion for planking by hand. This method of cutting was called pit sawing. The telltale saw marks of this cut are straight, irregularly spaced, and at a slight angle.

waste will be much greater. When viewed from the edge, the annual growth rings are almost at right angles to the saw cuts.

Quarter sawing was not pursued as merely an interesting way to cut wood. It produced a more interesting grain pattern in most woods and resulted in a board subject to less shrinkage, warping, and twisting.

In the 18th and 19th centuries, plain sawing was predominant; however, quarter sawing was common. An 18th-century pine table might have a plain-sawn board top because of the greater width that could be obtained, but the legs might be quarter sawn for strength. The use of quarter-sawn boards has been uncommon since the late 19th century.

Regardless of what manner a log was to be cut, the real problem was to be found in the work of sawing. The primary method employed to cut boards was *pit sawing*. With pit sawing, the log was placed either over stanchions of wood or, more commonly, a pit was dug in the ground as in Fig. 2-2. The log might be positioned in its entirety or debarked and squared. The log would be cut on a push-pull basis with one man on top and one in the pit. Appropriately, these men were known as the *sawyer* and the *pitman,* respectively. The top sawyer was considered the more skillful of the pair. He controlled the cut. Sawing was skilled work and sawyers had to work as pairs in order to become accustomed to each other's stroke.

The work of the pit sawyer was strenuous and not highly efficient. It would take two men 1½ hours to make a single cut in a 7-foot log. To the modern worker, the amount of labor and time consumed to produce a board in this manner is almost incomprehensible.

For the antique collector, there is wisdom in appreciating this aspect of the production of the raw material and there is safety in being able to identify the marks of the pit saw. Pit sawing leaves a distinctive straight saw mark across the face of the board. Pit sawyers attempted to maintain the saw as upright as possible. A slight degree of inclination was required for the process to work. Consequently, the marks will be slightly angled as in Fig. 2-2A. In addition to a slight angle, there will be some variation in the spacing of the strokes.

The marks of the pit saw make a strong statement with regard to the age of the piece. The beginning of pit sawing is lost in the sands of time. There is little need to be concerned with a starting date. The important question is how recently was the technique applied. As with most questions of technology, there is no precise answer—but there is an acceptable answer. Pit sawing was the primary method for turning timber into boards throughout the 16th, 17th, 18th, and early 19th centuries.

During the first half of the 19th century, pit sawing gave way to power mills. When pit saw marks are found on a piece, it can generally be assumed that the boards were cut prior to 1850. The word generally is used because in the conversion to modern technology there will always be backwashes where traditional hand modes of operation continue to be practiced long beyond their popularity.

Some older artisans have noted seeing the pit saw in operation in small English villages as recently as 1900. Pit sawing was utilized in parts of South America and Africa until World War II, and indeed, might still be carried on in some areas. Post-1850 survival examples of pit sawing are oddities and should not overly influence your judgments. When evaluating an antique piece, other aspects of style and construction should confirm whether or not the pit sawing was in period.

Pit sawing was a primary method of converting timber, but not the only method. Timber was also converted into plank by frame or gang saws. The frame saw used a series of vertical blades, as in Fig. 2-3A, to saw timber. With this method of sawing, multiple boards were cut at one time. Frame saws were the first power saws and were used as early as the 15th century in continental Europe. The early saws used horses, oxen, wind, water, and human sources of power. Although popular on the continent power frame saws never came into any predominance in either 18th century England or the Colonies. The manually powered frame saw (Fig. 2-3B) was widely utilized in the Americas. The manual frame saw lent itself to shop usage in the conversion of small timber. More often than not, the manual frame saw was used to convert previously sawn plank into board.

The saw marks left by the frame saw are similar to the marks of the modern band saw. Both the powered saw and hand-held frame saw will leave vertical stroke marks (Fig. 2-3C). The spacing of the strokes on the powered frame saw will be greater than that of the modern band saw. There will be some degree of irregularity in the spacing of the strokes of the manually operated saw.

Similar to the pit saw, when the marks of the manual frame saw are found on a board, it can be presumed to have been cut prior to 1850. The dating of the marks from a power frame saw is somewhat more difficult due to its adaptation to the age of power.

The type of sawing most recognizable to modern man is that of the circular mill saw. With this method, a squared log is placed on a carriage and moved into the rotation of a large circular blade (Fig. 2-4). The circular saw is not as recent an invention as one might think. It was patented in England in the late 1700s. The circular saw,

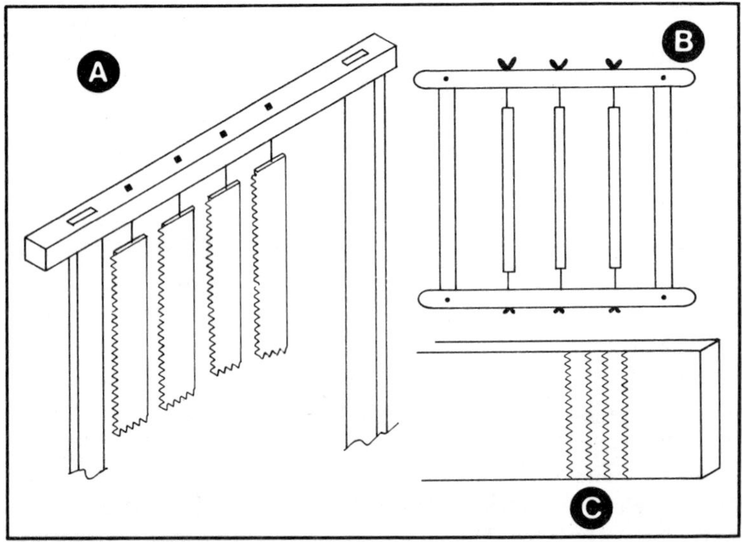

Fig. 2-3. Frame saws: (A) a power frame saw (gang saw) used to make multiple cuts. This saw was powered by wind, water or horse; (B) a manual frame saw used in the same manner as the power frame saw; (C) the telltale saws marks are straight, irregularly spaced and vertical.

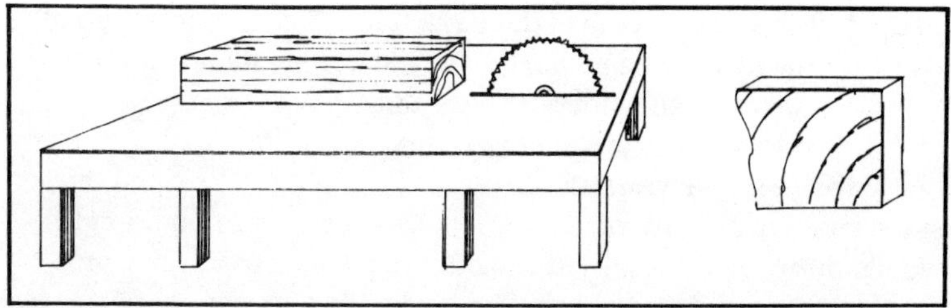

Fig. 2-4. A circular mill saw utilizing a rotary blade to plank the log. The circular mill saw leaves an arching cut pattern across the surface of the board.

similar to many woodworking innovations, lacked the existence of a power source to make its adoption practical. Hand-powered circular saws were used in the early 1800s to cut veneers because they were superior to hand cut veneers.

The adoption of circular saws paralleled the adoption and improvement of steam power. A steam saw mill was established for a brief time, near London in the early 1800s. The mill was short-lived because the local hand sawyers, who were not overly fond of the new machinery, burnt it to the ground. Although steam mills existed at this early date, the period usually accepted for steam-powered saw mills is 1825 to 1850. It can be assumed that 1825 marks the beginnings of the steam-powered sawing industry. Therefore, a limited amount of lumber on the market would have been produced in this manner. By 1850, it is assumed that steam-powered saw mills were widespread and producing a considerable amount of lumber near population centers.

When circular-saw marks are found on a piece of antique furniture, it is highly doubtful that the furniture was made prior to 1825. It is more likely that it was made after 1850. Even though steam-powered sawing was available by 1850, it does not mean that the entire woodworking industry shifted to a machine technology. Furniture in this period was still made, assembled, and finished by hand.

The steam-powered circular saw had limitations with regard to the size of log it could cut. A circular blade will cut to a depth of one-half the diameter of the blade minus the arbor and some allowance for the table. The lack of metalurgical development in the 19th century made it impossible to construct a blade large enough to cut through the really large logs. In some cases, the log was hand sawn and then power sawn. In other cases, the log was passed over the circular blade and then reversed in the carriage for a second cut. Another solution to the problem was the adaptation of steam power to the frame saw that planks the largest log. The important point is that the saw marks of a power frame saw can be found on furniture from the second half of the 19th century.

Collectors of historical trivia might find it interesting to know that, in the early days of steam-powered sawing in England, power saws were used only on hardwood. Hand sawyers could cut soft woods more economically than could the power saws. Sawing was the first area of woodworking to be mechanized because the old methods of production were inadequate to meet the demands of the growing industry.

Sawing was not the only method used to convert logs. Logs could also be split or, as it was known, *riven*. The process of riving had little practicality when it came to producing board stock—with the exception of oak. Oak splits exceedingly well along the grain. In the 16th and 17th centuries, oak was riven to produce planks as an easier alternative to sawing. By and large, riven oak is not found as an aspect of American country furniture.

Riving is important in relation to the production of turning stock. Pieces of squared wood were placed on the lathe to produce legs, spindles, and such. Riving was a simple process that involved using a wedge and maul (Fig. 2-5). The modern homeowner with a fireplace can easily relate to this process because it is identical to log splitting today. Riving, quite understandably, does not produce a perfectly square piece of stock; that is a point of significance. The artisan would eye up the stock for size prior to turning. Alas, the human eye is fallible. Frequently, the piece selected was a hair too small to produce a perfect round after turning (Fig. 2-5B). In cases such as this, a flat spot was produced on the turned stock.

Our woodworking ancestors are sometimes credited with a perfectionism that did not exist in reality. A man did not cut a tree, split a log, dry the stock and turn it on a lathe only to discard it because it was slightly out of round. If a piece only had a slight flat spot, the turner might reduce it to a smaller diameter. If the turner was making table legs, one leg would simply be thinner than the others (and as a rule not perceptible to the purchaser). Often the turner ignored the flat spot and proceeded with his decorative turning. When a piece was assembled, the flats would be positioned inward or to the rear where they would not be noticeable.

In the modern furniture industry, turning stock is sawn to perfect squares. This eliminates the problem. When flat spots are found on turnings, it is a positive sign of at least 19th-century origin. Of course, people then, as now, continued to rive stock for turning.

You are not likely to encounter many of these pieces. When saw marks are apparent, remember to keep the following in mind:

☐ Pit saw marks are prior to 1850 and frequently prior to 1825.

☐ Frame saw marks (hand operated) are prior to 1850.

☐ Frame saws powered by human, animal or steam sources can be found in the 18th and 19th centuries;

☐ Steam-powered circular sawing with distinctive radial marking is generally found from 1850 on. There is some possibility of finding examples from the 1825 to 1850 period. Examples from the 1800 to 1825 period are an extreme rarity and would probably denote English origin.

☐ Band saw marks denote modern origin and are generally found on pieces of this century.

☐ Riven wood is indicated by flat spots on turnings and denotes an origin prior to 1875.

DRESSING THE STOCK

Saw marks can be helpful in dating, but they are hardly appropriate for finished surfaces. When board stock was received from the sawyer or mill, it had to be prepared—or *dressed* as it was known in the trade.

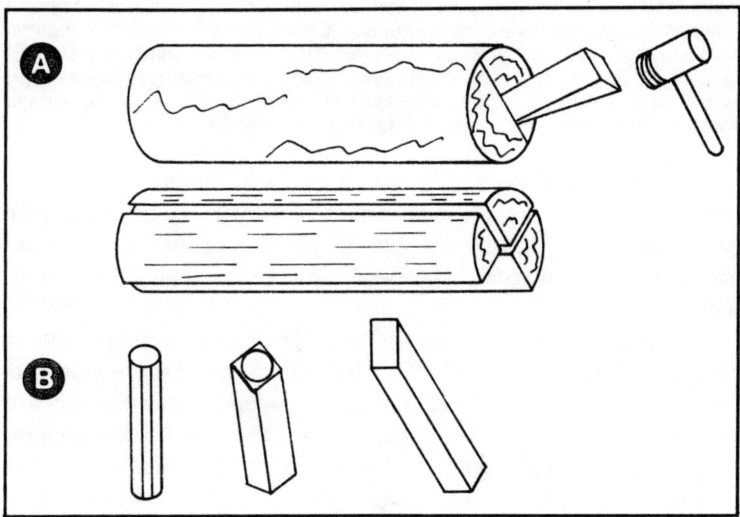

Fig. 2-5. A wedge and maul: (A) used to split (rive) an oak log. Turning stock (B) produced by riving often proved inadequate. This resulted in flat spots on the turning.

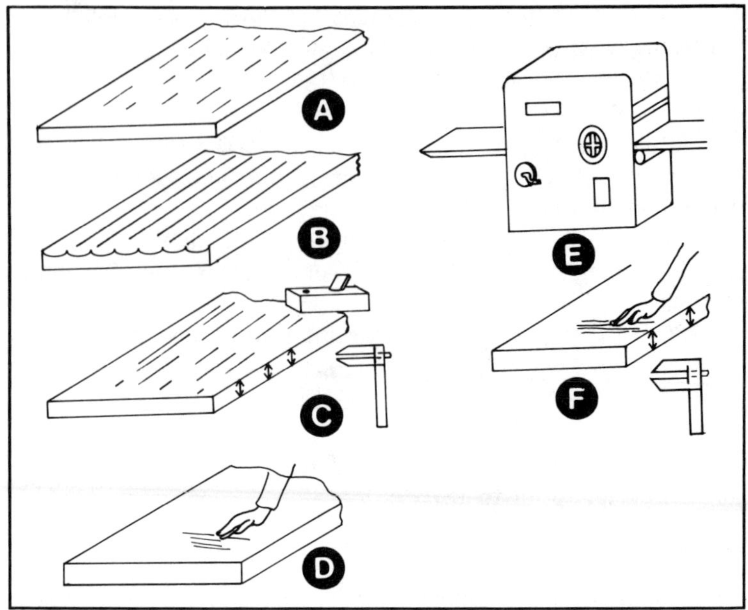

Fig. 2-6. Hand-sawn stock (A) often did not have parallel faces. The first step in dressing a board (B) was the use of a scrub plane. It removed stock with a concave blade like a gouge. The ridges of the scrub plane were removed with a jack and smooth plane (C). The face surfaces of the board would appear to be parallel. If measurements were taken at several points, variation would be evident. A hand rubbed across the surface (D) of a board planed in this manner can often detect the undulations of the hand plane. A modern machine planer (E) is used to dimension (dress) rough sawn stock. A machine planed board (F) would yield consistent measurements when taken at several points. A hand rubbed across the surface would detect no plane marks.

Boards were overcut to allow for, final dimensions, the removal of saw marks and to create two parallel faces. Mill sawn stock, because of the accuracy of the process, would have parallel faces. Hand-sawn stock often would not have parallel faces (Fig. 2-6A).

The dressing of a board was one of the most arduous tasks in the old-time cabinetmaker's shop. If the shop had an apprentice, this task was surely given to him. The first step in dressing a board involved the use of a scrub plane to bring the board to the general dimension desired. The scrub plane has a concave blade, somewhat like a gouge, that removes large quantities of wood in a single stroke. The scrub plane is run in the direction of the grain and leaves behind a distinctive channel (Fig. 2-6B). The next logical step in the preparation of a board was to remove the marks of the scrub plane.

There is no reason to presume that the cabinetmaker of yesteryear was any fonder of work than his modern day counterpart. The marks of the scrub plane were not removed unless necessary. Basically, the only surfaces that could be left so rough were backboards and bottom boards.

Scrub plane marks indicate construction prior to 1850. Thereafter, more precise mill sawing and the adoption of mechanical planing machines made it unnecessary. Although the scrub plane can be presumed to have been in active use until 1850, it was not fashionable, in the 19th century, to leave the telltale signs of the plane. Due to this aspect of fashion, scrub plane marks are not commonly found on pieces of the 1800 to 1850 period. When evaluating a piece of furniture, you can usually assume that scrub plane marks indicate 18th century origin if consistent with the design and construction of the piece. The absence of scrub plane marks on an 18th-century piece does not challenge its authenticity; it merely means that the maker chose to plane them out.

Removal of harsh plane marks was necessary for all finished surfaces. After using the scrub plane, the cabinetmaker would use a series of planes—usually a jack plane followed by a smooth plane—to bring the board to its final dimension and to remove all marks. Subsequent to final planing, scraping or some form of abrasive would be used to remove all traces of tool marks from surfaces that would be seen.

It is truly impressive to consider the skill and talent exhibited in the conversion of a log to usable board. No matter how impressive this process was, it was not perfect. No artisan, then or now, could hand plane a board to the degree that the overall dimensions would be the same at all points.

Assuming the board illustrated in Fig. 2-6C to be hand planed to three-fourths of an inch, a measurement taken with a caliper along its edges would show variations at several points. The variation might be as minimal as one-thirty-second inch or as much as one-sixteenth of an inch, but it will be there. Such slight variation as this is not visible to the eye. In addition, the use of hand planes might have left behind subtle undulated surfaces. The tips of your fingers rubbed across the surface of a board can often detect these wave-like changes (Fig. 2-6D).

The alternate to hand planing is mechanical planing. With modern planing, the stock is fed through pressure rollers and under a series of rotary cutters similar to the machine in Fig. 2-6E. After one surface of the board is trued, the board is reversed and trued to its final dimensions. Unlike the hand-planed board, if a series of measurements were taken across the edge of a mechanically planed board (Fig. 2-6F), there would be no variation. Likewise, a hand rubbed across the surface would yield no imperfection.

The first machine planers were produced in England about 1825. These were intended for use with metals. At least one Shaker community in America claimed to have a working machine planer for wood in the 1830-1840 period. It is fair to assume that there was no widespread machine planing prior to 1850. It is equally fair to assume that most stock was machine planed after 1875. For the purposes of dating, the following should be kept in mind:

☐ Well-defined scrub plane marks are found on backboards and bottom boards.

☐ Residual scrub plane marks (slight traces) can be found on the outer surfaces of some 18th-century pieces. This is most often seen with painted blanket chests of the first half of the 18th century.

☐ The absence of scrub plane marks does not mean a piece is not authentic.

☐ Inside and unseen surfaces usually exhibit some traces of hand plane marks.

☐ When measured with a calipher, hand-planed boards exhibit slight variations.

☐ The utilization of hand-planed boards indicates construction prior to 1875.

☐ Machine planed boards indicate, as a rule, construction after 1850.

MORTISE AND TENON CONSTRUCTION

Modern commercial furniture is constructed of veneered particleboard or, if better quality, veneered plywood joined together by an unfathomable collection of metal fasteners and mastic. Very high quality furniture and custom-made or craft-made furniture is still made in accordance with sound construction techniques used in the past.

No joining technique is more basic to furniture construction than that of the mortise and tenon. The principle of the technique is to join two pieces of wood together with or without glue. The use of shoulders at right angles in the joint allows for simple but true construction. The easiest explanation of the mortise and tenon is that it is no different than placing a square peg in a square hole.

The basic mortise and tenon joint is represented in **Fig. 2-7A**. From a piece of squared stock, material is removed from the top and from the bottom to leave a projection known as the *tenon.* The tenon is always at a right angle to the face of the stock, which is known as the *shoulder.* The tenon must have a shoulder to allow for proper fitting. A matching recess cut in the piece of wood that is to be joined is known as the *mortise.*

Figure 2-7B illustrates a haunched tenon that is commonly found in door construction. The haunched tenon allows for greater gluing surface. In addition, the haunch provides better protection from torsion. Figure 2-7C shows a double tenon that is somewhat more time consuming to make than a standard mortise and tenon. Where a large tenon is to be used, the double tenon provides greater strength. This was the option of the cabinetmaker. Either type can be found. Figure 2-7D illustrates a halved tenon that serves the same purpose as the other mortise and tenon joints described.

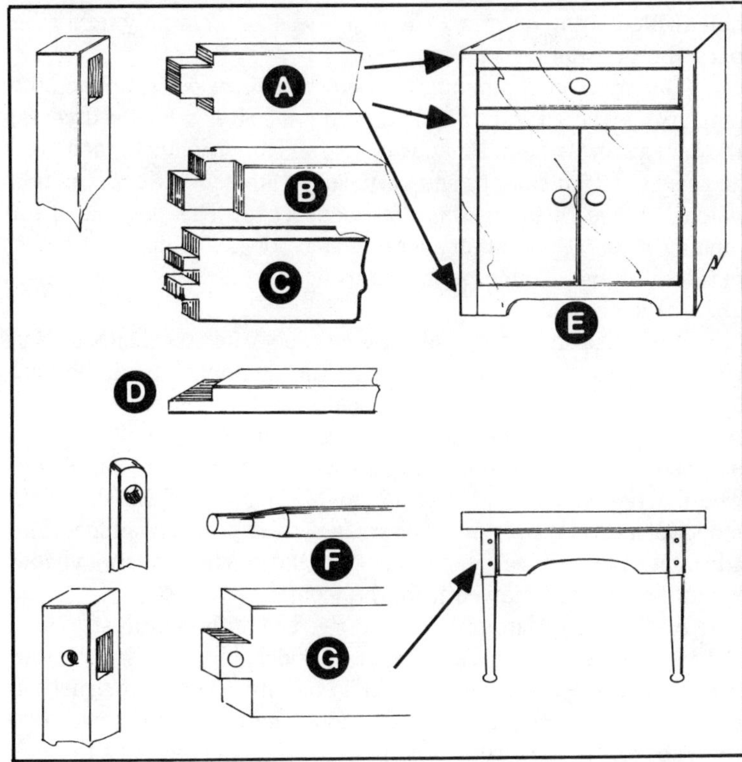

Fig. 2-7. Examples of mortise and tenon joints: (A) standard mortise and tenon; (B) haunched tenon; (C) double tenon; (D) halved tenon; (E) various points where a tenon could be used to construct a cupboard; (F) round tenon; (G) pinned mortise and tenon.

The cupboard illustrated in Fig. 2-7E would commonly have the cross members encasing the drawer and the bottom skirting board mortised and tenoned in the manner of the mortise and tenon shown in Fig. 2-7A. The doors of the piece would likely have a haunched mortise.

Figure 2-7F represents a round mortise and tenon as commonly found in chair construction. This joint is often referred to as a *doweled joint,* but it is properly a mortise and tenon even though it is distinct from the other types of mortises and tenons.

A variation of the mortise and tenon is the *pegged mortise and tenon* (Fig. 2-7G). Glue is not essential to a properly fitted mortise and tenon; however, when glue was not used it was necessary to pin the joint with a wooden peg. Pinning required only that a hole be drilled through the mated mortise and tenon and that a matched peg be inserted. In some cases, the tenon was drilled slightly shy of the hole drilled in the mortise. The result was an incredibly tight joint once the pin was driven home.

This method of pinning was known as *draw boring.* When the pins are extracted from a draw bored joint after a hundred years, they are severely bent. Pinned mortise and tenon joints tended to be an aspect of 18th century and very early 19th century construction when the use of glues was not widespread. The pegs used for pinning in the 18th century were square or hexagonal, but never perfectly round. Round pegs akin to modern dowels were a post-1825 development.

A mortise and tenon could also be used to join the dustboards in chest construction as in Fig. 2-8A. The dustboard is simply and appropriately fitted into a mortise cut into the chest side. A varia tion on this theme is the stopped mortise and tenon (Fig. 2-8B). The stopped tenon is fitted into the mortise from the rear of the side. The mortise stops an inch or so shy of the front of the side. The stopped mortise and tenon offers no structural advantage. The advantage of this join is aesthetic in that the mortises are not visible when the chest is viewed from the front.

Additional variations of the mortise and tenon are illustrated in Fig. 2-9. Figure 2-9A represents a bridal joint which, like the haunched mortise and tenon, is found mostly in door construction. Figure 2-9B is a double wedged tenon. The tenon is cut with two recesses and fitted through the mortise and is known as a through tenon. When the members are fitted, wedges are driven home. The tenon is expanded and this makes it impossible for the join to become separated. The wedged tenon, similar to the pegged mor-

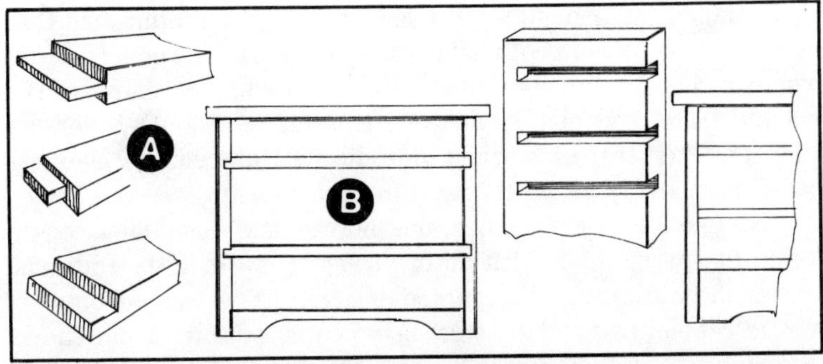

Fig. 2-8. A standard tenon or halved tenon (A) used for dustboard construction in a chest and a stopped mortise and tenon (B) used for dustboard construction. This joint has no structural advantage, but from the front, the join is not visible.

tise and tenon, was used instead of gluing.

When a through tenon was considered unsightly, a *hidden wedge* or a *foxed wedged tenon* was used. The wedges were lightly fitted to the tenon with the tenon subsequently driven home in the mortise to create another inseparable join. The foxed tenon has frustrated many a furniture restorer; there is no way to know it is there.

When mortise and tenon construction is employed on modern furniture, it is machine made. Drill presses can be fitted with mortising devices or special mortising machines can be used to replace the exacting handwork. The machined mortise, like the hand mortise, will have two parallel sides. The machined mortise will be rounded at each end and not square like the handmade mortise.

When a mortise was laid out by hand, a mortise gauge was used. The mortise gauge (Fig. 2-10A) is a simple device by which parallel lines can be scribed accurately on a piece to be worked. The cabinetmaker would make the scribe marks slightly longer than the intended mortise to allow for working room. Invariably, when examining an antique piece of furniture, one will find these marks by the mortise (as shown in Fig. 2-10B).

The mortise and tenon joint could be fitted dry, and therefore pegged or wedged, or it could be glued. The tendency in the 18th century was to work dry in country pieces. Very formal pieces were fitted either way. It is all too often asserted that glue did not exist until the end of the 18th century, but this just is not true. The ancient Egyptians used glue on their furniture and in one form or another glue has existed throughout man's history.

Animal and fish glues were used in the 18th century, but they were difficult to work with. Glues had to be dissolved or softened in water and applied to a warm surface in a warm environment. The simple truth was that it was often easier for the 18th century cabinetmaker to work without glue. In the 19th century, glue was used extensively for all forms of furniture joining.

In one form or the other, the mortise and tenon joint constituted the major mode of furniture framing in the 17th, 18th, and early 19th centuries. This method of construction was not optional for the cabinetmaker; there were no acceptable alternatives. Therefore, mortise and tenon construction should be evident in all forms of antique furniture construction. When examining mortise and tenon construction, keep the following in mind:

☐ Mortises and tenons were fit, for the most part, dry in country furniture prior to 1825.

☐ Dry-fit tenons will be secured by pegs or wedges.

☐ Irregular handmade pegs suggest an origin prior to 1825; however they might be later. The use of round dowels to pin a joint suggests a date no earlier than 1825, while 1850 is more likely.

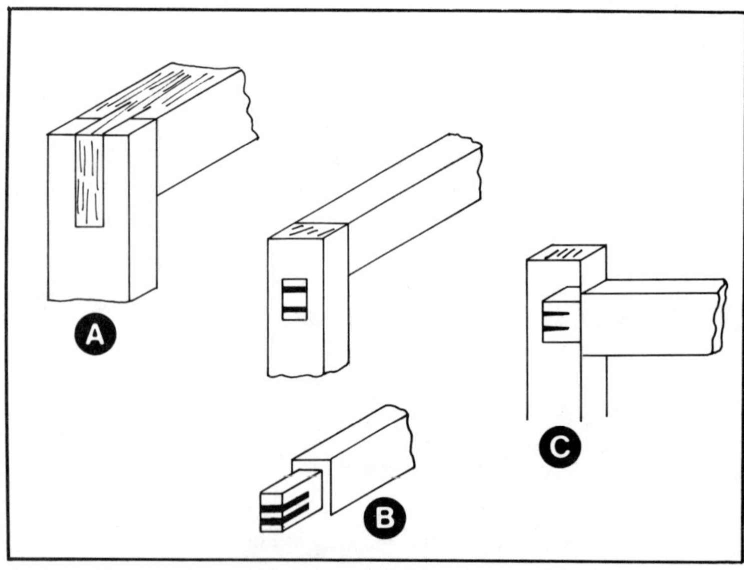

Fig. 2-9. Examples of tenons: (A) a bridal joint. This form of mortise and tenon is frequently used in door construction; (B) a double-wedged tenon; (C) hidden or fox-wedged tenon. Tenons were cut for wedges lightly positioned. When the tenon was driven into the mortise, the wedges were driven home, thus making an inseparable and hidden joint.

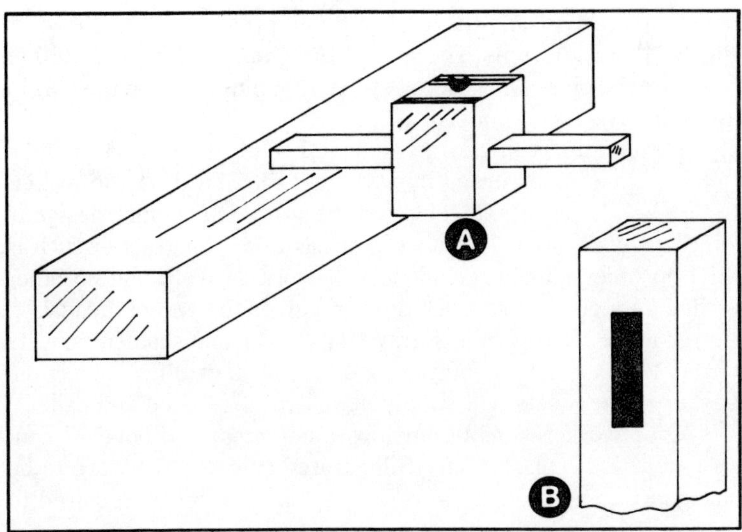

Fig. 2-10. A mortising gauge (A) used to scribe parallel lines for the mortise. Mortises were always cut within the marks of the gauge (B). Consequently, an overrun of the gauge will be apparent with a hand-cut mortise.

☐ Glued mortise and tenon construction was used in formal furniture from 1700 onward. Glued mortise and tenon construction with country furniture occurs mainly after 1800.

☐ Hand cut mortises and tenons should exhibit the parallel lines of the marking gauge.

☐ Machine-made mortises will have rounded corners and denote construction after 1850.

DOVETAILS

Like the mortise and tenon, the *dovetail* is another method of joining that is basic to historical furniture construction. The dovetail is not inappropriately named; its fan shape resembles the tail of a dove. The dovetail, like many other aspects of the woodworker's art, existed in ancient Egypt. For some unknown reason, the joint was lost to European craftsmanship, to be rediscovered only in the 16th century.

Essentially, the dovetail is another type of mortise and tenon. In this case, the tenon is not at a right angle with the shoulder. The almost triangular shape of the dovetail allows for an interlocking joint that will hold without the assistance of glue or the use of a pinning device. The dovetail joint consists of tails, pins, and mortises. Figure 2-11A represents a box or drawer construction where

43

dovetails are typically found. The flared projections, as shown in Fig. 2-11A, are the tails. The shaded, end-grain sections of the other piece are the pins. The spaces between the pins in which the tails fit are known as *sockets* or mortises.

Dovetailing is an unsurpassed method of joining in most situations. Its use is governed by style and the ability of the maker. Figure 2-11B represents a blanket chest of 18th century design in which dovetails are boldly used. With basic box construction such as this, no other joining technique will work as well, and no other technique requires this much time or skill on the part of the maker. Better-made blanket chests, traveling chests, and seamen's chests of the 18th and 19th centuries will exhibit dovetail construction. Lesser-made chests will simply be nailed or rebated and nailed.

Case work assembly employs other modes of dovetail construction. If the blanket chest illustrated (Fig. 2-11B) were to be changed into a chest of drawers, the top—no longer required to

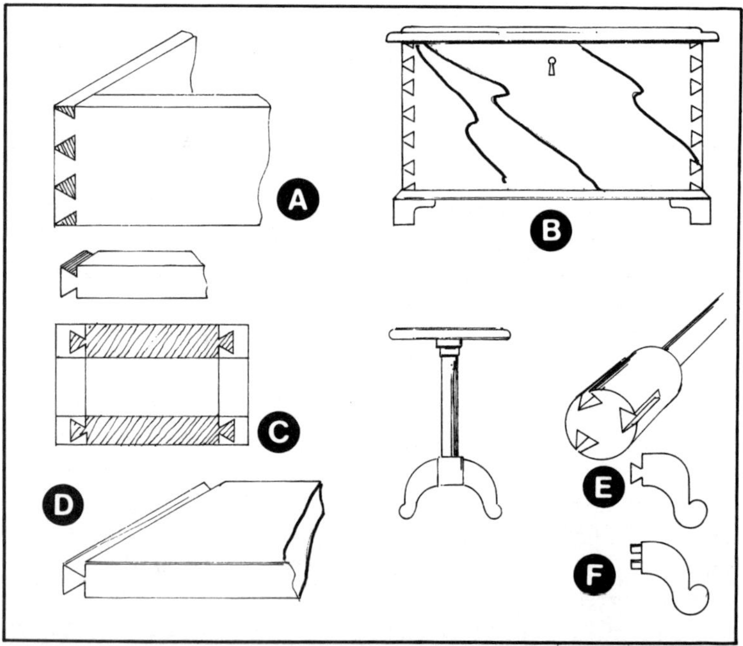

Fig. 2-11. Examples of joints: (A) dovetails used in typical drawer construction; (B) a blanket chest using dovetail construction; (C) a single dovetail used for framing, such as the top of a chest; (D) a sliding dovetail used for dustboard construction, table battens, etc.; (E) sliding dovetail used for leg construction on a pedestal table; (F) a dowel joint used as an alternative to a sliding dovetail for pedestal leg construction. This form is only found on pieces made after 1825.

open—could be dovetailed to the sides in its entirety. An alternative to dovetailing the entire top would be to dovetail simple cross members (Fig. 2-11C). The cross members would provide all the structural integrity necessary and allow for a simple top to be nailed on. The front of the blanket chest would no longer be required. This would be replaced by drawers. The stiles separating the drawers could be mortised and tenoned or stopped mortised as previously discussed. If the cabinetmaker was an exacting worker, the stiles and dustboards will be dovetailed to the sides of the chest in a manner similar to Fig. 2-11D.

In general, dovetail construction will be more evident in 18th century and early 19th century furniture when there was less reliance upon glue. Dovetailing tends to be less evident in the construction of 19th century country furniture where glued mortises and tenons were often substituted. A well-made drawer was dovetailed whether it was of 18th or 19th century construction.

Today, dovetails are still extensively used for drawer construction, but these are machine made. A dovetail machine was patented in England in the 1790's. Nevertheless, machines were not actively employed until 1850. Early machined dovetails, sometimes known as *bullet dovetails* or *bull's-eye dovetails,* were conical and easy to distinguish from handmade dovetails. By 1875, machine dovetails were made as they are today (and similar in appearance to handmade tails). With machine-made dovetails, the tails and pins are always the same size. The tails and pins are never the same size with handmade dovetails. Invariably, with handmade dovetails the pins are smaller than the tails and on occasion so severely tapered they appear to be disjointed. After a few minutes of study, anyone should be able to detect at a glance the difference between machine-made and handmade dovetails.

Dovetailing was also the primary method for attaching legs to pedestal tables and candlestands (Fig. 2-11E). Legs were almost always dovetailed in the 18th and early 19th centuries. On rare occasions, the legs might be mortised and pinned. From the second quarter of the 19th century, the legs might be doweled (Fig. 2-11F). Modern reproductions of this type of table will utilize dowels or a machine-made sliding dovetail. With machine-made dovetails, the mortise will be rounded at the closed end. This might not be easy to detect with the legs in place. In such a case, examine the dovetails for variation which will be evident if the item is handmade. In addition, slight saw marks should be visible where the cabinetmaker has overcut the mortises. To determine if legs have been dovetailed, you need only turn the table upside down.

Handmade dovetails are not a sure sign of antiquity, but when viewed in conjunction with appropriate style and wear they will strongly suggest antiquity. When examining dovetails, keep the following in mind:

☐ Dovetails were actively used in the 17th, 18th, and 19th centuries. They are still used today. It is difficult to date a piece on the basis of dovetails alone.

☐ Dovetails used in the 17th century tended to be large. In the 18th and 19th centuries multiple, fine dovetails were used.

☐ Machine-made *bullet* dovetails were employed after 1850, but dovetails were still hand cut in this period.

☐ Machine-made dovetails resembling hand-cut dovetails were employed after 1875. Machine-cut dovetails are uniform. The pins and tails are the same size.

☐ Hand-cut dovetails are laid out with a mortise gauge. Some trace of the gauge mark usually remains.

☐ The legs on pedestal tables were dovetailed until at least 1825. From 1825 onward, legs might have been dovetailed or doweled.

REBATES AND GLUE BLOCKS

Rebating was a commonly used method of furniture construction employed in conjunction with other techniques during the 18th and 19th centuries. Country furniture, in particular, used rebate construction to a greater degree because of the ease of making the joint.

A rebate is quite simple and merely involves removing a portion of wood at a right angle to the shoulder that will be created (Fig. 2-12A). This joint could be made easily and quickly with a specially made plane known, strangely enough, as a *rebate plane* or a *rabbit plane*. With modern construction, the rebate is made with a table saw, a radial saw, a router or a spindle moulder. When modern made, the wood surface is clean and smooth. When handmade, plane marks will be visible on the wood surface.

Rebating was a slightly more productive alternative to *butt joining* (which is the simple nailing together of boards). The chest shown in Fig. 2-12B could be butt joined with glue and nails. The problem with butt joining is that it involves gluing long grain to end grain which does not bond well. By creating a rebate, the gluing characteristics have not been changed, but the interlocking nature of the joint provides additional strength and resilience. The use of a rebate lessens the amount of visible end grain for a more attractive

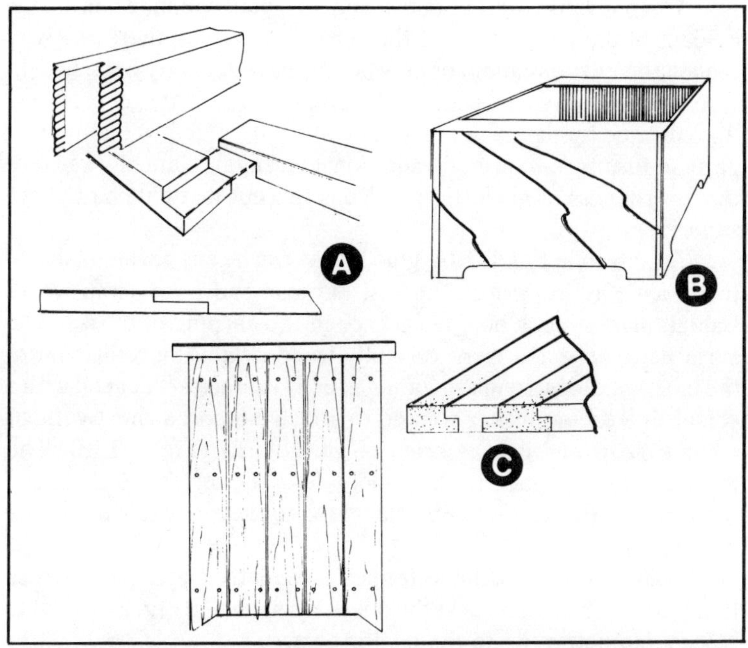

Fig. 2-12. Examples of lap joints: (A) a lap joint used for various modes of construction; (B) a nailed lap joint used for simple case construction; (C) a lap joint used for backboard construction. This is the most prevalent form of backboard construction.

appearance. In Fig. 2-12B, only the side panels have been rebated. All four panels could have been rebated, to provide some additional strength.

Rebating was used extensively to prepare backboards for furniture in the 18th and 19th centuries. There is one excellent reason for rebating backboards and that is shrinkage. All wood will shrink across the width of the grain over a period of years. When backboards are just nailed, shrinkage will in time create spaces between the boards ranging from one-eighth inch to one-fourth inch. This type of spacing is not only unsightly, but it allows dust to enter the piece.

By rebating, which is in effect overlapping, the shrinkage problem is solved. As shown in Fig. 2-12C, the newly fitted boards are tight and well sealed. When shrinkage occurs, gaps will appear, but the overlapping of the boards will prevent any open space. Modern furniture eliminates the shrinkage problem through the use of lightweight plywood or masonite backings that do not shrink. Such backings are used in single sheets.

When examining antique furniture, you will find shrinkage evident in the backboards. If the rebates are snug, there is every reason to believe that old or new boards have recently been fitted.

One area of construction frequently overlooked is *glue blocks*. As indicated by the name, blocks of wood are glued to the interior parts of furniture to provide additional strength. Glue blocks were the forerunners of modern angle irons (except that glue blocks are superior).

As shown in Fig. 2-13A, glue blocks can be any shape or size in that each was made for a special purpose and from scrap wood. Cabinetmakers took no special care in the shaping of blocks. The surfaces to be glued were carefully trued, while the remainder of the block would be rough sawn and usually thereafter reduced with a chisel. If a cabinetmaker wanted to attach a top to a chest without nailing, he would use a series of glue blocks (Fig. 2-13B). The blocks would be glued to the underside of the top of the chest and then the top fitted and the blocks glued to the sides (absent in the illustration).

Chair frames and table frames frequently suffer from stress that loosens the mortises at the posts. As shown in Fig. 2-13C, glue blocks join both rails to the center post.

This reduces the susceptibility to stress. Glue blocks are almost always found reenforcing bracket feet on a chest (Fig. 2-13D). Bracket feet are commonly mitered to make a neat, attractive joint. Nevertheless, it makes for a very weak joint because end grain must be glued to end grain.

Glue blocks are an absolute necessity with a mitered bracket foot. There were other methods used in antique furniture to reenforce a bracket foot such as dovetails, hidden dovetails and spline. These other methods, still used in conjunction with glue blocks, are not predominant in country pieces because they were time consuming. Many 18th-century pieces had finely dovetailed bracket feet. The plain miter, however, was more in fashion for the 19th century.

When examining an antique piece, you should easily be able to detect old glue blocks by their casual appearance and rough shaping. The cabinetmaker might have nailed or screwed the blocks in addition to gluing, but screwing was far less common. When glue blocks are employed in modern furniture, they are uniformly cut and screwed or stapled in place. When examining furniture bear in mind that:

☐ Nailed rebate construction is a simple form of construction used today and in the past. It is of little assistance in dating furniture.

□ Rebates were made by hand prior to 1850 and should exhibit the telltale signs of a hand plane. Machine-made rebates are clean and smooth.

□ Glue blocks were used extensively in antique furniture. Handmade glue blocks are all different and crudely shaped. They exhibit chisel marks or saw marks. Modern glue blocks are uniform.

DOWELING

The use of dowels was one of the major innovations in furniture construction in the shift to mass-produced furniture. The use of dowel construction allowed for furniture to be made more quickly and by persons of less skill. The inevitable consequence was less cost.

Doweling consists of boring corresponding holes in two wood surfaces and then joining them with dowels and glue (Fig. 2-14A). Doweling has almost unlimited applications and can be used to replace mortise and tenon, rebate, and dovetail modes of joining. Primarily, the dowel is a simple method of accomplishing what a mortise and tenon join does.

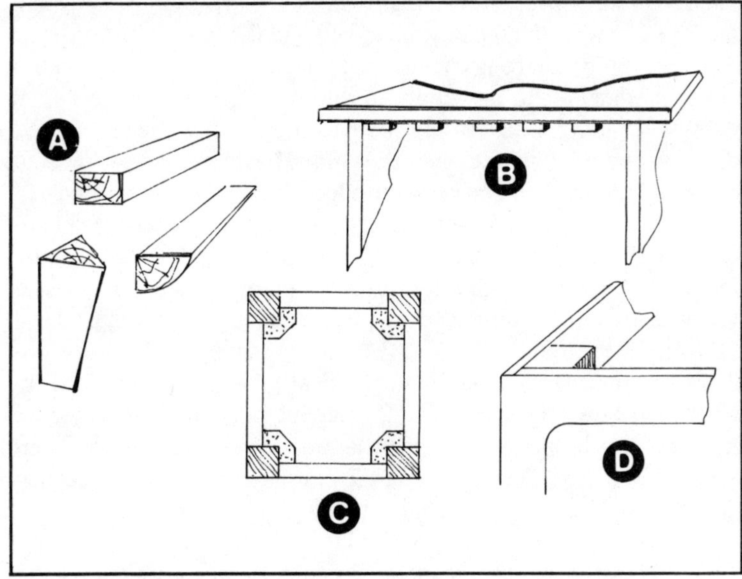

Fig. 2-13. Examples of glue blocks: (A) glue blocks were shaped to each use and always crude and irregular; (B) glue blocks used to secure and reenforce the top of a chest; (C) glue blocks used to reenforce mortised and tenoned chair rails; (D) a glue block used to reenforce a miter join on a bracket foot.

In Fig. 2-14B, a dowel replaces the traditional sliding dovetail for the attachment of the leg. To produce a sliding dovetail in this instance takes a high degree of skill and a fair amount of time. That is not true for the dowel. When the joint is completed, either method yields the same visual result. But in time, the doweled joint will separate while the dovetailed joint will not. Doweled-leg construction on pedestal tables can be seen on furniture built as early as 1825, but it more commonly is found on post-1850 pieces.

Figure 2-14C illustrates how a traditionally mortised door frame can be doweled (although the panel must still be mortised). This type of door construction can be found in some late 19th-century pieces, but it was an unusual and infrequently used method.

In Fig. 2-14D, dowels are used to replace a dado for the placement of a shelf in a chest or cupboard. This is not a common form of construction. When the builder lacked the skill or caring to make a proper joint, he would more often just nail the shelf.

Figure 2-14E illustrates two boards being joined by dowels. From the midpoint of the 19th century, it became increasingly common to join large surfaces in this manner. This method of joining still predominates today. When a large number of boards had to be glued, jigs were prepared so that the holes were drilled easily and quickly. When ready, the dowels would line the boards up perfectly for easy gluing. There is considerable debate among woodworkers as to whether or not doweling, in this case, is any stronger than plain-edge gluing. Logic would seem to suggest that the reenforced joint must be stronger, yet over the years I have seen more doweled joints separated than I have seen edge-glued joints separated.

If an open doweled joint is encountered, it might be possible to tell something of the age. In the 19th century, plain dowels—usually pointed at each end with a tool called a pointer—were used. The dowels are maple or birch and look the same as ones purchased in a hardware store today (Fig. 2-14F). Ready-made dowels were improved in this century and have vertical grooves or spirals (Fig. 2-14G) to allow for excess glue to squeeze from the joint. If one of these dowels is found, it means the piece is modern or has been repaired recently. The inverse of the statement is not true because plain dowels were used in this century and the last century.

Essentially, doweling was used for all types of furniture framing. The most frequently found application are table rails doweled into the leg post and chair rails doweled into the legs. This mode of construction might not have been as good as the mortise and tenon that preceded it, but it was still a sound form of construction. Much

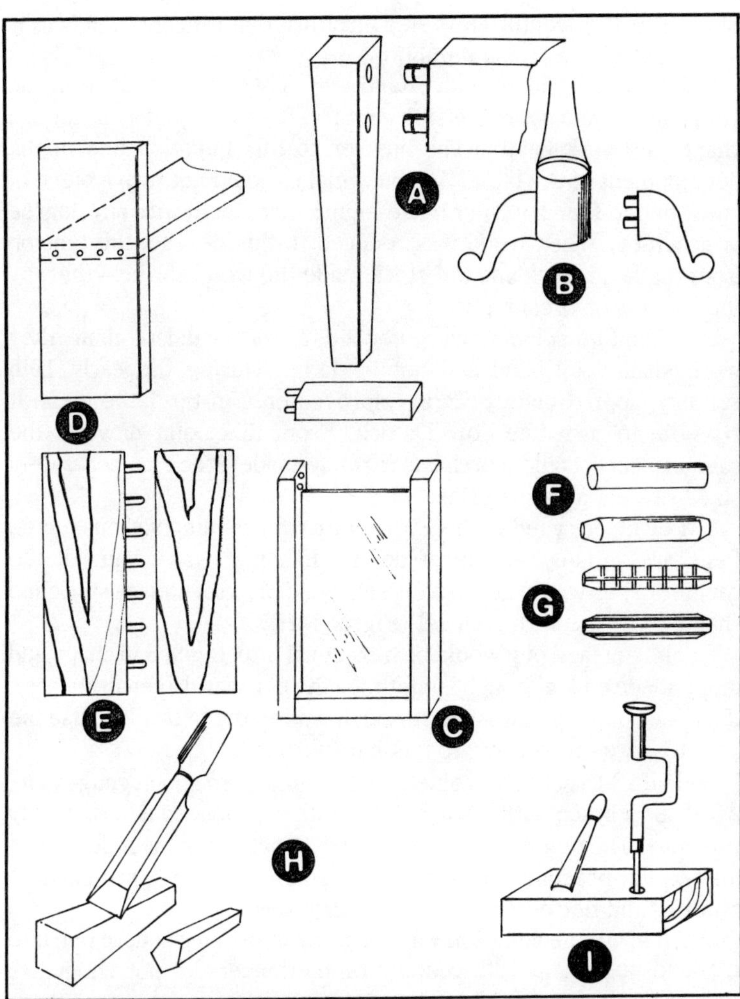

Fig. 2-14. A standard doweled joint (A) used for chair or frame construction. This mode of joining used as a simple alternative to a mortise and tenon joint. Dowels used for pedestal leg construction (B) can be used to replace a sliding dovetail. Dowels used for frame and panel door construction (C). This method of construction is rarely encountered. Dowels used for shelf construction in a cupboard (D). Dowels used to align boards for edge gluing (E). This was the dominant mode of joining in the post-1850 period. Standard dowels and pointed dowels (F) can be found in 19th-century pieces as well as modern pieces. Fluted and spiral dowels (G) so cut to allow glue to squeeze from the joint are only found in furniture made in this century. Pegs (H) were the 18th-century forerunners of dowels and were made by hand with a chisel. Pegs were square, octogonal, hexagonal or otherwise irregular, but they were never perfectly round as a dowel. In the 18th century, peg holes were made with a spoon gauge (I) or a simple spade bit. Both produced a somewhat irregular hole.

of the late 19th-century doweled furniture that remains stands as a testament to the joint's durability.

It is important to understand why doweling was done in the 19th century and not in the 18th century, It was not just a matter of a change in work habits. The answer to this question lies in the development of the lathe. A cabinetmaker could not turn a piece of stock to one-fourth inch or three-eighth inch round with any degree of accuracy. When wood was reduced to this degree, the tension from the head stock and tail stock made the wood spring—thereby throwing it or breaking it.

When fine spindles were needed, as for a windsor chair, they were shaped by hand and not by lathe. During the early 19th century, approximately 1825, improvements in the lathe made it possible to turn fine dowel stock. From this point onward, the cabinetmaker could purchase a ready-made stock of accurately sized dowels at a fair price.

Pegs were used in the 18th century for pinning various joints. Pegs are actually a type of dowel. If a peg was required, the cabinetmaker would take a well-seasoned piece of square stock and shape it to size with a chisel (Fig. 2-14H).

The finished peg would be hexagonal or octogonal in shape and taper at one end (although sometimes the peg was driven in square). If the size of the peg was imprecise, it was all the better because the hole that was to receive it was hardly round.

The 18-th century cabinetmaker would use a spoon gouge (Fig. 2-14I) or a brace with a spade bit. Neither produced a particularly true hole. The peg was oversized so the precision of the hole did not matter. For precision drilling, improvements were required in drill bits that did not occur until in the 19th century.

All in all, the situation was truly one of fitting a square peg into a round hole. The 18th-century cabinetmaker did not choose to make a peg by hand due to his love of labor, but rather because there was no alternative. When evaluating pieces with dowel construction, keep in mind the following points:

☐ In the case of antique furniture, if a perfectly round dowel is found pinning a join, it can be presumed that the piece is at least 19th century or has been repaired since the 19th century.

☐ If a piece uses dowel construction, it can be presumed that it was made, at the earliest, about 1825. But more likely that it was made after 1850.

☐ On a piece that has been doweled, there is often a slight separation between the rail and post after 50 or more years. If light can be seen between the rail and post, it must be doweled. If the rail and post are perfectly tight, look for the marks of the mortise gauge. The absence of this suggests doweling.

DRAWER CONSTRUCTION

There is a legendary scenario in the antique world of the expert collector who comes into a shop, walks to a piece, removes and examines the drawer, and then pronounces the piece as genuine. There is no doubt that one can judge much of the technical merit of a piece by the drawer. But as long as a piece can be constructed around a drawer, it is no sure guide to authenticity.

There is little difficulty in discerning a modern drawer from an antique one. A modern drawer will have hardwood sides and the back usually glued up from several pieces. The sides of the drawer will be machine dovetailed to the front. The drawer bottom will be a one-eighth inch piece of veneered plywood fitted into a groove on all four sides. The underside will have a guide that fits into a track that keeps the drawer in line. This simple drawer represents the culmination of hundreds of years of development. Sadly enough, this drawer is giving way to premolded, plastic boxes with wooden fronts.

Historically, the drawer has undergone a number of changes. An understanding of such changes can help with authenticating furniture. Figure 2-15A represents the side of a 17th-century drawer. The drawer side is rebated to the front and nailed. The side has a recess that fits into a guide on the chest. The drawer bottom is merely nailed on. This drawer is fairly crude, but in early 17th century England furniture was sparce and drawers were a luxury.

Throughout the 17th century, furniture proliferated—at least among those with money—and the drawer began to enter its maturity. By the midpoint of the century, drawers were fitted with a single, large dovetail (Fig. 2-15B). The drawer might or might not have been recessed for a drawer guide. If the drawer was not fitted for a guide, then the chest had runners and guides that kept the drawer true. The drawer bottom might have been nailed on or it might have been fitted into a groove.

By the late 17th century and early 18th century, guide recesses disappeared from the sides of drawers and the single dovetail gave way to multiple dovetails (Fig. 2-15C). As the 18th century progressed, dovetailing drawers became a means by which a craftsman demonstrated his art. A drawer might have four or six dovetails with the pins angled so sharply that hardly any wood remained where they joined the face.

This was a result of art and competition; in reality, such a great number of dovetails was not necessary for sound construction. In country furniture, the dovetailing of drawers was not as lavish in the 18th century and even less so in the 19th century.

All good quality drawers were dovetailed, but not all drawers were completely dovetailed and all drawers were not dovetailed. It was standard practice that when the front of the drawer was dovetailed so also was the rear of the drawer. It was common to use a lesser number of dovetails in the rear. Some makers dovetailed fronts while nailing the backs.

With country pieces, fine dovetails can be found. But many country furniture makers were jacks-of-all-trades lacking sophisticated skills. Consequently, drawers with nailed sides can be found with frequency. In the 19th century when the demand for cheap furniture for the working man grew, the simple nailed drawer became more common. In some instances, drawers were screwed or doweled. This was rather infrequent.

Dovetails do not provide precise information with regard to dating, but they do help establish the authenticity of a piece. A single, crude dovetail might suggest the late 17th century, but there is no reason why a 19th-century drawer cannot have a single, large dovetail. As with everything else, dovetailing has to be evaluated relative to the rest of the drawer construction and the other aspects of the piece.

Machine made, conical dovetails were making their appearance by 1850 and, by 1875, machine dovetails similar to hand dovetails were actively employed. Hand dovetailing was vigorous until at least the 1875 period, and could be found in commercial furniture until World War I. Even now, hand dovetailing can be found, to a very limited extent, in some commercial-production, heirloom furniture.

The message that a drawer has to tell is not only in the dovetailing, but also in the construction of the drawer bottom. Early and somewhat crude drawer bottoms were nailed on but, with the maturity of the drawer, bottoms were fit into grooves around the base of the drawer. Figure 2-16A shows a typical arrangement with the grooves running around the sides and front of the drawer. The grooves were made accurately through the use of a plough plane and were typically one-fourth inch to three-eighths of an inch from the bottom. The usual width of the groove was one-fourth inch.

A solid bottom board (Fig. 2-16A) was fitted to the drawer. The bottom board was chamfered on three or four sides to fit into the groove, while the overall thickness of the board was approximately twice the width of the groove. The use of a chamfered bottom board was adopted from the panel construction of the 17th century. The treatment of a board in this manner allowed for greater strength and appreciatively less work for the craftsman. The bottom board could just as well have been rebated instead of chamfered (Fig. 2-16B). There is no reason why this could not have been done on an 18th-century piece, but I have never seen it on pieces predating 1850.

The overall construction of the drawer, excluding the backboard, is shown in Fig. 2-16C and represents typical drawer construction from 1700 to 1900. In some instances drawer bottoms were reenforced with glue blocks, as in Fig. 2-16D, but this is not typical. During the second half of the 19th century, some modification of drawer construction was attempted (Fig. 2-16E). Rather than cut a recess into the drawer side, which naturally weakens it, runners were glued to the side to create the recess for the drawer bottoms. For decorative purposes, the runners would appear as quarter-round moldings. In many respects, this type of construction was sounder than the traditional construction, but it never caught on to any great degree.

Drawer backs tended to receive different types of treatment. The back could be grooved and dovetailed (hence the same treat-

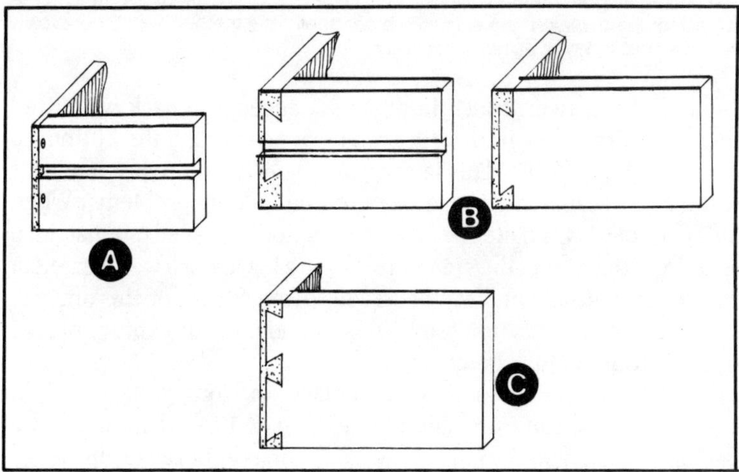

Fig. 2-15. A simple nailed drawer (A) with a side channel to guide it in place was a common form of drawer construction in the 17th century. A single large dovetail (B) with or without a guide channel was used in the late 17th century. A drawer constructed with multiple dovetails (C) as found in 18th-century or 19th-century furniture.

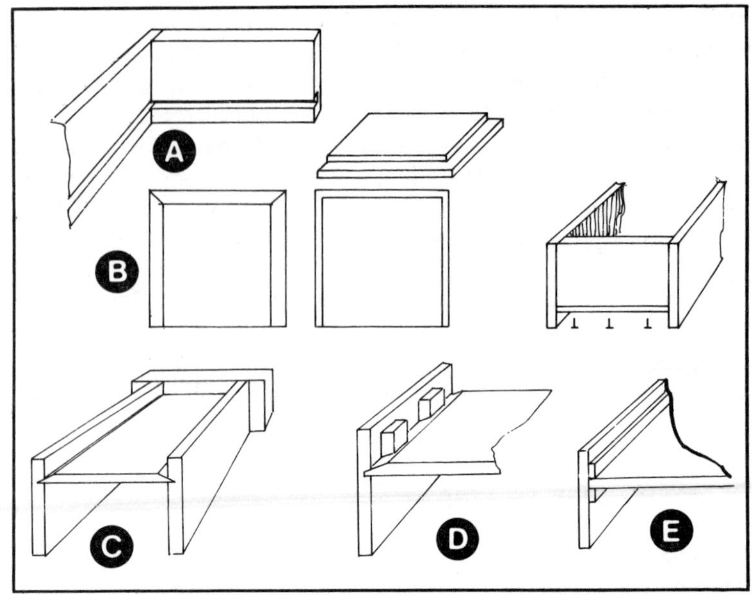

Fig. 2-16. Typical drawer construction (A) with a channel to allow the insertion of the bottom board. Bottom boards were almost always chamfered (B) to fit the drawer channel. Nevertheless, some were simply rebated. Rebated bottoms are usually found in the post-1850 period. A rear view (C) of a typical drawer prior to securing a backboard. Glue blocks (D) used to provide additional strength. This was an inadequate method of treatment. Glue blocks are used to form a recess (E) rather than weaken the side with a channel. This method was theoretically superior, but it never gained popularity.

ment as the drawer front). In other instances, the back was fitted above the drawer bottom with brads driven through the bottom to secure it (Fig. 2-16F). This latter example is the more predominant of the two because it eliminated potential binding problems. When the rear board was nailed, it was on occasion recessed one-half inch or so from the rear of the side rails. When a backboard was treated in this manner, less difficulty occurred in the fitting of the drawer. This form of construction tends to be found on 19th-century pieces and not 18th-century pieces.

When drawer bottoms were in place, the long grain would, in most instances, run from side to side (Fig. 2-17A). This was not a random decision on the part of the cabinetmaker because shrinkage problems were reduced. Wood shrinks across the grain. Consequently, it would pull out from the rear, but remain in the side grooves—leaving the drawer intact.

In Fig. 2-17B, the grain runs from front to rear. That is not a satisfactory arrangement for the reasons mentioned. This type of placement is most often found in pieces from the 17th century and the first half of the 18th century. But this is not a hard and fast rule.

Another form of bottom construction involved the use of a *mutin*. A mutin is a strip used to separate two boards (Fig. 2-17C). The use of a mutin allowed for smaller bottom boards, less subject to warping, while providing the maximum mechanical allowance against shrinkage. Drawer construction employing mutins was used on English furniture as early as 1790, but such pieces are encountered infrequently. This type of construction is more often found in post-1850 pieces and it is commonly found in post-1900 pieces. When evaluating drawer construction keep in mind the following points:

☐ Modern drawers use glued stock, plywood bottoms, and machine-made dovetails.

☐ Seventeenth-century drawers were usually constructed with just a single, large dovetail.

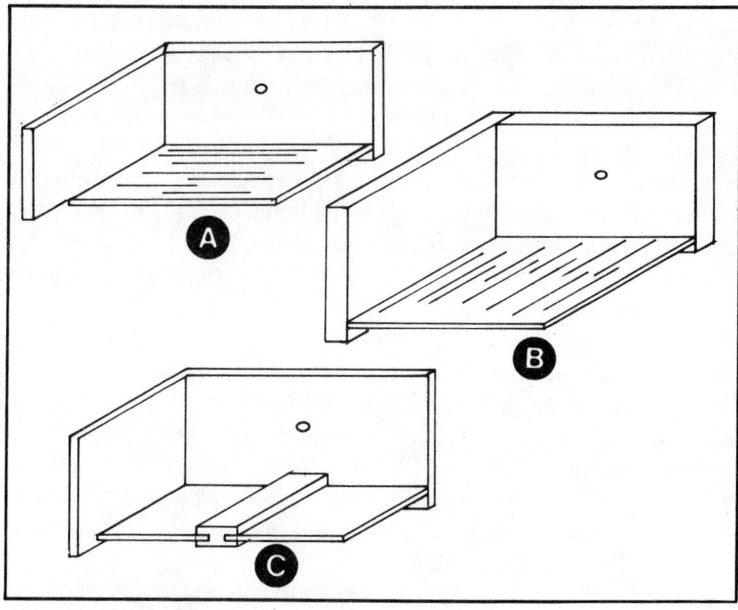

Fig. 2-17. The long grain (A) on a bottom board typically runs from side to side so that shrinkage will not pull it from the channel. Occasionally, the long grain is run from front to back (B). This is usually found on 18th-century pieces. A dividing board (C) called a mutin was used occasionally to add rigidity to a bottom. In England, mutins were used as early as 1790.

☐ Eighteenth- and 19th-century drawers frequently had multiple, fine dovetails.

☐ Not all drawers were dovetailed.

☐ Nailed drawer bottoms indicate early construction or crude construction.

☐ Rebated drawer bottoms (as opposed to chamfered) suggest 19th-century construction.

☐ Rear boards, which are positioned less than the full length of the side boards, suggest 19th-century construction.

☐ When a drawer bottom is positioned such that the grain runs from front to rear as opposed to from side to side, a construction date prior to 1750 is suggested. This is not an absolute rule.

☐ Mutins were used for drawer bottom construction on English pieces in the late 18th century. On American pieces, this mode of construction is most often found on pieces made after 1850.

DOOR CONSTRUCTION

There are all kinds of doors: house doors, Dutch doors, barn doors and a thousand variations only limited by the imagination of the maker. With country furniture, doors are limited to cupboards and washstands that have, thankfully, few variations.

The simplest door is the *plank door* (Fig. 2-18A). The plank door is a solid piece of wood fitted with hinges and attached to a proper opening. This type of door is usually associated with primitive, handyman pieces because the skill required was minimal. A number of well-made cupboards can be found utilizing plank doors. This suggests that there were some very talented amateurs. An alternate, and equally likely proposition, is that some country cabinetmakers chose to use this simple arrangement. The problem with this type of door is its high susceptibility to warpage. Plank doors can be found on 18th- and 19th- century pieces.

Another mode of simple door construction involved cleating boards together (Fig. 2-18B). This type of door is found on more primitive pieces, but it served its function well. The use of multiple pieces reenforced by cleats allows the door to expand and contract so that warpage is avoided. Cleated doors are found on cupboards of 18th- and 19th-century vintage.

The majority of cupboard doors found will be the framed panel type. The framed panel door, if properly made is unsurpassed for its function. Construction of the door requires a frame mortised together. Each member of the frame has a channel in which the solid panel will be fitted. When complete, the frame provides the requi-

58

site rigidity while the panel is free to float (expand and contract) in the channel. The framed panel door should be relatively free from problems associated with warpage and shrinkage. This style door was primary in the 18th and 19th centuries.

The panel inserted in the door was known as a fielded panel or a reverse fielded panel. The door panel was prepared in the same manner as a drawer bottom; it was chamfered on four sides to fit the channels. The chamfering also reduced the proportion of the face so that it did not look clumsy in the frame (Fig. 2-18C). Chamfering a door in this manner was known as *fielding a panel*. The door is referred to as a fielded panel door when the panel faces outward.

A cabinetmaker following the dictates of style could choose to reverse the panel (Fig. 2-18D). The panel would appear in the solid, slightly recessed from the edge of the frame. This style door was known as a *reverse fielded panel*. Both the fielded and reverse fielded doors were used in the 18th and 19th centuries. The fielded panel had more popularity in the 18th century. The reverse panel was more popular in the 19th century.

The usual construction for the fielded panel door was mortise and tenon. A number of arrangements such as plain tenon, through tenon, open tenon or bridal joint, or the haunched mortise and tenon (Fig. 2-18D) could be used. During the 18th century, these joints were often assembled dry on country furniture and they were pinned. The haunched mortise and tenon required gluing and was very popular during the 19th century. Pinned mortise and tenon suggest construction prior to 1825. The haunched mortise and tenon suggests construction after 1790. This is not a firm rule; it is a guideline.

On pieces made after 1850, framed panel doors can be found that are not fielded. The panels used are thin and they are directly fitted to the channel or they are slightly rebated to fit the channel. On some pieces, the panels are not solid; they are glued stock from several pieces. A glued panel can be found as early as 1850, but it is more likely a product of the 1870's or a later period.

Framed panel doors have never lost their popularity and they are still actively used. On the modern door, the bevels are made by saw or another machine that leaves a smooth surface. The remainder of the surface is true as a product of a thickness planer. On an old door, the marks of the plane should be visible upon careful scrutiny. Handmade mortises should be detected by tool marks and the telltale signs of the mortise gauge. When you are evaluating door construction, keep in mind the following points:

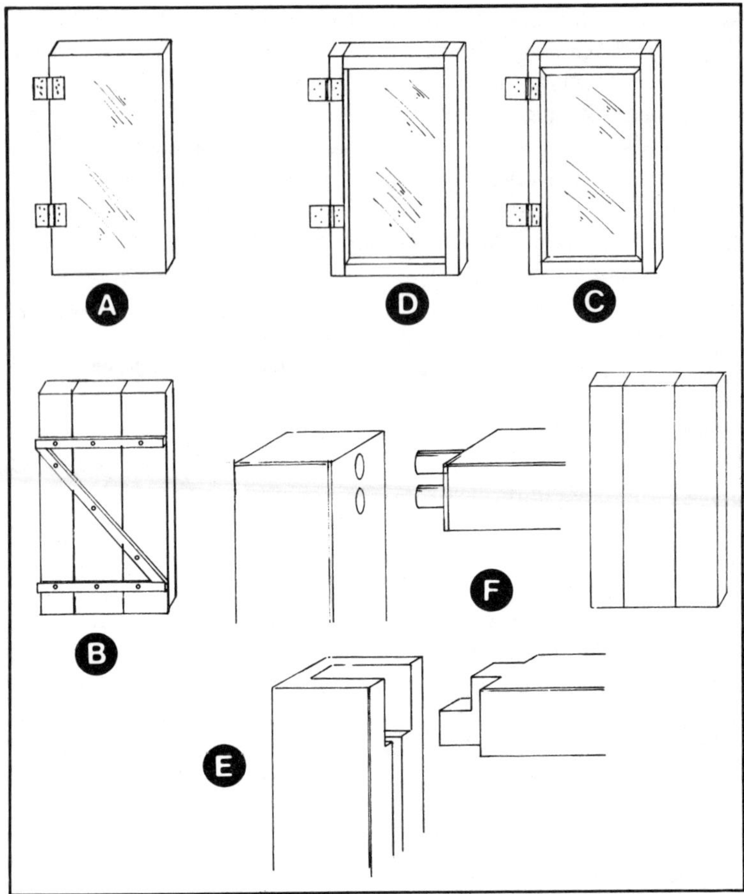

Fig. 2-18. Examples of door construction: (A) simple plank door cut from one piece of wood; (B) a cleated door made up of multiple boards held together with nailed battens where the nails were run through the board and clinched. (C) a frame and panel door with a fielded panel; (E) a frame and panel door with a reverse fielded panel; (F) a haunched mortise and tenon frequently used to join 19th-century frame and panel doors.

  ☐ Plank doors, cleated doors, and framed panel doors can be found on either 18th-century or 19th-century pieces.

  ☐ Fielded panels and reverse fielded panels were used in the 18th and 19th centuries. The fielded panel was more popular in the 18th century. The reverse fielded panel was more popular in the 19th century.

  ☐ The use of pinned mortises (hand-shaped pegs) suggests an origin prior to 1825.

☐ The use of a haunched mortise and tenon in door construction suggests a date of origin after 1790.

☐ Doors having solid, thin panels that are not fielded suggest a date of origin after 1850.

☐ Doors having panels made from glued stock suggest a date of origin of 1850 or later.

☐ Framed panel doors with machine-made mortises and tenons can be assumed to have been made after 1850.

CHAIR CONSTRUCTION

Most traditional furniture is *rectilinear*. That is a fancy way of saying it is composed of straight lines. One notable exception is the chair. The chair is frequently composed of curving lines, hence *curvilinear*. A chair can also be rectilinear. Chair construction is the same as that of other furniture except that some accommodation must be made for curvilinear function. Figure 2-19A represents a typical 19th-century chair known as a *rodback* or *country windsor*.

This type of chair, originating in the second quarter of the 19th century, uses mortise the tenon construction throughout. These are round tenons to accommodate the design of the chair. If the chair is carefully examined, you might find that the spindles are tapered and made by hand—indicating construction around 1825. If the spindles were the same throughout and obviously the work of a lathe, the chair would be dated more toward 1850.

With an early chair the spindles would have no shoulder and would be inserted between the crest rail and the seat. On a chair made later in the century, the spindles might have a shoulder. The chair legs would be lathe turned and could be adorned with ring turnings or be simply tapered. The legs might use a plain mortise and tenon or a *through mortise* with a wedged tenon (Fig. 2-19B). The leg could also be attached by a hidden tenon or foxed-wedged tenon (Fig. 2-19C). The through tenon was not popular in all regions of the country and you are likely to find more 19th-century chairs with plain or foxed tenons.

Stretchers were necessary for the stability of a chair and it might have one or two stretchers between each post (except for the rear which would only have one). The stretchers could have been handmade using a drawknife or made using a lathe. The ends of the stretcher would become the tenons which would fit the mortises in the chair legs. As shown in Fig. 2-19D, the stretcher might be tapered to fit the mortise or it might have been turned with a shoulder.

The seat of the chair would be one solid piece of wood and could be horseshoe shaped or saddle-shaped (Fig. 2-19E). The underside of the seat would be in the rough with saw marks or adz marks visible. The adz is a hatchet-type tool used to remove quantities of wood quickly. Solid seats would have been made throughout most of the 19th century. Toward the end of the century, as now, glued up stock was used. When a piece is presented as antique, you should always question the validity of a glued seat (other than as a repair).

Chairs must have a crest rail to hold the back posts together. Exceptions are ladderback chairs where the top rung functions as a crest rail, or a hoop-back chair that makes a rail superfluous. Variations in crest rails are limited because they must go on top of the posts, behind the posts, or between the posts. With the rodback chair the crest rail goes over the posts. The spindles are inserted into the posts. In Fig. 2-19F, the crest rail is placed between the posts. This chair back is late nineteenth century mission style. The crest rail might be mortised or doweled.

Figure 2-19G represents a crest rail that could be on a rodback chair in which the rail goes over the spindles and behind the posts. The rodback has rear posts as well as spindles. It would be impossible to insert the posts unless the crest rail was of unreasonably large proportion. In this case, a compromise is achieved in which the rear posts are lapped or recessed so that the rail can fit directly over the spindles. This latter arrangement produced very satisfactory results.

In Fig. 2-19H, the back of a mid-18th-century, New York Hudson Valley, splat-back chair is shown. With this chair, the builder could exercise a prerogative with regard to the attachment of the crest rail. As can be seen on the left of the chair, a standard rectangular tenon was used that was later pinned. On the right side, an alternative arrangement can be seen—that of a round tenon. If a round tenon is used, it would be continuous with the back post and not an inserted dowel. Either arrangement could have been used.

For a chair that did not have a solid seat, framing was required. Most framed 18th-century and first-half, 19th-century chairs used standard mortise and tenon construction (Fig. 2-19I). When a framed chair had round leg posts, as with a ladderback, round tenons were employed (Fig. 2-19J). Chairs such as this were invariably meant to be rushed or splinted.

During the 18th and early 19th centuries, the seat rails were rectangular in nature to provide a wide surface area for the rush.

Edges were rounded to prevent cutting of the rush. Toward the middle of the 19th century, round dowel stock was used for the seat rails.

Figure 2-20A represents a rush-bottomed ladderback chair with sausage and ball turnings, ball finials, and three arched slats. This chair is similar to one that might be found in the second half of the 18th century. The eighteenth century chair, however, would have been more likely to have four slats.

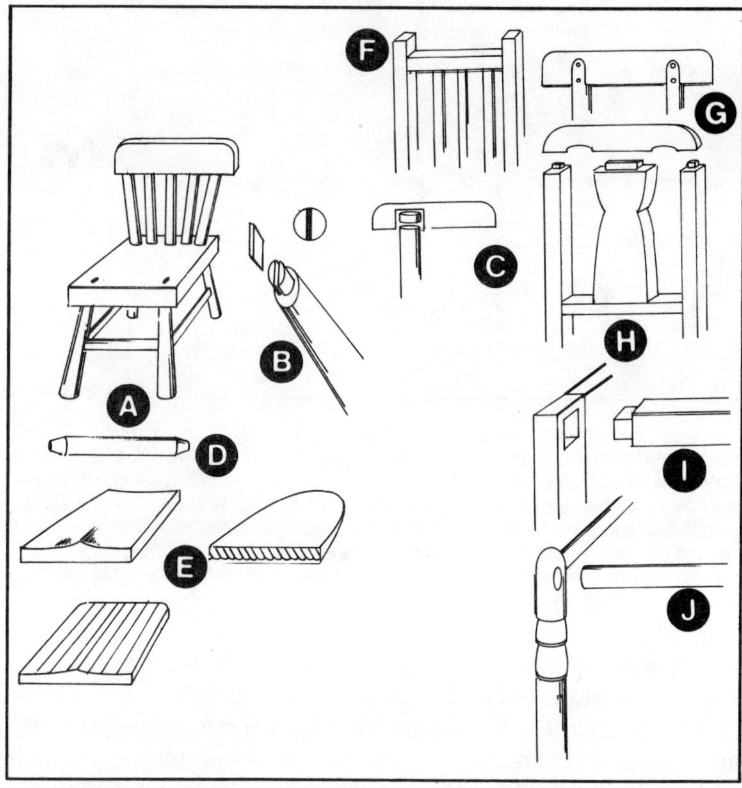

Fig. 2-19. A 19th-century rodback (country windsor) chair (A). A leg utilizing a wedged tenon (B). The tenon was run through the seat and wedged from the top. A foxed tenon used to secure a leg from the underside of the chair (C). A chair stretcher could have a lathe turned tenon or simply be tapered to fit the mortise (D). Saddle and horseshoe seats (E) made from the solid. Seats made from multiple boards suggest post-1850 construction. A chair crestrail (F) inserted between back post on a mission-style chair. A crest rail (G) attached to half lapped back post, commonly found on 19th-century chairs. A crest rail (H) tenoned to back post with either square or round tenons, commonly found on 18th-century chairs. A rectangular chair rail (I) attached with a plain tenon. A round chair rail (J) attached with a round tenon.

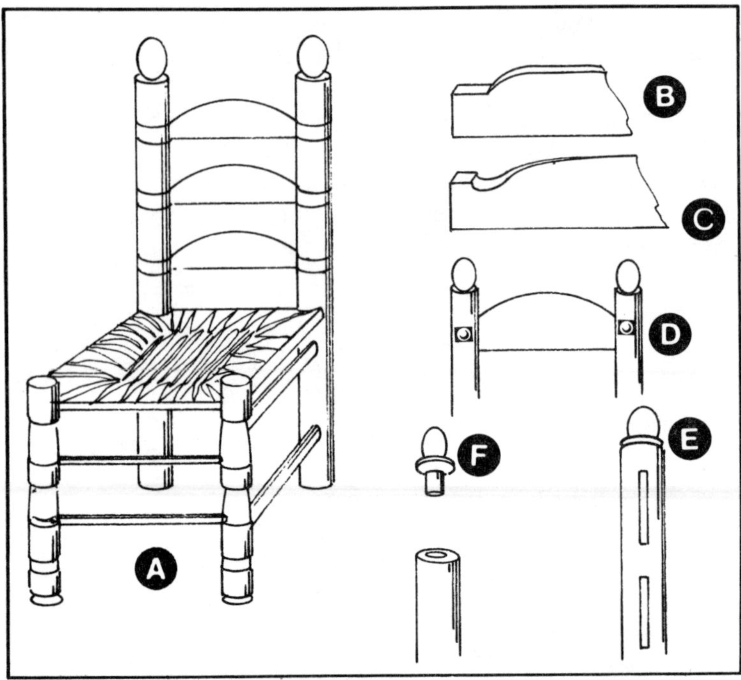

Fig. 2-20. Examples of chair construction: (A) three slat ladderback chair with sausage and ball turnings and flame finials; (B) standard mortise and tenon construction used for the attachment of the slat; (C) modified tenon utilized to provide additional strength found on 18th-century and 19th-century chairs; (D) wooden pegs used to pin the top slat to the rear post; (E) machine-made mortises (note that the mortise slots are rounded from the machine process); (F) a finial made from a separate piece and doweled into place (this was an occasional practice).

It is sometimes asserted as a rule that 18th-century chairs had four slats while 19th-century chairs had three slats. This has to be rejected on its face value. On the other hand, there is enough truth in the statement to accept it as a guideline. In the first half of the 18th century, the proportions of these chairs were heavy, with bold and elaborate turnings. Toward the end of the century, there was less elaboration and the chair assumed much lighter proportions.

In the 19th century, the ladderback became a more functional chair (the ancestor to the kitchen chair). The chairs of the 19th century assumed heavier proportions than their late 18th century antecedents and tended to have very little by way of turnings except an occasional ball and ring turning or a button foot. Finials, however, remained popular throughout the century.

The construction of a ladderback chair has remained rather constant. There are front posts and rear posts connected by stretchers and rails. There are some things you can look for to distinquish old chairs from new ones. The illustrated chair (Fig. 2-20) has rings located by each stretcher and slat. Usually there are two rings for a slat and one ring for a stretcher. Rings are frequently referred to as beauty rings, but this is most definitely not their function. The beauty rings are mortise marks provided to locate the mortises on each post so they will line up. The stretchers were marked with a single ring. A hole was drilled for a round mortise. The slats were marked with two rings to allow a rectangular mortise to be placed between them. In addition, the slat mortise would show the slight overrun of the mortise gauge (the same as with other mortising techniques).

Slats were and are mortised to the rear posts. Most often, a simple tenon (Fig. 2-20B) was used. Many exacting craftsmen preferred to broaden the tenon for additional strength (Fig. 2-20C). The top slat of a chair was always secured to prevent a chair from coming apart.

In the 18th century, a wooden peg was used to pin the mortise. In the 19th century, wooden pegs and nails were used to pin the slat. Wooden pegs are suggestive of an earlier origin for a 19th-century chair, but this is not a firm rule. On occasion, all slats were pinned; but this tells you nothing more than that the craftsman liked to work. The usual arrangement for pinning, whether peg or nail, was from the rear because it did not mar the looks of the chair.

Some craftsmen, however, preferred to peg from the front (Fig. 2-20D). This technique was especially popular among Shaker craftsmen, but it does not guarantee that a chair is the work of a Shaker.

Later chairs used machine-made mortises that are characteristically round (Fig. 2-20E). These mortises always appear to be somewhat oversized for the slats. On machine-made chairs, the slats are pinned with nails. If the nail is a modern round one, construction is indicated after 1875.

Chairs were the first pieces of furniture to be mass produced because no other piece of furniture was more in demand. The Hitchcock chairs and fancy chairs of the 1830's were essentially mass produced (although they were still made by hand). One chair producing area in England was turning out 1 million chairs per year, each handmade, as late as 1875. They were still underselling machine-made chairs! In America, machine-made chairs were made as early as 1850, but they are more common after 1875. The hand making of chairs did not cease with mechanization. Handmade ladderbacks were produced actively until World War I, and they are still being made in some areas.

The finials on ladderback chairs on occasion cause some confusion. More often than not, the finial was turned as a continuous part of the post. If a chair had a tall back post, it might be too large for the lathe. There are two solutions to this problem. One method involves shaping the finial by hand. It should be obvious, after examination, if the finials were hand shaped. Remember, even if turned on a lathe, there will be variations in size and shape because the turning was done by eye. The second, and problematic, solution is to turn a finial from another piece and mortise it into the post (Fig. 2-20F).

The problem is how do you know if the finial was made this way or if it was the work of an overzealous improver. The finial can be examined for wood and grain characteristics and color. The mortise can be checked to determine if it is out of round from shrinkage. But mostly all that can be done is to stand back, look at it, and decide if it looks right. When you are examining chairs, keep the following points in mind:

☐ Handmade chair spindles suggest an origin prior to 1825.

☐ Lathe made spindles suggest a date of origin of 1825 or later.

☐ Solid chair seats would be made of a single piece of wood. The seat will exhibit saw marks or adz marks on the underside.

☐ Chair seats made of multiple pieces of glued wood denote construction after 1850.

☐ Eighteenth-century ladderbacks often have four slats, but it is not an absolute rule.

☐ Slats were pinned with wooden pegs on 18th-century chairs. For 19th-century chairs, wooden pegs and nails were used. A wooden peg on a 19th-century chair suggests an origin in the early part of the century, but it is not a firm rule.

☐ Slats pinned with a modern-style round nail suggest a date of manufacture after 1875.

☐ Round slat mortises indicate machine work dating 1850 or later.

TABLES

Next to chairs, the most abundant pieces of antique furniture are tables. Unfortunately, tables are also one of the most often

66

restored antiques. Over the course of a table's life, the top receives all the wear and abuse while the base passes blithely through a sheltered existence. Quite naturally, a lot of table bases survive while a lot of tops do not. The antique collector must have some idea of how tops were made in order to ferret out the originals from the replacements.

Glue was available in the 17th and 18th centuries, but not commonly used for furniture construction due to the difficulty of using it. The 18th-century cabinetmaker had an abundance of good, wide lumber to pick from. Consequently, it was easier to make a top from one wide board than to attempt to glue together a top.

This is one area where old-time craftsmanship was not as good as modern construction. A top of several small glued boards is less likely to warp (which is another reason why a lot of old tops did not survive). Single board tops suggest one of those almost-but-not-always rules. On occasion, a top would be made in two pieces (but rarely more than two in the 18th century).

A number of different methods were used to join top boards. In Fig. 2-21A, the two boards are secured by *butterflies*. Butterflies are pieces of hardwood inletted into the underside of the table top. Given the angular nature of butterflies, the joint would not pull free and it was neat and glueless. This was a primary 18th-century method for joining table tops when a single board was not used.

Figure 2-21B illustrates a tongue and groove joint, a lap joint, and a doweled joint used to join table tops. The tongue and groove was used in the eighteenth century, but probably not as frequently as butterflies. If tongue and groove joining was employed, it was

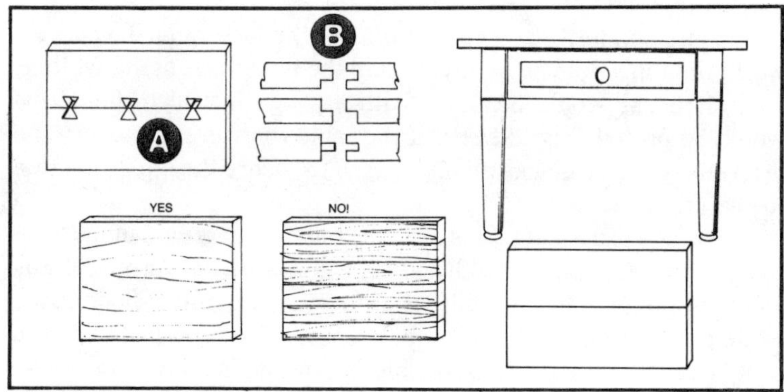

Fig. 2-21. A two-board top (A) joined with butterflies typical of 18th-century construction. Three types of joints (B) used for table top construction: tongue and groove, lap and doweled.

without glue. The tongue and groove top is secured when the top is nailed or screwed in place. While the tongue and groove holds the boards together, it does little to keep them together. In time, shrinkage will inevitably separate boards held together in this fashion.

The lap joint serves the same purpose as the tongue and groove and shares the same weaknesses. I have infrequently seen a lap joint used on 19th-century table tops, but never on an 18th-century top. I have not seen an original 18th-century table top that has been edge glued. The use of single board tops also extends to washstands and cupboards.

The dowel joint is totally a product of the 19th century. Doweled tops will be found mostly on post-1850 pieces. In the 19th century, the tradition of the single board top continued. The two board top became common. All the methods of top jointing used in the 18th century were used in the 19th century (although they were used infrequently). The primary method to top jointing was the edge gluing of boards. Multiple board tops (more than two) can be found in the 19th century. They conform to the general rule: as-early-as-1850-but-more-likely-after-1875. It is not likely that an antique table will have a multiple board top. If one is encountered, it should be subjected to the most extreme scrutiny.

Most country table tops were unashamedly nailed on. If not nailed, the top would be pegged (which was more of an eighteenth century practice) or screwed on (Fig. 2-22A). When nailed or screwed, the fasteners were positioned over the four leg posts, but to the inside corner, so that the fastener did not interfere with the mortise.

Some builders also secured tops to the side rails. To conceal work, the top would be screwed from the underside of the table. A conical recess would be made with a gauge in which the screw would be placed (Fig. 2-22B). If the table top were stationary (no drop leaves), glue blocks might be used to secure the top in addition to the other methods.

Antique drop-leaf tables are encountered in great number due to their popularity in the 18th and 19th centuries. The drop leaf was an exceedingly practical table; it utilized only minimal floor space while providing a great deal of table space. The drop-leaf table top could have a single board or double-board top like any other top— only now leaves were hinged to each side. There are three methods by which leaves were attached to tops: butt joint, tongue and groove joint, and rule joint. See Fig. 2-22C.

The butt joint—not really a joint because the board edges are left as is—was used in the 17th century and 19th century. This technique was unsophisticated and became outmoded in the 18th century. It was used again in the 19th with the proliferation of simple, country-made furniture. It is uncommon to find an 18th century drop leaf with a butt joint (some people suggest that it is impossible). If encountered, it should be treated with caution.

The tongue and groove was used in the latter part of the 17th century and the early part of the 18th century. This joint was fragile and subject to much breakage. The tongue and groove gave way to the rule joint. The rule joint has been used on better drop-leaf table construction from the 18th century until today.

Leaves would be attached with a full rule or half rule joint. A half rule, the convex projection on the table top, occupies one-half or less of the thickness of the board. The full rule joint, or just *rule joint* as it is known, occupies approximately three-quarters of the space. In the 18th century and the 19th century, cabinetmakers made this joint using a matched pair of hollow and round planes. Some slight tool marks might be visible on the rule joint, but mostly the joint has a quality of its own which is unlike the machine joint.

Rule joints were made by machine toward the end of the 19th century. Machined rule joints are almost always full rule and tend to broaden with a less severe slope. With a little practice, the machine rule joint should be easy to discern.

Table leaves were attached to the tops with a series of hinges. During the 18th century, three hinges were most often used. In the 19th century, two hinges became standard practice. This was especially true with country furniture (Fig. 2-22D). The hinge mortises on the underside of a table should reveal mortise marks and saw marks where the mortise was overcut. Mortises were cut with a saw on an angle (as shown in Fig. 2-23).

Two types of arrangements were used to support table leaves. The simplest method, as shown in Fig. 2-22E, was a simple arm on a single pivot (usually wooden). This method was not entirely satisfactory because the support rendered was somewhat minimal.

Another method was the swing leg or gate-leg, as shown in Fig. 2-22F. In the example illustrated, an additional leg was fitted to the side rail via a wooden knuckle hinge. The leg would be swung into position when the leaf was lifted—providing more than simple support. The knuckle hinge could have either a metal or wooden pivot.

Swing-leg tables did not always incorporate a third leg on each

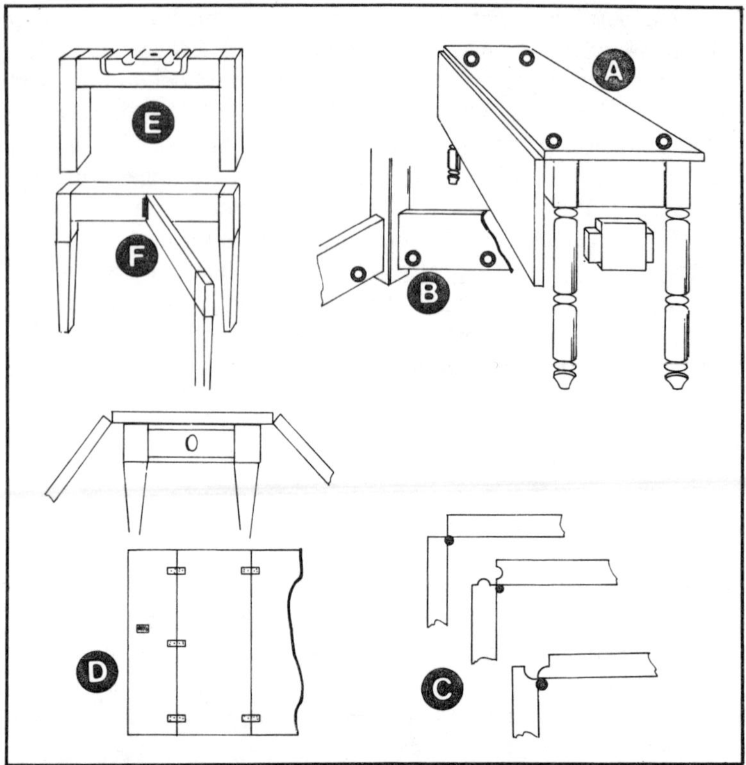

Fig. 2-22. Drop-leaf table construction. Table top (A) unashamedly nailed or screwed in place from the top side. A table top attached from the underside (B) will be screwed in place. Screw recesses will be made by a chisel and be conical in shape. Three methods (C) of leaf attachment: butt, tongue and groove, and half rule. Three hinges (D) were standard for the attachment of 18th-century tops. Two hinges became the rule in the 19th century. Wear marks as well as stop blocks should be evident on the underside of the leaves. A simple pivot arm (F) used to support a drop leaf. An additional swing leg support (F) from the drop leaf attached with a wooden knuckle joint.

side. In another variation, the opposite legs would be hinged and pivot into place. Whether a simple support or swing leg, the underside of the table should reveal an arched pattern of wear from opening and closing the table.

If there is not much overhang on a drop-leaf table, the eventual shrinkage during 50 to 100 years will pull the leaves so close to the table that they will not rest properly when closed. Shrinkage in this case gives the table the overall appearance of having wings. Although this condition might not be desirable, it does suggest age if not authenticity.

70

The construction of a table base follows the same principles of frame construction as mortise and tenon construction. A table base, other than a pedestal, will have four turned or tapered leg posts with front and side rails secured by some variation of the mortise and tenon joint. In the case of tables made after the midpoint of the century, the rails might be doweled. When you are examining tables, remember the following points:

☐ Eighteenth-century tables are almost always found with single board tops.

☐ Nineteenth-century tables are found with single and two-board tops. Two-board tops are more common. Two-board tops are frequently edge glued or doweled and glued.

☐ Tops glued up of multiple boards suggest an origin of 1875 or later (more than three boards).

☐ The tops on 19th-century country tables are frequently nailed.

☐ Drop-leaf tables using a butt joint are found in the 17th and 19th centuries, but they are infrequently found on 18th-century pieces.

☐ Drop-leaf tables using a tongue and groove joint suggest a date of origin prior to 1725.

☐ Drop-leaf tables made in the 18th century and better 19th-century tables use a half-rule joint or a full-rule joint.

☐ Machine-made rule joints are found on tables dating after 1875.

☐ Hinge mortises on drop-leaf tables should be handmade. Saw marks and marking gauge marks should be visible.

☐ The underside of a drop-leaf table should exhibit an arching wear pattern made by the leaf support.

Fig. 2-23. A table hinge displaying an overcut mortise typical of hand-cut hinge mortises.

CASE PIECES

Basic box construction items are referred to as *case pieces*. A typical case piece is a chest of drawers such as shown in Fig. 2-24A. The chest does not offer anything new as far as construction goes, but rather illustrates much of what has already been discussed. This chest has a single board top that is nailed to the frame. It might just as well be attached to a sub-top that is dovetailed to the base. The side of the chest is a single board (often referred to as a plank end or side). The majority of 18th-century chests will have plank sides.

A chest could also have a paneled side as shown in Fig. 2-24B. The panel construction of a chest is the same as door construction. Uprights and cross members are mortised and tenoned. The panel of a chest would be thin and not fielded. Paneled sides can be found on 17th-century chests, early 18th-century chests, late 18th-century chests, and on 19th-century chests. Paneled sides became very common in the post-1850 period.

The back of the chest would have standard backboard construction with rough-cut boards butted, lapped, or tongue and grooved, and then nailed (Fig. 2-24C). Tongue and grooved backs are more often found on 19th-century pieces than on 18th-century pieces. When the tongue and groove joint is made with hand planes, the tongue is frequently off center. If a builder had a well-equipped shop, he would have tongue and groove planes matched to each size board. If he did not, he would use the closest (which accounts for off center joints). In the post-1850 period, this joint was often made by machine and appears to be quite shallow when compared to hand-made joints.

The drawer dividers and side rails might be mortised or simply nailed to the sides (Fig. 2-24D). In Fig. 2-24 the runners are merely framed. In another instance the drawers might be separated by one solid board (as shown in Figure 2-24E). When drawer dividers are solid, they are referred to as *dustboards;* This is the function they served. With 18th-century pieces, dustboards are more commonly found on English chests. In the 19th century, the general tendency was not to use dustboards (whether English or American).

A variety of feet arrangements can be found on chests. These include ball feet, bun feet, turned feet, ogee feet, bracket feet, and, on high styles, a cabriole leg with pad or ball and claw. The most prevalent foot is the bracket foot. See Fig. 2-24. With this example, the bracket foot is created by shaping the bottom rail and the sides that are mortised into side rails. With the majority of 18th-century chests and later 19th-century chests, a separate baseboard molding and foot are fitted to the chest. When the feet are fitted in this manner, they are always mitered (as in Fig. 2-24F).

Drawer construction on chests will be of the variety mentioned earlier. The most basic construction will use simple nails. The better construction will have dovetails, and either handmade or early bullet dovetails (Fig. 2-24G). The number of drawers in a piece as well as the size will vary. In the 18th century, a chest of drawers almost always had four drawers. The top drawer could be divided into two smaller drawers known as *short drawers.* This configuration is known as *three long and two short.* When an 18th-century chest is found with three drawers, it is most likely adapted from another piece. This rule does not apply to tall chests in the high style. Nineteenth-century country chests frequently have four drawers. They do not vigorously adhere to any rule with regard to the number of drawers.

High-style pieces will have brasses in accordance with the style of the time. Eighteenth-century and 19th-century country pieces might have brasses, but more frequently they are found with simple wooden knobs. The most prevalent style knob in the past or present is the mushroom design (Fig. 2-24H). These knobs were attached in a number of manners. Following the sequence shown in the illustration, the first knob has a turned shank which is fitted into a hole bored in the drawer front. The second knob has a wooden screw. This arrangement involved threading the shank or fitting a threaded piece to the knob which is mostly the case. The hole in the drawer front is also threaded to mate with the wooden screw.

In some cases, the knob is fitted with a metal screw and screwed directly to the front of the drawer. The next knob shown is fitted with a plain screw that is inserted from the inside of the drawer. This arrangement is found on all modern construction using wooden knobs. It was widely used in the 19th century.

With pieces made prior to 1850, the wood screw will have a blunt end and not be pointed like the modern gimlet screw. The last knob shown has a threaded bolt that is fitted to the knob. The end of the bolt that is fitted to the knob will have an unthreaded, square shank. This knob is fitted through a hole in the drawer and secured with a nut.

If it is an 18th-century piece, the nut will invariably be round because it was easier to make. For a19th-century piece, the familiar square nut will be used.

When either the wooden shank, wooden thread, or threaded bolt are found securing knobs, antique construction is suggested. A

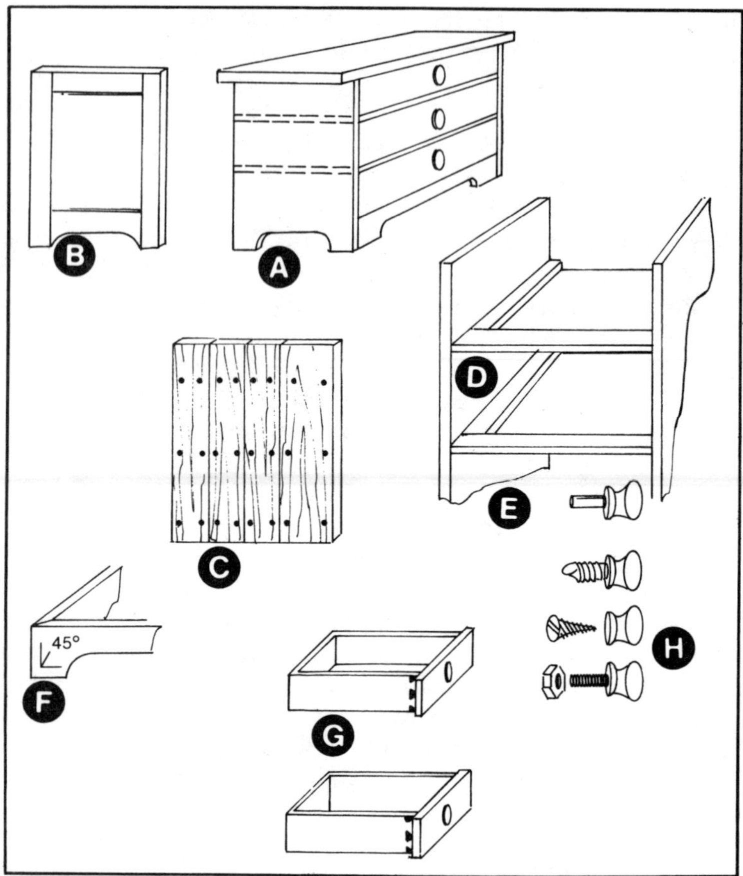

Fig. 2-24. Chest construction: (A) plank ended chest made from a single board; (B) frame and panel chest side construction found mostly in the 17th century and the 19th century, (very popular in the post-1850 period). (C) backboard construction butted, lapped, or tongue and groove (backboards could be vertical or horizontal); (D) drawer divider and runner made with framing members only; (E) drawer divider (dustboard) made from the solid or frame and panel; (F) mitered bracket foot; (G) hand-dovetailed drawer and machine (bullet) dovetailed drawer. (H) four methods of knob attachment: wooden shank, wooden thread, screw from the rear, threaded nut and bolt with either standard square nut or handmade round nut.

knob fitted with a simple screw might or might not be antique. When you are examining a chest of drawers, you should keep in mind the following points:

☐ Chests of drawers used plank construction or paneled construction in the 17th, 18th, and 19th centuries.

☐ The use of paneled chest construction proliferated in the post-1850 machine period.

☐ Chest panels made up of more than one board suggest an origin after 1850.

☐ Backboards on chests could be butted, lapped, or tongue and grooved.

☐ With hand-planed tongue and grooved joints, the tongue is frequently off center.

☐ Dustboards are commonly found on 18th-century chests, but they are infrequently found on 19th-century chests. English designs utilized dustboards to a far greater degree than did American designs.

☐ Eighteenth-century chests of drawers use a standard four-drawer arrangement (excluding tall chests). Chests with less than four drawers should be treated with caution.

☐ Nineteenth-century chests of drawers do not adhere to any rigorous standard with regard to the number of drawers.

☐ Country chests can be found with brasses, or with wood, glass, or porcelain knobs. Knobs attached with threaded wooden screws (dowels), round wooden shanks, or threaded metal bolts suggest a date of origin prior to 1850.

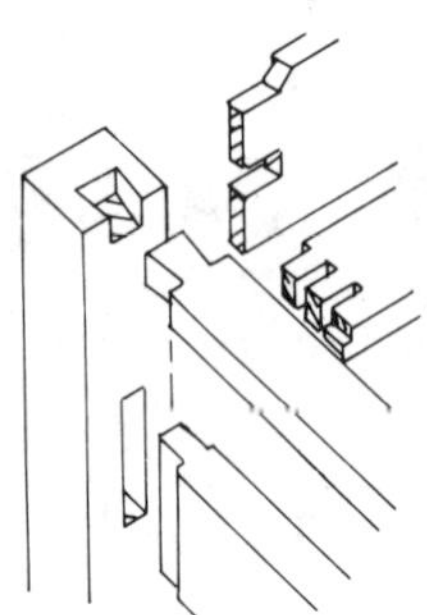

Chapter 3

Authenticating: A Guide to Age and Wear

The ability to determine what is antique and what is not antique is, for some, an art. There are those rare, talented persons who can view a piece from afar and detect a slight deviation in style; they can then announce the infamous work—*fake.* For the majority of antiquarians, the matter is approached from the more scientific basis of logic, order, and method.

There are four criteria for evaluating the authenticity of an antique. They must be used in conjunction. The first considerations should be design and style. Does a piece present itself in the style of the 17th, 18th, or 19th centuries? Did the style cease with the style period or did it have a later revival period that could be confused with it? If the piece is a later reproduction, does any part of it appear to be uncharacteristic? Craftsmen will often include, almost unconsciously, stylistic elements of the period they are working in when copying a piece.

The numerous picture books on the market can help the willing student develop a basis for understanding style. Visits to museums will complement and reenforce the knowledge gained from books. For country furniture, especially 19th-century furniture which has not yet come into its own, knowledge is best gained from constant visits to antique shops and local museums. If a local adult school or college extension program offers a course in the history of design, much can be covered in a short period of time.

To the novice collector, learning about styles appears to be an awesome task, but a considerable amount can be learned in a relatively short period of time. This is the type of study where the more you learn the more you become aware of how much there is to learn. It is a lifelong task and process.

The second criterion in evaluating a piece is construction. Methods of construction are associated with specific historical periods. All of these handwork methods can be found in modern, craft-made furniture, but almost never in mass-produced furniture—not even expensive reproduction furniture.

It is possible for a modern craftsperson to copy an historic style using all the correct methods of construction. It is unlikely, however, that he will not succumb to some modern labor-saving shortcuts. Given this possibility, the first two criteria are inadequate to assure the authenticity of a piece.

The third criterion to be applied is that of age, wear, and congruence. By congruence I mean the use of nails, brasses, or other hardware properly associated with the period of construction. When the telltale signs of age and wear are added to style and construction, you have the basic method of antique authentication.

This is the basic method, but no method is foolproof. There are expert forgers who can not only copy style and construction, but they can also reproduce the signs of wear and age to an alarming degree. Museums have been fooled and experts have been fooled. There are few expert fakers of this quality. The cost of their forgery limits it to a very small part of the antique market. The sad truth is that so many collectors know so little that sloppy forgeries are passed off upon collectors with ease. The constant and practiced use of authentication will result in the detection of most forgeries.

The last criterion is, alas, not one of science or method, but rather a little old-fashioned intuition. There might or might not be a scientific explanation for intuition, but whatever the case, it should not be ignored, and it should not be pursued with mystic fever. If you encounter a piece that meets the tests of style, construction, and wear, but still leaves you with an unnerving feeling that something is wrong, then perhaps it is best to decide against it. You might be detecting some inconsistency of which you are not consciously aware. If you are not prone to follow your intuitive sense, at least let this be cause to ruthlessly examine the piece.

The application of all or any of these criteria must be directed by logic and common sense. Common sense is the best tool in the arsenal of the antique collector. This is especially true with regard to questions of age and wear. If there is an upholstered armchair in the living room, what wears out first? The forward part of the arm does; the place where tactile persons grab and fidget.

If the chair is a wooden armchair used for 100 or 200 years, what wear are you going to see? The arm will be worn incredibly smooth by friction and hand oils. If there are wooden kitchen chairs with leg stretchers, what does the front stretcher look like? As a rule, it is scratched and worn from feet resting on it. If a chair is 100 years old, the wear will be the same, but there is a lot more of it.

What if an antique chair has two front stretchers and both are worn severely? There are two possibilities. One possibility is that the chair was alternately used by an average person and a midget. The second possibility is that someone has tampered with the upper stretcher to make it look old. Careful observation and the application of common sense can tell you quite a bit.

BOARDS

A single board in a piece of furniture can tell a great deal. Only modern lumber comes in perfect three-fourth inch or 1-inch dimensions. The boards used in antique furniture had to be hand dressed (planed smooth and parallel from the rough sawn board). No matter how good a cabinetmaker was, he could not perfectly dimension a board; it will never maintain an exact size throughout. These variations are not usually visible to the eye, but they can be detected by measurement.

A caliper, available in pocket sizes, can be used to measure a board at several points. If a board is hand planed, a variation of approximately one-thirty-second of an inch will be found. When hand planing, there is a tendency to taper near the edges. Consequently, the greatest variation will usually be found between the end and the center of a board (Fig. 3-1). A table top that measures a perfect three-fourths of an inch must be presumed to have been made after 1825, but more likely after 1850, when machine planed lumber was available.

Several years ago, I encountered a fine, demure, 18th-century gate-leg table in a small shop in England. The dealer insisted that the top was original. Consistent measurements were made at several points several times which lead to no other possibility than the use of modern lumber. Interestingly, the top was beautifully pegged and displayed slight plane marks and considerable wear. The hinge mortises on the underside of the table displayed clean, deep and strong saw marks that should have been softened by age—again suggesting recent work. I bought the table because it had a fine antique base and a darn good top replacement. The dealer still thinks the top is authentic.

A board surface that shows in the finished furniture will have been worked smooth. The final planing would have been with a fine-set, smooth plane that would have virtually left no marks. After the final planing, any tool marks remaining would have been removed with a scraper or abrasives. The key here is that all marks visible to the naked eye would have been removed. That does not mean all marks are gone. Inspection with a hand lens and flashlight might yield the telltale marks of the hand plane. The pocket-sized hand lens with built-in light is inexpensive and ideally suited for this purpose.

A table top or dresser top might have been refinished many times. This will obscure hand-tool marks so the test is not absolute. In many cases the human hand works as well as a pocket lens in determining whether or not a surface has been hand planed. The tips of the fingers run lightly over the surface of a board will detect the ridges or concavities left by hand planing. This skill can be learned with minimal practice.

The undersurfaces of boards will usually supply more information with regard to hand tooling. The average craftsman would not pay the same attention to the undersurface as the finished surface. Consequently, these surfaces tend to reveal more markings. A collector should have no hesitency in checking these surfaces. With a chest of drawers, the drawers must be removed and the piece inverted and illuminated. This might be a cumbersome task, but it is necessary.

It is worthwhile to develop an eye for wood and grain characteristics for when you are assessing a piece. Handcrafted furniture has an infinite advantage over mass-produced furniture in that the craftsman can select wood for its best grain characteristic. This advantage was even greater for an 18th-century craftsman or early 19th-century craftsman who had access to a large and select stock that simply does not exist today. The top of an 18th-century sideboard might be highly figured mahogany as compared to a

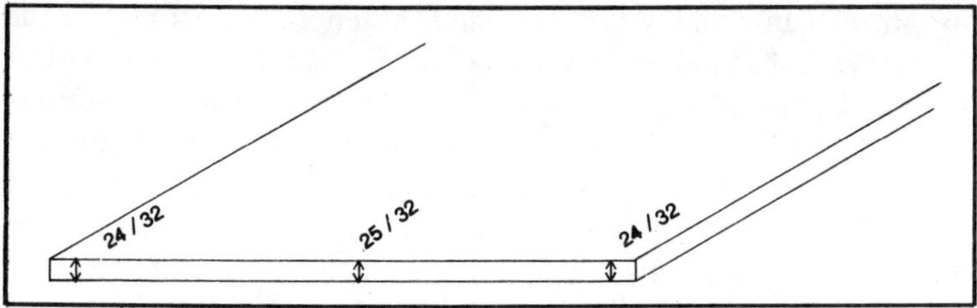

Fig. 3-1. A hand-planed board illustrating variation in thickness.

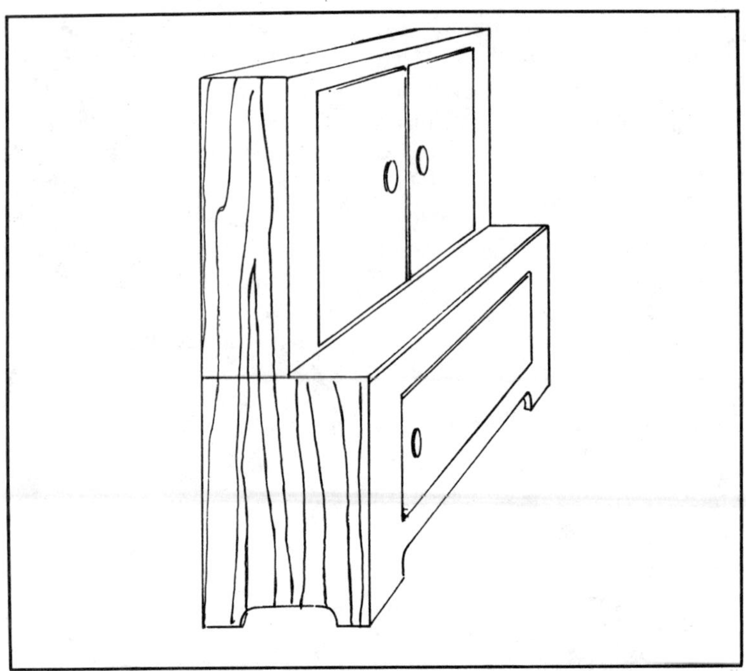

Fig. 3-2. A stepback cupboard made in two pieces with the plank side cut from one piece of wood displaying continuous grain.

modern reproduction that will have an opaque stain to obscure the variations in grain found in the glued stock.

If a cabinetmaker were making a secretary or a step-back cupboard in two pieces, he might select one long board and cut it for the two pieces so that the grain would be continuous from the bottom piece to the top piece (Fig. 3-2). This is especially true for high-style furniture and it is not uncommon with country furniture. The sides and top of a chest of drawers might be cut from one piece so that the grain is continuous from the left side to the top and to the right side. This careful selection of wood applies more to formal furniture than country furniture and is generally confined to the 1700 to 1825 period. Noting the continuity of grain or grain selection can be considered another factor in the confirmation of authenticity. The absence of these factors does not condemn a piece.

When authenticating antiques, a good place to start is at the back. The backboards and bottom boards of an antique piece of furniture can supply information that confirms or denies the originality of the piece. The backboards of almost any case piece were left in the rough; this included all varieties of chest of drawers, desks and cupboards. Pieces such as sideboards, sofas, and washstands will frequently have backboards that received some degree of attention. Like all rules, this is not exclusive. Some compulsive cabinetmakers did plane smooth the backboards of case pieces.

Saw marks can provide evidence that will suggest the age of a piece. Pit-saw marks, hand-frame marks, power-frame marks, and circular-saw marks might be encountered. The marks of the circular saw indicate early, modern construction (some time after 1825, but more likely after 1850). Because it was necessary for the artisan to bring the lumber to a uniform size, it was hand planed. When saw marks are found, they are usually found as traces not quite completely removed by the plane.

The backboards required no attention other than the dimensioning. The hollows of the scrub plane or the ridges of the jack plane should be evident on pieces made prior to 1850 (when machine planed boards were available.). On pieces such as washstands where there was some risk of the back being visible, the boards might be given a perfunctory treatment with a smooth plane. Rarely will they ever receive the treatment of surface boards.

On occasion, the backboards are legitimately painted. This is not common, and when found it should be on a piece that was painted in its entirety. At an Ohio auction I found an 18th-century country Chippendale desk in curly maple with red backboards. There was no sign of the desk ever having been painted. It is illogical to presume that the original maker or a subsequent owner would have painted the boards. Frequently, painted backboards are the product of a restorer who wants to disguise his work. When paint is encountered, the collector has to decide if it is consistent with the rest of the piece and if it is genuinely old paint.

Another technique of the restorer or faker is to stain backboards with an opaque stain. Occasionally, the stain is mixed with dirt or grime to achieve an old look. Stained backboards should always be viewed as dubious. There might be a genuine piece somewhere with stained backboards, but I have never seen one.

Backboards can be attached in a number of manners. The boards can be butted, lapped, or tongue and grooved. Very wide boards or a series of small boards might have been used. In addition, there might be a center mutin or a series of mutins spacing the boards. The boards might be positioned vertically or horizontally. The one thing that cannot be found—if the item is an antique—is a single, large, plywood back. Plywood did not come into use until after 1900. Interestingly, plywood on a conceptual basis, goes back to the Egyptians, but it was not commercially feasible to make until the 20th century.

The manner in the backboards are joined does not suggest a clue to the age of the furniture. With a tongue and groove joint, the difference must be discerned between the handmade tongue and groove—which is deep and on occasion off center—and the machine-made tongue and groove which is shallow. Machine-made tongue and groove construction can be found on pieces made after 1850. These pieces will typically employ a number of narrow boards. On some late pieces, a paneled back can be found (Fig. 3-3). A paneled back definitely indicates construction after 1850.

The use of very wide boards suggest early construction. Multiple smaller boards suggest later construction. This is a guideline and not a rule because either arrangement can be found. This is also true of horizontally positioned backboards in terms of early construction, but again this is not a rule.

Regardless of the method of joining used, shrinkage should be evident. When backboards were lapped or tongue and grooved, the maker had two purposes in mind: to prevent dust from entering the piece, and to allow for shrinkage. On any antique piece, backboards should no longer be a tight fit.

The degree to which any piece will shrink is governed by the moisture content of the wood, where constructed, as well as current environmental factors of temperature and humidity. Because of these variables, there is not a set rule as to how much a board will shrink; shrinkage of at least one-fourth of an inch is common. With tongue and groove construction and lapped construction, the joints will not have come apart, but the spacing should be evident.

If tightly fit backboards are found, the piece should be immediately suspect. When new backboards are fitted to a piece, any restorer worth his salt will position the boards to appear as if shrinkage had occurred. The restorer can imitate shrinkage, but rarely does he have a stock of old boards that are precisely the right length and width.

Generally, the problems of width can be worked out. But when it comes to length, the boards have to be cut. When you are inspecting a piece, check the bottoms of the backboards to see if they are freshly cut, or if they have been painted or stained to match the aged look of the backboards. If stained edges are found, it is reasonable to assume that the piece has been tampered with. Replaced backboards seriously detract from the value of antique pieces, but this does not mean that the remainder of the piece is fake or not worth having.

Another guide in assessing backboards is the thickness of the board. Modern boards come in standard thicknesses of one-fourth inch, one-half inch, three-fourths inch, thirteen-sixteenths inch, and 1⅛ inch. Hand cut and planed lumber did not conform to a precise standard. Fractional variations are commonly found. The thickness of the backboards can be measured with a caliper.

Backboards were attached to the frame of a piece in the traditional manner; they were pegged, screwed, or nailed. Backboards were pegged on some 18th-century pieces due to the high cost of nails. There is no reason why backboards could not be pegged on a 19th-century piece. This would be an extreme oddity. The same is true of screws. Nails have been the predominant method attaching backboards in the 18th century, 19th century and 20th century.

Nails used for backboards could be hand wrought, early machine nails, or modern, round nails. Hand-wrought nails and early machine nails can be found on pieces made prior to 1870. Modern round nails are found on pieces made after 1870.

When backboards are inspected, care should be taken to see if there are any desolate and orphaned nail holes (holes that have no purpose). Old floor boards and barn boards provide the most avail-

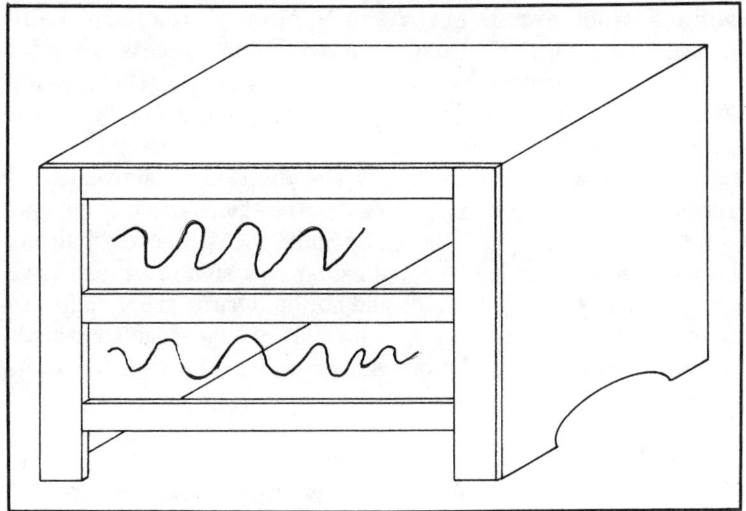

Fig. 3-3. Frame and panel backboard construction found on pieces made after 1850.

able sources for the replacement of backboards. When these materials are used, vacant nail holes from their former use are found. A restorer will use as many of these holes as possible, but they are not usually spaced correctly. Likewise, when a nail has been in the same place for one hundred years or so, a certain degree of oxidization (rust) will have occurred. As the nail rusts, the wood around the nail stains slightly. With some pieces where there has been severe exposure to moisture, there will be a heavy rust stain in a drip pattern around the nail. A rust pattern around a nail cannot be easily forged and is a good sign of authenticity.

The bottom board or boards are equally worth attention when inspecting a piece because they are rarely looked at or tampered with. Generally, most everything regarding backboards pertains to bottom boards. The thickness of the board is important, but it cannot usually be determined without taking the piece apart. The method by which the board was sawn might provide some information. With bottom boards, less care was taken to plane out the telltale marks of the saw. Bottom boards will be nailed unless dovetailed to the case or fitted to a recess. Again, the nails should be evident.

Backboards are used in multiples, whereas the bottom is usually fitted with a single board. On occasion, two boards are joined to form a bottom, but rarely more than two. When multiple bottom boards are found, a tongue and groove joint is employed. With a solid bottom board, shrinkage expresses itself in a different manner. If the bottom board is fitted to a recess, as with a drawer bottom, and not fixed at any point, it will float. That means it is free to expand and contract. With shrinkage, the board will have pulled out of one of the recesses. If the bottom board has been nailed, it is secured at all points and there is no allowance for shrinkage. The frequent result of this treatment is a crack somewhere along the length of the grain. Splits such as these should not be viewed as an inadequacy, but rather as a sign of authenticity.

As discussed, backboards and bottom boards supply information about a piece, but they are only part of a message and should never be viewed in isolation. A piece must be evaluated in its entirety.

SHRINKAGE

Shrinkage is a potent factor to be reckoned with in all wood construction. In simple terms, *shrinkage* is the contraction of wood as a result of a loss of moisture. When a tree is freshly cut, it has a high moisture content that is evidenced by its sappy nature and extreme weight. Having been denied its life source (the root system), the tree will loose moisture in an uncontrolled manner until it achieves harmony with its environment. As a result, the tree will be subject to numerous splits bisecting the growth rings. This phenomenon can be observed in a casual walk through any forest area.

When man adapts wood to his use, he merely replicates nature's process in a controlled fashion. The tree is cut into planks, which allows for moisture loss across a broader surface, and end grain is sealed to prohibit moisture loss at too rapid a pace. All in all, what is being attempted is to bring the wood to a point of diminished moisture and greater stability such that further shrinkage is limited. In modern terms, it is akin to purchasing prewashed and preshrunk jeans.

Presuming that wood is dried to a point of stability prior to its use (and that's not always a safe presumption), should additional problems be expected? The answer is yes. Wood can be brought to a point of relative stability, but the environment in which it is placed is not stable.

Invariably, wood will continue to lose moisture from years of being indoors. What is more significant is that wood will continue to change with the seasons. Wood will gain or lose moisture according to the moisture content of the air. Summer provides high moisture and expansion while winter means low moisture and contraction. Many an unsuspecting soul has purchased a piece of furniture in a high-moisture area such as England and brought it to a drier environment such as New York only to find that within a few weeks the piece was falling apart. There is no mystery to this. The move to lower humidity resulted in contraction. Stress to all the glue lines caused the piece to become unglued.

The first rule of shrinkage is that all wood shrinks across the grain (Fig. 3-4). The second rule is that all wood will continue to shrink to some degree after being employed in furniture. The third rule is that all wood will continue to expand and contract with changes in humidity no matter what you do to it. The last rule, to complicate matters, is that uneven absorption of moisture (one surface absorbing more than the other surface) will result in warpage.

This last point is all too frequently illustrated with table tops. A craftsman will finish the top surface of a table, for example, but rarely the underside. The finish on the top surface inhibits the

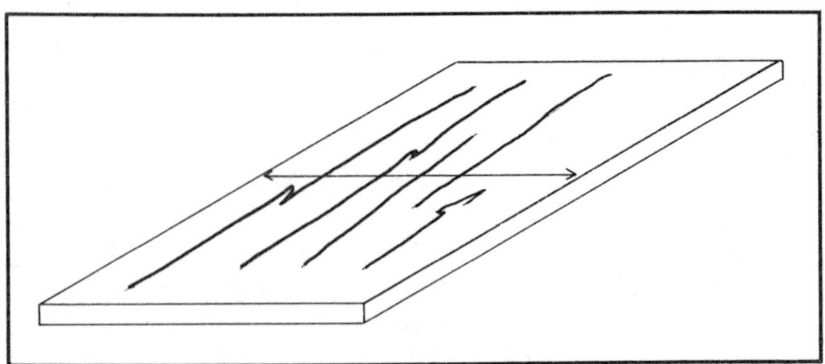

Fig. 3-4. Wood shrinkage across the grain.

absorption of moisture (the primary reason for using a finish) forcing greater absorption from the bottom. The consequence is a warped top leaf (Fig. 3-5). This effect is known as *cupping*.

Understanding and observing shrinkage is at the basis of authenticating antique furniture. Very few antique forgers can duplicate the effects of shrinkage adequately and, what is more important, few try. Without any shrinkage, a piece simply cannot be antique. A piece exhibiting shrinkage might not be antique, but it must be old.

At one auction I attended, the premier piece was a pewter cupboard in the style of the eighteenth century. The cupboard was unusually well shaped and in an old green paint. Old paint is to be cherished; "new old paint" can hide a multitude of sins. As I approached the cupboard, there was a smell of fresh paint. That in itself merited extreme caution. After careful scrutiny, the cupboard proved to be a very well done fake.

With country furniture, you do not often find a fake this skillfully done. The paint was marvelous and signs of wear were all in the right places. But there was not an iota of shrinkage. The backboards were butted and still snug. The shelves were snug against the back. And most importantly, no shrinkage whatsoever was evident in the doors.

The auctioneer did not refer to the cupboard as 18th century or 19th century. He did not describe it as old, but smugly announced that it was all original. The cupboard was probably not more than a week old and doubtlessly was all original. Most of the work on the cupboard was good enough to fool an experienced collector or dealer. A novice, who merely looked for shrinkage, could have determined that the cupboard was not authentic. The cupboard, unfortunately, sold for $1,000!

The effects of shrinkage are most apparent in any situation involving fixed points. By *fixed points* I mean the use of nails, screws, joinings or fasteners that prohibit the natural contraction of wood. The most common example of this is a table. A table top is fastened in four places, at the minimum, to maintain it in a stable position. Given wood shrinkage, there are only two options. The first is that some of the nails or screws holding the top have worked loose—allowing the wood to move. With the second option, the fasteners remain secure and the top inevitably splits (usually down the middle). If a top were made of two boards, as was the common practice with 19th-century tables, then the top would separate at the join.

In some cases, a combination of very well-seasoned wood and a stable climate will result in minimum shrinkage and no splitting. But you are likely to encounter more split tops than not.

Tables on pedestal bases are less likely to split because the manner in which they are attached allows greated latitude for the movement of the wood. Although this type of top is less likely to split, a liberal number of split tops will be encountered. Pedestal tables frequently have round tops. That poses an interesting question: should they still be round? The answer is no. If a top is initially cut round, but with age shrinks across the grain, it must be out of round.

Testing for roundness can be accomplished simply by measuring. If the table top, as shown in Fig. 3-6A, has a center point equidistant from all points, then the top must be recent. If such a center point is lacking, you can reasonably assume shrinkage. Fakers will attempt to duplicate this shrinkage by cutting a top and planning one section (Fig. 3-6B) so that when the top is rejoined it will be out of round. The reglued top can later be assumed as the

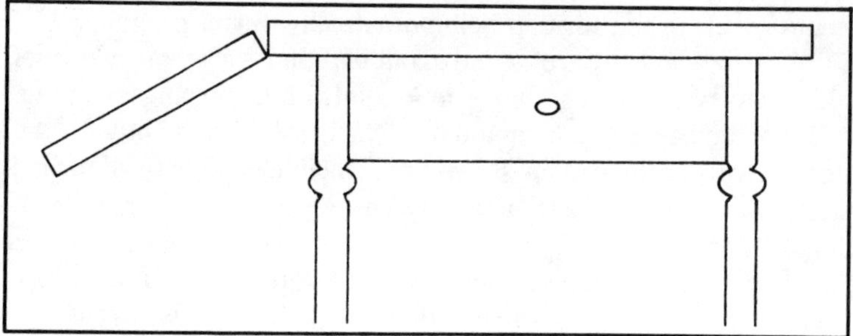

Fig. 3-5. A cupped leaf is the result of uneven absorption of moisture caused by only finishing one side of the leaf.

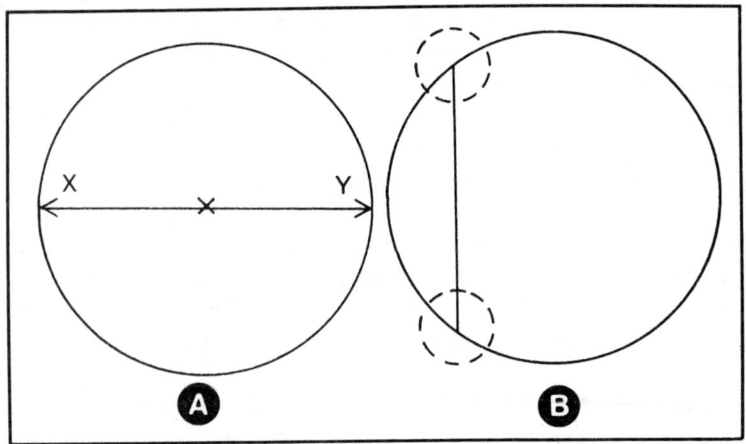

Fig. 3-6. A round top, if old, will no longer be round as a result of shrinkage (A). There will be no center point equidistant from all sides. Shrinkage is simulated by sawing the top and planing material from one leaf (B). The top is reglued and therefore it is out of round; however, a shoulder will be created that is not natural.

result of shrinkage. When this is done, a small shoulder is created between the larger and smaller sections. This is easily identified as the work of a modifier and not of age.

The principle of "once round but no longer round with age" applies to turnings as well as table tops. Turnings are produced by a tool—the lathe—that ran the gamut of primitive in the late 17th century to sophisticated, in the mid-19th century. Whether primitive or sophisticated, the product of the lathe of yesteryear was likely to produce stock slightly out of round the day it was new. When this natural tendency to be out of round is coupled with the effects of shrinkage, there is virtually no possibility of an antique turning being round. It should also be remembered that the method of preparing the turning stock often led to flat spots on turnings that would result in the turning being drastically out of round.

The determination of round or out of round is a simple matter of taking a measurement at two or four points of the turning (as in Fig. 3-7). Each measurement should be at variance with the other if the piece is truly antique. This shrinkage principle applies to all turned parts such as table legs, pedestal bases, bed posts, chair legs, spindles, etc.

There are numerous examples of shrinkage. In Fig. 3-8, a typical paneled door is shown. Because shrinkage is across the grain, the cross member of the frame must reduce from point A to point B. Consequently, there is now a ridge where the cross member is tenoned into the upright. Shrinkage of this nature should be found on every door of the type purporting to be antique. The degree of shrinkage will vary from door to door. Interestingly enough, the spurious pewter cupboard mentioned earlier lacked this type of door shrinkage.

The same type of shrinkage phenomenon is shown on the schoolmaster's desk in Fig. 3-9. Again, the cross member shrinks from points A to points B and leaves a shrinkage ridge where it is mortised into the leg post.

With ladderback chairs shown in Fig. 3-10, the slat will shrink and leave a portion of the empty mortise showing (as seen at point A in the illustration). This shrinkage ranges from one-eighth inch to one-fourth inch. Whenever I evaluate a chair, this is the first thing I check out. Remember, the mortise must be square. If the mortise is rounded, it is the product of a machine and later craftsmanship.

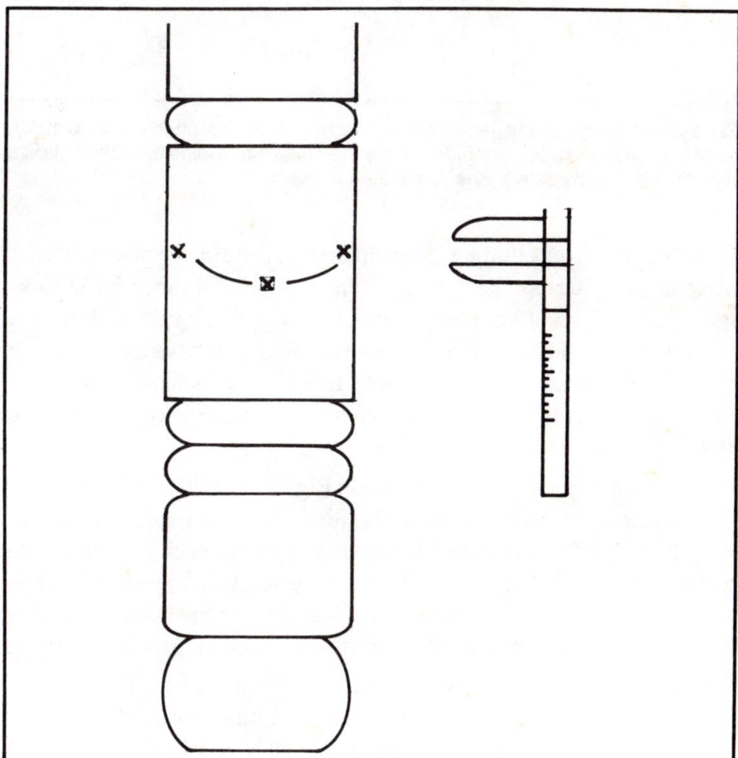

Fig. 3-7. Turnings are measured with a caliper for shrinkage to determine if a piece is old.

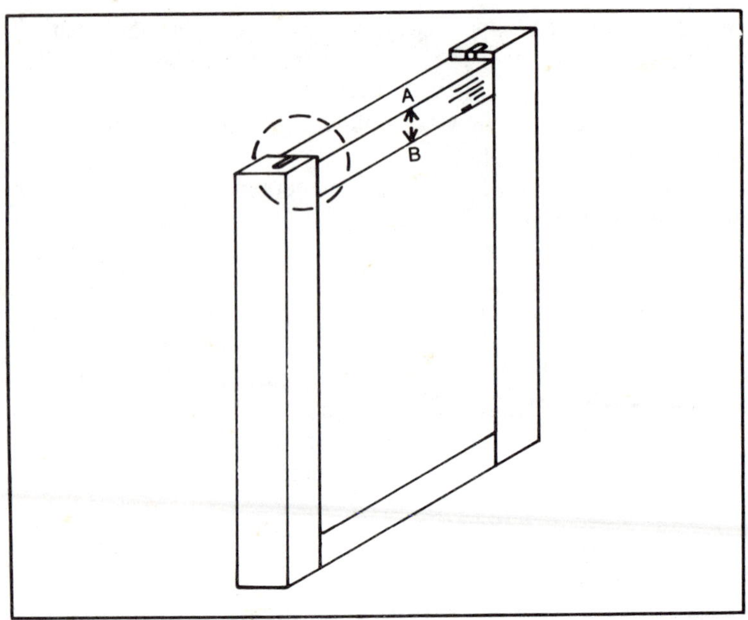

Fig. 3-8. With a frame and panel door the cross member will shrink from point A to point B. This will cause a shoulder where the cross piece joins the stile. This is a sign of authenticity rarely ever duplicated by forgers.

The important thing with shrinkage is the simple principle that wood shrinks across the grain. When evaluating a piece for shrinkage, the piece must be understood in terms of its relationship with other parts. In the aforementioned examples, you have a cross piece in which the grain runs from west to east and a side member in which the grain runs from north to south—thus making shrinkage apparent.

The simple nailed box, shown in Fig. 3-11, will exhibit no signs of shrinkage. As can be seen in the illustration, all sides of the box will shrink. After a hundred years or so of use, each will shrink to approximately the same width. The key to shrinkage in this case will be the bottom board of the box. Considering the bottom board is fixed at several points, it will have either cracked or pulled away at one side (as shown in Fig. 3-12).

Don't try to memorize the illustrations, but understanding shrinkage, and this one principle alone, can save you from countless financial disasters. Use your own home as a workshop. Walk around analyzing pieces and how they should shrink. One note of warning.

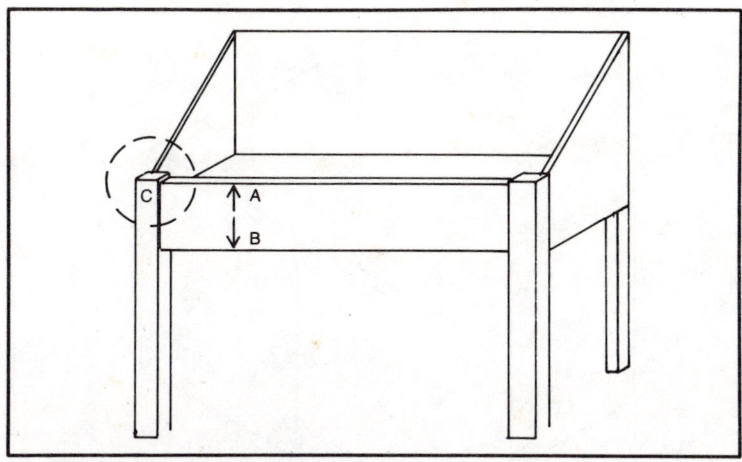

Fig. 3-9. Shrinkage across the grain from points A to B of the rail of a schoolmaster's desk forming a shoulder at leg joins.

Only do this with pieces of solid wood; pieces of veneered plywood do not shrink in this manner.

WEAR AND USE

Today, it is possible to purchase a piece of furniture as a statement of beauty and art. A piece such as this will be cared for

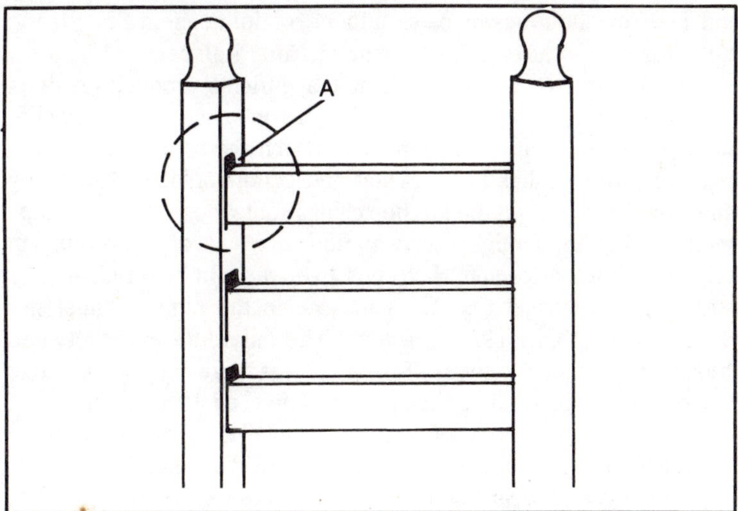

Fig. 3-10. The slats on a ladderback chair shrink, and this will leave the mortise somewhat oversized.

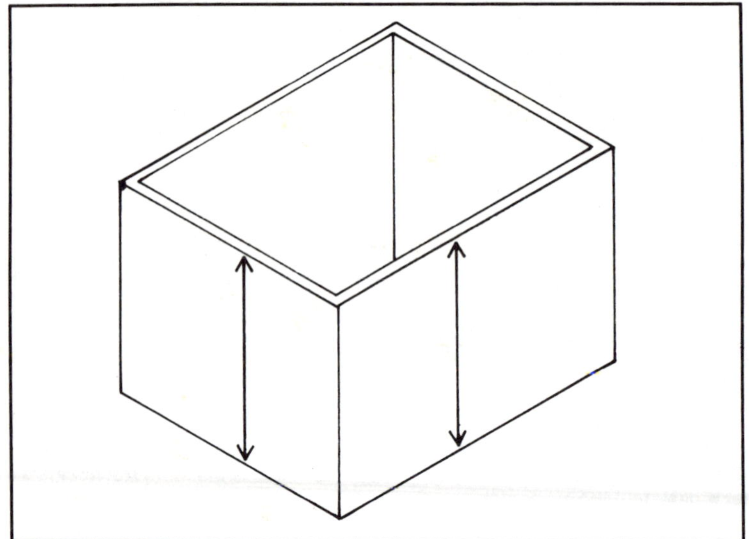

Fig. 3-11. Shrinkage will not change the box because all sides are continuous and they will shrink the same.

and protected from ordinary use or a neighbor's child. Historically, a piece of furniture was a functional item. It received a great deal of use and abuse. A piece of furniture that is purported to be 100 or 200 years old should exhibit considerable signs of wear. Signs of wear and use, or their absence, should be of immense value to the collector who is attempting to authenticate a piece.

Assessing wear and use is not a difficult proposition. It is merely a matter of observation and common sense. All of your life has been spent in an environment in which the wear and replacement of furniture has been casual and commonplace. How many times have the legs on the kitchen chairs come loose. Have the legs been worn by the family tilter who finds pleasure and adventure in using only the back legs? Have you ever thought of refinishing or replacing the bureau because someone in the family cannot get close to it without kicking the feet? The only difference between these everyday occurrances of wear and tear on an antique piece is repetition. Imagine what the impact of five or 10 generations of wear will be on a piece of furniture. Once a collector becomes attuned to this type of observation, a new world of insight is opened.

The signs of wear and use are most often apparent on chairs. There is no mystery to these observations. What piece of furniture receives more use? The usage of chests, beds and tables is minimal

92

next to that of chairs. If a chair has finials, look for those finials to be worn flat in the rear (Fig. 3-13). People like the security of walls behind them. Whenever possible a chair goes against a wall. Not all antique chairs will show such wear, but, oddly enough, most will.

If the finials do not provide information or if there are no finials, check the feet. The feet of an old chair should be well worn. The fibers should be compressed from years of use and smooth from grease, dirt, and abrasion. If lathe marks are still apparent, they should be worn smooth. On the other hand, if the feet are fresh and even, it suggests that the chair has been cut down. Some owner has compensated for uneven wear with a saw.

The wear on the feet tells you if the chair is old or tampered with, but not if it is antique. On an antique chair, the rear legs are often shorter than the front legs. This gives the chair a backward rake as in Fig. 3-14. People not only have a tendency to place chairs against walls, they also love to tilt back on the rear legs causing greater wear. This little custom was (and is) so prevalent that the Shakers made a tilting chair in the 19th century.

Any time that a chair has a stretcher in the front, it should be checked for wear. After several generations of use, the stretcher will be worn down in the center (as shown seen in Fig. 3-15). This is another one of those catchy human tendencies. The heels of both feet are placed on the stretcher or, more commonly, the heel of the right foot is placed there while the left foot is tucked under the right. Common sense must be your guide. If a stretcher is placed so high that it would be unlikely for anyone to place his feet on it, then it is unlikely that you will find wear. A collector once challenged the validity of a child's high chair because there was no wear on the lower stretcher; logic was obviously not his guide!

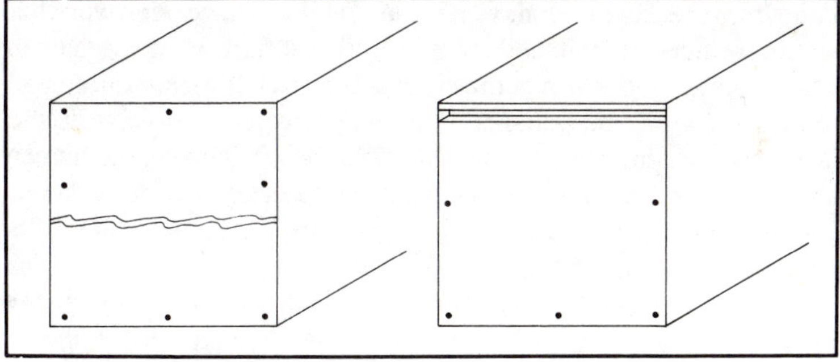

Fig. 3-12. Bottom boards that are stationary (fixed by nails or screws) will either split or pull loose from one side as the result of shrinkage.

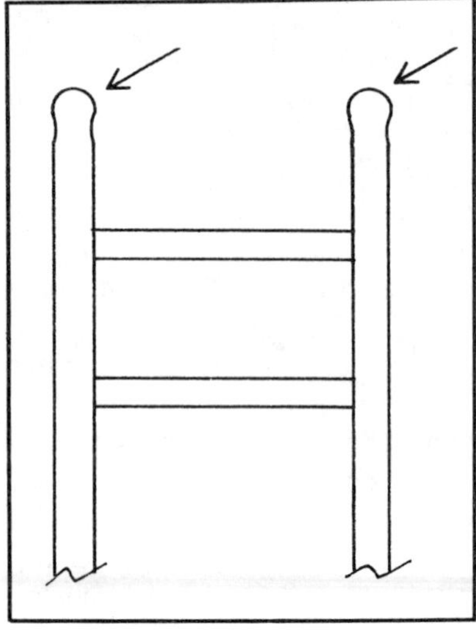

Fig. 3-13. Finials on ladderback chairs are often worn flat as a result of being placed against walls.

One note of caution. When antique fakers are at work, rarely do they miss duplicating this type of wear. Care must be taken to distinguish between wear and the work of a file and sandpaper. By the way, if the stretcher is very close to the floor, it usually means that the chair has been cut down.

You should have a growing awareness that the signs of wear on furniture are not only a function of accidents, but equally an aspect of human clumsiness and idiosyncrasies. Another one of those human idiosyncrasies revolves around the hands. People are tactile and sensual and they love to touch and feel things.

With old chairs, this compulsion to touch is apparent everywhere that is likely or comfortable for a hand to go. The hand rails on the armchair shown in Fig. 3-16 would have been manipulated from the day the chair was made. They will have been worn flat and magnificently polished from the oil and friction of the human hand. Likewise, the arm of the chair in the adjoining illustration will have been worn and polished in a similar manner. Even a simple ladderback chair without arms will yield the evidence of the human hand. On this type of chair, people have a tendency to tuck one or both hands under their legs and hold the tops of the front posts. This will produce a highly polished surface.

On case pieces such as chests or cupboards, wear again follows the prescription of logic. A chest of drawers has a top surface that is used constantly and should show evidence of scratches and abrasions from use. The top surface will be polished more often and

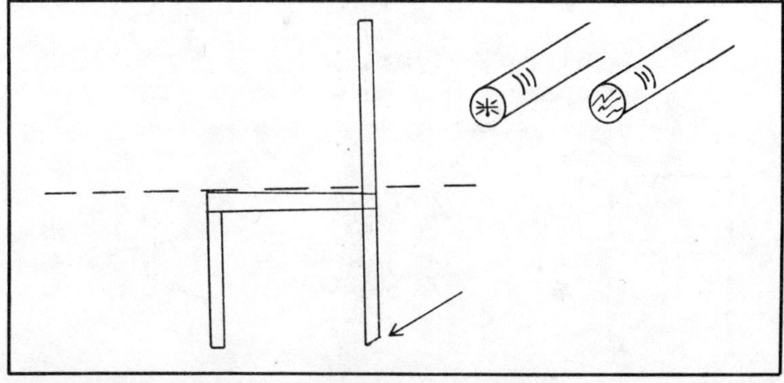

Fig. 3-14. Bottoms of chair posts might display vestiges of a lathe spur, but more often than not it will have worn away. Rear legs are worn as a result of back tipping.

should have a greater sheen than the sides. In addition, polishing might make it darker than the sides. If it has been kept in the sun, it will be lighter. In any case, the top surface is almost always a different color from the sides and shows far more use (unless the piece has been refinished).

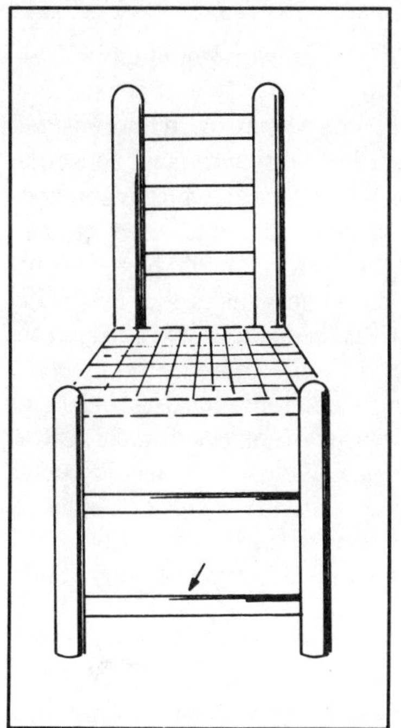

Fig. 3-15. Lower front chair stretchers are worn as a result of foot placement.

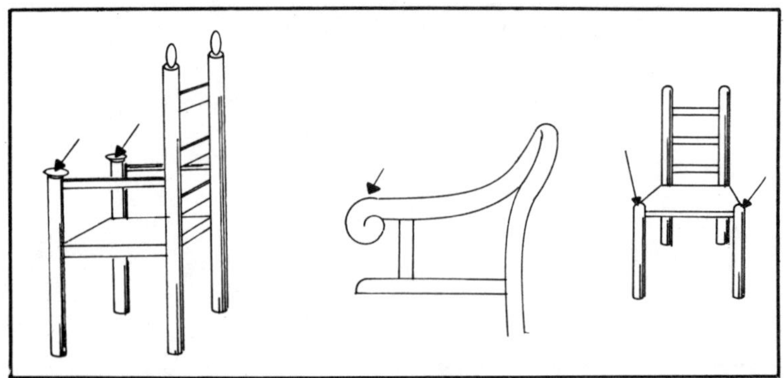

Fig. 3-16. Hand rails, arms, and front leg posts are worn and polished by the constant friction of human hands.

The feet or lower boards of chests will show nicks, abrasion, or damage. Another one of those funny human tendencies is to walk into or accidently kick a chest. Even if the owners are as graceful as a prima donna ballerina, the chest will suffer the slings and arrows of the broom or, in the modern household, a vacuum cleaner.

Whenever a piece of furniture has moving parts, these will show signs of wear. Just imagine if a drawer is only opened and closed once each morning and evening; that is 1460 times per year. Given a piece that is 200 years old, the drawer would have been opened and closed about 292,000 times. Not only is it reasonable that the drawer should be worn, but its survival is darn impressive.

An old drawer can be anticipated to be rickety as a consequence of use and the shrinkage of the bottom board (which stabilized the frame in the first place). The drawer runners, in effect the bottoms of the left and right side of the drawer, should be severely worn or replaced with new hardwood runners (as in Fig. 3-17). In this case replaced drawer runners should be looked upon as a sign of authenticity which does not detract from the value of the piece.

If the drawers have a molding around them such as a cock bead or thumb nail, it should be chipped, worn or replaced in spots. Often people leave drawers half opened (or half closed, depending upon your point of view). The tendency in this situation is to open or close the drawer by holding the top as opposed to the handles or brasses. It is not uncommon to find drawers with this type of wear. Such wear, however, is not severe.

On a case piece, it is wise to check the key escutcheons, knobs, or brasses. Over the years, brasses and knobs are often changed to update the style of the piece. The replacement of these items will, in some cases, necessitate the enlarging or reducing of a hole or the plugging of a hole. Modifications such as these do reduce the value of a piece, but they also tell you that a piece has been around long enough to be in and out of style.

If the knobs or brasses are original or if they have been in place for a long time, there will be an accumulation of dirt and polish around them. Very few people are so meticulous that they remove all the wax from difficult and unseen places. This is another one of those little human factors. Keyhole escutcheons are a good source for this type of information; rarely are they replaced. The removal of an escutcheon might tell you something about the original finish of the piece because it is likely that what you find under the escutcheon is original.

Over the years, a cupboard is likely to have suffered more abuse than a chest of drawers. After years of faithful service, chests seem to be relegated to basements while cupboards are sent to climatic oblivion in barns, outbuildings, and garages. Cupboards should be checked for rot in the feet as a result of a moist environment. In some cases, water marks can be found along the base line.

Cupboards, unlike chests, are the depositories of foodstuffs and morsels tempting to our furry, nose-twitching little friends. Mouse holes and teeth marks are found on old cupboards. The sneaky little rodent beggers are prone to make nice safe holes in the backboards. These holes were usually repaired with the lids from old tin cans. Doubtlessly, some future archeologist will devote a thesis to the primitive and probably religious practice of nailing tin to holes in wood. None of these aspects of wear guarantee antiquity, but rather they suggest use associated with a long period of time. When considered in conjunction with other factors this might confirm its antiquity.

The inside of a case piece should not be neglected. A very old or antique piece will have a musty odor that, once learned, will rarely be mistaken for something else. Fakers of antiques will leave

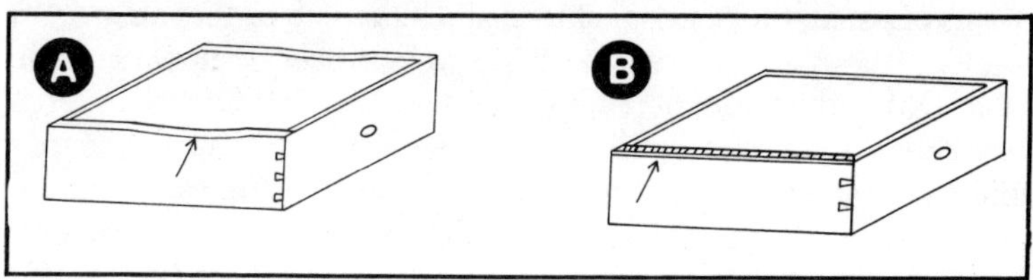

Fig. 3-17. Drawer runners (bottom of the sides) worn from constant usage (A). Drawers are frequently encountered with new runners glued into place (B).

an old piece of cheese in furniture to give furniture a seasoned and rancid odor, but this just does not do the trick.

The interior joinings—framing or rebates—should be jammed with dust, dirt, and debris. The debris that fills every crack cannot be removed by cleaning. Its absence suggests that a piece has been disassembled and reglued or that the piece is not old. In a chest, the guides that the drawers run on should be worn like the drawer bottoms. In a cupboard, the shelves should be stained and marred from use similar to a top surface. The underside of a shelf, however, should be free from such distressing.

If at all possible, chests, cupboards, tables and chairs, should be inverted to observe the coloration of the underside of the primary and secondary woods. All wood changes color in response to light and oxygen. A piece of cherry, when freshly cut, has a pink color. After years of oxidization, it develops a rich, soft, red/brown complexion.

The interiors of case pieces, by their very nature, are not as exposed as the exterior surfaces. These surfaces remain lighter than the exterior surfaces. Not only do the surfaces remain lighter, but they also develop a coloration or hue that tends to be consistent even when different woods are used. When the interior surfaces are checked for the depth of color and degree of sameness, useful information is gathered with regard to originality. If an interior is encountered with different coloration on side panels, supports, glue blocks, etc., the piece should be viewed as dubious.

A goodly number of years ago we were tempted to purchase a dressing table for our collection. The dressing table was 18th-century, English Chippendale, in mahogany, and with a patina that would knock the socks off of King Tut. From the exterior, the piece appeared faultless. When examined from the interior, the coloration of the surfaces proclaimed it to be a hodge-podge of old woods—many of which had not started life together. The salesman announced the absolute originality of the piece, save a few repairs that had been made in the shop upstairs. The salesman either had the brains of a snail (no disrespect to snails intended) or the integrity of a felon. The dubious dressing table was at best a simple antique table that had been expertly modified.

Everything that applies to chairs, chests, and cupboards applies to tables. The feet of a table will exhibit the same type of wear as the feet of a chair. The feet of the table are more prone to damage and replacement. If a table has a stretcher base (Fig. 3-18), it will be subject to the same wear as the bottom stretcher of a chair.

The top of a table will show the greatest signs of wear and use; this is evidenced by the number of tables with replaced tops. A table top will exhibit water stains and heat marks not found as frequently on dresser tops.

Where there are moving parts on a table, such as swing legs or gate-legs, greater wear can be anticipated. The wooden hinges upon which the gate swings should be loose and somewhat sloppy from wear. The underside of the table should be scored by the frequent movement of this gate. On a drop-leaf table, the half rule molding will be damaged or badly worn. This will be particularly true in the area of the hinges where there is a tendency to chip away.

Drawers on tables should exhibit the same type of wear as other drawers. When inverted, the table should display the consistency of coloration on the underside that suggests all parts started life together. Those areas sheltered from air, such as the undersurface covered by a drawer, should be somewhat lighter than the other surfaces. All in all, a table is not that different from any other piece.

The best guides to understanding the impact of wear and use upon furniture is logic, common sense, and observation, Your home provides an ideal laboratory for the application of these principles. Remember, no single thing establishes the originality of a piece and authenticity is no more than a reasoned, disciplined, and logical assessment of all available data.

FINISHES: ORIGINAL AND OTHERWISE

An original finish is the opiate of the antique collector. It is sought after, protected and fought over. Unfortunately it is often an illusion. The reality of an original finish is that only the person who made the piece knew what was original and even then he could not know what would happen in the years to come.

For example, the neighborhood cabinetmaker might have made a chest in 1750 and sold it as is or "in the white" as it was known at the time. The original owner of the piece might have done no more than oil the piece. In 1775, the owner bestowed the chest upon his son who decided it needed a face lift and sent it out to be varnished. Since 1775, the surface has been maintained and polished with regularity until a fine patina has developed. What expert, no matter how skilled, no matter what scientific technique he used, could disprove that this was other than an original finish, yet, it would not be. Even if a scraping were taken and the residual solids of the oil found microscopically in the wood fiber under

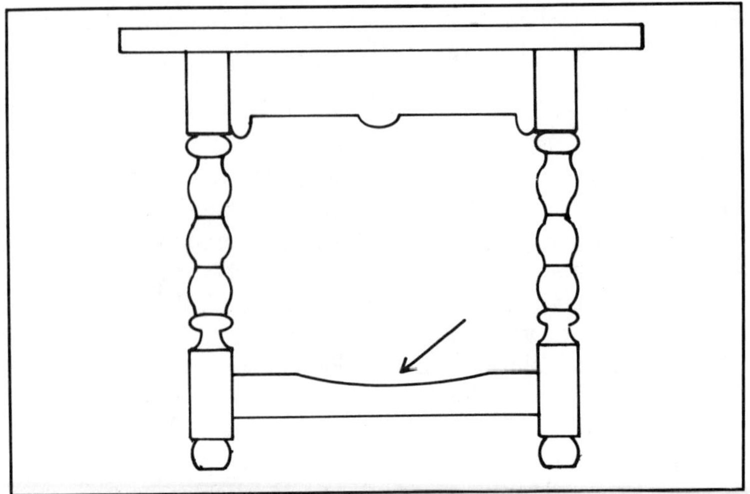

Fig. 3-18. Lower stretchers on tables wear similarly to chair stretchers. It depends upon the overhang of the top. A large overhang will prohibit wear of the stretchers.

varnish, nothing would be proven. Oiling before varnishing was one of many 18th-century practices. The intent here is not to be cynical, but rather to put matters into perspective. Avoid becoming obsessive. Old finishes are to be pursued and revered, but they are best understood as "old and possibly original."

Original finishes do not play a large part in the life of the collector of country antiques. They are mostly in the domain of formal furniture. The casual nature of country furniture has not promoted the preservation of original finishes that have been worn, painted, stripped or antiqued into oblivion. The most prevalent original finish for country furniture was paint. Country furniture was also varnished and shellacked like other pieces.

If a piece of furniture was not to be painted, the options for a finish were essentially the same in the 18th and 19th centuries as they are today. A piece then, as now, could be varnished, but the varnish would have been compounded from natural resins and not synthetics as today. The varnish of yesteryear might have used alcohol as a base; this was known as *spirit varnish.*

A piece might have been finished in shellac using an alcohol base that was a favorite for dark wood pieces such as mahogany. Lacquer was available as early as the late 17th century, but used only in special decoration work such as *Japanning.* The application of lacquer as a finishing material is primarily a 20th-century development. Furniture was, more often than is usually acknowledged, left unfinished to be subsequently waxed or oiled by the owner. Regardless of the finish to be used, furniture might or might not have been stained. When stain was used, it was produced from a natural product such as a berry or a root.

In the 19th century, a high gloss finish known as French Polishing became the rage. A French Polish was a shellac finish applied with a pad, known as a rubber, and a great deal of friction. The result was a super sheen. Many 18th-century pieces were done over in the 19th century with a French Polish.

By and large, the type of finish used does not assist you in determining the antiquity of a piece because most finishes were available during the last three centuries. Even when a finish can be dated, such as French Polish for the 19th century or lacquer for the 20th century, there is no way to know if it is an original finish. At best, you can determine if a finish is old or possibly original because that information ultimately enhances or detracts from the value of a piece.

To determine the age of a finish, discretely scrape a small area with a knife. If the finish is fairly modern, it will peel like a bar of soap. Old finishes, whether shellac or varnish, are brittle and will flake off. With time, varnish crackles in an alligator pattern that suggests age. Shellac will blush and haze with exposure to moisture (although new shellac will do the same).

If you have access to an ultraviolet light, experiment by exposing new and old finishes to it. Old finishes will have a greater florescence than new ones. Ultraviolet light is also a great way to detect well-hidden repairs and restorations.

Although a finish has been determined to be old, you still don't know how old it is. Realistically, the finish could be 80 years old or 180 years old and there would be little way to discern the difference. It is necessary to find additional confirming information. The removal of a knob, brass or escutcheon might reveal an original finish underneath that can confirm or deny your assumptions. Determining the originality or age of a finish ranges from difficult and elusive to the impossible.

The essence of an original finish is a fine patina. *Patina* can be defined as a surface appearance that has grown beautiful with age. A number of processes, such as oxidization, original and subsequent finishes, wax, natural oils, dirt, and friction produced by polishing, affect furniture surfaces. The magic ingredients of the formula are friction, dirt, and time. These factors, working in conjunction over a long period produce, a surface that is genuinely a beauty to behold. Of no meager importance is that a good patina also enhances the value of a piece.

It has been asserted that once you see a good patina you will never mistake it, and that a patina cannot be imitated. Generally, this is true. There is something marvelous, warm, and attractive about a patina that lets you spot it in a second in a room full of furniture. Whether or not patina, can be duplicated remains a debatable point. The interesting thing about being fooled is that you really never know it happened. You could witness 20 faked finishes and still swear that you never saw a faked finish. It is enough to say that a good patina is not easily faked.

Like an original finish, a fine patina plays a more important role in the collection of formal furniture. Select country pieces, especially those from the 18th century, can be found with original finish and patina, but the majority of country antiques will posses neither.

PAINT: ORIGINAL AND DUBIOUS

When you are dealing in the realm of country furniture, the key to original finishes is paint. This is both a positive and negative proposition. On the positive side, probably the majority of all country furniture was painted. The negative part of the proposition is that almost all country furniture, whether with a paint finish or a varnish finish, has subsequently been painted. Multiple paintings and strippings have resulted in the ruination of a considerable number of original finishes.

It is not difficult to understand why so much country furniture was painted. Country furniture was first and foremost a pragmatic venture; it was meant to be used. The country cabinetmaker was also concerned with the overall aesthetics of the piece, but this was secondary to the function. Once a piece was made, the simplest, fastest, most durable, and least expensive method of treating it was paint. To put a fine varnish or shellac finish on a piece, if it was appropriate, required skill that painting did not.

In metropolitan centers, where there were large furniture industries such as in London or Philadelphia, finishing was often a separate industry. If skill was not a factor, appropriateness was. Country furniture employed local woods that were not always thought to be attractive. Likewise, a number of woods might be used in a single piece. A good chair almost always utilized three different woods. A good windsor might use four or five. The simplest method for blending these various woods was paint.

The use of paint was surely a pragmatic consideration, but it was also an aesthetic one. In our modern homes, we tend to placate ourselves with somber brown wood tones or neutral beige. Our ancestors, lacking our accelerated life style, chose to use color to animate their environs. Paint was pragmatic, alive, and beautiful.

The problem for today's collector is to determine what is original paint, old paint and what is new paint. This is not always a simple proposition. Paint can hide more blemishes than the makeup of a French lady of the evening. For this reason, paint is dangerous and deceptive. A piece that is overly restored or rotted can be hidden under a coat of fresh "olderized" paint.

This creates a double bind for the collector. On the one hand, he cannot take the piece home and strip it before purchasing. On the other hand, it would be sacrilege to destroy what might be a good old paint.

Another problem for the collector is marketability. Although antique magazines tout, and correctly so, the value of original-painted furniture, it is salable in some areas but not in others. In Massachusetts and New Hampshire, painted furniture is at a premium. In any given week you will find more "original" painted furniture than existed in the last half of the 18th century. To give credit where it is due, there are some fine painters in New England.

One way to purchase original painted furniture is in the rough where it is buried beneath two or three coats of more modern paint. There should be no mistaking that stripping away several coats of paint is painstaking and frustrating, but it is also rewarding. When you strip the piece yourself, you at least know that what is at the bottom is original or old. To determine if there is an old coat of paint under fresh paint, a light scraping with a penknife will provide the requisite information. If the top coat is not terribly recent, it might be worn away in spots revealing an old finish underneath.

An alternate method of purchase involves buying a piece with an original, unrestored paint finish at auction or in a shop. But there are risks involved. One notable furniture restorer has declared that 90 percent of all the original paint finishes he has seen are phony. I am not as cynical as this gentleman; nonetheless, extreme caution is advised. When examining a piece, assess the overall presentation that it makes. If there is a paint finish purporting to be 100 years old, it should not be fresh and clean. The signs of wear and use that you would encounter on an unpainted piece should be apparent. The paint should be worn away in these spots. The bottom front rung of a chair should have little paint left. If a drawer or door were prone to being opened by hand, the paint should be worn in these spots. The bottoms of chairs, tables and chests should be scuffed from the knocking of feet. The top of a well-used table will have little paint left. People who imitate old paint finishes are aware of the primary wear areas. They will attempt to duplicate wear by rubbing the area with steel wool before the paint dries. This type of faked wear looks particularly sterile and it is easily detected with a little practice.

Nicks, dents, and scratches should be examined on painted furniture. If a piece is painted, but subsequently dented or scratched, then logically there will be no paint in the dent or scratch. With time, dents or other abrasions will darken from dirt or other substances. If you find the abrasions filled with the same color paint as the rest of the piece, you know it has been repainted.

Old paint, like old varnish, is brittle and tends to flake or powder off. New paint, no matter how old looking, is flexible. If you scratch a paint surface with a knife, recent paint will curl off like peeling a bar of soap. Old paint will flake. The basic ingredients of paint are a pigment, a vehicle and a dryer. The primary vehicle for paint, aside from modern latex paints, has been oil. Over a long period of time, the oil will completely dry and cause brittleness. The brittleness of a surface will tell you if it is old, but not that it is original.

When a restorer is trying to save an original paint he often will use a stripper carefully to bring him to the base coat. When the base is achieved, he will use a fine steel wool to even out the paint. This is known in the trade as *stretching.* In such a case, the old paint will have been revitalized to a degree. It will have more flexibility than a genuine old paint. This surface cannot truly be considered original, but on a relative scale it is more desirable than a stripped or newly painted piece.

With some pieces, such as cupboards that use nails in their construction other than for backboards, there will be telltale signs of discoloration. With time and moisture, the nails will oxidize and cause a deterioration in the paint surface around the nail. This deterioration takes the form of an oval or halo.

Painted furniture is wonderful and an asset to any collection, but it must be treated with caution and skepticism. There have been pieces done well enough to fool museums. If it is that well done, you will never know anyway.

NAILS AND SCREWS

Any original accessory or hardware on a piece of furniture, can assist you with dating and authenticating by providing corroborative data. The most reliable of these corroborative sources are nails. It is unlikely, but far from impossible, that a piece that is essentially nailed together has been dismantled and reassembled with new nails. Screws and hinges are more frequently replaced than nails. The least reliable indicators are knobs, brasses, and latches. They have a tendency to be changed as old furniture is modernized.

Nails are particularly useful in dating country furniture that is otherwise difficult to classify due to a lack of adherence to rigid rules of styles. A piece of furniture constructed with machine-made square nails has perimeters of origin established by the nails. Machine-made nails were not widely used prior to 1800 and they were not widely used, except for flooring, after 1870. Hence, you can conclude the period of origin to be from 1800 to 1870.

Nails fall into three categories: handmade or blacksmith nails, machine-cut square nails, and modern round nails. The most primitive of the three is the hand wrought, blacksmith-made nail. The origins of this nail are not known, but the type dates at least back to ancient Rome where it was known as a *clavus*. The hand-wrought nail was not difficult to make, but it was time consuming to make and therefore costly. The nail-making process generally involved the smith heating nail stock and hammering it to a point on the anvil. After that, it was placed in a device to form a head (known as a *header*). The cost involved in the process made nails an expensive and limited commodity. It was also an area of manufacturing that was receptive to technological innovation.

Much-needed innovation in the nail industry came in 1875 with the invention of Ezekiel Reed's nail-cutting machine. With this machine, nail stock could be cut and pointed in the machine. A second heading step was still required. Further developments in the machine led to a one-step process in the early 19th century. The cut-nail machine revolutionized the nail industry by making nails abundant and cheap for all types of construction.

The next major innovation in the nail industry was the modern nail known as the *wire nail*. Machinery for the wire nail was available in the United States as early as 1860, but the overall date for the common appearance of the nail was 1870. The modern wire nail quickly superseded all other forms of nail production, due to the ease of manufacture and cost, but it did not excede earlier forms of nails in quality.

For the purpose of dating an antique, it can be assumed that hand-wrought nails were actively made and used until 1800. After

1800, they did not cease to exist. The new machine-made nails were brittle and did not lend themselves to operations that involved *clinching* (bending the exposed portion of a nail over). Handmade nails remained in vogue, for clinching purposes, until at least 1875. For the most part, hand-wrought nails were not used in furniture construction during the 19th century. It is reasonable to assume that a piece made with blacksmith nails was made prior to 1825 and an origin prior to 1800 would be equally likely. A distinction is drawn here between the United States and other countries. Blacksmith made nails can be found in backboard construction and bottom board construction in 19th-century English, Canadian, and European furniture.

The cut, machine nail was made actively from 1800 to 1875 and was used extensively in furniture. The modern wire nail superceded the cut nail in the 1870 to 1875 period. The cut nail has remained in continuous production. The cut nail still remains the staple of the floor industry and is recognizable to most modern handymen as a flooring nail.

Cut nails and wire nails existed side by side as industries in the 1875 to 1900 period. Both style nails can be found in furniture of the period. In fact, both styles can be found on the same piece. Furniture made subsequent to 1900 appears to be dominated by wire nails. It is likely, however, that handyman pieces continued to utilize an abundant supply of machine cut nails.

A piece of furniture with machine-cut nails can be assumed to have been made at the earliest in 1790 if other considerations such as style and construction strongly suggest it. The most likely dates of origin for such a piece are from 1800 to 1875. Construction with machine-cut nails as late as 1900 is possible. Dating must also be based on elements of style and construction. Early machine-cut nails were made with a combination of machine and hand technology. The square, tapered shank of the nail would be formed by machine while the head was formed later, by hand, in the traditional blacksmith manner. If a cut nail has been headed by hand, a date prior to 1825 is suggested.

Modern wire nails clearly indicate a construction date after 1875 (and in many cases after 1900). Wire nails were in use in Europe prior to the United States; therefore, a date prior to 1875 might be indicated.

The problem for the collector is to determine what kind of nail was used in a piece. The blacksmith-made, rosehead nail presents the least difficulty. The rosehead nail is made with a minimum of three blows from the hammer. A distinctive mark is left on the nail (Fig. 3-19).

The rosehead nail seems to have the greatest romantic appeal to collectors, but it was not the only type of hand-wrought nail. The "T" or "L" shapes were used as commonly as the rosehead. These nails (Fig. 3-20), when in place, look remarkably similar to the machine-cut finish nail. On occasion, it may be necessary to remove a loose nail to be positive. There is usually at least one loose nail in an old piece.

Figure 3-21 illustrates a blacksmith T-nail, an L-nail, and a machine-cut finish and box nail. There is one difference between handmade nails and cut nails that is not discernible from the photograph. Handmade nails taper on all four sides, while a machine-cut nail tapers on only two sides. An additional difference is that hand-wrought nails are pointed, while machine-cut nails are blunt tipped. Numerous cut nails of different styles and for different purposes were produced in the 19th century. Examples are the clout, the hinge, the box, the finish, and the spike. All of these nails have heads with some variation of a rectangle or oval. Never are they perfectly round like the head of a modern nail. There should be no great difficulty in telling the difference between old machine-cut nails and modern nails.

With 18th-century furniture, the use of nails is restricted to backboards, hinges, and, occasionally, table tops. With 19th-century furniture, there is a proliferation of nail use. Backboards and sides will be nailed as will tops to dressers, cupboards, washstands, and tables. All nails, with the exception of the

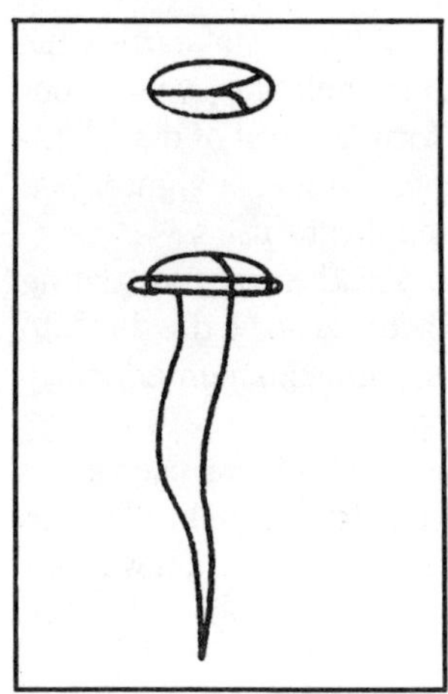

Fig. 3-19. A blacksmith-made rosehead nail displaying a minimum of three blows used to form the head. These nails are pointed and not blunt ended.

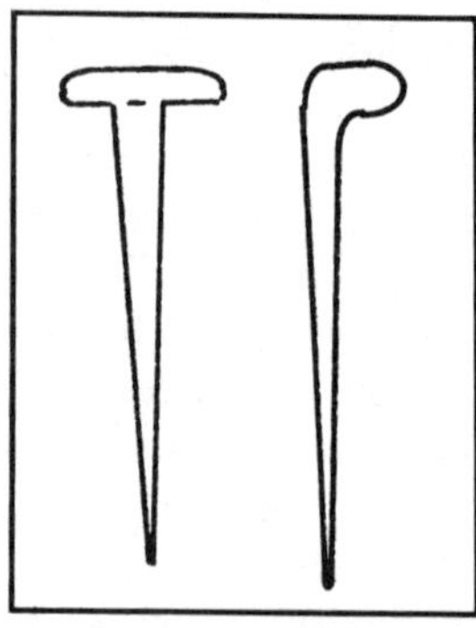

Fig. 3-20. Examples of T- and L-pointed, smith-made nails. These nails were used equally with rosehead nails.

backboards, will have been countersunk and filled with plaster. In most pieces the plaster filler will still be intact.

If a cut nail was used, the filled hole will have a rectangular or oval shape as did the nail. It is always wise to find one unfilled hole (and there usually is at least one) to double check what kind of nail is there. I know one dealer who made himself a square nail punch so that when a piece had modern, round nails, all that was necessary was a quick punch, a little plastic wood and, allacazam, the piece was 50 years older.

With time, nails will oxidize and rust. Handmade nails and early machine cut nails used a purer iron that was more resistant to rust. The process of rusting will stain the wood around the nail. With backboards, a slight discoloration can be seen around the nails. This rust staining is rarely ever duplicated by a faker. Because nails used on the face surfaces of furniture were countersunk and plugged, they will not oxidize because the filler prevents them from coming in contact with air and moisture.

With some painted pieces, usually simple cupboards, the maker might not have bothered to countersink the nails. Consequently, the paint will deteriorate and form an oval of discoloration in the area of the nail. This halo effect is a sure sign of age because fakers cannot, or do not try to, duplicate it.

Screws, like nails, can provide corroborative data for dating and authenticating furniture. Screw manufacture can be divided into four phases of development: handmade, machine augmented, early machine made, and basic modern.

There are positive references to wood screws being used as far back as the 16th century, but it is possible that they date back to the Romans. Regardless of how far back the screw originated, it was not commonly used until the end of the 17th century and early 18th century.

Screws were used as infrequently as possible because of the difficulty and labor involved in making them. Screw making involved the blacksmith shaping the shank, known as *swaging,* then heading the shank to form a rim, followed by the final shaping of the rim and the cutting of a notch. When this work was completed, the screw blank had to be threaded by hand with a file. It is easy to understand why screws were only used when there was no other alternative.

Handmade screws are often described as having little taper to the shank and a blunt end. This is not necessarily true because the blacksmith might have pointed the screw with a file. A better description of the blacksmith-made screw would be that it had uneven threads, little taper, and that it frequently was blunt ended, with an uneven or offset slot in the head.

Screw making increased in the fourth quarter of the 18th century with an advance in technology. This period of screw making can be called machine augmented. Hand-cranked lathes with threaded spindles produced relatively uniform threads. The Birmingham Directory (England) for 1770 lists at least two such screw makers. This stage of the industry lasted into the first quarter of the 19th century when water and steam power were employed to power lathes.

The screws of the hand-machined industry and early machine industry spanned from approximately 1775 to 1850. They were essentially the same type having a blunt ended screw of uniform spiral with little taper to the shank and a frequently off-center slot (Fig. 3-22). It was not a prerequisite that the slot be off-center. Because the slots were hand filed, it was often the case.

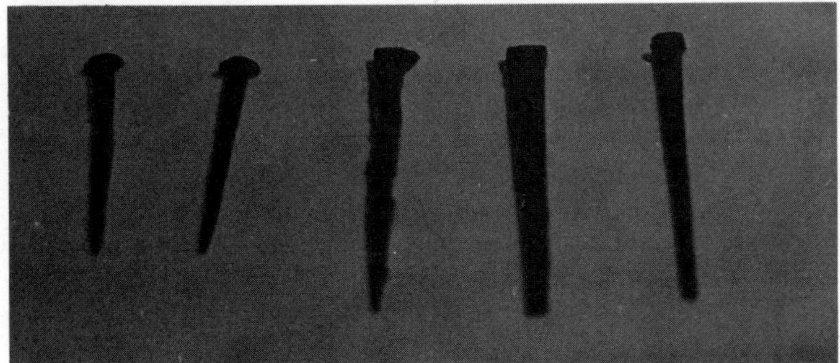

Fig. 3-21. Two blacksmith-made T-nails, an L-nail, a machine-made finish nail, and a box-head nail. Note that the blacksmith-made nails are pointed; the machine-made nails are blunt ended.

Fig. 3-22. A handmade screw, an early, modern machine-made gimlet screw, and a modern gimlet screw. Note that the handmade screw is blunt ended with uneven spirals. The early, machine-made screw has deep and well-made spirals when compared to the modern screw.

In 1846, Thomas Sloan, of New York, patented a machine to make a tapered and pointed screw known as the *gimlet screw*. The gimlet screw was in wide production by 1850, and it is not readily discernible from the modern screw.

When you are examining an antique piece of furniture, first check to see if any screws are slotted off-center. If some of the screws are off-center, then a date of manufacture prior to 1875 is established (but a date prior to 1850 is more likely). If you remove the screw and find that it has a tapered shank and a point, you can assume a date of manufacture after 1850. If the shank has a taper similar to a modern screw, but has a blunt point, it is probably a post-1850 screw trimmed. Some traditionalists preferred a blunt pointed screw, so they merely cut off the points from the gimlet screws. If, on the other hand, you find a screw with little taper to the shank, a blunt point and relatively even spirals cut deeper than a modern screw, you can assume a date of manufacture from 1800 to 1850 (with a possibility of being from the last quarter of the 18th century). If a truly handmade screw, hand filed, round, with even spirals is encountered, you can presume a date of manufacture prior to 1800.

If you are going to attempt to date a piece by a screw, you must be sure the screw is original to the piece. This is not as difficult as it may sound for each screw creates corresponding thread marks in the wood. If a screw has been replaced, there will be a second set of screw threads in the hole or a destruction of the first set. In either case, that would make replacement obvious. You should also come to some opinion as to how reasonable or acceptable screw replacement is. With a working part such as a hinge which suffers stress, it is understandable that a screw might have worked loose and necessitated replacement. If, on the other hand, the screws that hold a table top to a frame from the underside are all replaced, what is suggested? Screws securing table tops do not ordinarily work loose. Therefore, you should immediately suspect that the top has been repaired or replaced.

HINGES AND KNOBS

Hinges provide another source of supportive information for dating furniture. Hinges can be divided into three categories: hand wrought, cast, and machine-rolled plate.

Hand wrought, or blacksmith-made, hinges are principally a product of the 18th century. Any form of door construction requiring strength, whether for furniture or the building trades, would have used hand-wrought hinges. The primary patterns that were used then are still in use today, and they can be seen in the decorative hardware sections of most do-it-yourself stores. The H-hinge and H-and L-hinges (Fig. 3-23) were used on cupboards from 1700 to approximately 1825. There also were survival pieces produced throughout the 19th century.

In the 18th century, this hinge was attached with nails. In the nineteenth century, screws were more likely. Almost all hand-wrought, 18th-century hinges were intended to be used with nails. Consequently, the pilot holes were not countersunk for screw heads. That is a 19th-century characteristic.

In Fig. 3-24, a strap hinge and a butterfly hinge are illustrated. The strap hinge was used for chests and barn doors and was popular

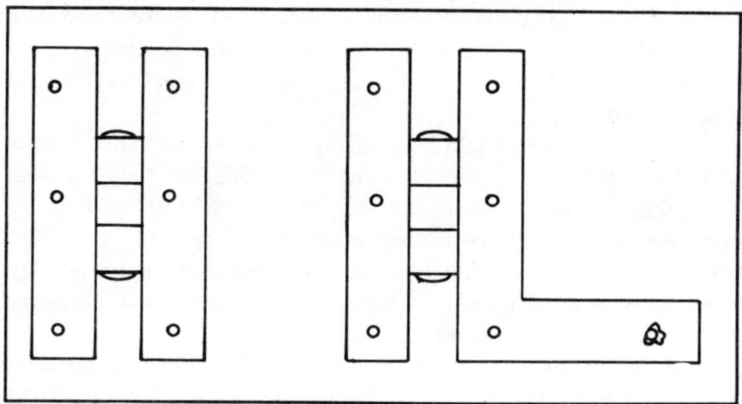

Fig. 3-23. Blacksmith-made H-hinge and H- and L-hinges. These hinges were attached with nails. Therefore, the pilot holes are not countersunk for screwheads.

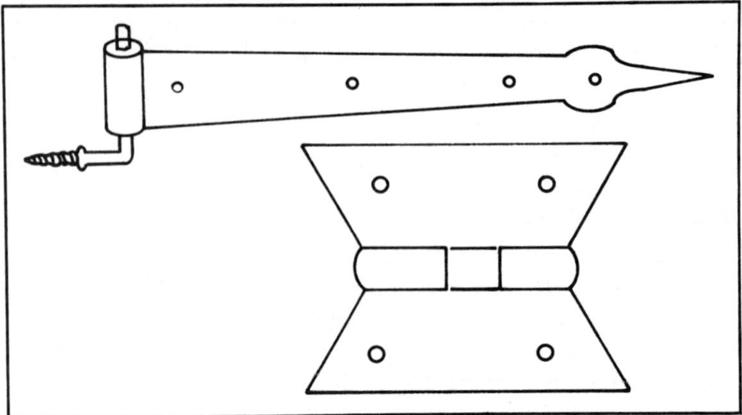

Fig. 3-24. Hand-forged strap hinge with pintle used for architectural construction and a hand forged butterfly hinge used for tables. These hinges were attached with nails.

in both the 18th and 19th centuries. In the 19th century, strap hinges continued to be hand wrought, but they were also available in machine-rolled plate hinges. The butterfly is one of the most classic of hand wrought hinges, and it was used on tables and doors from approximately 1700 to 1750.

The snipe hinge (Fig. 3-25) was used in chest construction from about 1700 to 1750. This hinge was no more than two cotter pins interlocked. It was not a durable hinge and most surviving examples are in sad condition.

The rectangular hinge (Fig. 3-26) was in use throughout the 18th century. This hinge is easily recognizable because it involved bending the iron around the pin. This caused a double sheet on each side of the pin. This was an extremely durable hinge. It is found on desks and drop-leaf tables.

Even a novice should have no difficulty in identifying a hand-wrought hinge. Hand-wrought hinges are uneven; they thin out toward the edges due to hammering. Marks from the blacksmith's hammer will be apparent throughout, but they will be subtle. Department-store reproductions of wrought hardware are grossly overstated and make it appear that every blacksmith was suffering from a neurological disorder.

Brass hinges were also available throughout the 18th century, but their shapes were restricted to rectangles such as butts. Brass hinges could be either blacksmith wrought or cast (the latter being the predominant mode). Cast-brass hinges are quite dissimilar from the more modern rolled-brass hinges. Cast hinges are thick and, no matter how well polished, have some surface irregularities from the casting process.

Cast brass hinges were used for furniture throughout the 18th century and 19th century. Hinges cast in two separate pieces and then joined with a separate pin are the old variety. Those cast in one piece with sealed ends and an internal pin are a 19th century innovation. There were two problems associated with these hinges: They were weak, and they required screws which were costly. The improvements in screw making toward the end of the century expanded the use of butt hinges.

Cast-iron hinges had greater strength than their brass counterparts and gained far more widespread use in casual furniture. Cast-iron hinges similar to cast-brass hinges are thick and they display the irregularity of the casting process. The cast iron hinge was stronger than the brass, but still relatively weak when compared with rolled plate hinges.

A number of sources suggest that cast-iron hinges did not come into use until 1800, but this is not the case. The cast iron butt hinge was introduced in England in 1775. The American Revolution might have impeded the transfer of technology, but doubtless the technology or the product was available in the United States by 1790. I have seen a number of pieces—that appear to be 18th century—with original cast-iron hinges that argue against rigid adherence to the 1800 rule. Cast-iron hinges will account for the majority of hinges that you are likely to find on country antique furniture.

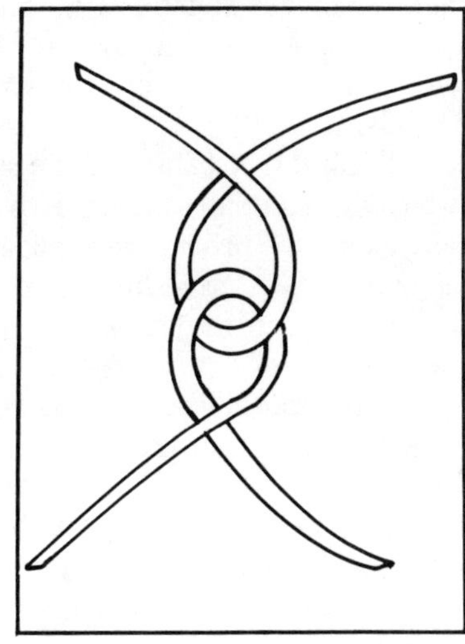

Fig. 3-25. A snipe hinge similar to a modern cotter pin was hand forged of malable iron and clinched to the adjoining surfaces. This hinge is seen mostly in chest construction prior to 1750.

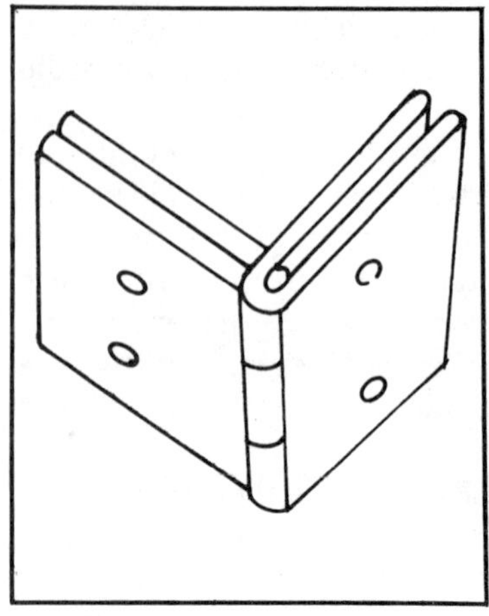

Fig. 3-26. A hand-forged rectangular hinge made by bending iron around a pin so that each half of the hinge will appear as a double leaf. These hinges thin out toward the edges as a result of the forging process.

Cast-iron hinges were available from 1775 or 1800, depending upon your point of view, and throughout the 19th century. Early examples of these hinges are cast in two parts and they are joined with a separate pin. Later examples have been cast in one piece, with sealed ends and an internal pin. Hinges marked "Patent" or "Baldwin Patent" date from about 1850. Cast iron hinges were intended for use with screws. Therefore, the pilot holes were counterbored to allow for screw heads.

For the purpose of authentication, cast-brass hinges can indicate either 18th or 19th century origin. If the hinges were cast in one piece, either brass or iron, a date after 1840 is suggested. The use of cast-iron hinges signifies 19th century construction in most cases. The information given by the hinges, when combined with the information provided by the screws, should narrow the dating periods.

The last type of hinge to be considered is the rolled plate hinge (which is essentially the modern hinge). These hinges were basically a machine product recognizable to anyone who has ever put a hinge in place. These hinges are far less attractive and romantic than their hand forged or cast cousins. Nevertheless, they are superior hinges.

I have read at least one source that suggests rolled plate hinges were available from 1820 onward, but I have yet to find a piece of this period with such hinges. This type of hinge was positively available, and in common use, by 1860. It is probable that these hinges did not come to any widespread manufacture until the broader application of steam power in the 1830 to 1835 period.

Brasses and knobs are still another source of information in dating a piece. They are the least reliable because people tend to modernize furniture by changing the knobs. Brasses are, for the most part, in the domain of formal furniture and not country furniture. But they were used on country as well. Sometimes there is nothing prettier than a New England blanket chest in old red with gleaming brass bails and a fine, brass keyhole escutcheon.

There was a rather infinite profusion of different shapes and styles of brasses used in the 18th century. For the most part, they featured a back plate with a bail (handle). See Fig. 3-27A. Or they had a bail with rosettes as in Fig. 3-27B. The bails were attached to brass posts (Fig. 3-27C) that went through the back plate and the drawer. The post was hand threaded and not tapered. The nut was round or hexagonal and obviously handmade.

The post was always a separate piece. This is unlike the cheap, modern reproductions where the post is part of the backplate. Brasses such as these can be found in the 1690 to 1825 period. Earlier examples (1690-1720) might have been attached with pins similar to cotter pins, or they might have utilized a simple tear drop as in Fig. 3-27D.

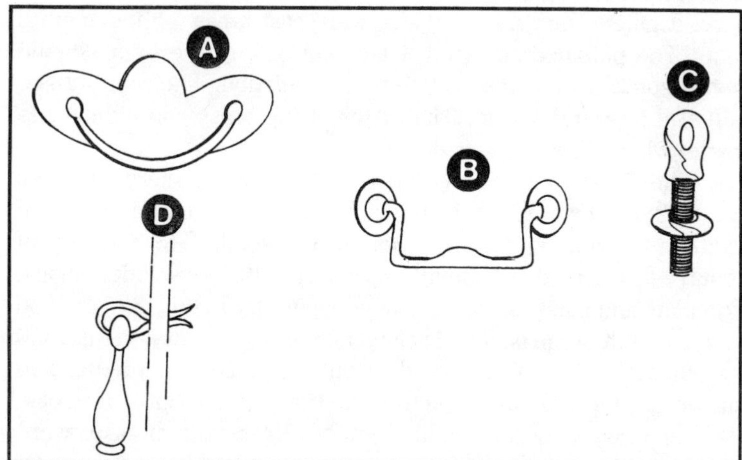

Fig. 3-27. Brass back plate (A) and bail (handle) typical of the hardware used throughout the 18th-century, although a great variety of shapes can be found. A simple bail (B) with rosettes of brass found from the mid-18th century through the early 19th century. A brass post and nut (C) used to attach the bail and back plate to a drawer. The shank will have no taper. The nut will be round and roughly cut. A simple brass teardrop pull (D) attached with a pin as found in the late 17th century and early 18th century.

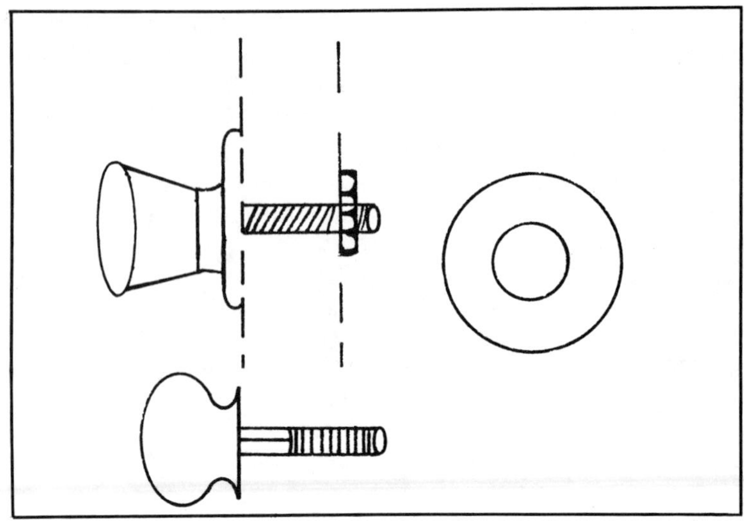

Fig. 3-28. A brass knob with rosette typical of the late 18th century and early 19th century. The knob would have a blunt-ended, hand-threaded shank with no taper. The mating nut was round and roughly made.

The styles and the dating of brasses is a lengthy subject that is covered in many good antique books; I will not belabor the point here. Eighteenth-century brasses were cast brass (although quite thin). The polished surface, or face surface, of the brass should reveal some surface imperfection or undulation. The rear surface will still be roughly cast. The edges of the brass will exhibit file marks where it was cleaned up.

The Sheraton period (1790-1825) introduced the brass knob (Fig. 3-28) that was to set the tone for the 19th century (although the medium for country furniture was to be wood). The majority of country furniture that you will encounter will have wooden knobs. Porcelain and glass knobs had some popularity in the 1825 to 1850 period, but they can be found at any point in the century. In the 1850 to 1900 period, machine-carved walnut and oak pulls were used on numerous pieces. In the 1880 to 1920 period of mass produced oak, stamped brasses loosely reminiscent of 18th-century brasses were widely used.

With 18th-century country furniture, wooden knobs were used more than anything else. Nevertheless, dating a piece by a knob is difficult. The clothespin style knob (Fig. 3-29A) and the basic mushroom style knob (Fig. 3-29B) were used. These knobs would most likely have been hand carved and not lathe turned. Consequently, variation will be apparent. Most of these knobs had a wooden shank with a slight taper for a tight friction fit. Toward the end of the century, a number of different methods (Fig. 3-29C) were used.

The first shown in Fig. 3-29 is the spike; it involves a pointed iron shank driven into the knob. Once in place, the shank would be clinched. This technique could be found in the 17th or 18th centuries, but it is uncommon because a wooden shank did the job as well.

The next method shown in Fig. 3-29 has a threaded metal shank in the manner of a Sheraton brass. The shank would have no taper and would be blunt pointed. The nut would be handmade. This type of arrangement can be found in the 1800 to 1825 period.

The next arrangement shown in Fig. 3-29 was widely used in quality work in the 1800 to 1850 period. This style utilizes a wooden

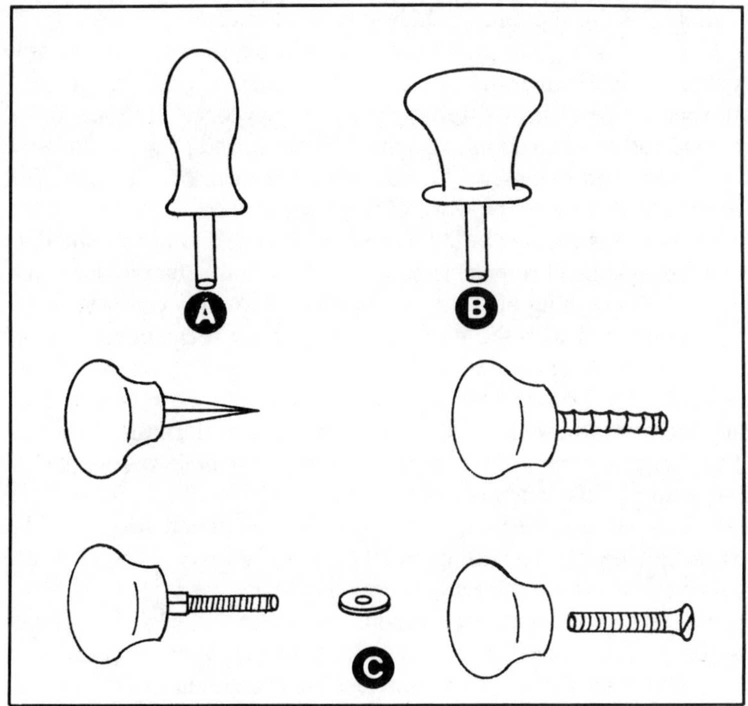

Fig. 3-29. Wooden knob attachments: (A) popular 18th-century clothespin knob attached with a wooden shank; (B) mushroom-style wooden knob used in the 18th century and the 19th century. (C) Four methods of knob attachment: metal spike, threaded nut and bolt, threaded wooden screw, and rear screw attachment.

screw, one end of which is fitted to the knob, while the drawer front was drilled and threaded to mate the wood screw.

The last attachment method shown in Fig. 3-29 was dominate during the 19th century and it is the primary method still used. This basic screw-from-the-rear method would have been used at any point in the 18th century, but it still remains predominently a 19th-century technique. With this arrangement, the screw will have to be your guide to age (if both screw and knob are original).

The wooden knobs used on 19th-century furniture were lathe turned, nicely made, and relatively consistent. Worthy of note is that Shakers continued to utilize press-fit knobs with wooden shanks.

GLUE AND PEGS

Glue and pegs are the stuff of which furniture is made. Well, this might not be Shakespeare, but it is accurate. A little understanding of the topic might help you authenticate furniture.

There is a great glue misconception that exists without any sound reason. Numerous antique books state that glue did not exist or was not used in the 18th century. Poppycock! Glue has been around and used since the ancient Egyptians, and probably longer. Glue was used extensively in the marquetry work of the late 17th century and the veneer work of the 18th century.

Glue was messy. It had to be mixed fresh and hot. It smelled like the dickens. It required a heated surface and a heated room. But more than anything else, it was, by the large, unnecessary.

Compared with the ease of sound joinery techniques such as dovetails, sliding dovetails, pinned mortise and tenon, glue was second rate. These jointing techniques and the infrequent use of glue dominated the first half of the 18th-century furniture making. The change that was to take place with regard to glue was not due to technology. Fashion was the reason.

The jointing techniques previously mentioned were visible from the exterior. The pins of a mortise were to be seen everywhere while dovetails were visible in the tops of chests, desks, etc. For whatever reason, an increasingly sophisticated society wanted furniture without these telltale signs of joining.

The impact of the change in fashion demanded the increasing use of glue because it was the alternative to exposed joinery techniques. This change started about 1750, but gained real impetus in the 1775 to 1800 period. It affected mostly high-society formal pieces. Simple country pieces continued to be made in the traditional glueless fashion throughout the century.

During the 19th century, the rules of the joining game changed. Concealed joinery continued to be the fashion. Nevertheless, there was a need to produce low-cost furniture for growing urban populations that could not make their own furniture. Glue lent itself to the concept of fast and cheap by eliminating some costly and time-consuming techniques. Country cabinetmakers and local handymen still used less glue than their urban neighbors, but the availability of machine-made screws and nails allowed construction without sophisticated joinery.

The glue used during the 18th century and the 19th century was one form or another of animal glue that leaves a thick, brown residue. The glue is very brittle and shatters easily. When examining an old piece, you will find that glue makes a few statements. If glue is apparent, the piece can be from the 18th century, the 19th century or the 20th century. If a glue other than animal glue is used, then beware. The piece has been disassembled and reglued or, worse, it is modern.

Pegs or wooden nails tell you somewhat more than does glue. Pegs were used in the absence of glue to secure a joint. Some insecure craftsmen might have glued and pegged a joint. Pegged joints were used extensively in country furniture until approximately 1825. After 1825, they are seen with less frequency.

The 18th-century cabinetmaker as well as the early 19th-century cabinetmaker did not have available dowel stock from which he could cut his pegs from square stock. These handmade pegs might be square, rectangular, hexagonal, or octogonal, but they were never perfectly round. The use of a round dowel to pin a joint, if original to the joint, indicates a date of origin after 1825.

Pegs were cut from well-seasoned hardwoods such as oak or maple. They can however, be found made out of walnut, cherry, birch, etc. With time and shrinkage, pegs will protrude from the surface of the wood. When pegs are encountered in this manner, it should be seen as a sign of authenticity and not shoddy workmanship. Antique fakers are aware of the shape of old pegs as well as the effects of shrinkage; they are simple to duplicate.

To repair a piece that is pegged, it might be necessary to drill out the old pegs. This is especially true if they were not originally drilled all the way through the mortise. A good restorer will replace the pegs with new, handmade pegs, but the use of dowel stock is acceptable. In a case such as this, the restorer will have also glued the joint. The presence or absence of glue should suggest whether or not the pegs are original.

To put matters in perspective, furniture assembled without glue and with the extensive use of dovetails, pinned tenons, and wedged tenons, is mostly a product of the 18th century (until 1825). Furniture assembled with glue or the extensive use of fasteners, such as nails and screws, is for the most part 19th century. These are gross overgeneralizations, but still basically true. When the information is combined with the other details mentioned in this chapter, the determination of age and originality should not be terribly difficult.

REPAIRS AND REPLACEMENTS

The originality of antique furniture is a simple determination of what has or has not been done to a piece, and what needs to be done to restore it to its original function. These two factors establish the desirability of a piece for your collection and the price that should be paid. The equation is not complex: as restoration increases, value decreases. The ideal is a piece that is sound, functional, attractive, and completely original. The reality is that you will encounter an increasingly small number of such pieces.

Textbooks on antiques often suggest quantitative approaches to the evaluation of antiques. Some sources I have encountered indicate that if there is more than 10 percent replacement, then the piece is no longer antique. Other sources have a replacement ranged up to 30 percent.

If you are going to assume a quantitative posture, it seems logical to go the half and half route. If 51 percent of the piece is replaced, it is no longer antique. But if 51 percent is original, then it is antique. This is logical, but it does not necessarily make sense. Neither does a quantitative approach.

The question at hand should be one of integrity. If repairs and restorations have not damaged the integrity of a piece, then in my opinion it remains antique. If the top to an elaborately turned gate-leg table is replaced, the table retains its primary statement and emphasis. With this type of table, the artistry and elaboration was in the turned base and not in the top. If the top to an original gate-leg table is acquired and fitted with a reproduction base, then the primary statement is gone.

If, on the other hand, you had a simple, basically functional tavern table with a breadboard top, the piece would lack a strong artistic or artisan statement. The merit of the piece would be found in the two centuries of wear that the top had received. Without the top it is of questionable value.

Very few people will agree on what maintains the integrity of a piece. It becomes a highly individualistic determination and it rightly should be. When the issue descends to cost, you must decide what it is worth and how much restoration is acceptable.

Discovering repairs and replacements is a matter of careful inspection and observation. It is possible for some replacements to be made that are almost beyond notice. These will be a small percentage of those encountered. The majority of repairs and restorations that you will encounter will be honest, straightforward, and observable.

When you are looking for restorations, it helps to know where to look. That's easy. Everywhere a piece of furniture is likely to wear or be abused is the place to look.

With tables, beware the replacement of a leaf or an entire top. Check the top for miscellaneous nail holes or screw holes that have no purpose and suggest prior installations. Check the coloration of the underside of the top and the inner portions of the frame; they should be the same. Are there scratches from one section to another that suggest the pieces have been together? Take a careful, if not dim, view of all breadboard tops on tavern tables; most are replaced.

Table legs should be checked carefully because they are subject to considerable wear. With turned table legs, are there extensions added immediately above or below a turning? These replacements can be hard to detect. Check to see if there is a glue line or if a knife blade can be inserted.

If a table has a drawer, check the runners and guides that should exhibit noticeable wear or be replaced. Is the drawer lining replaced (that is, the two sides and rear) or has the entire drawer been replaced? Tables are prone to losing drawers over the years. All pieces with drawers are subject to the same consideration.

When evaluating chairs, check the feet first. No one item of furniture is more likely to have extensions of the legs than chairs. If the chair is inverted, screws or pegs securing the additions might be noticeable. Check the stretchers because these often break. On a country ladderback chair, stretchers will not be uniform. Nevertheless, replacements should be detectable. Has an entire front or rear leg post been replaced? If a chair has finials, are they original or have they been doweled in? Remember that some old-time makers did dowel finials as a separate piece, but this was not common. The slats on a ladderback chair are rarely replaced. If it has high, arching slats, there might be some breakage along the top.

With windsor chairs or other spindleback chairs, check for the replacement of spindles. Remember, these spindles were made by hand and not by lathe until at least 1825, and not until 1850 in many cases. If a chair has arms, have they been replaced or have they been added? When a side chair has arms added to it, it looks ill-proportioned and is not as wide as a normal armchair. With a rocking chair, the rockers should be worn flat. If not, check for replacement. Are the lower stretchers close to the rockers? If the answer is yes, the rockers have probably been added.

If you have a chest of drawers in mind, remember that all knobs are suspect and all drawer runners and guides are to be checked. Has there been any drawer replacement? Are the backboards original or have they been replaced? You are more likely to see backboard replacements on chests than anything else. Are the feet worn and damaged? They should be. Has the entire foot been replaced? If in doubt, check the glue blocks on the underside. Do they look like they have been there for 100 or more years and has old, animal glue been used? Remember, the interior of the chest will not have darkened as much as the backboards or bottom board.

Cupboards, such as jelly or jam cupboards, are nothing but another variation of the chest of drawers. Be positive. Some unscrupulous lads have been known to remove the bottom three drawers from a chest and replace them with doors to form an instant cupboard. In this event, nail or screw holes and rebates should still be apparent on the interior surfaces.

Cupboards sometimes lack doors so check for replacements. If there are pegged mortises on the doors, check to see if the pegs haven't been added to increase the marketability of the piece. This is especially apparent when the cross members of the door have a shallow tenon. The upper doors of some cupboards are removed so that they can be described as hutch or pewter cupboards. Check to see if there are hinge mortises that have been filled in or covered with a molding.

Similar to chests, backboards on cupboards must be checked for replacement. Remember to look for rust around the nail holes and to check the bottoms for stain that would suggest that they have been cut down. Mouse holes are usually a good sign.

Jelly cupboards or other cupboards with drawers should be checked with the same precautions listed for pieces with drawers. Cupboards of this type often had splashguards; check for their loss or replacement. If a splashguard is missing, the top will fall short of meeting the backboards by one-half inch or so. With ventilated cupboards, check the tins. If original, they will have the remains of brittle and flaking paint on them. If the cupboard has been stripped, the inside surfaces should still retain paint. There should be an encrustation of dirt and debris wherever the panels attach to the cupboard. Beware of tin panels that are painted fresh brown inside and out.

Cupboard knobs are subject to replacement or modernization. Latches are subject to wear and loss and there are often signs of past latches. Check door hinges for replacement; the loss or damage of one is not uncommon. Similar to chests, the feet are subject to wear and replacement.

On traveling chests such as dovetailed seamen's chests, check for lid replacements and hinge replacements. A number of these chests had hand-forged strap hinges that have been removed and sold separately. When strap hinges are found in place, check to see that they are nailed and not screwed. Occasionally, bottom boards are replaced, but this should be obvious.

Beds are a simple proposition and not subject to a lot of replacement. They are, however, subject to a great deal of modification. Check to see that headboards, footboards and side rails go together. Artisans sometimes numbered the posts and rails to facilitate putting the bed together. Check side rails where they are mortised into the head or foot post to see if they are freshly cut. Many a bed has been put together with borrowed side rails. With high post beds, be especially careful to check that all posts are matched.

If your fancy turns to washstands, take the standard drawer and foot precautions. Splashguard replacement is fairly common with washstands; check nail holes. Does the back of the splashguard have the same color and texture as the adjoining surface? In the case of rectangular washstands with drawers and doors, make sure a 1920's Grand Rapids model has not had old backboards added for instant value and antiquity.

With simple benches, check to see that the supports are equidistant from each end or if one has been replaced or moved. Many of these fine, old benches were so long that they have been cut down to make two more salable benches. The same is true of the popular spindle back benches. Check to see if spindles have been replaced and if one arm has been added awkwardly.

Knowing where to look is a great help, but your actions should be guided by reason and careful observation. Don't be surprised if, no matter how carefully you examine a piece, you discover a great deal that you didn't previously notice once you get it home.

You are most likely to find restorations and replacements on pieces sold in antique shops. Most dealers cannot market a piece in the rough; they will rightfully restore it before putting it on the floor. When buying at a country auction and in the rough, you will find that restorations are not likely and the structural shortcomings are obvious. When you do encounter a piece at an auction that has been refinished and all spruced up, check it with double care. For some odd reason, whenever I encounter a piece like this at auction, it is doctored or overly restored.

There is also the matter of total fakes. A collector is more likely to encounter overly restored or modified pieces than total fakes, but they do exist. With complete fakes, the lack of shrinkage and the duplication of age and wear marks will be the key signs. The discovery of modified or built-up pieces requires a little knowledge and some imagination.

I know of one fellow who takes large, dovetailed wood boxes, removes one end, and scrolls the sides. The removed end becomes a seat, and voila, you have a primitive, antique, dovetailed wing chair. The wood will be old, the dovetails and nails proper, and the shrinkage authentic. In such a case, the signs of wear will be all wrong. The bottom of the newborn chair will show no signs of wear. The back will look like it had been walked on for a hundred years. The sides that have been freshly scrolled will be filed, distressed, and sanded smooth. But they will not have a mellow look of hundreds of years of use.

Careful observation should be enough to detect this type of fraud. A little knowledge will tell you that there is no original for this chair. This pseudo-wingback was the product of some modern builder's imagination. It will require a little imagination on the part of the collector to see what was done.

Whenever you are examining a piece, raise the question, "Could this have been something else?" Let your mind run fertile. Could a woodbox become a settle, a chest, a cupboard? Could a slope-front grainbox become a schoolmaster's desk. Could a broken, wooden shovel become a doughbowl?

If you allow yourself to see what could be, then you will know where to look to see what is. For practice, take a good picture book of antiques, study the illustrations, and fantasize what each could be with modifications. Involve your spouse or friends. Offer a price for creativity and have fun.

DEDUCTIONS: THE FINAL ANALYSIS

Once you have mastered the fundamentals, take your magnifying glass in hand, don your deerstalker cap, light your calabash pipe, and begin sleuthing. In reality, the authenticating of antiques is sleuthing in the time-honored sense of the great detectives. Sherlock's famed combination of observation, knowledge, and deduction is the course you should pursue. Antiquing has many facets that make it one of the greatest hobbies in the world. There is the intrinsic beauty and artistry of the object in conjunction with the historical presence and statement. Equally exciting is the hunt from shop to farm, treasure troves heaped with dust, do-dads, memoribilia, and the one gem-in-the-rough antique buried under a ton of debris awaiting adoption and restoration.

Once the treasure is found, there is the excitement of pitting your eye and reason against the ravishes of time and abuse. Your eye catches sight of the rosehead nail that quickens the pace of your heart. The empty hinge mortises and newly placed hinges speak to you of incredible use. There is no mistaking that this is the exciting part of the hobby. As Sherlock would say to Watson, "The game is afoot."

As you commence the search for antiques, bear in mind the foregoing observations and instructions as well as those that you will learn from other sources and experience. Try to maintain an awareness that no one thing confirms the antiquity of a piece, but rather the interplay of all the factors. By carefully assessing all factors, you can come to a reasoned, logical decision that will be correct most of the time. The safest posture is: when in doubt, don't. For those less conservative, risk-taking can lead to disaster or reward. Whether conservative or not, be consistent and methodical.

To assist with collecting, you should be armed with a basic tool kit. There are antiquing sets for sale, but because all the articles are readily available, you can assemble your own set and save money. Your tool kit should have a pocketknife with a large and a small blade, as well as one of the combination screwdriver/bottle opener blades. An inexpensive pocketknife can be found at any five and dime store, but if you have a few extra sheckles you can't do better than an official Swiss Army Knife that comes equipped with everything from a saw to a half-ton fork lift!

Antiquing brings you into a lot of dark places, so a light is essential. This is especially true for inspecting the interiors of cupboards and chests. You could use the six-volt lantern from your car, but it's a bit ostentacious. I recommend the purchase of a small penlight. A good idea is to pick up one of the inexpensive penlights that has a built-in magnifying glass. It can be used for examining detail.

A caliper is an absolute necessity for measuring table tops and other surfaces for the variation produced by hand planing. Standard calipers can be obtained at your local hardware store, but they are a bit awkward to carry around. If at all possible obtain a small, pocket-size one. If you can't find a pocket-size caliper locally, you can get a nice, brass one through one of the catalog houses that handles quality hand tools.

To complete your tool kit, find a tape measure, a pencil, paper and a magnet. You can use the magnet to determine if an item is brass or brass plated. Brass is not magnetic.

If someone in the family has talent with a needle and thread, you can have them make you a small roll-up pouch for your tool kit. But you can just as well put it in any type of bag. When working with your tools, you are better off placing them in your pockets or handbag so that you can be somewhat discrete when you enter a shop. Don't be surprised if, when you brandish your tools, the dealer comes forth with a medley of questions such as, "Is everything alright?" If the dealer doesn't appear to be at all purturbed, then it is probably a good sign. In any event, you can feel smug and professional with your tool kit!

When you become experienced with antiques, you will know what to look for without prodding. Until you do, it's wise to carry a checklist to jog your memory. I recommend you use something like the sample shown in Fig. 3-30. This one is broken into three categories: dating, indications of age, and financial considerations.

The first category should help you determine the range of possible origins such as first half of the 19th century, etc. This category also assists with the determination of originality and authenticity. The second category should help you decide whether or not you are dealing with a fine reproduction or a piece that has been knocking about for a hundred or two hundred years. The third category presents the question of restoration that is relevant to the desirability of a piece and that is a major financial consideration. The last item listed is intuition; it should be neither your guide nor ignored. Intuition works best in the negative. If a number of items

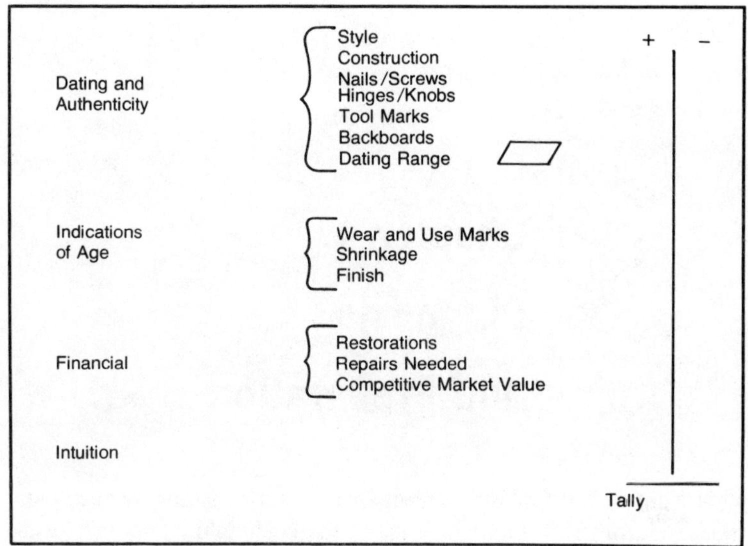

Fig. 3-30. A sample checksheet.

on your checklist weigh against the authenticity of a piece, but your intuition says yes, it is better to go with your observations and deductions. If your checklist works out well, but your intuition says no, then go with your intuition. You might not be right, but there is some aspect of yourself that is saying stop. If you follow your intuition in this instance, you will, at the minimum, avoid buyer's remorse and nagging doubts.

You can set up a checklist in any fashion you prefer. There can be a column for explicit notes or you can develop a point system. I prefer a simple yes/no column or +/− column. Whatever system you choose, after an assessment is made, there should be a neat column on the positive side. When there are checks in the negative column, there must be reasonable explanations or hypotheses for the inconsistencies. If you find yourself reaching for extraordinary explanations and circumstances to account for the difficulties, then something is wrong.

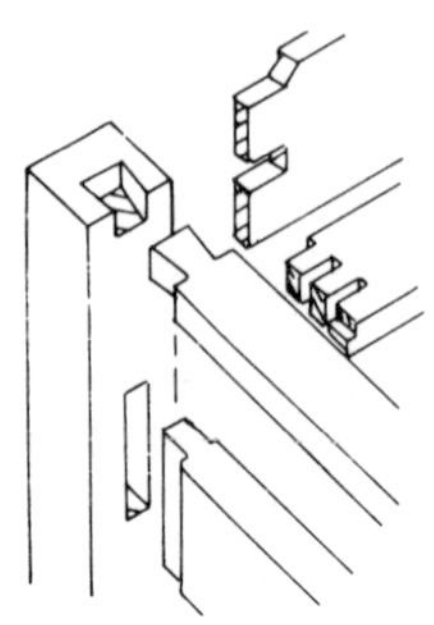

Chapter 4

Diagnosis

and Preparation

Restoring and refinishing antiques is not the same as restoring modern furniture. The techniques used in refinishing modern furniture are no different from one piece to the other, but with antiques you run the risk of damaging the value of a piece. With an antique—if you destroy the originality of a finish—it can never be redone. The risk is not one of accident or mishap, but one of purpose.

Each collector who sets out to restore furniture must decide upon an ethic to guide his actions. If you are a strict traditionalist and purist, the decision is simple. You do as little as possible. If you acquire a fine old table base with flaking red paint and no top, then that's the way you keep it. Frankly, you are going to have one heck of a time trying to serve tea on it. If you are somewhat more moderate, you will leave the old paint on the base and tastefully replace the top. On the other hand, if you are the devil-may-care type, you will replace the top, strip the base, belt sand it to remove all signs of age, beat it with a chain to make it look aged, and then put on umpteen coats of polyurethane until it shines like new plastic!

You will have to make your own decisions. At best, I can share some opinions with you. Our ancestors did not esteem rotting, broken down furniture; nor should we. Some things are junk even if it is antique junk. There has been a continuous tradition of restoring furniture that suggests people like pretty, clean things in their homes, but not necessarily new things. If you have a need for everything to look brand spanking new and shining, you probably shouldn't be collecting antiques. It will only frustrate you.

Original finishes and surfaces should be preserved if at all possible. There are three reasons for this: it looks better, it is worth

128

more, and it's a lot less work. Original finishes can be cleaned, polished, restored, or otherwise made to look beautiful. If you are not into old paint, the decision is simple. Don't buy it. If you encounter a piece of old paint and you like the shape and style—but you would prefer a pale refinished brown—please don't buy it and refinish it. Continue your search and you will find an antique piece that you like equally, but don't have to harm.

I do not believe that everyone's home should look like a museum. Some antiques belong in a museum and should not be tampered with. These decisions are not hard to make. The differences are obvious. Once you destroy a piece of history, it can never be undone. There is enough variety to suit everyone.

It is not necessary to become apprehensive over the weighty moral responsibility of finishing furniture. Most of the country furniture that you come in contact with will present few such problems. When you are buying rough furniture, you will encounter furniture in a few basic conditions: painted, some finish, or no finish at all. With painted furniture, other than original paint, there should be no indecision at all; it has to come off. An exception might be if there is a nice, old paint that is worth trying to save under the ten coats of white latex.

If the piece is not painted and some finish remains, a determination must be made whether or not the old finish can be repaired. More often than not the old finish can be saved. If not, it can be removed without any guilt feelings.

The category of no finish at all might present an ethical dilemma. The piece might never have had an original clear finish or it might have worn off. I have put finishes on a considerable number of pieces like this. I do suggest that if the piece is unique and valuable, it should be left alone.

DIAGNOSIS

Presuming that you have purchased your treasure and brought it home, the next step is to set it down in a comfortable place. Pour yourself a cup of coffee, relax, and study the piece from end to end before you do anything. This is a good time to confirm the suppositions that you made about the piece prior to purchase.

After examination, make a listing of all the structural repairs that are necessary. If the piece is painted, you will want to make repairs prior to the stripping. If repairs are not made at this point, paint residue will work itself into damaged areas—thus making gluing difficult. If the piece has a clear finish, you might want to do repairs at a later point. The general rule of thumb is to repair first.

Whenever a piece has a clear finish, there is a chance to resuscitate it. First you must determine what the finish is. This is not a Herculean task. There are limited possibilities: shellac finish, lacquer finish, varnish finish, oil finish, or wax finish.

Shellac Finish

It is best to test for a shellac finish first because the majority of clear finishes that you will find on country antique furniture are going to be shellac.

To prepare for testing the finish, it is necessary to clean a small area of dirt and wax that would impede testing. There are a number of ways to clean furniture, but some entail the risk of damaging the finish. For example, soap and water can be used to clean a varnish finish, but it will damage a shellac finish.

There is one all-purpose solvent that will not harm any finish; it is paint thinner. Paint thinner is not always best for heavy buildups of dirt and grease, but it will dissolve old wax, hand oils, etc. Paint thinner is also sold under the generic name of mineral spirits (and for less money).

If you don't have mineral spirits, turpentine will serve the same purpose. Select a small area in an obscure place on the furniture and clean with a rag dipped in mineral spirits. If the dirt or grease is persistent, you can dip a small piece of 0000 steel wool in the spirits and use it to rub out the dirt. Rub only with the grain of the wood.

When an area has been cleaned, you will be ready to determine the nature of the finish. Some finishes will dissolve in the vehicle in which they were originally compounded (shellac is one of these). The vehicle for all shellac is alcohol. Dip a cotton swab or a piece of cloth in alcohol and rub the portion of the old finish that was cleaned. As you rub, the finish will move under the rag and become shiny. Once you stop rubbing and the test spot dries, it should remain shiny. This will indicate that the finish is shellac. If the alcohol fails to affect the finish, then it should be tested with lacquer thinner. Shellac will sometimes dissolve in lacquer thinner, but not always. If a finish dissolves in both alcohol and lacquer thinner, you can assume the finish to be shellac. Lacquer will not dissolve in alcohol.

When you are testing for a finish, do not use rubbing alcohol; it's diluted and will not yield the desired result. Purchase a can of alcohol labeled *shellac solvent* or *alcohol solvent* from the local hardware store or chain store. Leftover alcohol can be used in the liquid fuel burner of your fondue pot; it's much less expensive than a special fondue fuel that is also alcohol. Alcohol, like all inflammable products, should (if at all possible) be kept in a garage or a shed. You must have adequate ventilation when using alcohol. Some people have been known to get a contact high in a room full of alcohol vapor; some have also been known to die as a result.

After you have determined that a piece has been shellacked, stick with mineral spirits as a cleaner. Shellac is a superior finish—with one exception. It has poor resistance to water. A glass left on a shellac finish will leave a ring from the condensation. A piece of furniture with a shellac finish left in a damp environment will blush; it will develop a cloudy film over the entire surface.

Where there is a severe buildup of grease and dirt, it might be necessary to risk the use of a mild soap and water solution. Use a gentle detergent such as a dish detergent. Do not inundate the furniture with water. Try to work with the suds. A soap and water cleansing might cause blushing, but if worse comes to worst, the blush can be removed. See the section on hazing and blushing later in this chapter.

Lacquer Finish

The process for testing a lacquer finish is the same as testing for a shellac finish. Clean a test area with paint thinner and allow it to dry. Instead of using alcohol for the test patch, you will use lacquer thinner. The lacquer thinner might take somewhat longer to penetrate the finish that does alcohol with shellac. Nevertheless, it will dry much faster. If the finish smoothes out and dries shiny, you know the finish is lacquer. Remember that lacquer thinner sometimes dissolves shellac and that it might be necessary to test with both alcohol and thinner to be positive of the finish.

Modern lacquers have been improved to the degree that they are relatively immune to water and alcohol, but all old lacquer finishes exhibit the same sensitivity to water as does shellac. When cleaning a piece with a lacquer finish, stick with paint thinner for cleaning purposes. If grease and dirt are tenacious, 0000 steel wool used with the thinner should loosen it up. Rub only with the grain.

Although lacquer did exist during the historical furniture period, you are not likely to encounter it on a piece of antique furniture. A lacquer finish can be found on some of the mass-produced furniture of the late 1800's, but it is almost exclusively a product of this century. Professional furniture refinishers use lacquer extensively due to the ease with which it can be applied by spraying.

Varnish and Other Finishes

Varnish is a clear finish similar to lacquer and shellac, but it differs significantly on a number of points. Varnish is immune to both water and alcohol and does not dissolve in its original vehicle (which is turpentine).

Testing for varnish is simple. If you have already tested the finish as indicated above using alcohol and lacquer thinner, but nothing has happened, then you have a varnish or similar finish. In the testing process, the lacquer thinner might damage the varnish (causing it to crawl), but it will not smooth out. This crawling effect merely substantiates that the finish is a varnish.

Varnish was used in the 18th century and 19th century for furniture, but accounts for a small percentage of the finishes found. During this period, spirit varnishes that used alcohol instead of turpentine as a vehicle were also used. Spirit varnishes will dissolve in alcohol and should be treated in the same manner as a shellac finish.

If a varnish finish has been established, a number of cleaning methods can be used. A mild soap and water solution can be used for heavy grease without fear of hazing or blushing. Commercially available dewaxers and cleaning solutions can be used with splendid results. Both turpentine and paint thinner can be used with positive results as with shellac and lacquer. If you want to get elaborate, you can mix a batch of special cleaning brew consisting of a quart of hot water, three tablespoons of turpentine and one tablespoon of vinegar. Another cleaning recipe that is renowned calls for hot water, turpentine, and linseed oil. I don't recommend the use of linseed oil in the cleaning process because it might inhibit some finishing approaches. Neither one of these recipes is likely to work better than paint thinner, but the old-timers like to talk about them.

With some refinished pieces, the finish might be polyurethane (a synthetic plastic varnish). For all intents and purposes, polyurethane will react as any other varnish except that it might not recoat as well. If a polyurethane finish is scuffed with steel wool and subsequently magnified, it will show a more severe pattern of abrasion than varnish. If you want to go around the house making test comparisons to determine what is varnish and what is urethane, then please feel free.

132

After testing, if you find that a finish is neither shellac, lacquer nor varnish, then it might be oil or wax. A waxed finish should be obvious. If you have any doubts, scrape it with your pocketknife; it should peel. Alcohol, paint thinner, and turpentine will all dissolve and redistribute wax to a degree.

The removal of a wax finish is a gruesome task. If you decide to tackle this type of job, the furniture should first be cleaned with a commercial brand dewaxer. Following the dewaxer, the furniture should be cleaned thoroughly with mineral spirits applied with a 00 steel wool pad. Once the surface is scrubbed with the steel wool and thinner, the excess should be cleaned with a paper towel. This process should be repeated over and over until there appears to be no trace of the wax.

In all likelihood, the cleaning process will force the wax deeper into the wood. That means you never really get all the wax out. When the cleaning process is complete, use a penetrating oil stain with a shellac finish. I recommend that you avoid all this mess and simply renew the finish with application of a couple of fresh coats of wax.

It is very unlikely that you will encounter a linseed oil or other oil finish. Linseed oil is the basis of oil paints and varnishes. Used in its raw state, it almost never dries. When further refined and with chemical dryers added it just barely dries. Linseed oil with chemical additives is sold as boiled linseed oil. When used on furniture, linseed oil forms a flexible surface that becomes harder as the oils evaporate. Given 100 years of drying, reapplication, and waxing, a beautiful surface will have been established. If you find an old oil finish such as this, it will either be so beautiful you will not want to disturb it or so worn that you will not know it is there.

PROBLEMS AND SOLUTIONS

If you are lucky, an old, clear finish on furniture will require no more than a good cleaning, followed by a waxing. Alas, life is perfidious and old furniture tends to be accompanied by an assortment of nicks, scratches and dents that drive the novice refinisher to dementia. Persons new to restoration have an almost biological drive to strip everything in sight and bestow a new spic and span finish. More experienced restorers take a longer view and become tolerant of slight aberations that are not all that noticeable.

There is not doubt that some furniture will look pretty scruffy when you purchase it. There is also no doubt that a great deal can be done to remedy the problems if you resist the urge to strip the furniture immediately. I am still amazed, after years of experience, to see pieces that look like they have emerged from a 10 year stint in the Black Hole of Calcutta become beautiful with modest cleaning and touch up.

Hazing and Blushing

Hazing and blushing are two words describing the same phenomenon. With this condition a white, cloudy film covers part or all of the finish. *Blushing* is the result of moisture damaging a finish. This does not usually occur under household conditions, but rather when furniture has been relegated to porches, damp basements, or garages. Shellac finishes are particularly prone to blushing. It can also occur with lacquer and varnish.

The remedy for blushing should be simple in most circumstances. Take a 000 pad of steel wool and dip in light mineral oil. Rub the lubricated pad in the direction of the grain. Mineral oil is available at any drug store. If you insist, boiled linseed oil cut with turpentine can be used or, in a jam, so can olive oil.

Rub the surface firmly but not brutally. Work only in the direction of the grain. Work a test area first and allow it to dry. If the blushing is gone, proceed to the rest of the piece. If the process is incomplete, switch to 00 steel wool which is slightly more abrasive. If steel wool fails, which it is not likely to do, you can attempt an old-time remedy of pumice.

To use pumice, prepare a rubbing block of hardwood that is at least 5 inches or 6 inches long. The wood block should have a piece of rubbing felt glued to the bottom, but it will suffice to wrap the block with a clean, soft cloth (preferably cotton). Once a rubbing block has been prepared, take 3/0 pumice and mix it with oil until a paste is formed. Work the pumice paste with the rubbing block, and only in the direction of the grain. When the rubdown is complete, wash the piece with water—but don't saturate. With a shellac finish, don't tarry because the water can damage the finish.

Under no circumstances should pumice be used without a rubbing block. When applied without the leveling pressure of a block, pumice can easily destroy parts of a finish. Even when using a rubbing block, the fast-action cutting power of pumice can eat through a finish. For this reason, I do not recommend it. Pumice is traditional; steel wool is easy, safe, and effective.

With either steel wool or pumice, the process is the same. What you are doing is using a fine abrasive to remove the top moisture-damaged surface of the finish. The use of oil reduces friction and prevents scratching the surface, this leaves a smoother, nicer finish than when you started. Furniture finishes are usually built up of several coats of finish. You don't have to worry about rubbing through, but it is a wise practice to recoat the piece with an appropriate finish. If you are satisfied with your initial rubdown, you might choose to clean the oil off, allow it to dry, and then wax.

Rings and Ink Stains

White and black rings are found on furniture as a result of water damage. A flower pot or a vase left on a table will eventually cause a black ring. Moisture will have worked entirely through the finish and stained the wood underneath. A water glass or wine bottle with a wet base left on a shellac or lacquer finish overnight will cause a white ring. Such water damage will not completely penetrate the finish. Varnish finishes have the greatest immunity against moisture. Nevertheless, they will also suffer water damage over a period of time.

White rings can be treated in the same manner as blushing. Take a 000-steel-wool pad lubricated with oil and rub lightly in the direction of the grain. If the damage forces the removal of most of the finish in that area, it will be necessary to build up a new finish in that area. See the section on worn spots later in this chapter.

Black rings and ink stains fall into the same category (and that is trouble). To remedy this problem, the stain must be bleached out. This requires removal of the finish. It might be possible to remove just the finish in the damaged area and bleach out the stain, but it is not likely. When you encounter this problem, you should assume that you have to remove the entire finish before dealing with the stain. Stains such as these are found mostly on table tops, desks, and dresser tops. There is no reason to remove the finish from the entire piece—just the top. If the black ring or ink stain is not too unsightly, give thought to living with it.

With an ink stain, once the finish has been removed, try removing the stain with a pumice and water paste. If the stain is not too deep, this will remove it. However, be careful not to create a hollow with the rubbing process. If the pumice has not removed the stain, then the procedure is the same as for a black ring. Take household ammonia and swab the top of the piece. Allow to dry and then repeat. Remember to open a window because ammonia can be terrible stuff. If you appear to be making progress with the ammonia, continue applications until the stain is removed. The ammonia functions as a bleaching agent which should remove the stain.

If ammonia has not removed the stain, oxalic acid will most likely do the job. Don't be alarmed; this is not the type of acid that is going to burn your clothes off. But it is poisonous so keep it away from children, dogs, and thirsty people. Oxalic acid can be purchased, in crystal form, from a hardware store or paint store. Mix a solution of 1 ounce of crystals with a pint of hot water. This is known as a saturate solution. The water should be stove hot and not just tap hot. Nevertheless, it should not be boiled. A stronger solution can be made with 2 ounces of crystals (for more stubborn stains). Brush on the solution. Allow it to dry and repeat if necessary. Oxalic acid is a bleaching agent. Cover the entire surface with the solution and not just the stain so that the overall surface will be bleached evenly. If the top surface has been previously stained, some of it will be removed or bleached out.

Once the oxalic acid has dried, there will be a residue that requires removal and neutralizing. If you fail to do this, the surface will not take a stain or finish properly. Some refinishers just give the top a good washing with fresh water, but this is not the surest approach. Mix a solution of ammonia and water, approximately 1 part ammonia to 4 parts of water, and wash the top carefully.

If ammonia is not available use white vinegar. It is somewhat a universal neutralizing agent. Do not dilute the vinegar. Between the oxalic solution and ammonia rinse, the wood fiber will be deeply saturated. Allow it to dry for a day or two prior to finishing. The various wetting processes might have raised the wood fiber such that it feels rough to the touch when you run your hand across the surface. In this case, rub the top briskly with 000 steel wool, or lightly sand it with 240-grit finishing paper.

Nine out of 10 times the oxalic acid will remove the stain in its entirety. There is always a slight chance that it will not. If some of the stain remains, scrape it with a cabinet scraper or a sharp knife, but only after the surface has dried. If all else fails, you can sand the top. Generally, it is better to live with the slight stain. With a medium to dark brown finish, the stain probably will not show.

There is a serious temptation to just sand down the top to get the job done. When you do, the end result is new wood and somehow that defeats the purpose of an antique. In any event, a new finish will be required when the top is dry. Select an appropriate finish listed in the chapters on finishing.

Scratches

Scratches constitute one of the largest problems on furniture with an old or original finish. With a little care, most novices should be able to reach a satisfactory compromise in the removal of scratches. This can also be an art. People who are experts at scratch removal and touchup can earn a living just doing that.

For scratches that are not deep, the abrasion method, (steel wool and oil) should suffice to remove the scratch. There are commercially made scratch removers sold at supermarkets and chain stores that are adequate for the purpose. The scratch-removal compounds are no more than a fine abrasive mixed with a lubricant. If you are hard pressed, auto compound will do the same job.

Deep scratches will not buff out; another treatment is required. For a shellac finish, make a wad of clean cotton, dip it in alcohol, and lightly rub the scratch. What you are doing is dissolving the original finish and spreading it into the scratch. Use a deft touch or you will make a mess of it and have to redo an entire top.

Old-timers used spirit of camphor to remove scratches from a shellac finish. The camphor had no value, but the spirit was alcohol and it dissolved the old finish. The process is the same for a lacquer finish except lacquer thinner is used instead of alcohol.

With a varnish finish, it is necessary to apply fresh varnish to the scratch, but not the entire surface. Use varnish directly from the can and apply it to the scratch with a fine pointed brush or a toothpick. Toothpicks work well and they are disposable. Try to keep the varnish in the scratch and not on the surface around it. More than one coat of varnish might be required to fill the scratch and bring it to the level of the old finish. When the varnish has dried for two to three days, rub out the scratch area with steel wool. The grade of steel wool used depends upon the degree of gloss of the existing finish. For a high gloss finish, use 000 or 0000 steel wool. For a satin finish use 00 steel wool.

The methods described above presume that the scratch is in the finish, but not through the finish into the wood. If the scratch is in the wood, a coloring agent will be necessary to blend it with the rest of the surface. There are polishes on the market described as polish and scratch covers. These are generally petroleum-based products with stains added. The scratch covers do work, but might inhibit some other things that you want to do. I don't recommend them.

There are a variety of ways to color and cover stains. One of the simplest methods is to take clear varnish and mix it with an appropriate color. Colors ground in oil, tinting colors (for oil paints) and Japan colors will all work satisfactorily. Do not mix an entire can of varnish; a teaspoon will do. When the color solution is ready,

Table 4-1. Basic Touch-up Colors.

Artist, Japan, and Universal Colors			
Sienna: yellow to brownish yellow Burnt Sienna: red to reddish brown Burnt Umber: brown Raw Umber: greenish brown			
Pine/Maple	**Cherry**	**Walnut**	**Mahogany**
Sienna Burnt Umber	Burnt Sienna Burnt Umber Sienna	Burnt Umber	Burnt Umber Burnt Sienna

cover the scratch with it using a fine brush or a toothpick. When the varnish has dried, rub it out with steel wool.

If you are intimidated by the thought of mixing your own coloring solution, buy a varnish stain and use it. The same process can be applied to a shellac finish by mixing shellac with alcohol soluble analine dyes and applying it to the damaged area. This is somewhat more difficult than the varnish approach.

For a simpler approach to the problem, obtain a large box of crayons and select one that is suitably matched to the color of the finish and rub it into the scratch. The repair can remain as is or it can be fixed with a coat of shellac. Mix one part shellac with two parts alcohol. Brush the shellac mixture over the scratch and allow it to dry for two to three hours. Then rub out lightly with 0000 steel wool. Only shellac will coat over wax.

For a still simpler method, mix a tablespoon of boiled linseed oil with a tablespoon of turpentine. Then add coloring. Linseed oil can be blended with universal colors, colors ground in oil, artist oil paints, or any penetrating oil stain. Rub this mixture into the scratch with a rag, rub off the excess, and allow to dry. The coloring material will take care of the scratch, while the linseed oil will dry and form a modest film over it.

If the scratch refuses to take a stain adequately, a solution is to use paint straight from the tube. Artist oil colors or one of the fast-drying acrylics will suit the purpose. With your finger, rub the paint into the scratch and allow to dry. Remember to remove any excess in the area around the scratch before it dries. Once dry, coat the paint with a mixture of 1 part shellac to 2 parts alcohol. Allow to dry and then rub down.

Using artist colors can be an easy or difficult proposition. It depends upon what kind of an eye you have for color. There are four basic colors with which you can match almost any finish. Table 4-1 lists the basic colors as well as combinations that can be used to match finishes. This is a trial and error process. You will have to play with proportions until you get the color you want. Use a piece of cardboard as a pallet for mixing. When the color seems basically wrong, don't add more color to try and save it—just start over. If you want to take an easy route, use premixed, furniture touch-up paints sold in some hardware shops. In my experience, these paints have been inadequate.

Dents, Gouges, and Cigarette Burns

A dent is the result of a sharp blow that compresses the wood fiber. Dents are almost the sole domain of softwoods such as pine because hardwoods are resiliant and they spring back. To remedy the problem, you must scrape away the finish and get down to the bare wood in the area of the dent. Once this is accomplished, wet a section of towel and place it over the dent. Take a household iron and apply it to the wet towel. This will force steam into the damaged area. When the heat from the iron dries out the towel, remoisten the towel and repeat the process until the dent works out. The steam expands the compressed fibers and they return to the normal shape. The first time that you do this, you will feel like a magician pulling a rabbit out of a hat! After the dent is repaired, it will be necessary to build up a new finish in the damaged area.

If wood fibers have been damaged and not just compressed, they cannot be repaired in the manner just outlined. The damage must be treated in the same way as a gouge or cigarette burn. The repair of a deep gouge or a cigarette burn requires the removal of a small area of the finish. It is best to scrape away the finish with a sharp knife. The hole is filled, plugged or patched, and then built up with a finish. The tendency here is to strip the entire top. This is not usually necessary. If this is the only way that you will ever get up the nerve to do the job, then do it.

The simplest and least adequate way to fill a gouge is to use a commercially available plastic wood. Plastic wood is fine for nail holes, cracks, and small blemishes, but it looks unsightly in large areas. If you decide to use plastic wood, build it up in layers and not in globs. Plastic wood is a cellulose nitrate product. It is no more than lacquer mixed with wood dust.

The professional standard for the repair of gouges and holes is stick shellac. Sticks of solid shellac come in a multitude of colors and they can be intermixed to match any furniture color and condition. When done properly, shellac-stick repairs are unobtrusive or not seen at all. If this sounds like a magic product, it is, but there is one serious drawback: it requires a great deal of skill. I don't recommend that you attempt a shellac stick repair on any piece of furniture that you care about. If you are a very talented amateur who likes a challenge, then all well and good. Practice on a junk piece first.

If you want to attempt such a project, it will require shellac sticks for patching, an alcohol lamp to melt the sticks, and a steel spatula—known as a burn-in knife—to work the shellac into the hole. You cannot use a candle to melt the shellac because the carbon from the candle will foul the shellac. You can, however, us a low flame on a propane torch.

Heat the spatula over the alcohol lamp until there is a warm glow. Then touch the spatula to the shellac stick to pick up some of the shellac on the flat of the blade. Force the shellac into the hole with the knife and repeat until the hole is filled. You will have to reheat the knife several times in the process. When the hole is full, smooth the patch with the hot knife and feather out toward the edge. When the patch is dry, which will be almost immediately, sand it with a fine emory paper wrapped around a wood block and lubricated with light mineral oil. When this work is complete, a new surface will have to be built up in the area of the patch.

All in all, shellac stick patching sounds easy, but it is not. Because they are pure shellac, shellac sticks dry shiny and favor high-gloss finishes that are not always appropriate for country furniture.

Wax filling is an alternative to shellac-stick patching. This is easily mastered by the novice and yields good results. A large box of crayons from a five-and-dime store should provide all the materials you will need. Select appropriate colors and shave some pieces into a teaspoon and melt over an alcohol lamp. You can mix colors in the spoon. When you think you have achieved the desired color, let it cool and harden because the dry color will be somewhat different from the molten color.

When the proper patch color has been achieved, use a spatula to force it into the hole or pour the molten wax directly from the spoon. When the hole is filled and the wax is dry, scrape the patch level to the surface with a knife. If the patch does not seem satisfactory, scrape it out with a knife and start over. Special furniture crayons with matched colors such as walnut are available at some hardware stores. Furniture crayons are harder than children's crayons, and they can be used with better results.

When the patch is ready, coat it with a mixture of 1 part shellac to 3 parts alcohol. Do not rub down the patch after the shellac has dried. Apply a coat of varnish to the patch area or to the entire surface. A wax patch is quite naturally soft as is the shellac finish that is applied over it. Should the wax patch be rubbed down, it will soften and damage. Hence the need for the varnish top coat to provide greater resiliance. Padding lacquer can be used over the shellac as well. After this has been accomplished, the piece can be rubbed down and waxed. Remember that only shellac will cover wax and that this must be the first step.

Cigarette burns are similar to gouges, but they do not tend to be very deep. If the cigarette burn is shallow, scrape it with a knife to remove the charred material. Then smudge on a paint that approximates the color of the wood and coat with a shellac mixture. A repair affected in this manner will be noticeable, but only to someone who is looking for it. If the burn goes deep, it should be treated with shellac-stick patching or wax filling.

Another method of treating large holes is to patch them with a wooden inlay. Newcomers are frightened by the awesome thought of cutting and fitting an inlay, but it is simpler to master than a shellac-stick patch. Give the method a try when the situation requires. Even if you botch it, you can still take it out and have it done.

WORN SPOTS AND BUILDING A FINISH

A fairly common problem with original or old clear finishes is areas where the finish has been totally worn away and a bare or raw spot remains. To remedy the problem, you must color the worn area and build a new finish to match the old finish.

Coloring the worn area, or "coloring up" as it is sometimes known, can be accomplished in two ways. The color material or stain can be applied in one operation and the finish material can be applied in a second operation. Alternatively, the coloring agent can be mixed with the finish material and applied at the same time.

The worn area can be colored with any commercially available stain, but one of the pure penetrating oil stains will yield better results. Different stains from the same manufacturer can be used to obtain the desired shade. You could also mix your own stain by adding universal colors or Japan colors to turpentine. Mixing your own stain allows for greater flexibility. You can control the depth of the stain and you can add small amounts of color for subtle changes.

The stain can be brushed on or wiped on with a rag. When it is brushed on, the stained area will be darker than if rubbed on. If the patched area is too light after staining, you can continue to add color until you reach the preferred depth. This is the best approach.

If the stained area is too dark, you have a problem because it is difficult to lighten up. If the stained area is too dark, rub it briskly with steel wool and turpentine, and then wipe clean. Some of the color should be removed in this manner.

When the stained area is dry, coat it with a mixture of 1 part shellac to 3 parts alcohol. You could also make a pad of clean, folded cotton moistened ever so slightly with boiled linseed oil. Take this pad and dip it in a mixture of 1 part shellac to 1 part alcohol and apply to the damaged area in a circular motion. Work quickly and do not overwork the area. This latter method avoids brush marks and in general blends the area in a better manner.

Padding lacquer is a marvelous product that can be used with simplicity to build up worn areas or otherwise patch a damaged surface. Padding lacquers are available from stores that sell professional finishing supplies.

Patching with shellac will work best with a shellac finish, but it will work under most circumstances on a small area of a varnish finish or a lacquer finish. You will already know what kind of a finish you have because you will have tested it.

When the coated area has dried, you can rub it down with steel wool to blend with the rest of the finish or you could give the entire surface a fresh coat of varnish. A new coat of varnish affects the originality of the finish, but—if the piece is going to get hard use—it might still be a good idea. Be sure the surface is clean of wax and dirt buildup before recoating.

Another way to approach this problem is to mix colors with varnish or to use a premixed varnish stain. This method is simple to use, but it is difficult to control the color or to remedy mistakes. If you choose this method, test your colors on a scrap piece. Brush the varnish stain on the damaged area and feather it out to the edges. Allow the varnish to dry for 48 to 72 hours. Then rub it down.

An old-time remedy for patching a finish is to mix equal amounts of boiled linseed oil and turpentine with a coloring agent such as universal colors or colors ground in oil. Linseed oil will also mix with most pure penetrating oil stains. Once the color is obtained, swab the mixture on and allow it to soak in. Then wipe it dry. Several applications can be made. The advantage of this approach is that it can be wiped off if the work is not going properly. When the finish dries, the linseed oil will harden into a layer over the patch with modest gloss. The entire process is done in one step and is relatively foolproof. The buildup, however, might take months of application.

A more modern approach to the linseed-oil patch method is to use one of the Danish oils, such as Watco, mixed with universal colors to the preferred shade. The method is the same as with the linseed oil only the Watco will dry faster and harder and with a better sheen. Minwax Antique Oil can be used as well as the Watco.

Regardless of the method chosen, the patching and buildup will be less noticeable if the entire surface is given a fresh coat of the original finish or varnish that will cover all finishes. The decision is yours and it should be based simply on what you see and feel. The final waxing that goes on after everything else also makes quite a difference.

ALLIGATORED FINISHES AND AMALGAMATION

Checked, alligatored, crazed, and *crawling* are all terms to describe a deteriorated finish that is marked by a cross-hatched pattern of grooves. If you want to be innovative, call it a crocodile effect; I haven't heard it called that recently. Whatever you choose to term it, the end product is a finish that has been subjected to direct sunlight or heat with a subsequent drying of the oils necessary for it to remain pliable. In the case of severe climatic changes, the deterioration might be such that the finish will simply crumble off. With a checkered finish, there are some remedies that can be attempted. With a crumbling finish, your best decision is to remove it.

Clear finishes such as shellac and lacquer initially use a vehicle in which the resins are mixed. Therefore, the secret is to use the proper solvent in which the finish will dissolve. For shellac and lacquer, this is no problem. Varnish is quite another story because it will not redissolve in turpentine (its original vehicle). The principle at hand is simple. You want to use a solvent to dissolve the damaged finish so that it runs into itself—thus evening out damaged areas. This process is called *amalgamation*. This is fairly straightforward work, but it does take a certain knack that can be developed with practice. Don't let the project scare you. The alternative is to strip the finish off. You can still do that if the amalgamation fails. In short, you have everything to gain and nothing to loose.

Amalgamation tends to work best with a shellac finish. That is just as well because it will account for the majority of finishes that you are likely to encounter. To start off, clean the piece carefully but gently. You must move all vestiges of wax and dirt, but you don't want to remove particles of the remaining finish. Next, pour shellac solvent (alcohol) into a container and select an inconspicuous place to begin your work so that you can get the hang of it. Some workers prefer to use a cotton pad for this work while others choose to use a brush. I recommend that you use a brush. You are less likely to get in trouble this way.

Wet your brush with alcohol and apply it to the finish with wreckless abandon. You can use diagonals, straights, or cross-hatched brush patterns—whatever suits your fancy. Once the alcohol is applied, you must even the finish with straight, overlapping strokes in the direction of the grain before it begins to harden or become tacky. Old shellac will loosen up quickly and harden quickly so you must work rapidly. If the finish seems resistant to the alcohol, but you are positive that it is shellac, then add lacquer thinner to your alcohol at the ratio of 1 part thinner to 4 parts alcohol. If need be, you can go with a ratio of 1 part lacquer thinner to 3 parts alcohol. In any event, the addition of the lacquer thinner should suffice to work out the problem.

When the piece has dried, there might be some uneven areas where the finish is more or less dense. You could try to work some of this unevenness out with 0000 steel wool, but you are better advised to apply a fresh coat of shellac. If at all possible, don't rub down the amalgamated finish prior to applying a new finish. An amalgamated finish is fragile and has a tendency to powder off on your steel wool. After the application of a fresh coat of shellac, you can decide if the results are satisfactory. If not, it is a simple task to remove the finish.

The procedure for the amalgamation of a lacquer finish is the same as for a shellac finish except that lacquer thinner replaces alcohol as the solvent. The thinner is brushed or padded on in the manner that suits you. Then it is evened with long, straight, overlapping strokes in the direction of the grain. Lacquer will probably take longer to soften than shellac, but it will also dry faster.

Lacquer is primarily a sprayed-on finish and not a brushed-on finish. Consequently, problems are encountered with brush marks. This problem is evident with an amalgamated finish so you will have to develop a light touch. In general, amalgamating a lacquer finish is more difficult than a shellac finish, but by no means impossible.

A newly amalgamated lacquer finish is less fragile than a shellac finish. Therefore, it can be rubbed down with steel wool to even it out after drying. It is less imperative to recoat a lacquer finish as compared with a shellac finish, but it is still the preferred course of action.

A varnish finish is an entirely different proposition from shellac or lacquer. Varnish will not dissolve in the original vehicle (turpentine). Another product must be used. A product known as amalgamater or varnish amalgamater should be used for this project. The method of application would be the same as for a shellac or lacquer finish, but application with a pad will probably yield better results than a brush.

You can attempt to amalgamate a varnish finish. As the saying goes, "Nothing ventured, nothing gained." On the other hand, I don't think it will work. When I encounter a crazed-varnish finish, I remove it and save the bother of a fruitless amalgamation step. Nevertheless, others tell me that it does work.

RECOATING AND FEEDING SOLUTIONS

More often than not, the revival of an old, clear finish will not involve the elaborate work outlined in this chapter. You bring a piece home, clean it with paint thinner, touch up the scratches with a little stain or wax crayon, and then wax with a good paste wax. Voila! You have a rags-to-riches story. A piece of furniture within minutes goes from looking like last Friday's fish to a desirable piece of furniture with a mellow luster.

If you want a little bit more out of a finish, you can always apply a fresh coat of the original finish. This is recommended for many of the treatments previously outlined. If you decide to give a piece a fresh finish, it is a simple task rarely requiring more than a few hours. Bear in mind that you should recoat with the finish originally used.

Varnish will go over shellac or lacquer, but not as well as it will over varnish. Lacquer might or might not take over varnish or shellac. Shellac should only be used over shellac. Don't bother to memorize this; you will only get confused. Just replicate the original finish and you will not have problems or anything to remember. It is important, however, to make sure that the surface is free from any residue of wax or dirt. Otherwise, the new finish will be botched up. Shellac tends to be kind with old wax residues, but why take a chance?

There are other approaches to sprucing up a finish and they are even simpler than applying a new finish. There are numerous products sold for this purpose. Examples are Elmer's Instant, Magic, Miracle Furniture Restorer, or Bertram's Zip, Dip and Shine. They are guaranteed to refinish furniture and remove warts. Some of the less pretentious products are called *feeding solutions*.

The basic principle behind miracle, do-it-all solutions and feeding solutions is one of protection—mostly from moisture. The original purpose of a finish is to inhibit the gain or loss of moisture. A feeding solution puts a finish over a finish. This lubricates the original finish and saves it from drying out. It also forms a thin, flexible film that further inhibits the loss or gain of moisture. A byproduct of this process is some additional sheen which dresses up a piece very nicely. A principal ingredient of these solutions is oil. There is no need to purchase what you already have at home.

To prepare your own miracle feeding solution, mix boiled linseed oil with an equal amount of turpentine. Apply this mixture with a pad of fine steel wool or with the palm of your hand. The friction from your hand can produce a better result. Swab the mixture on generously and work it into every crevice. After the mixture has soaked in, wipe it vigorously with old rags or paper towels to remove as much of the oil as possible.

Remember to dispose of the rags immediately. They will be highly inflammable and subject to spontaneous combustion. If you need to store them overnight, place them where they cannot do any harm.

Allow the piece to dry, usually three to five days, and then wax. If the piece in question has a lot of minor scratches that bother you, add some oil-based stain to color the mixture. When you rub off the excess oil, the pigment will rub off the top surface, but should remain in the scratches.

Don't allow the simplicity of this process fool you. It is really quite good and it will go over any old finish. You could choose to use only boiled linseed oil, because that is the active ingredient, instead of a mixture of oil and turpentine. You will find that it takes an immense amount of time to dry without the turpentine.

Another approach is to coat the piece with lemon oil. When it comes to furniture polishes, lemon oil is for all intents and purposes, nothing more than scented mineral oil. Save yourself some money and purchase a pint of light mineral oil from the drugstore; it will do the job. With mineral oil use it straight from the bottle. It is an acceptable product. Nevertheless, I think boiled linseed oil and turpentine will yield better results.

OLD PAINTED FINISHES

Old painted finishes are quite a different story from clear finishes. Frequently, the best course of action with a painted surface is just to leave it alone.

Your first course of action should be to clean the piece. Even this must be approached with caution. Do not randomly thrust

146

yourself at a piece with paint thinner and steel wool, but rather try different solvents on test patches of the finish. Try a simple soap and water solution first and then proceed to thinner and turpentine. Use a wad of padded clean cotton for your test and a different wad for each solution.

After testing, decide which solution has cleaned the best, but has not taken the paint off. This should be apparent by the amount of pigment left on the cloth after each test. If the original paint finish is crumbling (flaking off to the touch), there is nothing you can do. At this point, you can take the piece to a professional who specializes in paint restoration. Generally, he will have no remedy for the problem.

After cleaning, the next step is touchup. If a piece is badly worn, scratched, nicked, etc., some professionals will *stretch* the paint. Stretching involves the use of paint stripper to dissolve the old paint (similar to amalgamation). The softened paint is rebrushed or evened with steel wool. The result of this practice can be attractive, but it is unpardonable if there is any chance whatsoever to save the original paint. If no other option is available, stretching is a better alternative to stripping.

Painted surfaces can be touched up with artist oil paints with good results. But Japan colors, that dry flat, are more suited to old paint finishes. This is the type of work where you need an eye for color. If you don't have the aptitude don't do it. Perhaps you have at least one friend or family member who paints and who could assist you with this part of the task.

Areas where paint has chipped away leaving depressions can be filled with spackle compound, and then touched up with paint. For large areas where the paint has been worn away, an opaque stain can be made from Japan colors and turpentine, and blended into the area for color and the illusion of paint. This should be painstaking and careful work because errors become permanent.

Once you have cleaned and touched up a piece, the question remains: should you do more? In the past, a museum would oil a painted piece with linseed oil and then wax it. This practice has fallen out of favor because linseed oil will darken a finish. The modern rule is to leave it alone. But museums are moisture controlled and your home is not. A painted piece might begin to deteriorate in your home. This is especially true if the climate is radically different from where the object spent its previous years. If there is any question of deterioration, I recommend that the piece be brushed with boiled linseed oil and waxed when dry. This might make you an agnostic but certainly not a heretic, and you will be able to sleep at night.

With any piece of furniture—either a clear or painted finish—that you suspect to be original and valuable, seek advice before doing anything. You are not likely to come in contact with many pieces of this nature, but it is possible. Pursue a course of "better safe than sorry." Any reputable antique dealer should be both able and willing to advise you as to whether or not you have a great treasure. A professional antique restorer should also be able to provide the assistance you need to make a decision. Make sure it is an antique furniture restorer and not just a furniture restorer.

Chapter 5
Removing an Old Finish

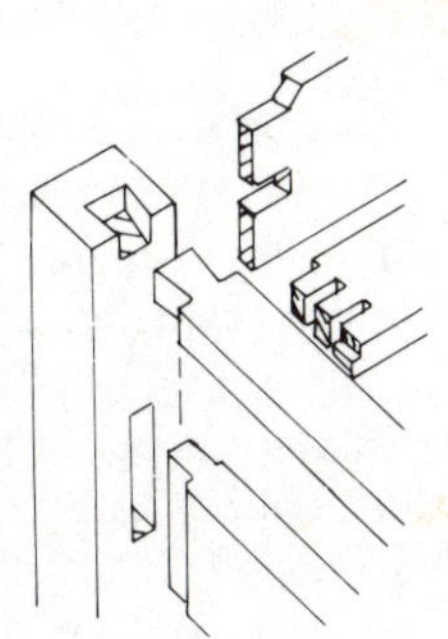

The population can be divided into two categories: those who like to strip furniture and those, like myself, who don't. Perhaps you are a kind of wild and crazy person who likes to dip your arms elbow deep in slime. Make no mistake about it; furniture stripping is a messy job at best. It is frequently frustrating and time consuming. I don't want to discourage you, but I also don't want to lie to you. The plain fact of the matter is that furniture stripping is a practical necessity. By doing your own stripping, you can save from 50 percent to 90 percent of the cost of a professional stripping job. Is is not only cheaper to do your own work, but also usually better. A professional furniture stripper cannot give an individual piece of furniture the same attention that its owner would. I have never sent a piece out to be done that has not needed some additional work when it was returned.

Furniture stripping might not be fun, but it is also difficult. The professional stripper might have a few tricks up his sleeve to simplify the work, but basically the amateur is as good as the professional right out of the starting gate. As with any other work, those who do meticulous and careful work will achieve much better results than those who tend to be shoddy.

Prior to entering the fantasy world of melting paints, remember—you don't have to do this. If you are not inclined to do this type of thing or if you have health problems that prohibit your involvement, you need not give up the hobby or endeavor. It is perfectly acceptable to send a piece out to be done. When the piece returns from the stripper, you can still do the repair work, apply the finish of your choice, and save money.

CHEMICAL METHODS

Furniture stripping can be divided into two methods: chemical and mechanical. Chemical methods of stripping dominate the field because they are the easiest and in many cases the most satisfactory.

Chemical stripping will require the assembling of a basic tool kit as illustrated in Fig. 5-1. Most of the articles can be found in your home or apartment, but those that cannot are inexpensive and locally available. You will need a small bowl or tin can to pour the stripper into. Because the stripper can corrode some metals, a glass container is better. A paint or other brush is necessary for applying the stripper. A 2-inch brush is ideal, but any size can be used. You can use an old brush that was used for paint or varnish, but once it is used for stripper it cannot be used for anything else. If a water-soluble stripper is used, a washbasin or bucket will be needed for the water rinse.

For your personal safety, you should have a pair of good rubber gloves. When stripper gets on your hands, it burns hotter than St. Elmo's fire. As you become acclamated to the product, it will burn less. Most manufacturers label their product as a skin irritant. Household rubber gloves are acceptable, but they will burn through after a few uses. You are better advised to pick up a pair of heavy-duty, neoprene gloves that are resistant to caustics. These gloves are worth the few extra dollars that you will pay. I have not tried the new type of disposable plastic gloves.

In addition to gloves, pick up a pair of glasses or goggles to protect your eyes from splatter. Many people cannot stand wearing goggles; a pair of spectacles with plain glass is usually preferred. If you normally wear glasses and they have the new plastic lenses, be careful. Some paint strippers will damage plastic.

The standard grab for stripping is an array of old work clothes. A plain wrap-around apron is also a good idea. Wear old shoes. When you strip furniture, you cannot help but walk in, through and over old paint residue. It will collect on your shoes. This not only ruins good shoes, but it can also make you awfully unpopular if you walk across the living room rug.

A paint scraper and a putty knife are necessary to remove the first coats of paint. The final coat of paint will be removed with steel wool. When removing paint, there is a tendency to gouge the wood with a paint scraper. The chances of this are minimized when a smaller putty knife is used. An old pocketknife or kitchen knife will add utility to your basic tool kit and will prove useful for corners and

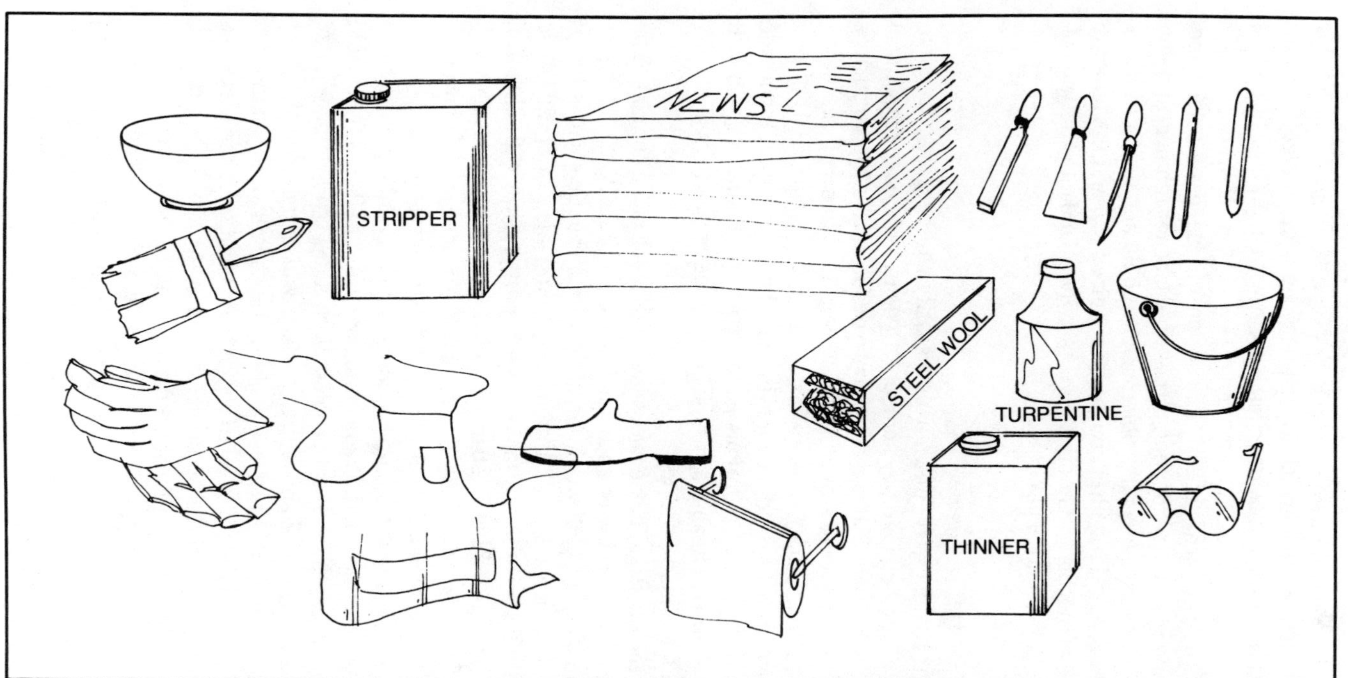

Fig. 5-1. A basic stripping tool kit consists of: a bowl, a brush, a pail, rubber gloves, an apron, goggles (eye glasses), old shoes, a putty knife, a paint scraper, a utility knife, a pointed dowel, a tongue depressor, turpentine (thinner), steel wool, newspapers, and paper towels.

difficult spots. Old dowels, tongue depressors, Popsicle sticks, or wood scraps are useful as special-purpose tools for getting into carvings or intricate places. Shape them with a knife or file to the shapes of difficult areas as moldings.

On the chemical side of things, you will need a stripper and other solvents such as alcohol, turpentine, lacquer thinner, or paint thinner. For some special problems, household ammonia or bleach (never to be used together) might be required. To add the icing to this cake of mechanical hodgepodge, provide abundant quantities of old newspaper and paper towels.

DIP STRIPPING

The easiest way, but not necessarily the best way, to have furniture stripped is to pay someone to do it. The most economical way to do this is to find one of the dip-type furniture stripping places that have proliferated over the last decade. These places go by various names such as Strip-Fast, Dip-Easy, Strip and Dip, etc. Most places will have dip somewhere in the description. If not, see if the advertisement mentions hand stripping. A hand stripper will always advertise his handwork. The absence of this phrase usually indicates a dipping process.

In the old days, these shops had a cold tank and a hot tank. The cold tank was filled with an alcohol mixture for shellac and lacquer finishes. The hot tank would be filled with a caustic such as lye. If the dipping wasn't well timed, you could kiss your furniture farewell. Today, the hot tanks have been replaced with chemical wash solutions similar to strippers sold for public use. But they will be in a less dilute form. With most of these processes, the furniture receives a water bath or it is hosed down after stripping.

Dip stripping is fast and economical, but it is not good as far as antiques are concerned. If someone has a set of 10- or 20-year-old kitchen chairs, there is no problem with a dip-type strip. With an antique, any trace of an original surface will be destroyed.

The harm in this process is not in the chemical, but in the stiff brushes (usually wire) used to remove the paint once the piece has soaked. The skill of the operator, as well as the type of brush used, will determine how badly abused a piece is, but you can count on a good surface being destroyed. The water bath or hosing does not help matters. The intense water pressure the piece is subjected to causes the wood grain to raise. In turn that necessitates sanding. Not only is sanding more work, but it means additional surface is lost. The water rinse also swells the wood joints and breaks the glue lines. When you take the piece home from the stripper, it will feel tight and secure. In a few days when it dries out, it will frequently loosen up. Dip-type stripping is a worthwhile process, but it just is not meant for antiques.

If you can't or don't want to do your own furniture stripping, find someone who does hand stripping. Hand strippers usually charge by the hour, but they will stick to an original estimate. In general, the cost of hand stripping will run about double the cost of a commercial dipping process. With small items such as chairs or drop-leaf tables, the discrepancy is not great. With large items such as cupboards it can be brutal. If the piece you are working on has any value at all, it is well worth spending the additional money.

COLD STRIPPING, SHELLAC, AND LACQUER

When confronted with a shellac or lacquer finish you need not bother with costly paint strippers. Shellac and lacquer can effectively be removed with their original solvents—alcohol and thinner.

To strip a shellac finish, put up a mixture of 3 parts shellac solvent to 1 part lacquer thinner. Swab this mixture with a brush, cloth, or steel wool. Only work a small area at a time or the alcohol will evaporate and the shellac will dry before you get to it. Once you have applied the mixture, take a 00-steel-wool pad, unravel part of it, and crumple it into a ball. To use a whole steel-wool pad would be costly and inefficient.

Dip the steel wool in the solution and apply it to the old finish. As the softened shellac is removed, the steel wool will gum up. Turn the pad as you work to expose fresh surfaces. When the pad is totally clogged, dispose of it and rip off a new section. Once the finish has been removed, dip a clean pad in fresh alcohol and give the surface a final going-over with long, overlapping strokes using the steel-wool pad. You should always work the pad in the direction of the grain. If the surface remains glossy after it is dry, you will know that the stripping process has been incomplete and that you will need to continue.

Alcohol stripping of an old shellac finish is fast and easy. The final surface might require an additional rubdown with 000 steel wool prior to finishing, but basically you will have an acceptable surface.

If you are working indoors, make sure there is adequate ventilation. Alcohol is combustible. If you have a buildup of fumes in an enclosed area, it might ignite. Alcohol vapors have been known to get a few unsuspecting souls a little tipsy. The vapors are dangerous for people with certain conditions such as bleeding ulcers. I don't use rubber gloves when working with alcohol. It only burns if there are cuts and abrasions on your hands. It will dry out your skin. To be on the safe side use gloves.

The process for the removal of lacquer is the same as for shellac except that you substitute lacquer thinner. Wet down the surface with lacquer thinner and allow it to soak in. Lacquer has a tendency to crawl. This permits easy removal with a paint scraper. You will be able to remove the bulk of the material. Do not try to get too close to the surface; you might gouge or nick it. Following the scraper, use the 00-steel-wool pad dipped in thinner for the final removal and cleanup. For the final cleanup, use a fresh pad with uncontaminated thinner and rub with continuous, long strokes— with the grain.

Lacquer thinner poses the same vapor threats as alcohol. Make sure if you are working indoors to provide adequate ventilation to protect your health and to prevent fire.

REMOVING PAINT AND VARNISH

Removing shellac and lacquer involves relatively simple work (even pleasant as stripping goes). Removing varnish will require a paint stripper usually labeled "Varnish and Paint Remover," but, similar to shellac and lacquer, new or old varnish finish will not be difficult to remove. Paint is an entirely different story. It can be as simple as eating a piece of pie or as difficult as splitting a diamond with a cold chisel. The type of paint and the condition of the surface painted determine how difficult the job of removing will be.

If the base coat was a refractory type, meaning "difficult," you are going to have a problem. This is another way of saying that there is a milk paint underneath. Likewise, if for some reason the piece has been stripped and repainted with a modern latex base paint, there will be hell to pay. If you are a lucky type of person, the kind who finds $10 bills instead of pennies on the sidewalk, then the surface will have been sealed prior to painting. In such a case it will be a breeze to remove. Basically, this can be a hard or easy task, but there is no way to know until you do it.

Paint stripping is best done on a warm spring day or cool summer day in the privacy of your own yard with the birds chattering and curious squirrels watching. Don't think these things are not

154

important. The nicer the environment the easier the task. As you move from yard to basement and basement to junk room, the task becomes less pleasant. Woe to the heroic apartment dweller who has to use the kitchen on Saturday mornings.

If you are working in the yard, try to work on a patio or in the driveway so that grass will not be damaged by the chemicals. When you work indoors, where most stripping is done (despite my good advice), a number of precautions should be taken.

The first and most important consideration is ventilation. The active ingredient in many strippers is methylene chloride. When you breathe in methylene chloride, it gets into the bloodstream and is metabolized as carbon monoxide. The high level of carbon monoxide can lead to insufficiency for various muscle systems. This is especially true for the most important muscle—the heart.

This is not the best relationship even for the healthiest person. For a person with a heart condition it can be fatal. IF YOU HAVE A HEART CONDITION OR SUSPICION OF A HEART CONDITION, DO NOT USE THIS PRODUCT. It would be wise to omit the stripping step in its entirety, but if you choose another product, please check the precautions on the label. A warning will always be there in the event of a potential problem. There is also wisdom in consulting your personal physician about the various work processes and chemicals involved. Doctors are not always aware of occupational health hazards. A mention of the chemicals involved might jog their memory.

Adequate ventilation must be provided. Adequate in this case means at least two windows in the room opened so that there can be cross-ventilation. If only one window is available, pick up a window fan to use in the exhaust mode.

You will have to select a paint stripper from the vast array of products on the market. Strippers can be broken down into the categories of liquid, semipaste, and paste, combustible, and noncombustible. All the products work well, but some have distinct advantages.

Semipaste strippers and paste strippers will cling to vertical surfaces, turnings, and carvings. Liquid strippers will be problematic in these areas. As an additional benefit, paste strippers will not evaporate as quickly as liquid strippers. Liquid strippers tend to be favored by professionals, but this is probably more a matter of cost than practicality because liquid strippers are less expensive.

When it comes to deciding upon a combustible versus a noncombustible stripper, I favor the non-combustible product 100 percent. Combustible products do not offer any benefit over the non-combustible ones and they are quite simply not as safe. Regardless of which product you select, don't smoke. If you are not worried about setting the place on fire, you should be worried about what you are breathing.

Some of the paste non-combustible strippers are water soluble. They can be given a final water rinse that saves money and produces good results. There is always a risk of raising the grain when you use water, but by and large, I have not had any serious problems with this. In the case of a veneered surface, it is best to avoid the water-rinse products. Some paste strippers contain parafin products and they require a final rinse with gasoline or lacquer thinner. Do not be overly concerned about a final rinse because it is a good practice regardless of which product you use. A final cleanup with lacquer thinner might cost an additional 50 cents or $1, but it is well worth the money if it avoids problems with the finish coat.

After all is said and done, I recommend that you start out with a non-combustible, paste, water-rinse product. You can try other strippers with subsequent projects and decide what is best for you. The type of stripper recommended will be of the methylene chloride variety mentioned earlier. Methylene chloride is a heavy chemical. When you are trying to pick from the various products, lift the cans and see which is heaviest. The heaviest can for the least money is the one you want. Whichever product you purchase, read the directions carefully and follow them in conjunction with my instructions.

With an indoor work space, lay out a large area with newspapers to catch debris, excess stripper, and rinse solutions. Make this covering at least three sheets deep. If you are an apartment dweller, pick up an inexpensive plastic dropcloth. Put the dropcloth down first, then cover it with newspapers. This will help you avoid costly accidents. I have seen one product on the market that is a large, rectangular, cardboard box with a small lip and fitted with a plastic liner similar to a small swimming pool. I have never tried this, but it seems like a good idea for those who have to work in confined apartment spaces.

With your work area properly set up, prepare the piece for stripping. If all areas are not to be stripped, mask off the appropriate areas with newspaper and masking tape. For example, you might have a ladderback chair with a good rush seat that you don't want to soil or you might be stripping a table that only needs the top refinished. You might want to mask off backboards to protect them from drippings.

Subsequent to masking, you will also want to remove anything that can be removed. With a jelly cupboard, for example, remove the drawers and then the knobs from the drawers. Remove the doors from the cuboard and do them separately. If the screws refuse to come loose, then leave the door alone and strip it as part of the cupboard (but mask the hinges). Use your common sense to make the piece as manageable as possible and your task as simple as possible.

Put on gloves, safety glasses, a work apron, and old shoes. Pour some stripper in a glass bowl or an old can, and ready your brush. Don't be surprised if, when you strip, the paint comes off the handle of your brush. After all, it is paint stripper. Dip your brush in the stripper and brush on as shown in Fig. 5-2. Brush the fluid on smoothly and in one direction only.

This is not a paint job. Don't crisscross or work the solution. Just get it on thickly and smoothly. The directions on the can will often indicate that you should pour directly from the can and flow the stripper on. This *might* work better, but it is an efficient way to use a very costly product.

You should be working only one surface at a time and that should be horizontal. Overambition can be your ruin if stripper is slopped on the top and all the sides. The stripper will drip on the floor while the remainder will dry and harden before you can get to it. One large surface might be too much to do at one time. Start with a small area, approximately 2 square feet. As your confidence grows, expand the area.

Let the stripper do the work. This will save your arm and your pocketbook. If the stripper is removed a few minutes after application, you will waste a lot of stripper and get frustrated in the process. Generally, the time required for the stripper to work is from 10 to 20 minutes. This is by no means a firm rule.

No two paints are alike. Some will take more time and others will take less time. It depends upon the number of coats. If the stripper starts to dry, regardless of how long it has been on, start removing it.

In a situation where there are multiple coats of paint, the first coat of paint literally soaks the stripper up and prohibits it from getting to the second coat. The first coat will have to be removed and the surface will have to be covered with fresh stripper. The

Fig. 5-2. Applying paint stripper with a brush. The stripper is brushed in one direction only.

second coat of stripper will, as a rule, work through the remaining layers of paint.

If you want to be really methodical about this thing, try a small test patch with the stripper and time how long it takes to do its job. Then you will have some basis for doing the remainder of the piece.

Once the remover has done its job, the bulk of the material must be removed. Some finishers prefer to do this with steel wool to avoid the risk of gouging the surface with a paint scraper. Frankly, this approach can take longer and cost a small fortune in steel wool. When there is only one coat of paint, and a thin one at that, I will use steel wool. For multiple layers of paint, I will start with a paint scraper and finish with steel wool. If you decide to go with steel wool, use No. 2 steel wool for the major part of the work and then switch to No. 1 or 0 steel wool for the cleanup. Generally, No. 2 steel wool is not recommended for use on furniture. It will scratch the wood. But it is acceptable when heavy layers of paint have to be removed. It is quite easy to gouge the wood with a paint scraper, but the odds of doing this are reduced when a putty knife is used. In either case, take a file and round the corners of your scraper or putty knife (Fig. 5-3), and avoid a potential problem.

Remove the paint with the scraper in any fashion that suits you—straight, sideways, on an angle, etc.—although fewer problems might be encountered with straight movements going with the grain (as shown in Fig. 5-4). As you begin to remove the paint, you have to decide what to do with it because it mounts up quickly. One solution to this problem is to cut newspaper into strips about 6 inches wide and use them to catch the paint residue. Just pile the

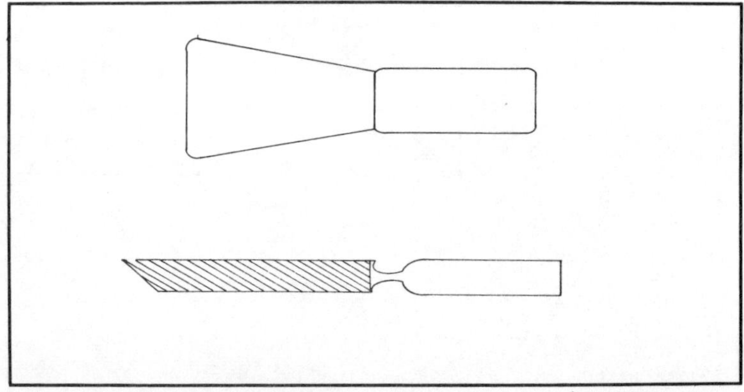

Fig. 5-3. Rounding the corners of a putty knife or paint scraper to avoid gouging.

goop on the newspaper until it becomes cumbersome, then dispose of it and take a new sheet. Make sure to set up a separate garage bag because you will want to get rid of this mess as soon as possible. A better approach to this problem is to fold some newspaper into a cone you can fill with the goop. Not everyone is adept at folding. Figure 5-5 should provide you with some idea as to how this is done.

On a very lucky day, all the paint can be removed with one coat of stripper and the paint scraper. You can count on this happening on any March night in a leap year during a full moon when it is hailing out! After the initial work with the scraper, you are likely to encounter a surface with small or large areas of residual paint. In the event of large residual areas, apply a second coat of stripper, allow it to work, and remove it with the scraper.

Fig. 5-4. Removing the bulk of the paint carefully with a putty knife.

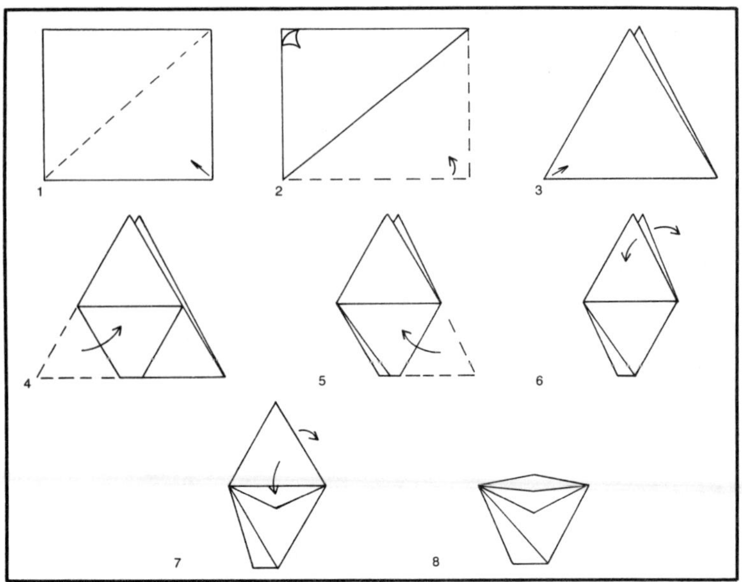

Fig. 5-5. A folding cone for paint debris. Take a square piece of newspaper and fold in the manner of the numbered sequence.

When the bulk of the paint has been removed from the residual areas, regardless of how many coats of stripper it took, take a pad of No. 1 steel wool or a pad of 0 steel wool, dip it in the stripper and rub these areas vigorously until the paint is completely removed (as shown in Fig. 5-6). Small areas that are totally resistant to the stripper might be encountered. To remove these areas, take a knife and—holding the cutting edge at a right angle to the surface—use it as a scraper to gently remove the paint. Do not use the cutting edge of the knife or you could damage the wood surface.

With all the paint removed from the surface, dip the steel-wool pad in the stripper and give the piece a final once-over—working with the grain. If the stripper used accepts a water rinse, perform this last step with water and make sure all paint residue is gone. Rinse the piece the way you would your car, but afterward dry it off with old rags or paper towels before the wood soaks up the water. Some strippers will require a final rinse with gasoline or lacquer thinner. Use lacquer thinner; it's a bit safer. Even if the product does not call for a final lacquer rinse, it is a good practice. Allow the piece to dry at least 24 hours before applying a stain or finish.

Most stripping jobs will require one or two coats of stripper and a final rub of the trouble spots with steel wool. Do not assume,

160

however, that all projects will be like this. Some stubborn paints will require three or four coats of stripper before you get to the bottom. With stubborn paints, put the stripper on thickly and let it stand for the maximum possible duration.

With any given stripping job, there will be trouble areas such as crevices, moldings, turnings, and carvings. These are not serious problems; people just think they are. These trouble areas call for a little more time, creativity, and patience. For crevices, use the point of a dull knife to remove the stripper and paint residue. You can work all day with steel wool and not get this material out, but with a knife it's a matter of seconds. With moldings, carvings, and turnings, remove paint in the normal fashion with steel wool. You obviously cannot use a scraper in these areas.

After the bulk of the paint is removed, recoat these areas with stripper and allow it to soak. In fact, you can allow it to dry. When the stripper begins to dry, apply a thick, fresh coat and allow it to work. By now these areas should be an oozing mass with little paint adhering to the wood. Take a 00-steel-wool pad or 000-steel-wool pad, which is finer than you have been using, and clean the area up. The finer steel-wool pad is less likely to damage delicate areas and the added flexibility of the finer pad helps to work in and out of tight areas.

The steel-wool pad will not be able to remove all the material. Take an old wood scrap, dowel, tongue depressor, or whatever and point it with a knife. Use it to get into tight areas. Become a creative toolmaker and adapt each stick to your special need: point, hook, concave, or convex. If need be, you can cut the entire profile of a molding into a thin piece of wood and use it to clean up the molding.

Once the piece dries, you might see paint deep in the crevices of carvings that you could not reach. Do not fret yourself into oblivion or take up sackcloth and ashes; this problem has a simple remedy—paint. When the piece has been stained or colored, a little paint is mixed, usually darker than the stain, and applied to the

Fig. 5-6. Paint residue (the bulk of the paint has been removed) is removed with fresh stripper and steel wool.

recessed areas of the carving. This is done by professionals all the time and it adds a little charm to the piece. The recessed areas in the carvings should be darker from years of use.

Turnings should be treated in the same manner as carvings. Once the bulk material is removed, soak them in multiple coats of stripper and go to town with a softer steel wool. For the tight areas between the turnings, take burlap and cut into thin strips. Wet the burlap with the stripper and pull it back and forth through the turnings the way you would buff your shoes. There is just enough abrasion with the burlap to remove the paint, but not enough to hurt the wood. Burlap can also be used instead of steel wool for paint removal and cleanup on flat areas (so can wood shavings). Burlap is available at hardware shops and garden centers; don't go out and purchase 300 to 400 pounds of potatoes!

Similar to carved areas, turnings that have paint residue can later be painted with a paint somewhat darker than the stain. A professional finisher will invariably shadow the areas between the turnings with pigment or special stain to simulate the look of age. This type of color and shadow work is legitimate for an antique when refinishing and can be undertaken without hesitation.

After the piece is stripped, it might or might not have a final surface ready for staining or finishing. The stripping process is, after all, both a chemical and abrasion process. Therefore, it tends to leave surfaces a little on the rough side. If the surface is smooth to the touch, there is no need to go further. If it is rough, some remedy must be attempted. If at all possible, sanding should be avoided. This is not always possible.

Steel wool is a better alternative to sanding because less of the original surface will be disturbed. Smoothing out a surface in this type of situation calls for working backward. Start with a smooth pad and work to a rougher one. Take a 000-steel-wool pad and rub a small area of the surface vigorously with the grain. If this produces a smooth surface, there is no need to search further. Rub down the entire piece with the steel wool. In the event that 000 steel wool does not work, try 00 steel wool. If the 00 steel wool works, rub down the piece and return to the 000 steel wool for a second rubbing.

In most cases the steel wool will work. If not, try a 240-grit finishing paper. If the 240-grit paper fails, work 220-grit paper and then try 180-grit paper. It is rarely necessary to go below 180-grit. When sanding, use a sanding block. A block can be made out of any piece of scrap wood. You could use an electric finishing sander on large surfaces to ease your work load, but do not use a belt sander. Do the last sanding by hand and without a block so that you can move in and out of the subtle undulations found on hand planed surfaces. After the 240-grit paper has been used, rub the piece down with the 000 steel wool. Wipe down the entire piece with a rag dampened in paint thinner to remove all vestiges of sandpaper and steel wool. By now you should have a final surface ready and worthy of a finish.

Removing Paint with Lye and TSP

There is probably no one topic of wood stripping that is more controversial than using lye as a paint remover. Professionals are divided into two camps. There are those who say yes, preferred always, and those that say never, not under pain of eternal execration. I say yes for the professional and experienced home worker, and no to the novice.

To be sure, nothing cuts through heavy layers of old paint as quickly and inexpensively as lye. On the other hand, lye can darken or ruin a piece and it has greater injury potential to the user than other types of stripper. I will outline how to work with lye in the event that you need to someday, but remember, I don't recommend it for beginners. Be careful when using lye because it is a caustic. But it is also not worthy of the horror stories that are bantered around.

When working with lye, you must work outdoors or in a basement that has a floor drain. The work is preferably done outdoors on a patch of the yard where you don't care if the grass ever comes back. Lye will not work very well in the cold weather. You should pick a day that is 70 degrees F or above.

Working with lye will necessitate the use of a few items that are not in your basic stripping tool kit. A cotton mop, a long-handled scrub brush and a 9- to 10-quart galvanized pail will be required. An enameled pail can be substituted for a galvanized pail, but *never* use an aluminum pail. When aluminum comes in contact with lye, a toxic gas is formed.

Set up your project and put on rubber gloves, safety glasses, and an apron. Have a hose conveniently hooked up nearby to wash yourself down in the event of a bad splash. The hose will also be needed to wash down the piece after the lye has done its work.

Take your 9- to 10-quart galvanized pail and fill it with 5 quarts of cold water. Add to the water approximately 40 ounces of lye. Remember to add the *lye* to the water and not the water to the lye if you want to avoid a splash back in the face. The lye mixture will froth violently; that is why you need a pail at least double the volume of the water. The lye mixture can be used at this point, but it helps to add a cup of wheat-based wallpaper paste. The wallpaper paste will give the solution a little body so that it clings to the surface.

Swab the mixture on with the mop and stand ready with a paint scraper. You simply cannot know how long to leave the lye on. If you leave it too long, it will burn the wood and damage the wood fiber. After 20 or 30 seconds, test the paint with a scraper and continue to test it until it's ready; then go to work.

Ideally, you should work one horizontal surface at a time. But given the nature of lye, this is difficult to do because it will drip to sides and backs. The choice is yours, but it is probably wise to attempt to strip the entire piece at one time.

When the finish has loosened up, use the hose to wash it down. Don't set the nozzle for a stray pattern. Try for the maximum pressure so that as much of the paint as possible is removed. Next, take the paint scraper and remove the stubborn residual paint. Following use of the paint scraper, work the long-handled brush vigorously to remove any traces of paint or lye.

It is necessary to neutralize the lye so that it will not continue to eat at the wood or ruin subsequent finishes that are applied. The appropriate neutralizing agent for lye is vinegar. Wash off the long-handled brush so that it can be used to scrub the piece with the vinegar. Use the vinegar freely and make sure that it drips into all cracks and crevices. These can be problems later if not neutralized.

One of the problems encountered with lye stripping is that it turns some woods darker. The treatment is fairly kind to pine, hickory and maple (tuning them just a tad darker). In some cases the effect is attractive. Lye is said to destroy cherry or open-grained woods such as mahogany, oak, and chestnut. It will darken these woods, but it should not destroy them. In the event that the wood has been darkened, apply liberal amounts of household bleach after the water rinse, but prior to the vinegar neutralizer. In most cases, the bleach will return the wood to the desired shade. If this doesn't work, try a solution of oxalic acid after the piece has dried. The one wood I have had difficulty with is chestnut. It was not ruined, but it was made a shade dark.

By the time you have finished stripping the furniture, the piece will have been subjected to considerable amounts of water (in the lye mixture and the water rinse). Allow the piece to dry in a warm place for at least two to three days. Outdoors is fine, but not in the direct sunlight which might foster some warping. Inevitably, the combination of the water and the caustic lye will raise the grain of the wood. Therefore, the piece will require sanding prior to staining or finishing. You should also check the piece for sturdiness because the water might have caused disintegration of some of the glue joints. Just one final note of caution. Do not use lye on clear finishes; it's both foolish and unnecessary. And do not use it on veneered pieces.

Trisodium phosphate, commonly known as TSP, is a product similar to lye, but just not as strong. It is a difficult product to find on the shelves. Yet, it is the active ingredient in many household cleaners and it is used for water softening. If it is not available at the local hardware store, try a large paint supply house. TSP can be used in its own right to remove paint (in many cases), but it will not remove paint as well as lye will.

The application process for TSP is basically the same as for lye. There is no sense in using it as a primary paint remover. Nevertheless, it does have some other applications. If you plan on doing a lot of stripping and if you want to save a few dollars, then TSP is your product. Use a commercial paint remover for the top layers of paint and then switch to TSP for the residential paint and cleanup. A lot of money spent on stripper can be saved this way, but it is hardly worth the mess and effort for the weekend furniture stripper. The real value of TSP is in removing stubborn paints, such as milk paints, that resist other treatments. TSP is also good in situations where white or black paints have penetrated into the wood and ignore plain stripper.

The method for application of TSP is similar to that of lye. Work outdoors in warm weather. Protect yourself with gloves, safety glasses, and an apron. Have your hose in a standby position. Mix 1 pound of trisodium phosphate crystals in a pail with 5 or 6 quarts of hot water. Use *hot* water not cold water as with lye. Swab the solution on with a cotton mop and allow it to stand for about 1 minute. Take a long-handled brush and scrub the piece. If the paint comes loose, continue the work. If not let it stand a little longer. If there is no response to the TSP, then give up. It is not going to work on that particular paint. If the solution appears to be working, it might take several applications to remove the paint.

When the paint is removed, dip the long-handled brush in a pail of fresh water, preferably hot, and scrub the piece thoroughly. As a final step, hose the piece down. Make sure the water reaches all cracks and tight spots. Trisodium phosphate, similar to lye, might darken the wood. In such a case, the wood should be treated with bleach. After the final washdown, allow the piece to dry for two or three days—then sand as appropriate.

Milk Paint and Other Headaches

Paints that are difficult to remove are called refractory paints. Nine times out of 10 this is going to be a milk paint, but not all stubborn paints are milk paints. This should not overly concern you because the procedure for removal will be the same in any case.

Removing milk paints and the like is a headache by anyone's standard. The best way to approach a milk paint is to decide not to remove it. Layers of recent paint can be removed leaving the milk paint surface. This approach saves a great deal of work and generally enhances the value of the piece.

Alas, not everyone wants painted furniture; first things first. Take your pocketknife and scrape away a small area of paint from the piece so that you can see the base paint. If you encounter the characteristically red, green, or blue milk paint, you should think twice prior to purchasing the piece and taking on the work load. If the base coat is black, give the matter very serious consideration. Rarely will you ever get it all off the wood. Paint stripper has a tendency to force old paint into the pores of the wood. This will stain the wood the color of the paint. Even when a piece with a black-base coat is brought to a dip stripper, it will come back with a grayish hue and black streaks. With a black paint, you are best advised to scrape the paint off.

Coping with milk paints will involve a trial and error approach. After you strip a piece with a commercial stripper and find that the base coat is impervious to the stripper, you can attempt removal with trisodium phosphate. Occasionally, TSP will work on milk paints, but more often than not it doesn't.

Failing to achieve success with TSP, try using alcohol applied with a steel wool pad (in the direction of the grain). Allow the alcohol to soak into the surface even if it dries. Should the paint be susceptible to alcohol, it will rub off as opposed to lifting off. Rub hard and wipe with paper towels. Alcohol, like TSP, is a hit-and-miss product lending itself to less than frequent success. You could try lacquer thinner or turpentine to remove the paint. These generally do not work, but there might be a first time.

The most success in removing a milk paint will probably be found with the use of ammonia. Remember to allow for adequate ventilation if you don't want to play havoc with your nasal passages. Use household ammonia full strength and swab it on in any manner that you find convenient. Allow the ammonia to sink in for 5 to 10 minutes. Take a pad of 0 steel wool dipped in ammonia and rub vigorously (with the grain). Wipe the surface with paper towels. The towels should be colored by the paint as you work. Repeat this process until all of the paint is removed. When finished, rinse thoroughly with fresh water.

On a good day, all of the paint will be removed leaving a workable surface. On a bad day, the wood will be stained the color of the paint. There are several options at this point. The first is to burn this book and condemn the author to oblivion. Another option is to take the piece to a dip stripper or a professional hand stripper. Before you agree on a price, have them guarantee they will remove the staining because chances are they won't be able to do it. A disreputable avenue that can be taken is to belt sand the entire piece until you get to fresh wood. This course of action is not in the spirit of antiques and it seriously reduces the value of the piece. I suspect that many professional finishers, in moments of frustration, have resorted to sanding—though few will admit it.

The most viable approach to this problem is to bleach the piece with a household bleach or a two-step bleach sold by shops that handle professional finishing supplies. The bleach will not remove the stain, but it will lighten it up somewhat. If ammonia has been used on a piece, the piece must be rinsed thoroughly prior to application of a bleach. Ammonia releases toxic chloride gas from the bleach. Do *not* use the products in conjunction.

The next step is to select a stain that is compatable with that of the residual color in the wood. With a brown, there is no problem— just go to a darker brown. With traces of black or green in the wood, a dark walnut stain will usually do the trick. With red, try a wet test (see the section on finishes) to determine if the color is acceptable as is. If the red is not acceptable, it can be toned down with a walnut stain or brought into the cherry/mahogany family with a red-brown stain.

The biggest bugaboo of all of the residual paints is white paint. No matter what color stain you choose, the white is going to show through with an undesirable milky effect. For this problem you might try your luck with a wipe-on glaze or a varnish stain. If one of these remedies has not worked (and at least one should), then you can always mix up a batch of milk paint and repaint the piece.

Refractory paints are not the source of all problems. Some original stains can be quite problematic. Mahogany stain used in the early part of this century is particularly tenacious and leaves wood a deep red after the finish has been removed. For this type of problem, a household bleach or a two-step bleach should do the trick. In some other cases, berries, herbs or, roots might have been used as a powerful natural dye. Bleaching might help somewhat with these stains, but it will by no means eradicate them. For this type of problem, follow the approaches listed for opaque stains. Use darker stains, glazes, or varnish stains.

End grain, as found on tops of tables, dressers and cupboards, can be a terrible problem if you let it be. The porous nature of end grain results in its drinking paint if it has not previously been sealed. You can strip day and night—and for that matter until the cows come home—but you will not get all the paint out. Some workers sand the paint out, but it takes a lot of work and might require the removal of up to one-eighth inch of wood.

There is no reason for all this labor. Just take some artist colors, mix them to match the stain you will be using, and paint the end grain. End grain is always darker than the other surfaces so it doesn't have to be a great match. This remedy looks fine and is used by most refinishers.

Wax Finishes

The weekend refinisher is not likely to come across too many wax finishes, but there are some out there. You should have some idea as to how to deal with them. Americans don't tend to like wax finishes, but the English are inordinately fond of them for country pine pieces. The English also find the idea of darkening or staining pine abhorent and heathen.

I do not think it is possible to remove all the wax from a piece when the wax has moved deeply into the wood. Nevertheless, there are ways of working within the context of the problem.

Take 00 steel wool and paint thinner and wash the piece down, drying with paper towels as you go. Natural waxes, as opposed to silicone waxes, use turpentine as the basic vehicle to dissolve the waxes. Mineral spirits can be used to dissolve the wax. Mineral spirits or turpentine can also be used to clean and remove wax buildups on furniture around the house.

Following cleaning of a piece with mineral spirits you can use a commercial dewaxer that is dissolved in water. If a dewaxer is not available, try Spic and Span (it has TSP as one of its primary ingredients), but remember to rinse thoroughly with fresh water. The whole purpose of removing the wax finish is to provide a surface that can be stained.

With the appropriate cleaning and drying you *should* be ready to stain. Wrong. Doubtlessly, the waxes have permeated the wood. No matter how nice the surface looks, it will inhibit most stains that you might use. In such a case, an alcohol based stain with aniline dye would work adequately. It's not the type of product the average person happens to have on the shelf. There is no need to search the wilds for a special stain. Minwax, available just about everywhere, will do an adequate job. Minwax is quite compatible with old wax finishes. It does tend to favor the lighter, less full-bodied shades.

After the stain has been applied, allow the piece to dry at least 24 hours (48 hours if it still feels tacky). Following the stain application, only one product can or should be used and that is shellac. Shellac is the only finish that will coat a surface that has a wax residue. It is a natural for this kind of problem. Apply at least two coats of shellac solution comprised of 3 parts alcohol to 1 part shellac, rubbing down between each coat. When the piece has been sealed with shellac, you can decide to finish the job with shellac or go on to varnish. When this work is completed, you will put on a fresh coat of wax and wonder if all the work was worth it!

If you are the type of person who likes to cut corners and make life a little simpler, there is an old trick that can be used for wax finishes. After the wax has been basically removed with the mineral spirits, take some good, brown paste shoe polish or mix brown, black, and cordovan to suit your fancy. Rub the shoe polish in vigorously with a rag and then buff with a brush. Allow the wax to dry and then put on a layer of new, clear paste wax. Buff to a luster. You can obtain good results with this method and save some elbow grease.

Stretching: The Easy Road to an Original Paint

If you have never heard of *stretching* a paint, don't feel bad because it is mostly a trade term. Stretching a paint means exactly that. An old paint is expanded or extended to cover a broader surface. If a dealer has a seaman's chest in old red paint, but the paint is badly marred, chipped, and worn away in some areas, he could use a solvent to dissolve the paint and redistribute it over the entire surface. The result is fairly appealing and far more salable. Some would like to say that this is a legitimate restoration, but it's not really. The chest should be left for someone who will appreciate it as is. The reverse side of this coin is—if it is a choice between stripping and stretching—I would elect the stretching because at least the original character of the chest is maintained.

Stretching is more acceptable, at least in my opinion, when it is the inevitable product of stripping. For example, you are stripping a cupboard with four coats of white paint on it. When the final coat of white is removed, you find underneath a beautiful powder blue paint. Ideally, you will remove all of the white paint neatly, leaving the blue painted surface. This is an ideal occurrence, but infrequently reality because there will be streaks of white here, there, and everywhere. The thing will look like an unholy blue and white mess.

Museum restorers approach this task with a cotton swab working only a square inch at a time. Few amateurs or professionals have this type of patience or tenacity. The usual treatment in this case is to stretch the original paint. This will blend or hide the residues of the old surface paints.

If you want to save an old paint in this manner, the first thing to do is to prepare a test patch. Scrape an area with a knife to determine what the base paint is. This allows you to know if there is something there that you want to save and it provides the basic incentive for the project. Next, put some stripper on another area and stand by with your paint scraper ready to test the paint. When the top coat has crinkled, try removing it with the scraper to see if you can work to the bottom coat. If not, allow some more time and try again. Time the entire operation starting from when you put the stripper on.

This is a trial and error process, but you want to get to the bottom and know how long it takes. You do not want to use a great deal of pressure to remove the last layer or you could damage the painted surface underneath. It might be possible to accomplish this task with one application of stripper. If need be, remove the top coats of paint and apply more stripper. Remember to time the work. Inevitably, some of the original paint will be removed. This is the nature of the process. When doing this type of work, do an entire surface—such as the top of a table or side of a cupboard—at one time.

The goal of this process is to leave a perfect surface. If that's what you have, give thanks to your ancestors and leave it alone. Chances are that the surface is not perfect and that there are residues of the top coats of paint everywhere. Make sure that you have removed as much of this paint as possible with the scraper. Then proceed to take a pad of 0000 steel wool dipped in stripper and use it to level the now soluble original paint. Be as light-handed as possible so that you do not rub through the paint to bare wood.

170

Work with the grain and spread the paint until all surfaces are covered. Where residues of the top paint are encountered, blend them carefully with original paint until an acceptable hue is obtained. Blending the paints will lead to some light or dark spots. It depends upon the color of the original and subsequent coats of paints, but variation should look acceptable.

When the piece is dry, the surface might appear rough or show marks from the steel wool. In such a case, it can be rubbed down with dry, 0000 steel wool to smooth it out. Allow the old paint to dry at least a week before you attempt this, and watch the work carefully to see that the steel wool is not removing too much of the original paint. If you like your painted furniture with a sheen, rub in a mixture of half turpentine and half-boiled linseed oil and allow to dry. For a final finish, put on a layer of paste wax and buff to a soft luster.

MECHANICAL STRIPPING

Furniture stripping falls into two categories: chemical and mechanical. Mechanical stripping is essentially a heat or abrasion process that involves such sundry techniques as sanding, scraping, torching, and sand blasting. In almost all cases, chemical stripping is the preferred method for antiques because the abrasion methods will destroy the original surface and all hope of a patina. The principal value of the mechanical method is speed and cost.

I mention these techniques briefly so that you will have some general knowledge of how they work, but also to warn you of their potential harm. Abrasion methods can be used on relatively new furniture without detriment to the value, but even then I feel that chemical methods are preferable.

Scraping

Scraping is the one abrasion method that can have some valid application with regard to antiques. This is also the method preferred by many old-timers. This is especially true for those in New England who are renowned for their lack of extravagence.

Scraping involves the use of any sharp object—such as cabinet scrapers, knives or paint scrapers—to remove a clear or paint finish. Actually, the preferred tool of the scraper people is a chard of broken glass. Glass is inexpensive and when a new edge is needed you just break another piece. With a fairly recent finish, this process is laborious and you would doubt the sanity of anyone who indulges in it. With an old finish, especially one that is crumbling or powdering, this method can be extraordinarily fast and effective. The problem encountered with this technique is that, no matter how good you are at it, a pattern of overlapping striations will be left on the surface and sanding will be necessary. What remains of the original surface after scraping will be lost to sanding.

There are times when scraping is the preferred route to the restoration of an original paint. When the mechanical bond between an original paint and subsequent paints breaks down, due to the deterioration of the latter paints, they can be removed by scraping. In simple terms, when the newer paint is flaking off a light scraping can get you down to the original paint without any damage to it.

With this type of situation, scraping is the preferred and most acceptable method for returning an original paint. If the later paints retain their elasticity this method will not work adequately. The operator will have to apply more pressure to the scraper than can be controlled. There will be damage to the original surface underneath.

If you are trying to save an old paint finish, give this method a try. Otherwise, relegate the information to the recesses of your mind where it can be retrieved in moments of desperation.

Sanding and Sand Blasting

Most refinishing projects call for some modest sanding before a final surface is achieved, but sanding is never recommended for removing a clear or paint finish. To be sure, there is some weekend worker out there who got a brand spanking new belt sander for Christmas and is now ready to take on the world with it. With the belt sander, a painted chest of drawers can be brought down to bare wood in 20 minutes as opposed to the 4 hours that might be spent with a stripper. But the value of the piece will be sadly diminished and the historical character will be lost forever. If you want something with new wood, buy new. Please don't ruin an antique. I know of one "restorer" whose hands were never soiled by a chemical. He just churned pieces out with a super sander and sold them as fast as he could finish them. There is no accounting for taste.

The use of a powerful finishing sander to remove a finish is no more acceptable than the use of a belt sander. There will be times when light sanding has to accompany the finishing process, such as after lye stripping, but the general rule of thumb is sand as little as possible as often as possible.

If you decide to strip a piece of furniture by sanding, presumably a non-antique piece, allow for ventilation and use a respirator. When an old lead paint is broken up, thousands of minute toxic particles are sent into the air. These particles can harm you directly or find their way into the environment and be carried on in plant life cycles. You might not believe it, but people have developed lead poisoning from chips of house paint that have fallen into the garden during a scraping and restoration project. The lead was absorbed through the root systems of the plants and vegetables and subsequently eaten.

Use of flap sanders and rotary strippers falls into the same (unacceptable) category as belt sanding. Flap sanders are superbly effective in preparing new work, but they will damage the surface of old work. Rotary strippers (circular objects with 10,000 wires coming out of them) will also damage the surface. Besides, they are not terribly effective.

Sand Blasting is a method used by some refinishers to strip large quantities of furniture. It is difficult to believe that a technique abrasive enough to resurface concrete can be controlled enough to do furniture. But apparently it can. Sand blasting is not a technique that you would use on antique furniture.

Blow Torches and Hot Irons

Heat is another method used to remove old paint finishes. Most home handypersons have some familiarity with the use of a propane torch to strip the porch steps or whatever. When you are working on a house, this is the only route to travel because it is the only one economical for large areas. If you recall such experiences, you will remember that the wood was gouged, nicked, charred, and occasionally set afire.

If you apply this method to furniture, the general results are going to be the same. Actually, I have seen some talented people who can remove paint on furniture with a torch using a spreader tip. Such persons are both gifted and lucky. There is no reason to assume this risk. Chemical stripping is more effective and just as fast. The few dollars saved by using a torch are simply not worth the risk.

Electric hot irons work on the same principle as propane torches except there is far less risk of burning a surface. Burning can be avoided by the use of the hot iron, but there still will be the profusion of nicks and scratches associated with the process. Save your torch for the start of the next Olympics and spare your furniture.

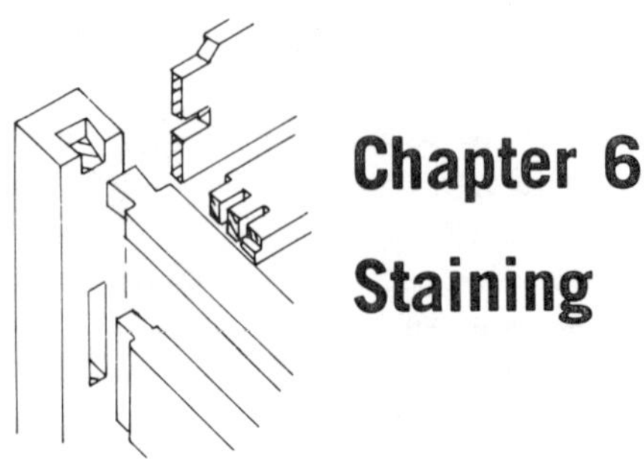

Chapter 6
Staining

Staining is one of the most abused aspects of furniture finishing. Weekend craftspersons are all too often concerned with stripping the piece and getting a nice, shiny finish. They consider staining to be an intermediate step that is something to be slopped on from a can as quickly as possible. Even cabinetmakers who build new furniture often become obsessed with the creative process and relegate the choice of stain and finish to an afterthought.

Staining is something that can be done satisfactorily by almost anyone who is willing to pay modest attention to detail. It is also an art that draws upon knowledge of colors and light and the creative use of both. The final outcome of a restoration project can be affected more by the staining process than the finish that will eventually be put on.

Some purists will suggest that antique furniture should never be stained, but this seems a little ridiculous. Furniture was stained in the 17 century, the 18th century and the 19th century. There is no reason why it should not be stained now. Thought should be given to how staining will affect the originality of the piece.

After all is said and done, the first rule of staining is: don't stain unless you have to. In their natural state, woods such as walnut, mahogany, and cherry do not need a stain. Actually a stain will only obscure their natural beauty. Light woods such as pine, maple, poplar, and oak need some stain to enhance the grain pattern and give depth to the wood. With antique pieces, factors of time and use might have colored wood enough to make stain unnecessary or harmful. There is a simple test that can be made to determine whether or not to stain. This will be discussed shortly.

The second rule of staining is: never under any circumstances use a commercially available mahogany stain. I doubt that there has been any other product in the history of furniture that has destroyed so many projects or disappointed so many people. It would be more appropriate to hold a cocktail party in a nuclear reactor than it would be appropriate to use mahogany stain on furniture!

The third rule of staining is: never use a stain without testing it on a scrap piece first, especially a maple stain. There is a not-very-subtle message here. Commercially prepared stains can be dangerous. I am not advocating that these products be abandoned, but rather that they be used with caution.

SURFACE PREPARATION AND FILLERS

Prior to staining, all repair work should be done, all stains should be removed, and cracks and nail holes should be filled. The surface should be smooth, free of dust, and without any wax or natural, hand oils. If there is any doubt as to how clean the surface is, wipe it with mineral spirits, turpentine, alcohol, or lacquer thinner. Lacquer thinner is generally the best product to use. This is especially true if a chemical stripper has been used. Lacquer thinner will also dry the fastest.

How smooth the surface should be is a factor that you will have to determine. The depth of stain will be controlled by the type of stain used, the type of wood, and the relative abrasion or polish of the natural wood surface. A coarse surface will drink a stain deeply. A modestly smooth surface will accept less stain and a very smooth surface will accept still less. For the staining properties of wood, see Table 6-1.

WOOD FILLERS

Some open-grain woods will require filling prior to finishing. These are the woods with large, visible pores such as oak. If you do not fill the pores on these woods, the surface stain will look uneven and the finish coat will never truly be smooth because it will not be capable of filling the gaps. Wood fillers, excluding patch products such as plastic woods, are divided into two categories: liquid fillers and paste fillers. I will not discuss liquid fillers because the finishing product selected will serve the purpose of liquid filler. In addition, most woods specified for liquid fillers can be used without any fillers.

The application of a paste filler is not difficult and does not require any super skill. But practice does help. For some odd

Table 6-1. Staining Properties of Common Woods.

Good	Moderate	Poor
Pine	Oak**	Maple
Popular	Chestnut	Oak**
Birch	Hickory	
Mahogany*	Ash	
Walnut*	Beech	
Basswood	Butternut	
Gum		
Cherry **		

*Probably should not be stained

**Staining properties will vary with species of oak. Common oaks found today are American white and red, English oak, and Japanese oak.

reason, many woodworkers and finishers find this work distasteful. If I can avoid filling a wood, I will, but it is also a reality that has to be faced.

Mahogany, walnut, ash, chestnut, elm, hickory, and oak traditionally require a filler. This is a formidable list but it can be simplified. Filler is recommended for walnut, but I have rarely ever seen a good piece of walnut that needs it. The walnut encountered in 18th-century furniture and early 19th-century furniture will not require filling. Some inferior walnut used in late 19th-century furniture will need filling.

Mahogany is a study in itself and it can be divided into a number of categories such as old Spanish mahogany, Honduras mahogany, African mahogany, and Phillipine mahogany. In most cases Spanish mahogany, only seen on good, 18th-century pieces, and Honduras mahogany can be used without filling. African mahogany, which came into use in the middle part of the 19th century, has a larger pore structure than Honduras mahogany. With African mahogany, it is a 50-50 proposition, depending upon your judgment, if it needs filling. Phillipine mahogany, sometimes called Luan, is not a true mahogany, but it is quite similar. Phillipine mahogany is mostly a product of the 20th century and it has large pores that always need filling. When properly filled and stained, Phillipine mahogany and Honduras mahogany cannot easily be distinguished. You are not likely to encounter Phillipine mahogany on an antique piece.

As the list of problem woods pleasantly diminishes, you come to ash, elm, and hickory. Elm is not commonly used in American furniture except as a secondary wood. Ash and hickory are woods used for their flexibility and mostly in chairs as stretchers or steam bent parts. As a rule, these woods are not filled on antique pieces.

The process of attrition reduces your concern to two types of wood; oak and chestnut. Oak will be found in 17th-century, 18th-century, and 19th-century country pieces as well as Victorian-formal pieces and mass-produced pieces. Chestnut as a primary wood will be found almost exclusively in late 19th-century Victorian furniture and mass-produced furniture.

If you encounter an oak, mahogany, or chestnut piece that needs filling, the product to use is paste wood filler. Paste fillers can be purchased in most large paint stores. You are likely to get a better filler from a professional finishing products supplier. The better fillers are silex (crushed rock). Some fillers have silica; it is not as good as silex, but it is acceptable. The least acceptable fillers are those made of gypsum or calcium carbonate. The other ingredients in fillers are linseed oil, varnish, and dryers. The fillers that are primarily varnish are better than those that are primarily oil. Brick dust and plaster of paris were once used as fillers.

Paste filler comes in a neutral gray shade. Some suppliers will offer them in walnut and mahogany colors as well. Japan colors and colors ground in oil can be used to color the neutral filler. If these products are not available, oil stains can be used. The filler will come in a thick paste that must be reduced with turpentine or mineral spirits to a cream-like consistency before it is worked into the wood. If you are using an oil stain to color the mixture, add it prior to the turpentine because it will reduce the mixture somewhat. With Japan colors or colors ground in oil, add them after the turpentine. Follow the product directions for reducing the paste filler.

If the work piece is going to be stained, it should be sanded and stained prior to the application of the paste filler (as shown in Figs. 6-1 and 6-2). When the stain has dried, apply the reduced and

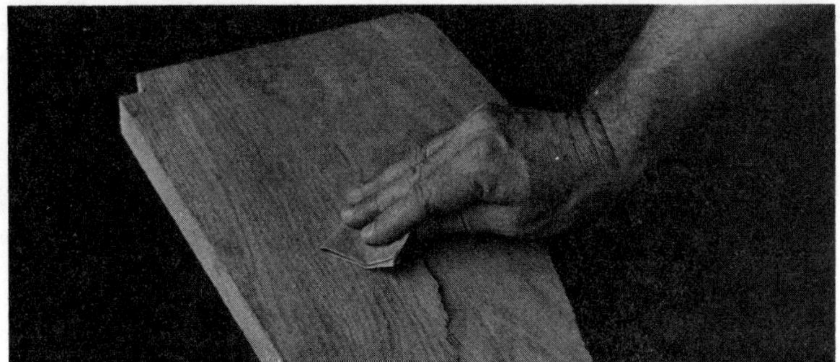

Fig. 6-1. Preparing an oak board for filling.

Fig. 6-2. Staining is accomplished prior to filling unless there is to be a natural finish.

colored filler with a stiff bristle brush. Work it across the grain and into the grain as shown in **Fig. 6-3**. The finishing strokes should always be with the grain. Allow this mixture to dry until the gloss wears off (or approximately 15 minutes). Then take a piece of burlap and rub it across the grain to work the now-partially-dried filler well into the pores of the wood (as shown in **Fig. 6-4**).

Take a fresh piece of burlap and wipe across the grain a second time to remove the excess filler from the wood surface. Take still another piece of burlap and wipe the piece with the grain. If all has gone well, the pores will be filled and no excess will remain on the surface. If some excess does remain, give the piece a final wipe with a clean, cotton cloth along the grain. If the filler has pulled out of the pores, it means that the paste was thinned too much. If this problem occurs, there is no choice but to remove all the filler with turpentine and start over again.

When the filling process is complete, allow the piece to dry for 24 to 48 hours prior to attempting any other work. When dry, sand lightly with a 220- or 240-grit paper and seal the piece with a coat of 1 part shellac to 4 parts alcohol. The shellac uses a different solvent from the filler—alcohol as opposed to turpentine—and therefore it will not remove the filler or coloring. A wash coat of varnish, a mixture of one-half varnish and one-half thinner could be used. Do not apply a coat of full strength varnish to a filled surface or the filler could be pulled from the pores of the wood.

Never use a wash coat on a surface that is going to be filled prior to the actual filling. Once filled, the final finish must be one of the traditional finishes (shellac, varnish or lacquer). Natural oil,

Danish finishes, and penetrating oils will not work effectively on this type of surface.

WET TEST AND COLOR RESTORATION

Whenever you read anything about woodwork or finishing you are bound to encounter the mystical term *wet test*. This is not a matter of alchemy with dilute mixtures of 5 parts nitric something or other, but a simple matter of rubbing a wood surface with a little water. If you want to impress your friends, call it a hydrogen/oxygen solution.

Prior to staining a surface, you will want to determine what it would look like without a stain, but with a finish. The simplest and most effective way to do this is to rub a small area with water. The wet spot will look approximately the same as it would with a shellac or varnish finish. I have seen some incredibly drab surfaces come to life this way. If there is already a beautiful hue or tone inherent in the wood, why gum it up with stain. Pine is a wood that usually requires a stain, but with time it mellows and tones. A wet test will show whether or not this color can be brought out.

If the wet test shows promise, but you feel that just a wee bit more depth or color is needed, you can use a rejuvenator. Take boiled linseed oil, add to 6 parts of pure gum turpentine, and work it well into the wood with either a rag or your hand (as shown in Fig. 6-5). When the piece is coated, wipe off as much of the mixture as you can with a clean rag. Another approach to rejuvenation is the use of a dilute coat of shellac (1 part clear shellac to 5 or 6 parts alcohol). There is not a set rule to the proportions of this mixture. Some will

Fig. 6-3. The paste filler is mixed to a cream consistency and applied with a stiff brush in the direction of the grain.

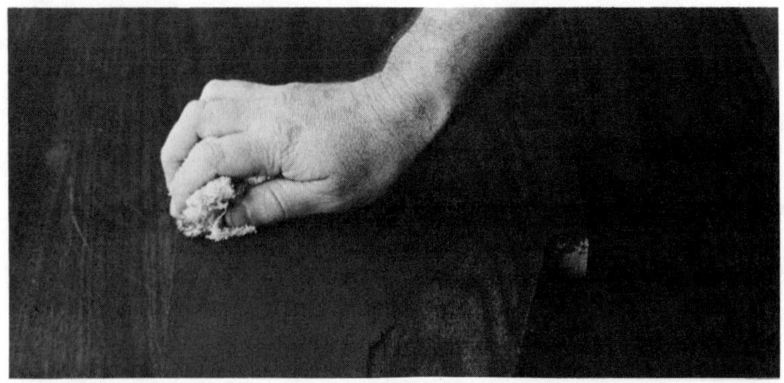

Fig. 6-4. Filler is allowed to dry for 15 minutes. The excess filler is removed with a piece of burlap first rubbed with the grain, then across the grain. A final rub with the grain is given.

go as strong as 4 parts alcohol while others will insist on 8 parts alcohol. Somewhere in the middle seems to be a safe route to take.

Either one of these solutions will give the wood a greater depth and somewhat more color than is indicated by the wet test. If you decide upon this approach, but find that you are not satisfied with the results, there is no problem because the piece can still be stained. Make sure there is absolutely no smell of turpentine coming from the piece prior to staining or finishing. The turpentine and linseed oil mixture has some slight advantage over the shellac mixture. It can be bottled and kept on your shelf for a few weeks; the alcohol mixture will spoil. The oil mixture is compatible with oil and sealer finishes. The shellac mixture is best followed by a traditional finish.

Experiment with these approaches before jumping the gun on a stain. You might well be delighted with the results.

WASH COATS AND SEALER COATS

I am reluctant to tell you about *wash coats* for fear of leading you down the primrose path of destruction. Wash coats are used to control the depth of penetration of a stain where necessary. Wash coats are especially good for very dry surfaces such as an old, weathered pine bench that would soak up stain more quickly and deeply than a sponge. When the stain takes this quickly, it will dry blotchy, uneven, very dark, and altogether undesirable.

A wash coat would retard the absorption of the stain by sealing the wood well below the surface (rendering an even stain cover). On a surface that is not dried out, this will unnecessarily prohibit the penetration of the stain and make it difficult to achieve the final color desired. A wash coat should only be used when circumstances suggest that there is a need to limit the depth of penetration of the stain. The majority of jobs encountered will not require a wash coat prior to staining.

Wash coats are also used on coarse-grained woods such as fir. With fir, the soft portions of the wood drink stain deeply while the hard portions resist. Hence the *tiger grain* of the wood is unnecessarily emphasized. The use of a wash coat diminishes the unsightly tiger-grain effect. With fir, a lightly opaque and pigmented stain is used to further conceal the natural grain. The stain can be followed by a finish coat that has been pigmented for the same purpose. This is a lot of work to make fir or fir plywood attractive. But don't worry. Antiques are not made out of fir plywood.

The best all-around wash coat is clear shellac cut with 6 or 7 parts of alcohol. This is a fairly safe solution and should not cause any problem even if the decision to use a wash coat was injudicious. The wash coat is brushed on and will be absorbed almost as soon as it is applied. The surface will dry to the touch within minutes, but allow at least an hour's drying time prior to staining. It is best not to use a water stain over a shellac wash coat because it could play havoc with the alcohol. I have used water stains in this manner without problem, but it is still wiser not to. A shellac finish, a lacquer finish, or a varnish finish can be used over a wash coat.

If you plan to use tung oil or a modern Danish oil finish, prepare your wash coat of 1 part boiled linseed oil to 5 parts of turpentine and rub or brush on. Wipe the excess from the surface and allow to

Fig. 6-5. A color restorer, made of 1 part boiled linseed oil and 6 parts turpentine, is rubbed on a faded chair.

dry for 24 to 48 hours. There should be no smell of oil or turpentine prior to staining. A Danish oil as well as traditional finishes can be used over this.

Sealer coats are used after staining to seal the surface so that the stain does not bleed into the final finish. The most traditional sealer coat is shellac mixed somewhat stronger than a wash coat (perhaps 1 part shellac to 4 or 5 parts alcohol). The sealer coat should impart little or no sheen to the surface. You can shellac, lacquer, or varnish over this surface.

Some people insist that you cannot use shellac under a varnish surface. This is just not true, but it cannot be argued that the final finish will make a better bond if it is the same as the sealer coat. For varnish, you could use a mixture of 50 percent varnish and 50 percent turpentine applied with a brush. Allow this sealer coat to dry for 48 to 72 hours. When the sealer coat is dry, rub down with 000 steel wool or 220-grit paper, clean, and apply a final finish of varnish. This is a lot of waiting time considering the shellac sealer would have been dry in a few hours. It's your choice!

There is a product known as sanding sealer that is made especially for lacquer finishes. The sanding sealer brushes on easily and dries quickly without lap marks. The surface is ready to be lightly sanded within 2 to 3 hours. In some cases, you might be able to varnish over a lacquer sealer. Follow the manufacturer's instructions on the label. Sanding sealer is not only good underneath a lacquer finish, but it makes a rather nice finish by itself.

Some manufacturers sell specially prepared sealers for shellac and varnish. The shellac type is difficult to find and it is expensive. These products work well enough, but they are costly and unnecessary. The shellac and varnish sealers are less expensive and they are easily prepared.

A PLETHORA OF STAINS

Staining, in its simplest definition, is a method of coloring wood. There are three basic methods of coloration. The first is chemical action. If oak is exposed to the fumes of ammonia, it will turn brown. Lye will turn cherry wood brown or black. In both of these cases, a chemical reaction occurs between the wood and the solution producing a color change.

The second method of coloration is dying. This involves the dye permeating the wood fiber and changing its color.

The third method of coloration is staining. Staining employs a solution of particles of pigment that are forced into the wood surface. The particles are so small that no matter how much the surface is rubbed, coloring material remains in the pores of the wood. Although only this last method is truly staining, all of the above are included under the general category of stain. Some commercial products will use pigments and dyes.

The application of all stains is basically the same. Stain is brushed on profusely and then wiped off after it has been allowed to penetrate. The furniture should be stained one area at a time in a logical fashion. For example, a table should have each leg done separately, then the side rails connecting them, and finally the top. In the case of a drop-leaf table, each leaf should be stained separately and then the center should be stained. Areas not intended to be stained, such as the underside of a table, should be masked off. The piece should be checked for drips constantly during the staining process.

Stain can be wiped on or sprayed. Spraying is a highly effective way to stain with some products, but it does not necessarily achieve better results than a brush-on stain. There are special wipe-on stains that have a thick body, but almost any stain can be wiped on. When stain is wiped on, there will be less penetration. Hence there will be a lighter surface.

With all staining, the end grain must receive special attention. The porous nature of the end grain will result in its taking a stain very deeply. To remedy this problem, the end grain should be covered with a dilute stain or a wash coat of shellac that will seal the grain prior to staining. If the end grain becomes problematic, it can be covered with Japan colors or oil colors matched to the primary stain.

Water Stains

Water stains are not popular with home craftspersons. This is true mostly because they don't know such a thing exists and because water stains are not available at hardware or department stores. Primarily, water stain refers to water-soluble, aniline dyes. But anything that can color water can be used as a stain. For example, a very strong tea can be used to impart a mellow color to old pine. Dry colors used to color cement can be mixed with water to form a stain. Artist water colors or acrylic colors can also be diluted with water to make a stain. At any rate, the message is simple: water plus color equals a stain.

You can fool around and mix your own stains. It's fun, but basically the commercially available water stains are super. Stain powders come in at least seven different colors. All of them can be intermixed when made up to provide an enormous variety of colors. The depth of these stains can be controlled by adding more or less water, and they have an extremely long shelf life. These powders are dyes that are permanent and they are among the clearest available. These are also the most inexpensive stains available. You have an unbeatable combination.

There must be some dark cloud associated with the sunshine of water stains. Water in any form applied to a wood surface swells the fibers, causing a little coarseness. This is known as *raising the grain.* For this reason, most sources don't tout water stains. But it isn't really such a problem.

With new woodwork, after the piece has been sanded, it is wetted down (rubbed lightly with a rag soaked in water). This action causes the grain to raise. After the piece is dry, it is sanded lightly until smooth. By purposely raising the grain and sanding, the grain-raising effect of the water stain is minimized. Consequently, all that is required after staining is a light rubbing with steel wool.

With antique pieces, the grain does not lend itself to raising a great deal, but the same process will work. Moisten the surface with a wet rag or paper towel (don't soak it), allow to dry, and sand with a 220- or 240-grit finishing paper.

After the stain has been applied, a gentle rubdown with 0000 steel wool should yield a perfectly acceptable surface. If a water-rinse stripper has been used on the piece, there is no need to wet the piece down because the water rinse will have well accomplished this.

Water-stain powders are available from professional finishing supply houses and they are available in 1-pound tins. Some companies make them available in 1-ounce packages for the occasional user. Each can of stain powder will have directions for mixing, but the general rule is 1 ounce of powder added to a quart of boiling water. When the stain is cool, it is ready to use and it can be reduced by the addition of more water. If your local tap water is hard, use spring water or distilled water.

When you are applying water stain, use a clean brush and wet it with tap water. Take the stain on your brush and apply the stain in long continuous strokes with the grain (as shown in Fig. 6-6). Each brush stroke should overlap the other. Work quickly because the wood absorbs the stain readily. Don't be stingy with the stain. After a surface has been covered, wipe it vigorously with a clean rag and go on to the next surface. After staining, allow the piece to dry for at least 24 hours. If the stain process has raised the grain, rub down the piece with 0000 steel wool and go on to a finish.

Water stains dry completely flat with a somewhat murky appearance that alarms most first-time users. There is really no problem. Once a finish is applied, the area comes to life brilliantly. Water stains are compatible with any finish you might choose to use.

Non-Grain-Raising Stains and Spirit Stains

There is a group of stains known as non-grain-raising (NGR) stains. This is a particular type of stain and it should not be confused with oil stains labeled non-grain-raising.

NGR stains are highly favored by professional finishers because they use water-soluble, aniline dyes with a special solvent that contains no water and, consequently, does not raise the grain. The problem with NGR stains is that they are best sprayed on. Brushed on NGR stains dry almost as quickly as they are applied. And they leave lap marks in the process. You don't have to worry about accidently picking up one of these stains at the local hardware or paint store because they are only available from professional houses.

I don't recommend that you use an NGR stain. If you do, you must also purchase some reducer and retarder made by the same manufacturer as the stain. The reducer is used to control the depth of the stain. The retarder will help when you brush on the stain. When you are working a large surface, use a large brush to reduce the chances of lapping.

Fig. 6-6. Water stain is applied with a brush in long, continuous, overlapping strokes. Excess stain is wiped off with a rag.

If the stain will not go on without lap marks, wipe the surface with the solvent, reduce the stain with the solvent and try another coat. There is no need to wipe the surface after application because it will be dry by then. NGR stains will dry completely somewhere between 3 minutes and 30 minutes and they are compatible with any subsequent finish. This product takes practice to use and it costs at least twice as much as an oil stain.

Spirit stains represent an earlier stage of evolution in non-grain-raising staining. Spirit stains utilize alcohol-soluble, aniline dyes mixed with alcohol. Spirit stains dry even faster than NGR stains and they have the same lap mark problem. You can't shellac over a spirit-stained surface because the shellac will pick up the stain and the stains have a nasty habit of bleeding through finishes. You really shouldn't want to use spirit stains, but if you like a challenge, alcohol-soluble dyes are available from supply houses in 1-pound tins. You will have to add your own spirit.

Alcohol-soluble dyes have another convenient capacity. They can be added to shellac to give it a little color when you are doing patch work or cover-up work.

Oil Stains

Oil stains are most commonly recommended for beginners and for good reason. They are safe, effective, and moderately priced. Oil stains are divided into two categories: penetrating oil stains and pigmented oil stains. Basically, both categories of stain employ oil, turpentine, dryers, and coloring material.

Penetrating oil stain has a coloring agent that can be a dye. It is in a clear liquid form as opposed to the slightly opaque pigments found in pigmented oil stain. The penetrating oil stain has greater clarity and better penetration than the pigmented types and it is preferred in many instances. Penetrating oil stains will always be marked as such or as pure penetrating oil stain. These stains are becoming increasingly difficult to find. One company that still manufacturers them is Cook and Dunn.

Penetrating oil stains are non-grain-raising and they can be brushed or wiped on. When brushed on, the excess must be wiped off with a rag. These stains can be reduced with thinner and they are readily intermixable within the color ranges of one manufacturer. Penetrating stains are compatible with any finish. Some Danish-type oil finishes, however, might lift a little of the color. If a penetrating oil stain has been made with aniline dyes, it must be sealed with a dilute coat of shellac prior to application of a varnish finish. Product instructions should indicate whether or not this is necessary.

Pigmented oil stains use opaque pigments similar to colors ground in oil. These stains might not always be marked "pigmented." If the directions call for the product to be mixed before using, you can be sure it is a pigmented stain. On some occasions, it is desirable to avoid stirring up the can because the basic solution might have enough pigment in it. Try some on a scrap piece of wood. If you want more color, then stir the contents of the can. Pigmented stain is often preferred for antique work because the opaque nature of the pigmentation tends to hide some minor blemishes.

The procedure for applying a pigmented oil stain is the same as for the penetrating type or other stains. Brush the stain on liberally in the direction of the grain and allow it to soak for a minute or two. Then wipe dry with a clean cloth as shown in Figs. 6-7 and 6-8. Both types of stain require a 24-hour drying period. The pigmented stain can be lifted slightly with some types of oil finishes.

Pigmented oil stains also come in a variety known as pigmented wiping stains. These stains are somewhat thicker and they have a heavier concentration of pigment. They are even more opaque and should only be used when you are attempting to obscure rather than highlight the grain of a piece.

With oil stains, and all stains for that matter, the logical procedure should be from the lighter shades to the darker shades. If perchance your stain coat is too dark, rub the piece with fine steel wool and paint thinner, and wipe clean with paper towels. This procedure will not remove the stain entirely, but it should lighten it somewhat.

Varnish Stains

Varnish stains are used by the uninformed, and possibly lazy, or by those who are trying to conceal something. Varnish stains are no more than varnish mixed with pigment to give it an opaque nature. Because the coloring material is in the finish, the wood is never really stained. Varnish stains are available in hardware and paint stores, but they can be made by mixing small quantities of oil stain with any varnish that can be thinned with mineral spirits or turpentine.

Varnish stain is really an awful product that more often than not yields an ugly surface. Applied in one thin coat, it is barely acceptable. Applied in thick or multiple coats, it is the same as using paint. The only acceptable use of varnish stain is to conceal a surface such

Fig. 6-7. The application of an oil stain in the same manner as a water stain.

as a chest where an original white paint has bled through the stain coat. Even in situations that require some type of opaque covering, a wiping glazing that you prepare yourself is more desirable.

If you decide to use varnish stain, cut it with 1 part turpentine to 3 parts stain and brush on as you would any varnish. Allow the varnish stain to dry for 72 hours and rub down with 000 steel. Apply a final coat of clear varnish and allow to dry an additional 48 to 72 hours. Rub down with 00 or 000 steel, clean, and wax. This will not make varnish stain attractive, but it will look a heck of a lot better than if you followed the directions on the can.

Sealer Stains

Varnish stain is an attempt at a one-step finishing product. It fails admirably. Sealer stain is an attempt at a one-step finish. it succeeds admirably. Sealer stains might have a wax added to them to provide luster or they might use a dilute oil or resin base. Minwax is probably the best known of these products. It is available in a pleasant range of colors and it brushes on with ease, free of lap marks. When the stain coat dries, it can be rubbed with 000 steel wool and buffed to a mellow luster using a good paste wax. Minwax stains can be intermixed with each other and tinted with colors ground in oil. This stain does not provide a high-gloss finish, but it is nonetheless pleasing. If more is desired from the finish, it can be followed by Minwax brand Antique Oil which is a polymerized tung oil. The antique oil is a fine product that will give the surface more sheen and body. A shellac finish can be used over Minwax. If a varnish or lacquer finish is to be used, however, a sealer coat of shellac should first be applied.

188

Minwax stain and finishing products are especially good for wood finishing due to their simple and safe application for beginners. They are also pleasing to experienced workers.

It is possible to make your own sealer stain with little difficulty. Minwax Antique Oil or Watco Danish Oil Finish, an oil resin base product, can be mixed with colors ground in oil or universal colors (water based) and applied with a rag or brush. These approaches work especially well. They can be wiped off before drying if you don't like the color. See the section on foolproof finishes.

MIXING AND MAKING STAINS

After stripping a piece of furniture and preparing the surface, the average person makes his way to the local hardware store or paint store to purchase a can of stain. Once in the store, he is confronted with an array of cans, colors, labels, and instructions. There are multiple color charts, but even the novice knows you can't depend on a color chart. The clerk might have a Ph.D. in astrophysics, but never seems to know very much about the product being sold. Questions receive answers like, "Yeah, they're all good," or, "My Uncle Burt used that one on a snowy day in May and had good results."

Products will be purchased, taken home, tried, found disgusting, shelved, or given to an unloved relative. After some time, the purchase of a lot of brands, and a considerable expenditure of money, the weekend finisher will finally find a product that he likes and will use it for the rest of his life.

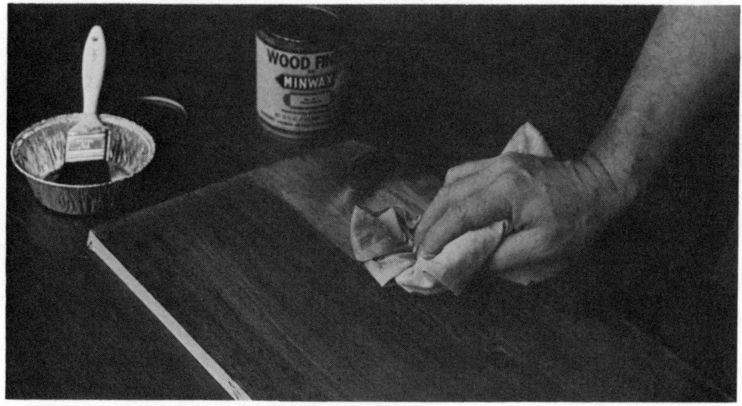

Fig. 6-8. Excess oil stain is wiped from the surface with a clean rag after a minute or two of absorption.

What this indicates is that people are persistent, occasionally a little silly, and that color is a very personal thing. Even after I find a brand I like, I will be dissatisfied (as my courage develops) with the colors and I will begin to experiment with a little of this and a little of that until I find something I like better. There is nothing wrong with this. But why not start at the middle, as opposed to the beginning, and save money and effort.

Mixing Commercial Stains

Despite the variety of stain colors available in commercial stains, there are only three colors that are important: walnut (which is brown), maple (which is yellow/brown), and mahogany (which is red or red/brown). Working with these three colors you can make almost any wood tone you want.

The only one of these stains that should ever be used by itself is walnut. Mahogany stain is the ugliest red or red/brown that you have ever seen. Every can should bear a label reading, "Warning—Horror—Use only as part of another product!"

If you like yellow furniture, then maple stain is for you. I have met people who like it, but *they* would probably bestow a decoration award upon the Black Hole of Calcutta.

There are red maple stains that are actually red/brown and acceptable. What this boils down to is that people like brown, and that variations of brown comprise the world of furniture colors. By intermixing stains and reducing them with turps or thinners, you can achieve the individual color or variation that pleases.

Mixing commercial stains as well as mixing your own stains is a trial and error process. Use some type of basic measuring device, a spoon or whatever, and make notes as you go. When you achieve a color that you really like, record it on an index card and save it for future reference. I must admit that I don't think I have ever mixed the same color twice.

Oil stains can be intermixed freely, but only mix stains made by the same manufacturer. Oil stains can be tinted with colors ground in oil and Japan colors to achieve the desired color. And they can be reduced with mineral spirits or turpentine.

Water stains can be reduced with water and intermixed freely, and they can be tinted with universal colors. The range of water stains is such that there should be no need to use other than a water stain to achieve the desired color. NGR stains can be intermixed and reduced with a special reducer made by the manufacturer. They should not be tinted with additional colors.

Table 6-2. Basic Stain Colors.

Walnut: Brown
Maple: Yellow-brown
Mahogany: Red /red-brown

MIXING GUIDE

Color	Wood	Stain
Light brown	Pine / maple	Walnut reduced
Medium brown	Pine /maple /cherry	Walnut reduced
Yellow-brown	Maple /oak	Walnut & maple
Red-brown	Maple /cherry /mahogany	Walnut & mahogany reduced
Deep red-brown	Mahogany	Walnut & mahogany
Drak brown	Walnut	Walnut

Tinting Products	Color	Name
Universal colors*	Yellow	Raw sienna /yellow ocher
Japan colors**	Red /red-brown	Burnt sienna
Colors in oils**	Walnut-brown	Burnt umber
Artist oil colors**	Green-brown	Raw umber

*May be used on water stains
**Use for oil stains only

To get you started on your mixing project, Table 6-2 represents a basic mixing guide. Please remember that this is only a starting point and that you must experiment and test colors on scrap wood.

Making Stains

Many professionals prefer to make their own stains. This might sound sophisticated, but in reality it is not. It is no more difficult to make your own stain from scratch than it is to mix commercial stains. When working with your own stain, you can obtain precisely the color you want while only mixing the small quantity you need.

To make an official oil stain, take coloring material as needed and add it to turpentine, boiled linseed oil (1 part oil to 5 parts turpentine) and a tablespoon of Japan dryer (as shown in Fig. 6-9). If this seems a little bothersome, don't worry about it. The unabashed truth of the matter is that you can omit the linseed oil and dryer and the stain will work almost as well. You can also substitute mineral spirits for the turpentine because it will save you money and the stain will dry faster. Could anything be easier than just mixing coloring material with mineral spirits? There is no catch. That's all there is to it.

When it comes to coloring materials, chances are that anything that will color the turpentine will make a stain. Berries, tea, brick dust, tobacco, food coloring, fabric dye or whatever else suits your fancy. You can experiment with these things because it's fun. For your furniture, it is best to stick to tried-and-true coloring agents because they come in standard colors that simplify mixing.

The best known of the color agents is Japan colors. Japan colors are ground pigment mixed with Japan dryers. Used directly from the can, Japan colors can be used to touch up furniture, cover burn marks, and match end grain. Japan colors can be used to color glazes for antique toning and cover-up work. They also tint shellac. Thinned slightly, these colors make an excellent flat paint that matches up with old milk paints very well. With additional thinning, they also make an excellent stain.

Japan colors are a super product and they can be found in any professional finishing shop. They are just not for the weekend craftsperson. These colors come in half-pint cans and they have a reasonably good shelf life. For the occasional user, they will probably dry up on the shelf. Japan colors cannot be treated as disposable items because they are too darn expensive. You are not likely to find them at even a large paint store, but they can be obtained from catalog houses or professional finishing supply houses.

Colors ground in oil serve the same purpose for weekenders as to Japan colors for the professional. This product is similar to Japan colors, but the pigment is less pure and ground in oil instead of a dryer. They come in tubes, they have a longer shelf life, and they are less expensive. Colors ground in oil are primarily intended to tint

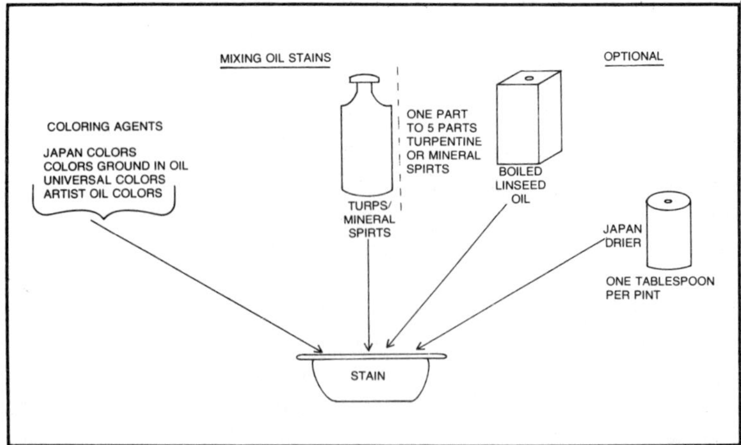

Fig. 6-9. Turpentine, boiled linseed oil, Japan driers, and coloring materials are shown as the basic ingredients of a homemade oil stain.

oil-base paints and they can be found in large or better paint supply houses.

In the past, you could pick these up in local paint stores, but they are giving way to universal colors and water-based paints. To make a stain, mix these colors with turpentine or mineral spirits using only small quantities at a time. Brush this stain on as you would any other stain, but you must constantly mix the stain or the pigment will fall out of solution. When you test this stain, allow the test piece to dry because the wet and dry colors will vary more than a commercial stain. Colors ground in oil can also be used to tint varnishes and make glazes.

Both Japan colors and colors ground in oil can be added to commercial oil stains to increase pigmentation. A highly opaque stain such as this can be useful when some degree of coverup is required.

The next product down the line is universal colors. This product comes by its name honestly because it will tint almost anything; Danish oils, varnish, oil paints, water stains, and water paints. Universal colors can be mixed with turpentine or mineral spirits in the same manner as Japan colors or colors ground in oil. Generally, I feel that colors ground in oil make a better stain. If universal colors are all that is available to you, they will do the job.

In a pinch, artist oil colors can be dissolved in turpentine to make a stain. The particle size of the pigment is larger in this product. Consequently, it tends to streak and not work as well. Remember, you are only bound by the limits of your imagination and creativity.

For all of these products, the methodology is the same. Mix the basic color with turpentine until the preferred depth of color is attained. Then tint with other colors until you have precisely the shade you want. Work on a small scale and record your proportions. Then make up the large batch when the proportions are known.

If the color goes awry in your sample batch, don't try to save it; you will go crazy and fail. Start a new mixture. After a stain is made up, test it on a sample piece of wood—preferably the same type of wood as the project—and allow it to dry because the wet and dry colors will be different.

When you are finally ready to stain the work piece, select a remote area and try a little of the stain again to see if it matches what you had in mind. The mixing chart shown in Table 6-3 should help start you on your way, but this is a direction not a road map. Combine it with common sense and observation.

Table 6-3. Mixing Guide to Homemade Oil Stains.

Wood	Primary Pigment	Secondary Pigment
Walnut	Burnt umber	-
Light walnut	Burnt umber	Reduced
Mahogany	Burnt umber	Burnt sienna
Mahogany (red)	Burnt sienna	Burnt umber
Cherry	Burnt sienna	Burnt umber/raw sienna
Pine (light)	Raw sienna/burnt umber	Reduced
Pine (medium brown)	Burnt umber	Raw sienna
Maple (light)	Raw sienna	Raw umber
Maple (red)	Burnt umber/burnt sienna	-
Maple (brown)	Burnt umber	-
Oak	Raw sienna	Raw umber
English oak (dark)	Burnt umber or Raw umber	Black

Water stains are best made up from commercial aniline dyes, but like oil stains they can be made from anything that is water soluble. Most noteworthy of the available products for water stains are blending stains and matching stains. These are products intended for use with padding lacquers in repair patch work. These products are water-soluble and they will make adequate stains. Dry colors that are used for coloring masonry materials will also make acceptable stains. Artist water colors or acrylic colors will readily dissolve in water for an acceptable stain. But they impart too much gloss to the surface and they are the least adequate mixing products for a water stain.

SHADING

The goal of some refinishers is to give a piece an overall sameness with an even, consistent color throughout. This might be all well and dandy for new furniture, but it is boring and inadequate for antiques. If an antique piece with an original finish is examined, considerable variation in color will be found. Tops of pieces will be lighter than sides due to polishing and due to bleaching by the sun. Tight areas such as those around turnings or moldings will be found to be darker from the accumulation of oils and polishes. Any area constantly touched by human hands will be worn and show color changes. The lower stretcher of a chair will be a light tone in worn areas, but as the stretcher moves to either leg post it will turn into a deeper brown—perhaps with a touch of red.

When a piece is stripped, all the color changes and variations of age are, unfortunately, also stripped away. Returning these shades to antiques in the staining process can make the difference between an acceptable job and a great job. There is no denying that this work is best done by persons with some artistic talent and a strong sense for color. If you are not one of those lucky people, then you will have

194

to travel the hard path of trial and error. Study will help to overcome this obstacle, but not book study. Make trips, with paper and pencil, to museums and study furniture and its color changes. Take appropriate notes. You will be surprised at how much detail you can see.

One of the principal methods of shading is the use of a wipe-on glaze to darken those areas that would normally accumulate dirt and darken with age. This work is fairly simple and effective. See the section on glazes.

Glazes work well for the dark areas, but they cannot handle the problems of toning down or highlight. For this work, take Japan colors or colors ground in oil and mix them on a pallet (a fancy term for an old piece of cardboard). Mix the colors directly from the tube as if you were going to do an oil painting. When the preferred color is achieved, mix the pigment with a little turpentine into a paint-like consistency, but not a thin stain.

Work the color into the selected areas with an artist brush. Or even better, use your fingers. Make sure to feather it by working it thin at the periphery so that it blends with the rest of the finish. Then wipe off the excess with a clean rag. These changes in color should be subtle. Work from light to dark. If the toner is too dark, rub it with 0000 steel wool and turpentine and wipe clean before it dries. With a little time, work, and patience, you will get the hang of it.

If only universal colors are available, mix them from the tube in the same manner as the colors ground in oil. To dilute the coloring material, use Watco or a penetrating oil finish as opposed to turpentine. If these products are not available to you, use a mixture of 1 part boiled linseed oil to 2 parts turpentine or 1 part varnish to 2 parts turpentine. Work the universal colors in the same manner as the colors ground in oil.

The shading process can begin as soon as the primary stain has dried to the touch. Once the shading has been applied, allow the piece to dry for at least 24 hours. If the preliminary stain is a water stain, allow it to dry overnight before beginning the shading work. In any event, shading is exacting work. But you will find the time and effort well rewarded.

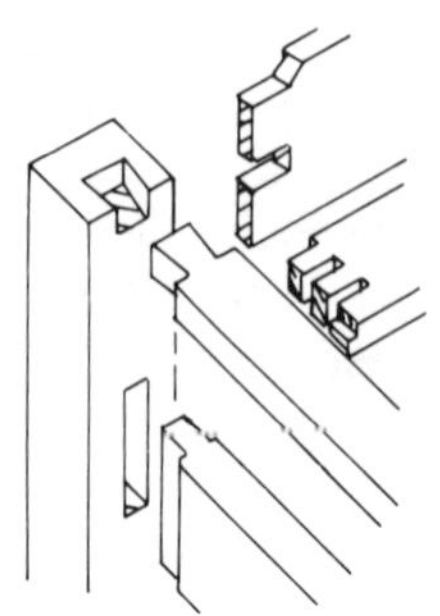

Chapter 7

Foolproof Finishes

Of particular interest to weekend restorers is a new generation of finishes that I like to call *foolproof finishes*. A wise man once said that there is nothing safe in the hands of a fool, and he was right. Suffice it to say that these finishes will offer the best opportunity for a fool to succeed. For the rest of us who are frequently less talented than we would like, but who are not fools, these finish approaches offer all that we could want: speed, simplicity, little possibility of error, and positive results.

The secret to these miracle finishes is oil. That is not surprising because oil has been the basis of furniture finishing for the last 200 years. Only recently have some of the problems been worked out.

LINSEED-OIL FINISH

Linseed oil is not a new finish, but it is the one that almost everyone has heard of. Few things elicit such awe and respect as a linseed-oil finish, but that's alright because most of the time it's a varnish finish moonlighting as an oil finish. Despite the famed value of a linseed-oil finish, I don't know any professional finisher who uses it except some of those patient fellows who make gunstocks.

Linseed-oil finishes are simple to apply and they are alcohol and heat resistant as well as beautiful. There are a few problems associated with linseed oil. It takes about six months to apply and then it never really dries.

Our ancestors used linseed oil as a finish because it was available and there was a lack of simple alternatives. The modern finisher has preferable alternatives. Therefore, I don't recommend

196

the use of a linseed-oil finish. For traditionalists, I will cover its application.

First, obtain a supply of boiled linseed oil. I stress *boiled* linseed oil because if you use plain linseed oil, there will be no hope of your project ever drying. Boiled linseed oil, oddly enough, is not boiled. It has chemical dryers added to it to assist the drying process. In the old days, the oil was boiled. Please don't try it. It is dangerous, incredibly messy, and the smell will lead your neighbors to take community action against you.

Not even the most traditional person uses linseed oil straight from the can. Mix 2 parts of the oil with 1 part turpentine. Some people prefer 3 parts oil to 1 part turpentine. There is no rule to govern this mixture. Basically, the turpentine acts as a vehicle to distribute the solid content of the oil so that it can permeate the wood with greater ease.

In any event, swab the first coat of the oil mixture on the piece and allow it to soak in for at least an hour. After an hour or so, wipe the piece as dry as possible with clean rags. Remember to dispose of the rags carefully. Wait approximately 2 weeks while the piece dries. Then repeat this first step application. Wait for the second coat to dry, usually in the vicinity of two to four weeks, and apply a third coat. Do not swab the third coat on, but rather apply it with your fingertips or with a wad of cloth. Apply sparingly, working it into the wood as much as possible. After this coat is applied, rub off as much of the oil as possible with clean rags. Treat this like a buffing operation as if you had waxed the piece. When the third coat has dried, apply a fourth coat in the manner of the third. At some distant, time when the fourth coat has dried, take 0000 steel wool and buff a small area of the surface. If after buffing you are satisfied with the luster, then fine, you are basically finished. If you are not content, keep applying the finish.

Some people claim that at least twenty coats are required. When you have arrived at some final point where the finish meets your needs, buff, wax and take a well-earned rest. Do not be surprised if on a very hot, humid day some of the oil bleeds through and the finish feels gummy or tacky. That is the nature of a linseed oil finish. This is a beautiful finish, but I just don't think it is worth the work.

Special Home-Brewed, Linseed-Oil Finish

It should be apparent that I have been trying to discourage you from using a linseed-oil finish because of the problems. But there are some ways to cheat. This approach doesn't quite fit my definition of a foolproof finish, but it does qualify as an almost foolproof finish.

Prepare a mixture of 1 part boiled linseed oil, 2 parts varnish (not spar varnish) and 3 parts turpentine. Mix this up in a glass jar and allow it to stand for a few hours. The jar must be stopped up. Swab the piece of furniture with this mixture—using either a brush or a rag—and allow it to soak for about two hours. Then wipe off the excess with a clean rag.

Allow this first coat to dry for at least a day. Then brush on a second coat. Do not swab on this second coat, but work it into the wood with the brush and allow it to soak and dry for another day. Apply a third coat with a wad of rag, sparingly, using a lot of elbow grease and pressure.

There should be no residue after this third coat, but if there is, wipe it off. If the finish is so tacky that it will not wipe, wet your rag with mineral spirits and this should do the trick. Allow this last coat to dry for two to three days and then buff with a 0000 steel wool pad. Prior to buffing, hold the palm of your hand with pressure to the surface for about 5 minutes. If the finish has not become tacky, you are ready to buff. If it has, allow greater drying time. After buffing, apply a coat of good paste wax.

This modified linseed-oil finish lends itself to all the desirability of an oil finish, but it cuts out much of the work. If you really want to cheat, I have heard of one gent who adds a tablespoon of linseed oil to a pint of varnish to give it the right smell and texture. But somehow that's just not in the spirit of things.

Here is one note of caution regarding the stain coat used under a linseed oil finish, (whether a true oil finish or the home brew that I have recommended). If an oil stain has been used, then the linseed oil might lift some of the stain. The pigments of the stain will dissolve somewhat in the oil or turpentine base of the finish. This isn't fatal. The stain coat will not be removed, but it will become just a shade lighter. Water stain, alcohol stain or NGR stains that employ aniline dyes are best used under an oil finish. They will remain undisturbed. If color loss becomes a problem, add some coloring material to the oil mixture in the form of colors ground in oil or by the direct addition of oil stain.

TUNG OIL

Tung oil, sometimes called China wood oil, is produced from the nuts of the tung tree. Similar to linseed oil, tung has a long history of involvement with wood finishing. Nevertheless it has escaped popular attention until recently.

Tung oils clearly fit the category of foolproof finishes. They wipe or brush on easily and dry quickly. There is no chance of lap marks or drips. Tung oil is also heat resistant, water resistant, and alcohol resistant. This is clearly the kind of finish that should not trouble even the most inexperienced worker.

All tung oils are not the same. The one you choose will make a difference in the final finish achieved. There are three distinct categories of oil: plain tung oil, tungseed oil, and polymerized tung oil. Plain (pure) tung oil is the least commonly available and most expensive of the three categories. This should not cause you great concern because this oil used by itself will never dry and it will cause you considerable headaches.

If you want to use pure tung oil, reduce it with at least one-half mineral spirits and brush it on or wipe it on. Allow the finish to dry and repeat coats as necessary to achieve the preferred luster. Each coat might take from 3 hours to a day to dry. After the final coat has dried, buff the piece with 000 or 0000 steel wool.

Tungseed oil, or tung oil varnish as it is sometimes called, is basically pure tung oil cut with mineral spirits or other agents to assist with the penetration and the drying process. In effect, when you mix tung oil with mineral spirits as described above, you are making a tungseed oil. You are generally better off with the commercially made tungseed oil than the homemade product because it contains special chemical dryers that work well. To use a tungseed oil finish, apply in the manner described for a tung oil finish.

The last of the three types of tung oils is a polymerized tung oil that is heat treated to change the molecular structure of the oil. This process increases the drying time. To use the polymerized tung oil, brush or pad on in quantity. Allow the oil to soak in and then remove the excess material with a clean rag. Allow to dry. Repeat this step until the preferred depth of finish is achieved. After the final coat has dried, buff with steel wool and wax. Directions for the use of a polymerized tung oil might change from one brand to another, so make sure to read the directions printed on the can.

The question remains as to which of the tung oil products is best to use. Plain tung oil can be dismissed due to the drying problems. The real choice is between tungseed oil (tung oil varnish) and polymerized tung oil. The tungseed oil will dry slightly faster than the polymerized tung oil, but the latter has a higher solids content. What this means is that it will take more coats of the tungseed oil to equal the finish of the polymerized tung oil. The variance in drying time is insignificant. Logic suggests that you should select the polymerized tung oil, but who said that you always have to be logical? I prefer the tungseed oil, but this is solely a matter of preference and you should feel free to choose either product.

Remember that an oil finish will have a tendency to pick up an oil stain. It will not affect a water or alcohol stain. If a penetrating-sealer stain such as Minwax is used, it will severely impede the drying time of the tung oil finish. It is not a good practice to use sealer stains or products with a paraffin base in conjunction with tung oil.

The home-brewed, linseed-oil finish mix previously discussed will also work well, if not better, with tung oil. Mix 1 part pure tung oil with 2 parts varnish and 3 parts turpentine to constitute the brew. Brush or swab on the mixture liberally and allow it to soak for 15 minutes, then wipe the excess with a clean rag. When the first coat has dried, usually after a day or so, apply a second coat in the same manner. Two coats will prove to be sufficient in most cases, but you can continue to apply the mixture until you obtain the preferred depth of sheen. Allow the final coat of the mixture to dry for 2 to 3 days and buff with 0000 steel wool followed by a good waxing.

Tung oil products do not work on an evaporation principle such as varnish. They are chemically reactive when combined with oxygen. Because these products work with an oxygen, a partially used can will combine with the oxygen remaining in the can to form a hard layer of film. In a short period of time the product can be ruined. To remedy this problem, transfer the tung oil to smaller cans as used, so that the can is always filled, or place marbles in the can to raise the liquid level to the top.

Tung oil is a substantial product well worth your interest and enthusiasm. A wonderful soft luster or hand-rubbed finish can be developed with it in a simple and efficient manner. If you find you cannot develop as high a gloss with this finish as you would like, then you can shellac or varnish over it. Varnish would be the preferred product over a tung oil base, but shellac will make a mechanical bond and it will work adequately.

DANISH OILS AND THE LIKE

There are a number of finishes under the generic name of Danish oils, penetrating finish, or rubbing oils. Primarily, all of these finishes are oils with polymerizing agents or resins added to them. Some are super while others are less impressive. One type of finish works primarily on an evaporation process. The liquid vehicle dries out and leaves a solid. The other type of finish is chemically reactive as with tung oil. The chemically reactive finishes are by far the better products.

If you went to an old-time cabinetmaker and said you wanted a hand-rubbed Danish-oil finish on your furniture he would say, "Yup no problem." When you left the shop, the old-timer would take some varnish and mix it with an equal amount of turpentine and, presto, he would have a Danish oil to be hand rubbed into the finish.

In this case, the Danish oil would be no more than dilute varnish. So are some of those sold on the market today. Successive coats of the dilute varnish penetrate the wood deeply and they eventually build up to a fine finish. The dilute varnish is applied sparingly with friction so that rubbing between coats does not become necessary.

Some other Danish oils combine penetrating oils, such as linseed oils or tung oil, with natural resins and dryers. This process also works and it is approximately the same as the homemade, oil-varnish-thinner mixtures mentioned earlier. In any event, all of the Danish oils meet the ease and simplicity test. There is almost no way that you can mess up one of these finishes, but there are other far superior Danish-oil-type products.

WATCO AND ANTIQUE OIL

As foolproof finishes go, Watco Danish Oil is one of the best available in the marketplace today. Watco brushes on without drips or lap marks and dries to the touch in a few hours. Watco is a penetrating resin and oil product; linseed oil is converted into a resin with the subsequent addition of solvents and dryers. This oil is a chemically reactive product that dries completely and deeply in the wood fiber. The result is that the wood is made stronger.

Watco and similar products are far superior to the dilute varnish type of products. Some quality cabinetmakers that I know will give their custom furniture a coat of Watco prior to a final finish of lacquer. These people are perfectionists and they simply feel that a sealer coat of Watco is better than sanding sealer.

Watco, like other oil type products, should be used over a water stain, a NGR stain or an alcohol stain. Watco has a line of their own stains that are compatible with the product. If you like, you could mix colors ground in oil or universal colors with the Watco to make your own sealer stain. This method has many adherents because it allows a great deal of control over the staining process.

Fig. 7-1. Watco oil is brushed on either with or across the grain. Nevertheless, the last strokes should be with the grain.

Brush the oil on liberally and cover all surfaces (Fig. 7-1). Once the piece is coated, use your hand or a wad of clean cloth to work the oil into the wood. Use circular, figure-8 movements or cross-hatch movements, but make the last strokes with the grain. At this point, you do not walk away from the project. Stay right there to watch. The wood surface will ignore the oil in some areas. In other areas, the wood will soak up the oil and dry.

As some areas dry out, apply additional oil so that the surface remains uniformly wet. This touch-up work should be accomplished within the first 30 minutes. The next step is to remove excess oil from the surface of the project. The wipe-down should occur approximately 45 minutes after the finish was started. Don't wait more than an hour. This is not 45 minutes after you touched up the dry spots, but a total of 45 minutes starting from when your brush first touched the work surface. Use clean rags and wipe down the entire piece as in Fig. 7-2. Make sure there are no traces of the oil. Wisdom dictates that you wipe the piece down a second time with fresh rags.

The only thing you can do wrong with this finish is to leave the oil on the surface more than the allocated hour. In such a case, the surface will remain tacky. If the surface remains tacky after an overnight drying period, you will know that an error has been made. But is isn't a fatal one. Wet down the entire piece with fresh Watco and wipe it clean with dry rags. The new coat will dissolve the old one and bring you back to ground zero. Allow the piece to dry and start the application process over again.

Presuming that the first application of Watco was successful, allow the piece to dry for 24 hours and rub it down lightly with 0000 steel wool. After the rubdown, apply a fresh coat of the oil in the manner outlined previously. Don't be as liberal with the application of the oil.

There is no rule as to how many coats of finish will be required because it is a matter of taste. One coat of the finish is not likely to be enough. Three to four coats seem to suit most users. I have heard of some finishers using upwards of 15 coats, but then there are workoholics in every profession.

After the final coat of the finish has dried, there are a few options available to you. The simplest option is to take 0000 steel wool and rub down the entire piece. Follow the rubdown with a good coat of paste wax. Another approach, albeit somewhat more complicated, is to take a 400-grit wet/dry paper and dip it in some fresh Watco and proceed to rub down the piece. The extremely fine-grit, wet/dry paper used in conjunction with fresh Watco, that serves as a lubricant, will polish the surface and leave a smooth-as-silk finish. Immediately following the rubdown, wipe the piece dry with fresh rags and allow it to stand an additional 24 hours. After drying, apply wax and buff.

The third option is to apply wax with a pad of 0000 steel wool. The cutting action of the steel wool will be minimized by the lubricants in the wax, but the overall effect should be one of a satin smooth finish. Make sure, as with any rubbing-down process, to rub only in the direction of the grain. Following the wax rubdown, buff the piece to your heart's content.

Another product of high quality that is comparable to Watco Danish Oil is Minwax Antique Oil. The Minwax product is a polymerizing tung oil and it is different than the Watco Oil. But the

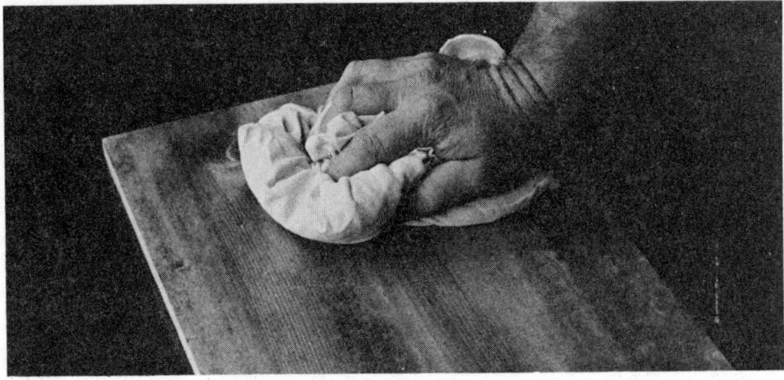

Fig. 7-2. After 45 minutes' drying time, the oil is wiped from the surface with a clean rag.

overall effectiveness of the product is the same as the Watco product. The Minwax Oil dries somewhat harder and with more sheen than the Watco Oil. The nice part about the Minwax Antique Oil is that it is compatible with Minwax stains and it can be purchased at most good hardware stores. On occasion the Watco Oil can be difficult to obtain. The Antique Oil is applied in the same manner as the Watco oil.

Both Watco and Minwax Antique Oil will provide a more than adequate finish, but they do not provide a high-gloss mirror finish. If the finish proves to be less than preferred, you could lacquer or varnish over either product. It is not advisable to shellac over a Danish-oil-type base product.

Watco Oil and Minwax Antique Oil represent the best efforts of science, to date, in making wood finishing both simple and foolproof. I am confident that this type of product offers the greatest possibility of ease and success to the amateur refinisher.

SANDING SEALER

Sanding sealer is a product primarily intended to be used as a finish preparatory to the application of a sprayed lacquer finish. This is a nifty little product that qualifies as a fast and simple finish all by itself. Sanding sealer is heat resistant and moisture resistant and withstands wear and abrasion well. It is not alcohol resistant. There is some possibility of lap marks with sanding sealer, but they are minimal when compared to those left by almost any other brush-on finishing product. They can be avoided with modest care.

Sanding sealer can be applied over any type of stain or wood filler, but the surface should be smooth prior to the application of the sealer. Sealer is ready to use from the can under most circumstances. If it appears thick, add a smidgen of lacquer thinner, say, half an ounce to a pint of sealer. Apply the sealer with a clean brush; use the largest size appropriate for the project. Work the sealer into the wood with any stroke that suits your fancy, but make sure to level the finish with overlapping strokes with the grain (as shown in Figs 7-3 and 7-4). As with any other brush-on finish, it is best to work on horizontal surfaces. Don't be impatient. Work one surface and allow it to dry to the touch. Then turn the piece and work another surface. The additional time spent in this manner will produce results.

A sanding sealer finish will dry in as few as one and one-half to two hours and it will be ready to work in three hours. It is best not to push the drying time and allow the finish to dry overnight. When

Fig. 7-3. Sanding sealer is brushed on first with the grain and then it is worked across the grain.

dry, the finish will have to be rubbed down. With sealer, you must use sandpaper and not steel wool. Use a 220- or 240-grit finishing paper to accomplish the rubdown. Working with the grain at all times (as shown in Fig. 7-5). Residue from the sandpaper can be cleaned up with a rag lightly dampened with mineral spirits.

If the first coat of sanding sealer has provided the depth of finish and sheen that you want, then finish the job off with a coat of wax. If the sanding sealer has not provided as much of a finish as you had planned on, you should *not* apply a second coat. It will only gum up the works. This problem can be easily remedied by the application of a coat of lacquer or varnish, but not shellac over the base coat of sealer. In most cases, sanding sealer yields a soft, lustrous finish

Fig. 7-4. The final sealer brush stroke is with the grain.

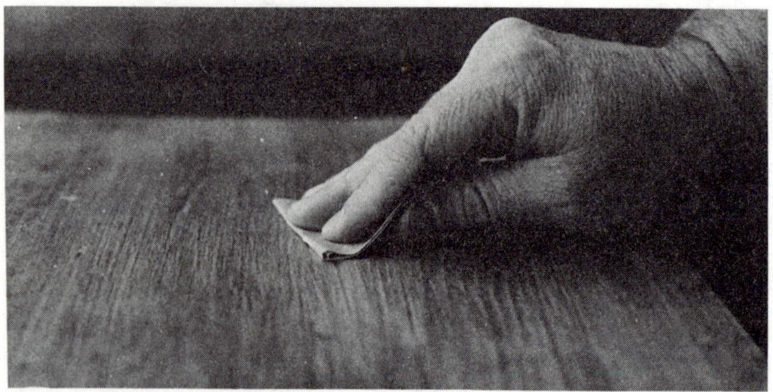

Fig. 7-5. After three hours' drying time the sealer is lightly sanded with a 240-grit finishing paper.

that is very attractive. This is a simple finish that allows for little possibility of error.

WAXING AND HOT WAX

There seem to be few things in life that discourage people more than waxing. I actually enjoy waxing a piece of furniture. After all your preparation and work, the final truth is revealed with the waxing. Whether you do or don't like waxing isn't important because all furniture should be waxed. With each refinishing job, the final finish should be waxed. This is necessary not only to protect the furniture, but also to bring the finish to its final depth and sheen. In addition to the initial waxing, all furniture should be waxed at least once a year (twice a year is preferable).

There are three reasons why furniture should be waxed. The first reason is cosmetic; a waxed surface looks better than a boring, disinterested, unwaxed surface. Far more important than cosmetics is the matter of moisture. The primary reason for putting a finish on a piece of furniture is to add to its stability by retarding the loss or gain of moisture. Wax serves as a secondary protective system in sealing the wood and preventing further loss or gain of moisture. Wax also protects furniture from the direct assaults of spilled liquids such as alcohol and water.

The third function of wax is to protect a furniture surface from abrasion. The constant use of furniture naturally results in scratching and scuffing. This can be greatly reduced by the use of wax. Somewhere in your neighborhood there must be one person who is out every couple of weekends washing and waxing his car. Surely there is another neighbor who has never disturbed the virgin dirt on his car. Look at the two cars and then decide how necessary wax is.

Which wax to use always poses an interesting question. There is the handy liquid wax, the resistant old paste wax, or the new super-silica spray wax that buffs itself to a luster while the can does a soft shoe back to the shelf. Well, for a start, discard the modern silicone waxes. These new waxes, in some instances, have ingredients that can damage a shellac finish. They provide no more protection against moisture than other waxes and no protection from abrasion. The silicone waxes also play havoc with a finish and wood surface if you ever have to strip a piece. Keep plastic waxes for your plastic furniture!

Liquid waxes are basically soft waxes reduced in turpentine or a similar petroleum product. These waxes provide a decent sheen and protection from moisture, but virtually no protection from abrasion. Because liquid waxes are thinned waxes, the surface coat provided by a single wax job is far less than that of a paste wax. Consequently, you must wax more often. By process of elimination, we arrive at old-fashioned paste wax. I endorse it wholeheartedly. Paste waxes offer the maximum protection from moisture and abrasion while requiring less attention than any other form of wax. Paste waxes require a little more work than liquid waxes because they employ harder waxes. In the long run, they are worth the effort.

Most paste waxes are made of the same ingredients, but the proportions differ. Commercial waxes are made of carnuba, beeswax, paraffin, and turpentine (as a vehicle). The better waxes are the harder ones that have a greater percentage of carnuba—a wax derived from a palm leaf. As the carnuba content of a wax goes down, the paraffin content goes up. Hence there is less cost. There are some very fine, hard, English furniture waxes on the market, but you need to just about take out a mortgage on the house to purchase an 8-ounce tin. Most brands don't break down the contents on the label. I can tell you that Treewax, Butcher's Wax, and Bowling Alley Wax are all good, reasonably priced waxes.

There is no art to applying a good wax job, but neither should it be treated with contempt. Take a clean piece of rag, cut it into a workable pad, and rub it through the wax until the rag is saturated with wax. Apply your wax pad to the wood surface in a circular motion—covering all areas. Recoat the pad with wax as necessary. Don't slop the wax on; a thin coat is better. I have been told that the professional manner to apply wax is to prepare a wad of several layers of cheesecloth wrapped around a quantity of wax so that the heat and pressure of the hand forces the wax through the cloth and onto the wood surface. I will stick to a plain piece of cloth. When you are finished applying the wax, leave the cloth in the can where it will be ready for use next time. Remember to fit the lid of the can on tightly.

The natural tendency in waxing is to buff the wax off almost as soon as it is applied. But that only defeats the purpose. If you buff the wax immediately. it will be easier to work because you are removing most of the wax with your buffing rag. Manufacturers' instructions usually indicate that you should start buffing when the wax is almost dry. The drying time for paste wax ranges from 20 to 30 minutes, but you are better off buffing on the late side than the early side.

When it comes time for buffing, I like to employ a three-rag system. The first buffing is done with a clean cotton cloth and it is for the purpose of removing excess wax that has not dried. For buffing, the rag is moved in a circular motion with a medium pressure. Immediately following this buffing comes the second buffing with a clean cotton rag. The heat and friction of the second buffing will develop a soft luster. The third and final buffing is accomplished with a soft flannel rag. The flannel buffing produces a rich sheen that makes all the work worthwhile.

Allow your rags to dry out after the buffing process and then store them until the next use. You can get several uses out of a set of rags before they have to be washed. Through the course of the year after the waxing, an occasional buffing will return the piece to a nice sheen.

Buffing wheels, consisting of a circular rubber pad and a lamb's wool cover, are available as attachments for electric drills. The buffing attachments might serve many functions, but one of them is definitely not buffing furniture. An electric drill develops too high an RPM for waxing purposes. Consequently, the heat build-up melts the wax while the centrifugal force hurls it all over the place. The end result of this approach is a botched wax job and a gummed up wool pad. If you had thoughts of simplifying your project in this manner, put those thoughts to rest unless you are willing to purchase a special wax buffer that operates at a suitably low RPM. The special buffers will work adequately, but not as well as your hand. Save yourself a few dollars.

Brown Wax

Paste waxes fall into three color ranges: yellow, amber, and a reddish/brown. Some furniture finishers prefer to use dark waxes that will hide nicks and scratches (a not-altogether-bad idea). You are not likely to find brown wax on the shelf of the local store. You will probably have to make your own. It only takes a few minutes to make your own wax, but you have to be careful if you don't want to burn the house down.

Take a cup of commercial paste wax and place it in a pan. Add a tablespoon of turpentine and a tablespoon of brown paste shoe wax. Ideally, the melting should be done with a double boiler that will minimize any fire hazzard. If you don't have a double boiler or if you don't want to use the one you have, then substitute a small saucepan with a lid.

Place the saucepan over the lowest heat possible on your range and allow the mixture to melt. If the mixture starts to smoke or crackle, remove it from the heat and allow it to cool down for a minute or two. Then place it back on the heat until it melts entirely. Should the wax mixture superheat and catch fire, just place the lid on the pan and the fire will shortly go out.

Once off the range, the brown wax mixture should be allowed to cool and harden. The heating process and the subsequent cool-down will have resulted in the evaporation of some of the turpentine that is necessary to maintain the flexibility of the wax. To remedy this problem, add a small amount of turpentine to the wax and mix until you obtain the normal consistency of the wax. Apply the brown wax in the same manner as you would any other paste wax. Leftover wax can be placed in an old jar and kept for the next use.

A Wax Finish

Wax serves the same purpose as a furniture finish. It protects the wood surface from gains or losses in moisture. For that reason, wax can be used as a finish. There is no finish more foolproof than wax. Wax is simple, fast, efficient and it will cover any stain coat after a sufficient number of applications. The wax will buff to a pleasing, soft luster. A wax finish only provides modest protection against alcohol and heat, but that is not a real problem because you need only to rewax the piece to restore the finish.

There is nothing radical or amateurish about deciding upon a wax finish. It was a common form of furniture finishing during the 17th century, the 18th century, and the 19th century. The one thing to bear in mind before deciding upon a wax finish is that it will play havoc with future attempts to finish the piece in any other manner. Once wax permeates the wood fiber, which it does well, it will give you a bear of a time trying to get it out. By working with turpentine, alcohol stains and shellac, however, the problem can be overcome—but it is work. Don't be overly discouraged by this. Once you have opted for a wax finish, there should be no need to ever consider another finish.

Prior to waxing, make sure the surface is clear of dust and hand oil by wiping it with a rag dampened in mineral spirits. After the mineral spirits have dried, you can proceed to the wax step. There is, however, an optional step that can be taken to provide better results. Brush on a wash coat of shellac consisting of 1 part shellac to 5 parts alcohol. The wash coat of shellac will seal the wood and allow for a little more body in the final wax finish. If you ever decide to change the finish, the wash coat of shellac will lessen the potential of problems. Allow the shellac coat to dry for at least three hours.

Once the shellac coat has dried, pad on your wax in a circular motion and work the wax well into the fiber of the wood. Allow the wax to dry for 20 to 30 minutes as you would with a normal waxing operation. Then buff the wax with a clean rag. Buff the piece a second time with a new rag. Do not go on to a third buffing with a polishing cloth. Allow the wax to dry overnight. Prior to applying the second coat of wax, brush with an application of wax in the same manner as the first coat was applied. Apply at least three coats of wax in this manner (allowing a day between each). Follow the last coat with the three-rag buffing process previously outlined. If after the final buffing you are not happy with the body or luster of the finish, continue to apply coats of wax in the same manner as the initial coats. But it probably will not change very much. Buff the piece at least once a week for the first few weeks after the final coat of wax has been applied. If, at any point, the wax appears to be wearing thin, apply a fresh coat of wax. Provide your antique treasure with a fresh coat of wax each year, or as often as warranted, and it should last a lot longer than you will.

Hot Waxing

Hot waxing is one of those little tricks used by professionals, but is not mentioned to any great degree in articles or journals. Hot waxing is another way of applying a wax finish to a piece of furniture. It yields far superior results while requiring no more effort or talent.

By melting wax, the deep penetrating qualities of a liquid wax are duplicated without sacrificing the hard wax content of a paste wax. Hot waxing works best on open-grained hardwoods such as walnut, mahogany, or oak. With a hot-wax finish, there is no need to use wood fillers because the wax will fill the pores. We have a late 18th-century walnut table in our kitchen that went from shabby to beautiful with the application of a hot wax finish. The table gets two coats of fresh paste wax each year and it remains lovely even with hard use.

For the application of a hot wax, follow the same preparation steps as required for a wax finish. The wood surface should be as smooth as possible and cleaned with mineral spirits prior to the wax application. Seal the wood with a wash coat of shellac and allow it to dry for three hours. It is not necessary to rub down the shellac coat once it has dried.

The components (Fig. 7-6) of a hot wax are paste wax, shoe wax, mineral spirits or turpentine, and a suitable vessel for mixing. It is not essential to color the hot wax, but it is a good practice because the color material will cover small scratches and abrasions that would otherwise be noticeable. With a mahogany finish, use cordovan shoe paste wax. For an old English finish, add a small amount of black shoe paste wax. Mix a cup of paste wax with a tablespoon of turpentine and a tablespoon of brown shoe wax (for most wood colors). If only a small amount of wax is required, the proportions can be halved.

Place the mixture in a double boiler, if available, and heat until all the wax is dissolved. When the wax is liquid, stir lightly. If a double boiler is not available, put the wax mixture in a small pyrex bowl or similar container and place it in a saucepan partially filled with water. The water should help to dissipate the heat build-up, but make sure the stove burner is set to its lowest position. If the wax superheats, it will burst into flames. Watch the mixture for smoking or crackling. In such a case, the pan should be removed from the burner immediately. Keep the lid to the pan handy so that it can quickly be dropped in place to smother a fire. When the wax is hot and liquid, pad it on generously with a clean piece of cloth. Work the wax quickly because it will cool rapidly and begin go coagulate. If the wax thickens too much during the application process, reheat it and finish the application. Unused wax, once cooled, can be used for a future project or mixed with turpentine to form a brown wax.

Allow the hot wax to dry for two to three hours; then brush it vigorously with a shoe brush. If there are thick patches or globs of wax that resist the shoe brush, apply a little heat and they will work out. A hot comb or a blow dryer can be ideal for this purpose. Following the brushing, use the three-rag buffing system to bring up

Fig. 7-6. Colored shoe wax, paint thinner, paste wax, and a suitable melting vessel are the ingredients of a hot wax.

a beautiful sheen. Apply a coat of fresh, paste wax the next day and buff in the usual manner. If at any point the finish begins to wear through or become dull, just apply a fresh coat of wax. If you have never seen a hot-wax finish, you will surely be impressed by the warm, soft sheen that can be achieved with wax.

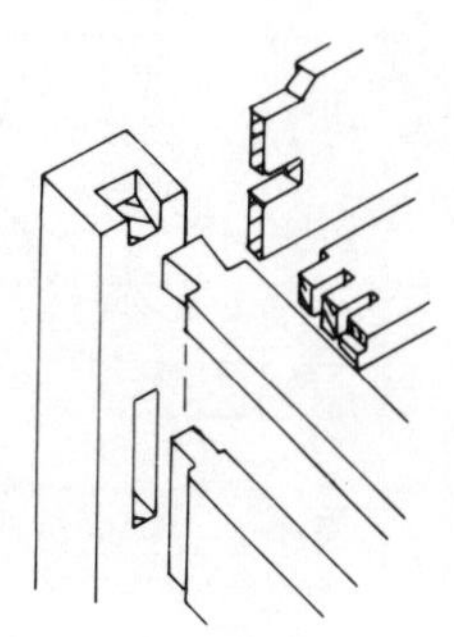

Chapter 8
Traditional Finishes

One comment frequently heard from do-it-yourself finishers is that they don't want their project to look like an amateur-night special, one that looks like polyurethane was poured on straight from the can—replete with specks of dust, air bubbles and runs. Your friends and relatives might utter words like "marvelous" and "wonderful" when they look at the finish job, but they are really thinking that they would rather decorate their homes with plastic TV tables than have something looking like that.

There is one secret to a smooth, lustrous finish that looks like a professional job and that is *rubbing down*. Almost every type of finish needs to be rubbed down so that the surface is smoothed and leveled between each coat and after the final finish coat. Regardless of what type of finish you choose, rubbing down more than any one thing will make the difference between a project that looks professional and one that looks amateurish.

RUBBING DOWN AND ABRASIVES

The most traditional and well-known abrasives for finish work are pumice and rottenstone. Pumice is crushed volcanic rock. Rottenstone is decomposed limestone. Pumice and rottenstone were the abrasive products used during the historic and antique periods. These products are still preferred by many professionals. I do not recommend them for the occasional finisher.

Pumice comes in different grades of coarseness (see Table 8-1). For rubbing down a finish, 3/0 is most commonly used. If you decide to use pumice, a rubbing block must be prepared. Pumice is a

Table 8-1. Abrasives.

Pumice Grades	
1/0, 2/0, 3/0, 4/0	
4/0 is the finest.	

Rottenstone	
One grade for polishing.	

Steel Wool	
4/0	—For final rubdown for high-gloss finish.
3/0	—For final rubdown; rub down between coats.
2/0	—For rubdown between coats.
1/0	—For stubborn problems such as lap marks, etc.
No. 1	—For furniture stripping.
No. 2	—For furniture stripping; top layers of paint only.
No. 3	—Not for furniture.
4/0 is the finest; No. 3 is the most coarse.	

powerful abrasive; it has the potential of cutting through the finish to the wood surface with ease.

Pumice must be used with the rubbing block to avoid mishap. The block can be made from a scrap of wood approximately 3 by 5 inches. Glue a piece of felt to the bottom of the block and wrap the block in a clean cotton cloth.

Pumice can be used with either water or oil as a lubricant, but only with oil in the case of a shellac finish. In general, oil—usually a high grade mineral oil—is recommended because it reduces the cutting action of the pumice more than water would. The risk of rub-through is thereby lessened.

When the block is prepared, dip it in a small pan filled with the oil and then in another pan containing a layer of pumice. Apply the pumice to the finish with a reciprocating movement in the direction of the grain. Work lightly, evenly, and carefully. To the degree possible, have the successive strokes of the rubbing block coincide as you move across the width of the surface (but avoid overlapping). In this case, overlapping might wear the finish too thin in the lapped areas. When this process is complete, remove the pumice residue with a clean rag moistened with water or oil and then buff the surface with a clean, dry rag. It is best to use pumice only after the final coat has been applied. If used between coats, it might hamper the bond of the subsequent coats.

Rottenstone is not a cutting abrasive (as is pumice). It is a polishing agent. If you want a high-gloss finish, then rottenstone is the final step for you. In most cases, especially with regard to country furniture, a rottenstone polish is not necessary. Prior to applying rottenstone, allow the piece to dry at least 3 days after the pumice rub because the finish might have been softened. Apply the rottenstone in the same manner as the pumice, but use water as the lubricant instead of oil.

Following the rottenstone polish, clean with a moist rag, and then use a dry rag. Allow the piece to dry an additional three days. Please bear in mind that I *do not* recommend the use of pumice and rottenstone by novices. Pumice entails the unnecessary risk of destroying your project. Sandpaper or steel wool will fulfill the same functions as the pumice, but without any risk of harm.

Sandpapers

The principle products used for between-coat rubdowns and for final rubdowns are sandpaper and steel wool. Either can be used with little risk or fear of working through the finish. Sandpaper is more popular than steel wool.

Purchasing sandpaper is not always the easiest task in the world. There are many varieties: aluminum oxide, garnet, flint, open coat, closed coat, etc. Sandpaper is made of four substances, flint, garnet, aluminum oxide, and silicone carbide. To simplify matters, omit the flint papers. These are the least expensive and the most readily available at local hardware stores. Flint paper was great in the old days when there was no other choice. Compared with garnet or aluminum oxide papers, it just does not match up. Flint paper wears down very easily so it becomes a matter of being penny-wise and pound-foolish.

The principle products you should be concerned with are garnet paper and aluminum oxide papers. The garnet papers are the red/brown papers. The aluminum oxide papers are tan/beige. Aluminum oxide is the harder of the two papers and it is preferred for machine sanding. You can use either.

Sandpapers are graded according to the degree of abrasion such as 1/0, 2/0, 3/0, etc. The more zeros in the grading, the finer and less abrasive the paper. Sandpapers are marked by grit as well as by grade. The grit markings indicate the number of grits per square inch. The finer the paper, the higher the grit number. A high zero number will accompany a high grit number. Most hardware stores sell sandpaper by the grit number and not by the grade.

Sandpapers are divided into three categories: cabinet papers, finishing papers, and wet/dry papers. The difference between these designations is the paper used to form the backing. Cabinet paper has a heavier backing than finishing paper and it is associated with the lower grade and grit numbers. The thinner backing used with finishing paper allows for greater flexibility. Wet/dry papers are silicon carbide papers with a waterproof backing and are associated with the very fine grits used for polishing. These papers, as indicated by their name, can be used with lubricants.

Gradings, grits and such stuff might sound complicated at first, but they're not really. Table 8-2 lists sandpapers by grade and grit. Spend a minute or two studying it and matters should be cleared up considerably. There will be no need to use all the papers listed for refinishing. After stripping a piece of furniture, use a 180-grit (fine) paper followed by a 220-grit (very fine) paper.

If the surface is particularly rough, start with a 150-grit paper and work to a 220-grit paper. For rubbing down between finish coats, use a 220-grit (very fine) paper, a 240-grit (extra fine), or a 280-grit (extra fine) paper. The final finish coat is rubbed with a 240- or 280-grit paper.

If a mirror-like polish finish is preferred, the final coat is rubbed with a 320- or 400-grit wet/dry paper and oil. The final rubdown with a wet/dry paper follows after a rubdown with the extra-fine-grit sandpaper. The wet/dry paper serves the same purpose as rottenstone in providing a polish finish.

Table 8-2. Sandpapers.

Grade	Grit	
1/0	80	
2/0	100	Cabinet Papers
3/0	120	
4/0	150	
5/0	180 fine	
6/0	220 very fine	Finishing Papers
7/0	240 extra fine	
8/0	280 extra fine	
-	320 polishing	
-	400 polishing	Wet/Dry Papers
-	500 polishing	
-	600 polishing	

Paper backing graded:
    A: soft and thin for finishing papers.
C & D: thicker backing for cabinet paper.

When rubbing down a piece between coats, use a sanding block to assure even pressure and a level surface. Sanding is always done in the direction of the grain. All residue from the sanding process must be cleaned prior to applying another coat of the finishing material. When using a wet/dry paper for a final polish, water or oil can be used as a lubricant. Be sure to clean oil residue carefully and allow the finish to dry for two to three days before waxing. Don't throw away your sandpaper when the job is complete. Worn pieces of sandpaper can be used for turning and carvings.

Steel Wool

If sandpaper is the simple alternative to pumice, then steel wool is the simple alternative to sandpaper. Steel wool is effective, readily available, economical, and easy to figure out. People steer away from steel wool because they remember the bundle of tangled wire in pop's tool box that could rip rust from old pipes and send spiny wire bristles into your hands. To be sure, No. 3 steel wool will do this, but extra-fine steel wool can be rubbed across a baby's bottom, or your finest furniture, without leaving a mark.

Steel wool comes in grades 1 through 3 and 1/0 through 4/0 (see Table 8-1). No. 3 steel wool is never used on furniture unless you have a grievance to reap on it. No. 2 steel wool can be used to remove difficult paint, but preferably the top layers only because it will scratch the wood surface. No. 1 and 1/0 (0) steel-wool pads are predominantly used for paint removal, while 1/0 (0) and 2/0 (00) are used to remove an old shellac, varnish, or lacquer finish.

For rubbing down between coats 2/0 and 3/0 (000) steel wool can be used—although 3/0 is most commonly used. A 3/0 or 4/0 pad is used for the final rubdown. A polish effect can be obtained by using light mineral oil and a 4/0 pad for the final rubdown. For a greater sheen, the 4/0 rubdown can be followed by a rubdown with a lubricated wet/dry paper.

Steel wool can be a problem with some open-grained woods such as oak or hickory, if the grain has not been filled, because the steel wool can catch in the pores of the wood. Steel wool should not be used for rubbing down sanding sealer. Noting these exceptions, in most cases steel wool is easier to use than sandpaper.

To rub down with steel wool, unravel the pad so that it can be broken into smaller wads (as in Fig. 8-1). To use an entire steel-wool pad is a plain and simple waste of money. As a steel-wool pad becomes clogged, rotate it to clean surfaces. Then turn it inside-out and do the same.

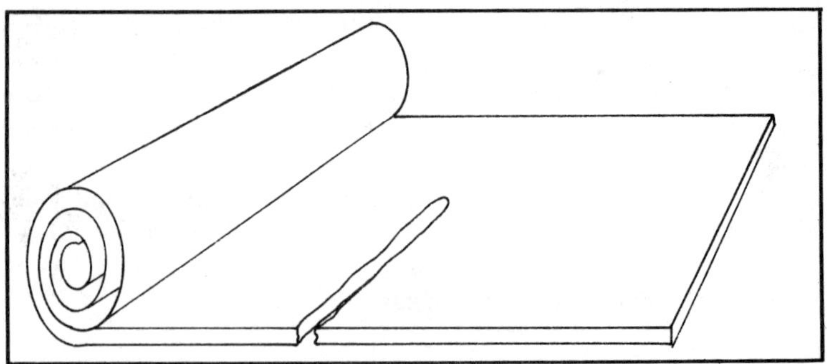

Fig. 8-1. Steel wool is unrolled and ripped into wads for maximum economy.

As with sandpaper, the steel-wool pad should be used with a reciprocating motion in the direction of the grain. Successive strokes of the pad can overlap because there is a little fear of rubbing through the finish. It is difficult to tell someone how much pressure to exert on the pad. It's the sort of thing that you have to get a feel for. Start with the same pressure you would use with a scouring pad on a frying pan and work up or down from there.

When rubbing down a finish, it is best to work outdoors in good sunlight. Indoors, a good overhead light will do the trick. After a surface is rubbed down, lift the piece slightly from different sides to expose the surface to light from different angles. Moving a piece in this manner will reveal snags or other imperfections that were not noticeable with the overhead light. It is necessary to remove all snags prior to the application of a second coat of a finishing material. When removing a snag, don't be afraid to switch to a coarser grade of steel wool or sandpaper if it will do the job. Don't recoat until it is removed because subsequent coats will repeat or amplify the snag.

Turnings present less of a problem for steel wool than they do for sandpaper due to the flexibility of the steel wool. When rubbing down turnings, rotate the steel wool piece around the circumference of the turning. Turnings were originally sanded on the lathe as the work piece turned between the centers. When rubbing down, you want to replicate the original smoothing motion. If the finish material has built up in tight areas between the turnings and cannot be reached with steel wool, then use 240-grit sandpaper folded so that it can be drawn through the problem area. Use the sandpaper in the same manner that you would use a buffing rag on your shoes (pulled back and forth).

After a piece has been rubbed down, all traces of the steel wool must be removed prior to recoating. A clean rag and a soft bristle brush should easily remove any traces of the wire bristles. If a problem is encountered, a rag dampened with mineral spirits should do the trick. If you choose to clean up a varnish finish with mineral spirits, allow the piece to dry for three or four hours before recoating. The mineral spirits might have softened the finish ever so slightly. Cleaning up a shellac finish with mineral spirits sometimes causes a slight surface blush. The second coat of shellac will remove the blush or, in the case of a final finish, the wax job will remove the blush.

I prefer to wax a piece of furniture after the final rubdown. Some professionals incorporate the final rubdown and wax job into one step. To accomplish this, dip a pad of 000 steel wool in your paste wax and apply it to the finish. Remember that you must work in the direction of the grain.

Allow the piece to dry and buff in the usual manner. Using wax and steel wool together will reduce the cutting action of the steel wool somewhat and produce more of a polish finish. There are commercially available rubbing compounds for furniture such as Furniture Rubbing Compound and Patina Rub. The commercial products mix fine abrasives with the wax to accomplish the task, but they are actually no better than steel wool and wax. If you decide to use a rubbing compound, keep in mind that they must only be used after the final finish coat and not between finish coats because the wax and oils will impede subsequent recoating.

Rubbing down a finish is the key to a professional-looking job. Nevertheless, it is only secondary to the finish used.

SHELLAC

One of the most traditional finishes in the marketplace is shellac. In recent years, for some unknown reason, I have heard shellac finish described as tricky or difficult. Actually it is one of the simplest and most rewarding finishes that can be found. Shellac, when properly used, is applied in multiple, thin coats. This allows for far more control than almost any other method of finishing. Applying successive thin coats of shellac builds a deep, luxurious, soft finish that is unparalleled. If shellac is applied directly from the can, the way thousands of students were shown in shop classes, it will produce as sickening a finish as ever has been seen.

There are advantages and disadvantages with a shellac finish. Shellac is easy to use, beautiful and forgiving in the event of a mistake. On the other hand, the finish it produces is easily damaged by heat (a hot teapot), alcohol (a spilled drink) and moisture (white ring from a water glass).

All of these potential problems are minimized by the use of a good paste wax. The shellacked tables in our living room have seen countless spilled wine glasses and hot teapots without any damage to date. Most of the formal antique furniture on the market today designated "original finish" has a shellac finish that argues well for its tenacity. What this all boils down to is that shellac is a great finish for everything but heavily used table tops that are better varnished. In those cases where additional protection is warranted, it isn't necessary to varnish the entire piece—just the top.

Shellac is a natural material made from the resinous secretions of the *Laccifer lacca*, an insect found in the Far East. Lac secretions are processed as flakes and are mixed with alcohol to form the shellac that is found on the shelves of neighborhood stores.

All shellac flakes, are not the same. There are bleached, unbleached, highly refined, dewaxed, etc. The original quality of a shellac flake does make a difference in the final outcome of the product, but there is no way that you can determine quality from the label on the can. The safest course to pursue is to purchase only highly esteemed name brands from professional finishing supply houses. Off-name brands might be as good as the name brands, but there is no way to tell.

When shelf browsing, you will encounter white shellac and orange shellac. White shellac is made from bleached flakes and it is somewhat harder than orange shellac. Orange shellac is made from unbleached flakes and it is usually recommended for antique pieces because the amber color is thought to enhance the antique look. I prefer white shellac for new and antique pieces, but this is strictly a matter of taste. Some sources recommend a compromise of a mixture of half-white and half-orange shellac, but I don't consider it to be a sound procedure.

Shellac will also be found with mystical markings on the cans such as 4-pound cut or 3-pound cut. These markings refer to the ratio of shellac flakes and alcohol. A 3-pound cut means that 3 pounds of shellac flakes have been mixed with a gallon of alcohol. A 4-pound cut means 4 pounds of flakes were used. As far as the consumer is concerned, the difference is negligible and should not be worried about.

Shellac has a short shelf life. In about a year, it undergoes a chemical change that impedes its drying time. Shellacs are marked with an expiration date on the top of the can. Be careful not to purchase a short-dated product. If you have any doubts about your shellac, try it on a scrap piece and check for drying properties.

Considering the shelf life of shellac, you are best off purchasing only small quantities that will be used for the project at hand.

The ideal way to purchase shellac is in flake form so that small quantities can be mixed as needed. Shellac in flake form has a long shelf life and it can be purchased from professional supply houses. If you encounter shellac flakes, you might want to experiment with Button Lac. Button Lac flakes are a very low grade of flake that makes a dark brown shellac mixture used for cover-up work, or patching on an antique piece. Button Lac is similar to the type of shellac that was used in the 18th century. It is appropriate for antiques. If you use Button Lac, it will be necessary to strain the shellac through fine cheesecloth after mixing because there will be some undissolved solids content.

As is the case with shellac, alcohol too should be purchased in small quantities. Over a time alcohol, can absorb too much moisture. This would affect the shellac mixed with it. When you are working with shellac, purchase a name brand *shellac solvent* (as it is known in most areas). This product might be known as *alcohol solvent* as well. You do not want to use rubbing alcohol. It is almost all water. Nor do you want to use methanol. It is common wood alcohol. Methanol will make shellac brittle.

The secret to a shellac finish is to apply it in multiple thin coats. To do this, it is necessary to dilute shellac with additional alcohol. The standard mixture is 1 part alcohol to 1 part shellac. Nevertheless, I recommend that you start with a 2 to 1 mixture (2 parts alcohol to 1 part shellac). I prefer a 2 to 1 mixture, but, when you become experienced with the finish, you can attempt a 1 to 1 mixture.

It is best to mix the shellac in a clean jar so that it can be stopped up to avoid evaporation between coats. Remember to stir the shellac before pouring it from the can. The shellac can be measured by eye, if you have a good eye, but an easier method is to purchase an inexpensive glass baby bottle with graduated markings. After use, the baby bottle can be cleaned with alcohol and put away for the next use.

Shellac is a brush-on finish. You will need a clean, two-inch brush. Do not take an old paint brush from the basement or from Uncle Harvey's workroom and clean it up. Regardless of what finish you choose to use, you will need a separate brush to be used for that finish and that finish alone. You can purchase a high quality brush and clean it after each use or you can purchase a quantity of inexpensive brushes and dispose of them after each project.

When you are working on a shellac project, place the brush in a separate jar with sufficient alcohol to cover the bristles. Store your brush in this jar while waiting for the finish to dry. Cover the jar with a piece of aluminum foil, as in Fig. 8-2, to inhibit evaporation. If you decide to save your brush, rinse it in the jar of alcohol after the final use. Then discard the alcohol and replace it with fresh alcohol—cleaning the brush a second time.

Following the second cleaning, wrap the brush in newspaper and fasten it with elastic bands or masking tape. Make sure to label the brush "shellac only." When the brush is removed for its next use, rinse it with lacquer thinner prior to use. I am aware of another (somewhat dubious) method for taking care of your shellac brush. After you are finished with the brush, wrap it in a paper towel and squeeze the excess shellac from the brush. Then wrap the brush in newspaper. The brush will invariably harden when it dries. Nevertheless, you need only place it in alcohol for 15 minutes prior to the next use and it will soften up. I have tried this method without experiencing a problem.

Having mixing your alcohol and obtained a brush, you are ready to start your shellac finish. With any brush-on finish, the best result is obtained by working horizontal surfaces. A horizontal surface is particularly important with shellac because the water-like consis-

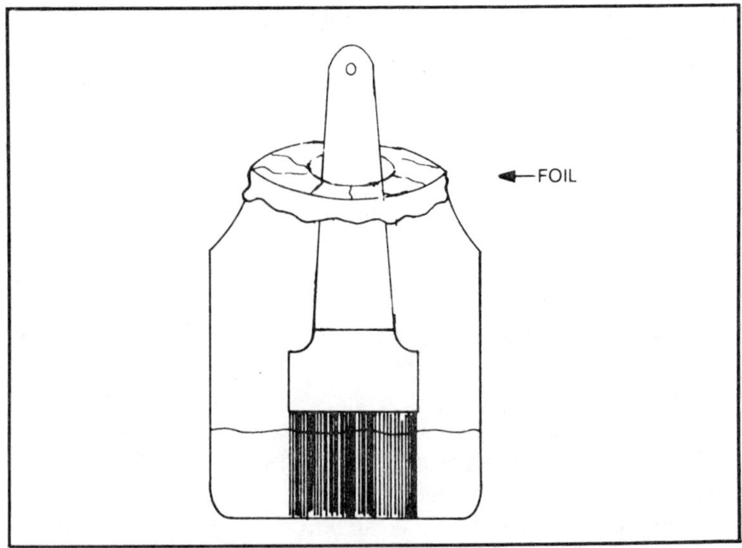

Fig. 8-2. When in use, a shellac brush is immersed in alcohol. For overnight storage, the lid is capped with aluminum foil pierced for the brush.

222

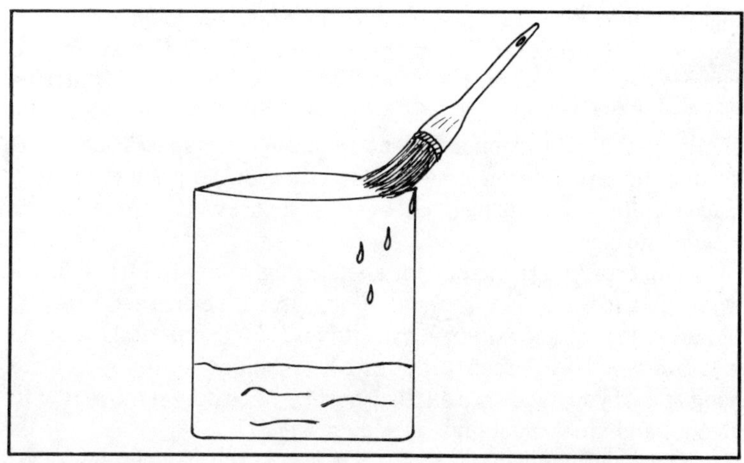

Fig. 8-3. When you are shellacking, the brush should be pulled across the rim of the shellac container to remove excess shellac. The brush should be loaded, but not dripping.

tency of the dilute shellac will cause runs on vertical surfaces. The pack period for shellac—the time in which it will become dry to the touch—is from 15 to 45 minutes. There should be no difficulty in waiting for a surface to dry so that the piece can be turned. The surface to be coated should be clean and free from any dust, hand oils, or abrasive residue. If there is any doubt about the cleanliness of the surface, clean it with mineral spirits and allow it to dry.

If the work piece has not been sealed, start by applying a wash coat of shellac as outlined previously. The key to applying shellac is in the speed and the brush stroke. Dip the brush in the shellac mixture, to half the depth of the bristles, and then press the brush against the side of the jar as you would a paintbrush in order to remove excess shellac (Fig. 8-3).

When the brush is removed from the jar, it should be loaded with the finishing material, but it should not be dripping. Apply the brush to one corner and brush in one long continuous stroke. With shellac, the brush is not worked as it is with paint or varnish. The brush is moved in only one direction, as shown in Figs 8-4 and 8-5, and not moved back and forth. The finish is applied in the direction of the grain, with each successive stroke overlapping the prior stroke slightly, until the entire surface is covered as shown in Fig. 8-6.

It is important to work quickly with shellac because it dries so rapidly. Only one area should be finished at a time, and then in a logical order. With a drop-leaf table, for example, do one leaf, then the center section, and then the remaining leaf. If drawers are involved, remove the drawers and do each one separately. The table can be inverted and each leg finished. With turnings, apply the shellac in the same manner as you would use sandpaper. That means around the circumference as opposed to with the grain (Fig. 8-7). Each stroke of the brush should overlap the previous stroke as with a level surface.

The brushing technique for shellac might seem a little complicated, but it really is quite simple and it can be learned in a few minutes. Prior to starting your first piece of furniture, take a scrap piece of wood and practice the brush technique until you get the hang of it. If you mess up a shellac job, you need only remove it with alcohol and steel wool and start over again.

Once the shellac wash coat has dried, rub it down with 000 steel wool (Fig. 8-8) and apply a coat of the 1 part shellac to 2 parts alcohol mixture. The first coat of shellac will probably dry to the touch in 15 minutes, but allow it to dry at least three hours before applying a second coat.

After the first coat has dried, it must be rubbed down with steel wool—as must each successive coat. If the shellac is properly dry, it will show up as powder on the steel wool and the surface. If the steel-wool pad gums up while rubbing, it means the shellac has not dried sufficiently. In that case, stop and allow additional drying time. Continue to recoat the piece until the desired depth of finish is achieved. An average finish requires from three to four coats of shellac, but it is not uncommon to use as many as seven or eight coats to achieve a high-gloss finish.

Fig. 8-4. Shellac is brushed on, if possible, in one continuous stroke with the grain.

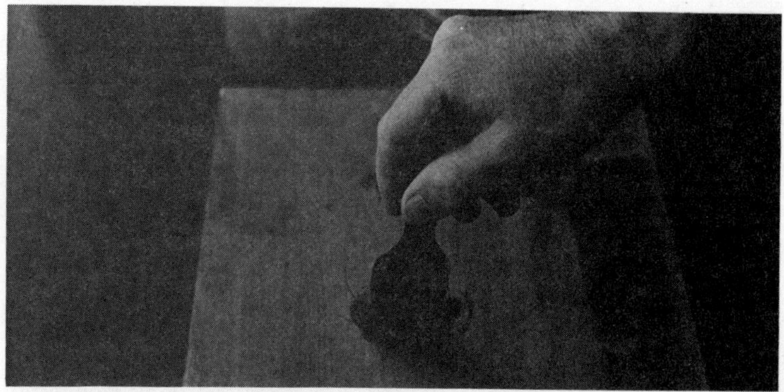
Fig. 8-5. With shellac, each successive stroke overlaps the previous stroke.

When to stop shellacking is a matter of taste. When the last coat applied has a solid sheen after rubbing down, then it is time to consider stopping. Allow at least three hours' drying time between coat of shellac prior to rubbing down and recoating. Allow the final coat to dry overnight before rubbing down.

If you are in no particular rush, allow each coat of shellac to dry overnight. For a polished surface, rub the final coat with 0000 steel wool and light mineral oil or a mixture of half-boiled linseed oil and half turpentine. Wipe the excess oil from the piece and allow it to dry, and then wax.

The best place to do your shellac work is outdoors. The air is healthier, the light is better, and you save on electricity. Whether you work indoors or outdoors, you must work in a warm, dry environment. Shellac is anhydrous; it is gravely affected by moisture. On damp days or in damp environments, shellac might take longer to dry and might turn white once it has dried. The simplest remedy to this problem is to wait for a dryer day, but not everyone's schedule allows this luxury. If drying or blushing become a problem due to moisture, mix your shellac with lacquer thinner—not alcohol. Lacquer thinner will work well as a vehicle for shellac, but it will retard the drying time. If the steel wool gums up, allow at least six hours (or longer) for drying time before recoating. The room should be well-ventilated when you work indoors with alcohol or lacquer thinner.

French Polish

A French polish has magical connotations in the world of furniture finishing as the ultimate art of finishing. A French polish historically is a super-high sheen finish achieved through the use of shellac, friction, and oil. French polishing was a popular finish and the rage of the 19th century; it has not been held in high esteem during this century. Many 18th-century pieces of furniture were French polished in the 19th century. In modern times, a French polish also refers to a special product made for this use. See the section on lacquers.

Some people say a French polish is easy to apply. Others say it is difficult. I definitely think it is difficult and not the type of thing that you should fool around with until you have a lot of practice. Before applying a French polish, make sure the wood surface is absolutely smooth. It should be sanded, wet sanded, and resanded. If there is the slightest open grain to the wood, as with walnut or mahogany, it must first be filled with a paste-wood filler. In the 19th century, plaster was used as a wood filler.

To apply the finish, a wad of soft, clean cotton—folded until it's at least an inch thick—should be prepared. Alternatively, a center of folded cheesecloth wrapped with several layers of cotton can be used. The pad is soaked in linseed oil and squeezed dry. Then it is dipped in a mixture of 1 part shellac to 1 part alcohol. The pad is applied to the surface in a circular or figure 8 motion.

Once applied, the pad cannot be removed from the surface without leaving a mark. This means only small areas can be worked at one time. This method works well for small table drawers and the like, but when an entire table top is to be done the work is brutally exacting if a blotchy surface is to be avoided.

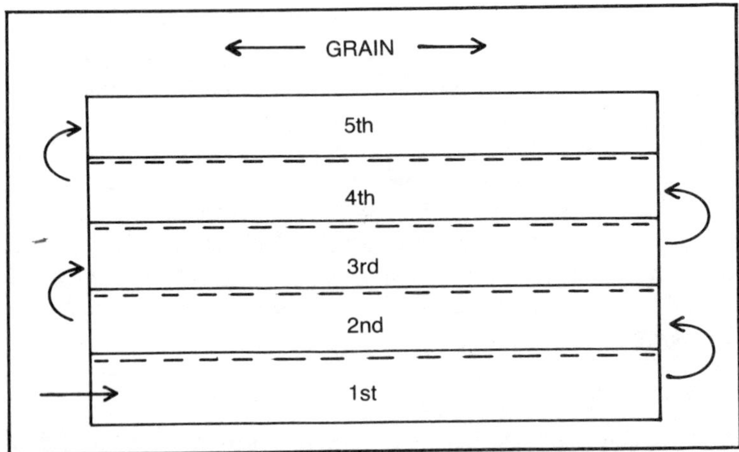

Fig. 8-6. Shellac is applied with overlapping strokes in the pattern shown.

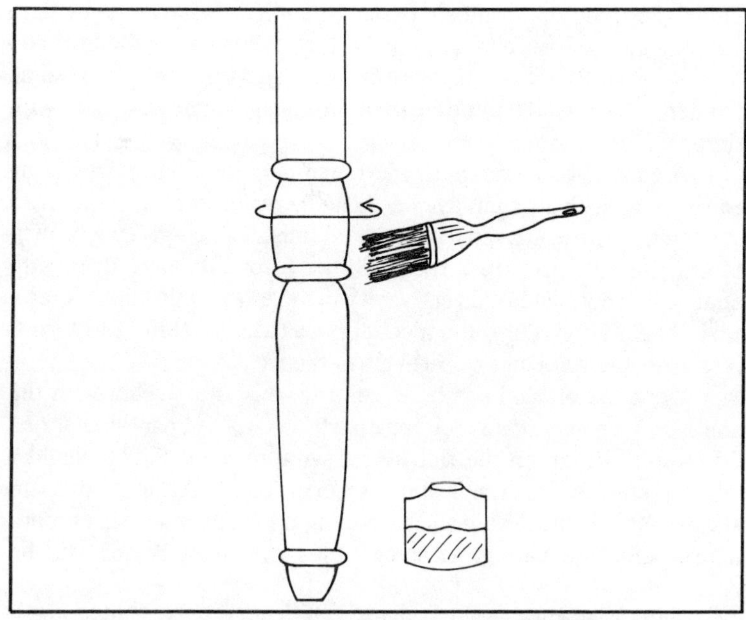

Fig. 8-7. With turnings, shellac is brushed on across the grain.

Although mastery of a French polish might require exacting skill and practice for entire top surfaces, it can be used effectively to build up a small damaged area of a furniture finish. The technique for patching can be mastered without too much difficulty.

Tinting

Occasionally, it becomes necessary to conceal surface imperfections with a finish coat. A particular piece might have too much variation in the grain and require toning down, or a change in pigmentation from residual paint might require attention. Repairing a worn area in an antique finish might require toning to match an original finish darkened with age. With modern furniture, this problem is handled by adding pigments to lacquer so that each successive coat is slightly opaque. If you examine newly made furniture, you will notice that hardly any grain is visible due to the pigmented finish.

The use of orange shellac instead of white shellac will provide some minimal tone (should it be needed). As mentioned earlier, the use of homemade Button Lac shellac, which is dark brown, will add considerable tone to a finish. When more tonation is required, some coloring agent must be added to the shellac to produce the requisite effect. Japan colors or alcohol-soluble aniline dyes can be used to tone shellac. Of these two products, the aniline dye is the best and most logical. The dyes that are in powder form can be mixed as needed and have an unlimited shelf life. Japan colors will spoil with time.

Aniline dyes come in a wide range of colors, but most tinting can be done with a walnut dye because the majority of all stains are a variation of brown. Even a cherry red finish can be given a brown-tone finish. To prepare a tint, mix the alcohol-soluble dyes with shellac solvent, but not directly with the shellac. Only slight coloration should be given to the alcohol because any attempt to turn it into a deep-stain color will result in failure.

Once the alcohol has been colored, mix the alcohol with the shellac for a standard mix (either 2 parts alcohol to 1 part shellac or a 50-50 mix. Brush on the tint in the same manner as you would a regular shellac finish and allow to dry. The addition of dyes to shellac retards the drying and hardening time. Allow for six or more hours before recoating. In some cases overnight drying will be required.

The tinted shellac will dry different from regular shellac and it will be subject to more snags and streaks. So great care must be given to the rubbing down process. A light touch is in order when rubbing down this finish in order to avoid rubbing through the finish to the lighter wood tone underneath. Tinted shellac builds up faster than regular shellac so fewer coats are required. After the final coat, rub down and wax as you would with any other finish. The ability to tint can be a powerful technique in your refinishing arsenal. It is wise to first practice the technique on scrap wood.

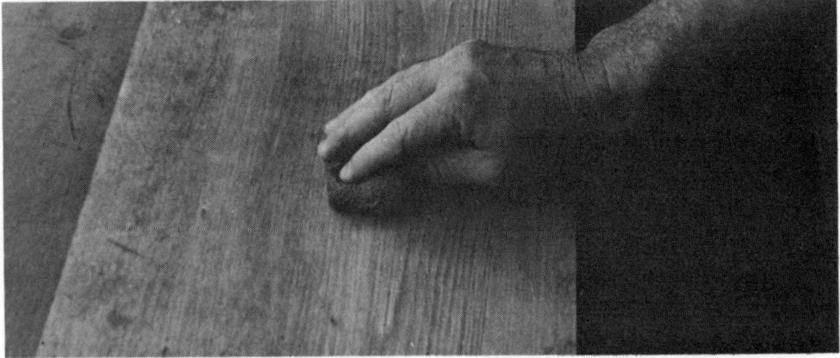

Fig. 8-8. After the requisite drying period, shellac is rubbed down with 000 steel wool. If properly dry, the shellac will appear as a white powder on the pad of steel wool.

VARNISH

Varnish is the king of finishes. It is tough, alcohol resistant, heat resistant, and moisture resistant. In addition to its superb wear qualities, varnish can be rubbed to a beautiful, soft luster or a high-polished sheen. No other finish offers as much as varnish (although modern alcohol resistant lacquers are getting close).

Varnish is undoubtedly a superior finish, but there are some dark clouds among the rays of sunshine. Varnish takes more care in application than other finishes. It requires extended drying times. The average drying time for varnish is three days, but five days is safer and not uncommon. You don't have to be an Einstein to calculate that three coats of varnish can take 15 days of drying in a warm, dust-free environment. Home craftspersons, in general, are too impatient to allow for the necessary drying times. This results in many botched jobs.

One approach to minimizing the problems associated with varnish is to only apply it to those surfaces that need the extra protection that varnish provides. The tops of tables and dressers that receive the most wear can be varnished. The remainder of the piece can be shellacked or given some other appropriate finish. Top surfaces can be built up with multiple coats of shellac until the preferred sheen is achieved and then given a final coat of varnish for protection. This will reduce the total project time.

Not all varnishes are the same and that means there can be considerable variation in the finished project. Varnish consists of solids suspended in a solvent. After varnish is brushed on, the solvents evaporate and leave a thin layer of the solids that form the finish. Varnishes that have a higher solids content provide more of a finish with a single coat. Therefore, they are better and they are more expensive. Some varnishes are labeled so that the solids content can be determined, but others are not. A good rule of thumb for varnish is that inexpensive products represent no bargain. Purchase known and reliable brands.

Varnish can be made from natural resins such as linseed oil or from synthetic substances such as alkyd resin. Or they may be a combination of natural and synthetic resins. There is no discernible difference between the two types of resins and either can be used with good results.

Phenolic resin, commonly known as *spar varnish*, should be avoided at all cost. Some finishing books and numerous hardware store clerks will tell you to use spar varnish for your furniture. They are misguided. Spar varnish is wonderful for use outdoors. Spar varnish hardens on the surface, but not throughout the finish. This provides an elasticity that can survive the extreme expansion and contraction produced by outdoor environments. This type of elasticity is not necessary for indoor furniture and the lack of a totally hardening product will result in a gummy finish.

The type of varnish that you want will be labeled just "varnish" or in some cases "floor varnish." Read the label carefully and be sure that it is not spar varnish. Rubbing varnishes are sometimes encountered on the shelves and they are no more than varnishes with a high solids content. A rubbing varnish dries very hard and it is suitable for a high polish finish.

Varnishes are labeled according to sheen such as high gloss, eggshell, satin, rubbed finish, etc. With satin- or rubbed-look varnishes, chemicals are added to the varnish to control the final sheen. These chemicals extend the drying time of the varnish and they are not necessary. The final sheen of any finish can be controlled by the grade of abrasive used for the rubdown. Consequently, it is best to purchase a plain varnish that is high gloss.

Another type of varnish (probably the most popular these days) is the plastic varnish known as *polyurethane*. The new plastic varnishes are all the rage today and I am positively against them. At the risk of sounding cynical, if you want plastic then buy plastic. But don't try to make wood look like plastic! On a less emotional note, I question the value of the polyurethanes.

Regular varnish and plastic varnishes are heat-, alcohol-, moisture- and abrasion-resistant. Why is the plastic better? Plastic varnishes are harder and more wear resistant than regular varnishes. This has meaning for floors and bar tops, but certainly not for furniture where the additional hardness just is not needed. The hardness of the plastic finish makes it harder to rub down so that a soft sheen can be difficult to attain.

When compared under magnification, surfaces that have been varnished with regular varnish and polyurethane varnish will show different abrasion patterns after being rubbed down. The polyurethane finish will show a far more severe abrasion pattern. In the long run, polyurethane will wear better but show more wear. If a polyurethane finish needs work after years of use, it will not patch well nor will it bond well with additional coats. It is also difficult to strip. I admit that I am prejudiced about this product and that many professionals don't share this prejudice. If you want to use polyurethane, by all means go ahead—and ruin your project with it!

Once you have chosen the varnish product, purchase only a

small quantity because it does spoil. It is wise to strain the new varnish—as well as varnish that has been around—through a fine mesh prior to using it. There might be solids in the varnish that can ruin a project if they are not removed.

Prior to applying the first varnish coat, you should seal the wood in order to avoid uneven absorption of the varnish. If the varnish is applied without a prior sealing coat, the finish will not be ruined, but more coats of varnish will be required. If the wood has not been sealed, the direct application of varnish to a surface that has been oil stained could result in some of the stain being lifted. The use of a sealer coat will undoubtedly avoid many problems.

There is always much talk in the world of finishers as to what is the proper sealer coat for a varnish finish. As a rule, product labels will tell you to use the varnish straight from the can or to thin the first coat with a little turpentine. Most often, the consumer will be instructed not to use the varnish in conjunction with shellac. Many professionals use a sealer coat of shellac. This is one of those issues of practice and custom working in contradiction to theory. Varnish will not chemically bond as well with an undercoat of shellac as it will with an undercoat of varnish. Nevertheless, there is a strong mechanical bond with the shellac. I have never had a problem using shellac as a sealer coat and I do not know of anyone who has.

For a shellac sealer, use a dilute coat of shellac proportioned 1 part shellac to 2 parts alcohol. Allow the fresh coat of shellac to dry overnight and rub down with 000 steel wool. If you are uncomfortable with a shellac sealer, varnish can be used as a sealer by mixing 1 part varnish with 1 part mineral spirits. Brush on the varnish sealer, allow it to dry for two days. Then rub down with 000 steel wool or 7/0 finishing paper.

Regardless of which sealing approach is undertaken, it is imperative that all traces of the steel wool or sandpaper be removed as well as any dust or dirt that has accumulated on the piece. A good, clean dust cloth is suitable for the purpose, but some workers prefer to use a *tack rag*. Tack rags can be purchased commercially prepared from a good paint store or you can make your own by soaking a piece of clean cotton in a mixture of one-half varnish and one-half mineral spirits. When removed from the solution, the rag is squeezed dry and placed in a sealed jar, until needed, to avoid evaporation.

Varnishing must be accomplished in a dust-free, dry environment. If you attempt to varnish in a room in that you have previously sanded, the project is doomed. If the piece is placed in the basement, it could be subject to settling dust loosened by walking on the floor above. You will have to figure out which is the most dust-free place in your home. The work place must be dry. Excessive moisture will inhibit the drying of the varnish. The temperature of the work place should never go below 70 degrees if the finish is to harden properly.

Varnish can be brushed, sprayed, or padded on with a cloth. Brushing is the preferred method of application for both professionals and weekenders. There are many precautions traditionally associated with the application of varnish. Examples are that it must be flowed on or that it should never be mixed, etc. I recommend that you pay more attention to the instructions listed here than those written on the can or told to you by a friend.

The first taboo to be violated is that of thinning. Product directions will indicate that no thinning is necessary or to thin only when necessary. Varnish doesn't have to be thinned, but it works much better and you avoid problems if you do thin it. There is no exact rule as to how much the varnish should be thinned, but 1 ounce of mineral spirits to a pint of varnish seems to be a working relationship.

You shouldn't need more than half a pint of varnish for one coat on an average sized job. Pour off half a cup and add one-half ounce of mineral spirits. Prior to mixing the varnish, pour it through a fine mesh to rid it of any solids.

Thoroughly stir the mineral spirits and varnish mixture. When the varnish is mixed, it will froth. That might present some difficulties. I am told that when varnish is frothing the air bubbles will transfer with the varnish and dry as pit marks. Too many people have reported this problem for it to be ignored. I have never experienced the problem. Following the dictum, "better safe than sorry," allow the varnish to settle prior to applying the finish.

Apply the varnish with a standard 2-inch brush that is clean and has never been used for any product other than varnish. It is a good idea to rinse the brush (new or old) in lacquer thinner prior to use to remove any dirt or dust particles that might be loaded in the bristles. Dip the brush to the depth of about one-third of the bristles and tap the brush on the container as you remove it to shake loose excess varnish. Tap the brush on the metal binding and do not drag the bristles across the edge of the container as you would a paint brush.

Apply the varnish to the surface briskly and work the varnish into the wood. Forget nonsense about flowing the varnish and make sure the entire surface is covered. First apply the varnish with vertical strokes in the direction of the grain (Fig. 8-9) and then rework the stroke across the grain (Fig. 8-10). After the surface has been covered thoroughly in this manner, use the tip of the brush to even out the finish (Fig. 8-11).

First stroke across the grain with the tip of the brush and then finish with long strokes in the direction of the grain. Don't worry if some brush stroke marks show. The varnish will run into itself and level out (obviating the brush strokes). Turnings should be worked across the grain and then tipped off with the brush. Long, uninterrupted, vertical sections of the turnings can be worked with the grain. If your brush becomes stiff from the drying varnish as you work, dip it in paint thinner to return its flexibility.

As with other methods of brush-on finishes, applying the finish to a horizontal surface will test your patience, but improve your results. The average dry-to-the-touch time (tack time) for varnish is three to five hours. Be absolutely positive that the surface is dry before inverting a piece. When a piece is to be turned over, it is best to pad the area with newspapers and then cover it with an old sheet. The varnish is still soft at this point and it can be damaged by unnoticeable debris on the floor. This is a problem that can be prevented by the newspapers. If the newspapers are not covered by the sheet, they might stick to the varnished surface.

After a surface has been coated and begins to dry, you might notice a speck of dust or a foreign particle here or there that will result in a surface imperfection. If you try to remove the dust speck with a tool, whether it be a fine needle point or a jack hammer, you

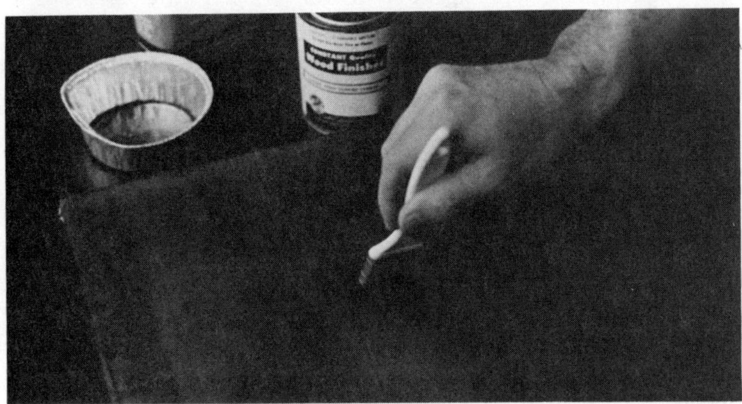

Fig. 8-9. Varnish is diluted slightly with thinner and brushed on in the direction of the grain. The varnish is worked vigorously into the grain.

Fig. 8-10. The varnish is rebrushed across the grain to insure coverage of all areas. Fresh varnish is not added to the brush.

will damage the finish. To remedy this problem, you need a pick stick or brush. Cut a length of one-half dowel to 6 or 7 inches and point one end with your pocketknife.

Next, place a few drops of varnish on an old piece of tin or any thin metal and heat it with a match until it starts to harden. When the varnish has a rubbery consistency, roll it into a ball and place it on the pointed end of the dowel. You now have a pick stick that can be used to lightly touch the surface and remove dust spots. Another variation of the tool is to take an inexpensive artist brush, dip the tip in varnish, and then heat the varnish with a match until rubbery. The match must be held sufficiently distant so that the tip of the brush is not burned.

A plain and simple truth about varnish is that it takes a long time to dry. More varnish jobs are ruined by impatience and insufficient waiting time than are ever ruined by poor technique. Some manufacturers suggest that their product will dry in eight to 10 hours. Perhaps it will under laboratory conditions, but never in your home. Varnish should be allowed to dry (at the minimum) 48 hours before rubbing down or recoating. And 72 hours is a safer amount of time that is generally necessary.

After waiting the requisite drying time, stick your thumb nail into the varnish finish. If the finish marks, it is not dry and it should be allowed to dry at least another day. If varnish has been applied under damp or moist conditions, it will take three to five days to dry. There is absolutely nothing you can do to shorten this drying period—just be patient.

The application of three coats of varnish can take a long time.

This is why I prefer to build up a finish with two to three coats of shellac and top it off with a final coat of varnish.

When the first varnish coat has dried, it must be rubbed down as with a shellac finish. Rub down the varnish with 000 steel wool or 7/0 finishing paper (according to your preference). If a second coat of varnish is required, recoat in the same manner as the first coat. Once the final coat of varnish has been applied and has dried, it can be rubbed down in the manner that suits your taste with regard to sheen.

For a soft, luster/low-sheen finish, rub down the piece with 00 steel wool or 6/0 finishing paper. Use 000 steel wool or 7/0 finishing paper for an average sheen. If slightly more sheen is required, use 0000 steel wool lubricated with light mineral oil for a second rubdown. If a high polish effect is desired, use 300-grit paper or 400-grit wet/dry paper and mineral oil for the second rubdown. The finisher is very much in control of the rubdown process and can work to suit his taste. Whichever method of rubdown is used, the piece should be cleaned of any residue and given a paste wax and buffing.

Varnishes, similar to shellacs, can be tinted to tone down a finish. Commercially prepared varnish stain can be used for this purpose, but it generally has too much opaque pigment and yields poor results. Varnishes can be tinted with Japan colors, colors ground in oil, or blending stains with good results. A small amount of oil stain can also be added to varnish to produce a tint.

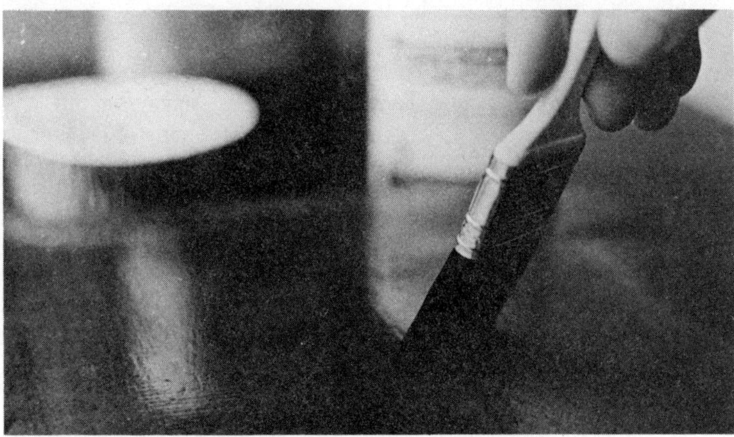

Fig. 8-11. The final stroke of the brush is made with the tip of the brush and in the direction of the grain. This last stroke levels the varnish.

LACQUER

Lacquer is the staple finish of the modern furniture industry and of a multitude of professional refinishers. The widespread use of lacquer is not whimsical. It is a hard, durable product that lends itself to efficient mass production. Lacquer dries to the touch within a few minutes and can be recoated within two hours. This is a decided bonus to anyone who has ever finished a piece of furniture. The miracle of a lacquer finish is accomplished by spraying multiple thin coats of lacquer to build up a finish. Lacquer is an ideal spraying finish. That makes it viable for production work and problematic for home use.

The spraying of lacquer is simply not a task that can be undertaken by the weekend craftsperson. To start with, the cost of a spraying outfit would hardly be warranted by the occasional user. Recently a number of spraying kits have come on the market for less than $100. But they will not do the work of better professional equipment. Aerosol spray units, that you load with your own finish, are available, but they are not adquate for the task.

If your money is invested in spraying equipment, an area will have to be designated as a spraying room with appropriate backdrop and super ventilation system or the work will have to be done outdoors. Lacquer thinner consists of acetone to a large degree. That makes it one of the most volatile of finishes and not particularly pleasant to breathe. All in all, lacquer spraying is not a preferred method for home refinishers. If you have your mind set upon this sort of thing, buy a compressor, read the instructions, and practice. Spraying is a skill that can be learned with practice.

Brushing Lacquer

The brushing of lacquer is an alternative to spraying, but it is not a particularly positive alternative. The fast drying of lacquer is not a problem when sprayed, but when brushed on the quick drying properties make avoiding lap marks extremely difficult.

To brush on lacquer, you will need a special brushing lacquer that has retardants added to slow the drying. Brushing lacquers are not available in the average paint store, but they can be purchased from a professional finishing supply house. I have been told that a teaspoon of castor oil added to a pint of spraying lacquer will render it a brushing lacquer, but I have not tried it.

As with other finishes, a clean brush that has been used for nothing other than lacquer is required. Brushes made of some synthetic materials such as nylon will dissolve if left to stand in lacquer thinner. A natural bristle brush or a brush labeled for use with lacquer will be required. If possible, a 3-inch brush should be used for large surfaces because you will want to cover as large an area as possible in a short amount of time.

Prior to applying the brushing lacquer, you must seal the wood surface. The ideal product for this work is sanding sealer. Sanding sealer is brushed on, allowed to dry, and sanded lightly. This makes a perfect undercoat for the lacquer. If you don't choose to use sanding sealer, a sealer can be made by mixing brushing lacquer with an equal amount of lacquer thinner. The sealing mixture is brushed on generously so that the surface of the area being worked is drenched. Work only one surface at a time. After brushing the mixture, take a clean rag and wipe the surface to distribute and remove the sealer. Allow the sealer coat to dry for three to four hours and sand with 7/0 finishing paper.

When it comes to brushing on lacquer, the operative word is "élan" (vigorous spirit and enthusiasm). Dip your brush in the brushing lacquer, this time undiluted, and apply it to the surface with long strokes in the direction of the grain. If at all possible, try to continue from one end to the other without rewetting the brush. If necessary, even out your stroke with the tip of the brush. The second stroke should overlap the first stroke slightly, as should the third, etc.

Work the surface as quickly as you possibly can without being reckless. The lacquer coat will be dry and ready to be worked in four hours. If the sealer coat and the lacquer coat have been applied within the same day, allow the piece to dry overnight. The sealer coat and the lacquer coat should be sufficient to meet most requirements. If an additional coat is required, sand the surface with 7/0 paper and recoat in the manner of the first coat. There is always some potential of a second coat of lacquer softening the first coat when it is brushed on. That is why it is better to let the project stand with one coat of lacquer. The final coat of lacquer can be rubbed down with 000 steel wool or polished for a higher-gloss finish.

Brushing lacquer is a troublesome finish at best. There is no reason to use it unless you find it necessary to recoat an already lacquered surface.

Special Brushing Lacquer

There is a wonderful alternative to standard brushing lacquers called Deft Clear Wood Finish. Deft is a nitrocellulose product (a lacquer). It does not however, have the problems normally associated with a brushing lacquer. Deft has modified their product with coconut oil and other ingredients that seem to eliminate problems with brush strokes. This product has a low solids content that invariably has something to do with the elimination of problems, but also means that more coats are necessary to provide an adequate finish. Deft provides good protection from moisture and abrasion and it is alcohol resistant and water resistant when three or more coats have been applied. The Deft product is as volatile as any other lacquer. It requires cautious use as well as adequate ventilation.

Deft is used without a sealer coat and it is applied directly from the can without thinning. The easiest method of application is with a brush. It can be sprayed or padded on. Use a clean brush and brush the finish on with even strokes in the direction of the grain. Overlap each stroke until the working surface is covered. Then even the finish with the tip of the brush. Apply this product liberally and make sure the entire surface is covered evenly.

If your brush becomes stiff as you work the finish, dip it in lacquer thinner. The finish will be dry to the touch in 30 minutes and will be ready to recoat in two to three hours. When the surface has dried, sand it lightly with 7/0- or 8/0-finishing paper, and recoat.

If the sandpaper begins to gum up, allow additional time for drying. The manufacturer indicates that the finish can be recoated after two hours, but it is a good practice to allow four to five hours between each coat if more than two coats are to be put on in one day.

At least three coats will be necessary to provide protection from alcohol. More coats might be necessary to achieve the sheen you desire. Rub down the final coat with 000 steel wool or 0000 steel wool for a nice sheen. For a polished surface, follow the final rubdown with a wet/dry paper and oil or a rubbing compound as you would a varnish finish.

Deft is a good product to use anywhere that a lacquer finish is needed and it is also a simple-to-use, good-all-around finishing product. The only thing I don't like about Deft is the coconut smell that can permeate a room in minutes. That is a small price to pay for a good finish.

Padding Lacquer

Padding lacquers are used extensively in professional refinishing shops, but they are not generally known in the do-it-yourself refinishing market. Two well-known products are Qualasole, made by H. Behlen & Brother, New York, and Pad-Lac, marketed by Albert Constantine and Son, New York. These products are similar, but the Qualasole is harder and more durable than the Pad-Lac. Pad-Lac is less expensive and easier to use. These products are used for patch work or a modern, French-polish finish.

When modern refinishers talk of French polish, they usually are referring to a finish built up with Qualasole. Some will argue that this finish is not as good as the original shellac finish, but none can argue that it does not produce as high a luster with much less work. I cannot think of a piece of country furniture that would look appropriate with a French polish. If you have something that you want to put a mirror-like finish on, then pick one of these products. Padding lacquers have a long shelf life. You can keep them for years without fear of spoilage.

To apply a modern French polish, seal the surface of the wood with a coat of shellac (as described in the section on Sealers). Prepare a rubbing wad by folding about a half inch of cheesecloth or cotton and wrapping it with a clean piece of white cotton or linen (Fig. 8-12).

Wash the cotton prior to use with warm water to remove all traces of lint, and allow it to dry. Wet the pad with lacquer from the bottle, but do not soak it. Tap the pad against the palm of your hand to disperse the lacquer (Figs. 8-13 and 8-14) and apply the pad to the surface. Use a circular motion or a figure 8 to work the lacquer over the surface. Increase pressure as you go (Fig. 8-15).

When it becomes necessary to rewet the pad, slide it from the surface, as opposed to lifting it, so that a mark is not made. When working, the pad should always be in movement. Padding lacquers

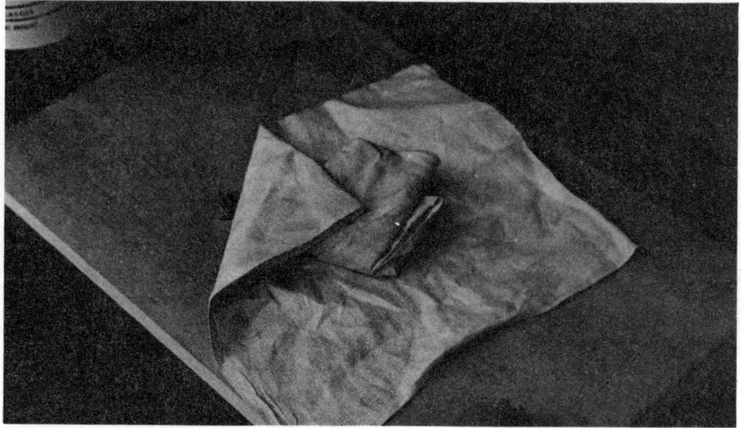

Fig. 8-12. A wad for padding lacquer is prepared by wrapping a clean piece of linen around a 1-inch core of folded cotton or cheesecloth.

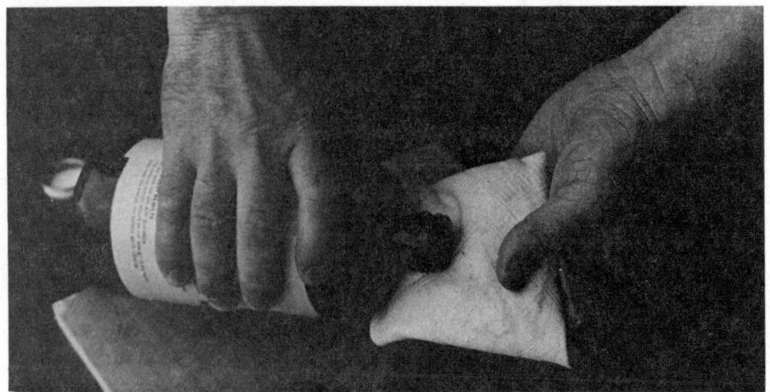

Fig. 8-13. The padding lacquer is directly transferred to the pad.

work on a friction and heat basis. The pad will become difficult to move as you work that is as it should be. To remedy this problem, a few drops of boiled linseed oil can be added to a stiff pad.

After one thin coat has been applied, allow the surface to dry for two hours and apply a second coat. Unlike other finishes, this is not rubbed down between each coat. After the final coat is applied, put a few drops of Qualasole on the pad and stroke the pad lightly, going with the grain, to remove any marks that might be present. For an even higher gloss, the finish can be rubbed lightly with a pad dipped in Qualasole Solvent. Rub down the final coat with a pad of 0000 steel wool and light mineral oil. Then clean and wax the surface.

Padding lacquers are rarely used to provide a finish on a new piece, but they are used extensively to build a new finish over an old, damaged one. Padding lacquers can be used over shellac, lacquer, or varnish. Varnish finishes with minor checking can be saved with Pad-Lac. Mix Pad-Lac with an equal amount of Pad-Lac Solvent and apply to the surface with your pad.

The surface should previously have been cleaned of all dirt or wax using mineral spirits. In this case the Pad-Lac and Solvent should act as an amalgamator. Allow the surface to dry for 4 hours and then sand lightly with a 400-grit wet/dry paper used dry. Clean the surface and apply fresh coats of Pad-Lac or Qualasole in the manner described. This technique might not always work, but if it does, you have saved a finish and a great deal of work.

The real value of these products is in patching a worn finish. If a small area of finish has worn through, a padding lacquer can be applied, to just that area, with ease even by a beginner. It is applied

240

with a pad. The worn area is built up until it matches the rest of the finish. Then it is allowed to dry and rubbed with steel wool.

Once the worn area is patched, some workers prefer to give the entire surface a going-over with the lacquer. Padding lacquers can also be used with special powder stains to add necessary color to a worn area, a nick, or a scratch.

Blending Stain Powders are used with Pad-Lac, while Match-O-Stain Powders are used with Qualasole. Stain powders come in standard colors, such as walnut and mahogany, and they can be intermixed to a desired shade. To use the stain powders, apply the padding lacquer to the patch area and allow it to dry for two to four hours.

When it is time for the second padding, dip the pad in the lacquer, dab some stain powder on the pad—but only a minute amount— and apply it to the patch area with a circular motion. If too much stain powder is used, the area will streak. Allow the stain coat to dry for four hours, and then apply a clear coat of the padding lacquer. When the clear coat has dried, apply another stain coat. Work in this manner—clear coat and stain coat—until the preferred color has been achieved. The final coat should always be a clear coat. When the patch job is complete, rub down the patch and wax the piece.

The skills required to use padding lacquers can be acquired with only a modest amount of practice. Using the lacquers with a

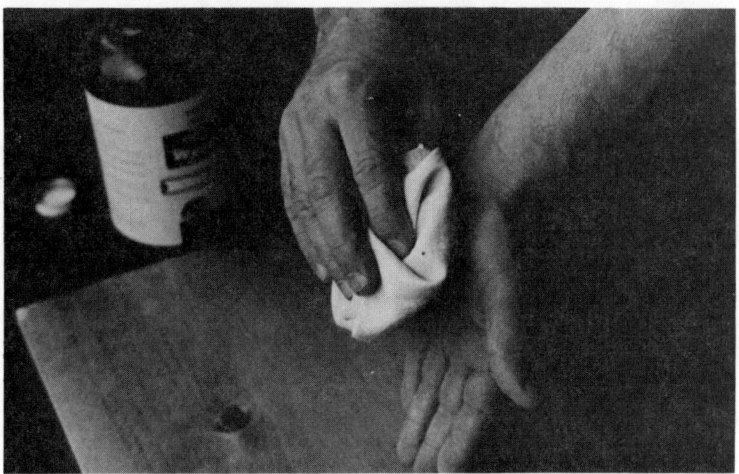

Fig. 8-14. The lacquer pad is hit on the hand to disperse the liquid throughout the pad.

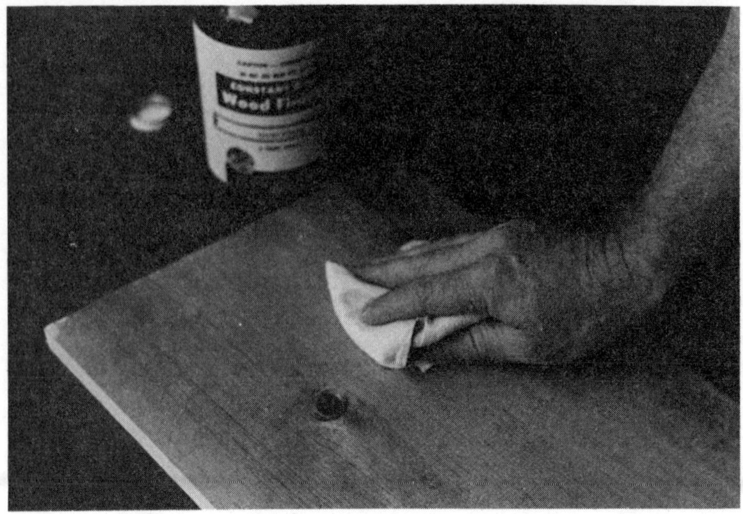

Fig. 8-15. The pad is applied to the work surface with a figure 8 motion, but it is not lifted from the surface. The pad is slid from the surface when it is time to replenish the lacquer.

stain powder requires much more practice before you get the hang of it. But it is well worth all the effort you put into it.

Chapter 9
Glazing, Aging, and Faking

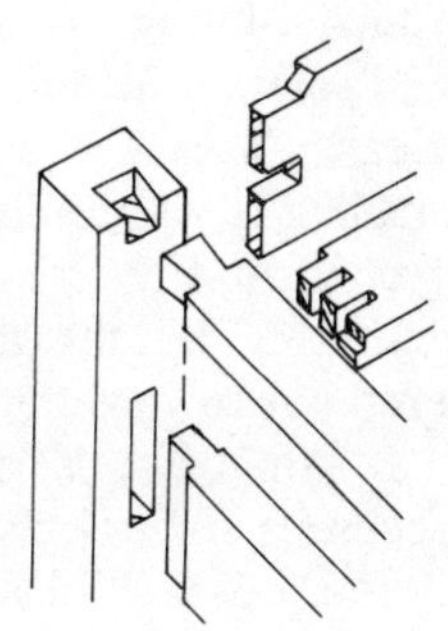

It would be nice if every refinishing job were simple and straightforward, but, alas, that is not the case. On occasion, paint will have filled surface imperfections that render the stain job unsightly. Or paint residue will have bled through the stain causing an ugly mess. Whatever the problem, it is helpful to have a few tricks up your sleeve. Recently, I refinished a water bench that had a badly pitted and marred surface from years of use and abuse. All of the surface imperfections had been filled by the many coats of white paint that it had seen in its lifetime. One way to remedy such a problem is to use a belt sander and remove an eighth-inch of wood. This would leave a flat, clean surface. Belt sanding is the easiest approach, but not a good approach because it would result in a piece that looked brand new. What is the sense of buying something with the appeal of age and wear if that age is only going to be removed?

As an alternative to belt sanding, the recesses of the bench could have been picked clean with a fine pointed instrument such as an awl, ice pick, or dental pick and then filled with wood putty. This is an acceptable method, but you need the patience of a saint and a lot of spare time. With this particular bench, I did pick and patch some of the larger areas, but most of the smaller areas were left as is. Being somewhat of a lazy fellow, I chose to apply a wipe-on glaze to the surface. The glaze filled the cracks so that, when the surface was wiped, the glaze remained and covered the paint areas. The use of the glaze did not damage the surface of the bench, It was applied in 15 minutes with considerable ease. The moral of this story is to choose the best method and the easiest method.

FURNITURE GLAZES

The primary use for glazes with furniture is to shadow areas and provide a finish with both depth and interest. Glazes are also used to cover imperfections in a surface and to simulate wood grains in faking. A glaze, simply defined, is a coloring agent in a clear vehicle. In this simple sense, the only difference between a glaze and a stain is the quantity of the coloring agent. Stains are relatively clear; glazes are relatively opaque. The easiest glaze to use for shading is just a mixture of turpentine and Japan colors or colors ground in oil. The glaze is brushed or wiped into turnings and corners. Then the glaze is worked well into the surface and feathered out toward the edges.

When dry, the area is left as is or buffed with a rag so that only recesses and not high spots will be glazed. Following the buffing, the surface is shellacked carefully to seal the stain. If a varnish finish were applied directly to this glaze, it would be removed in the brushing process.

Glazes can be made of anything that your fertile imagination conjures up, but the basic professional glaze consists of a coloring material, varnish, and mineral spirits. Of course, no one agrees what the proportion of mineral spirits to varnish should be. Workers who prefer a thin glaze use about 3 parts mineral spirits to 1 part varnish. Those who like a thick glaze that really grabs choose to mix 2 parts mineral spirits to 3 parts varnish.

Which mixture to choose is a matter of personal preference and experience. A good starting point and compromise is a 50-50 mixture of mineral spirits and varnish. That should prove satisfactory in most circumstances. As you might well imagine by now, no one agrees how much coloring material will be needed in a glaze. To get started on a right track, mix 3 tablespoons of mineral spirits with 3 tablespoons of varnish. The varnish can be a natural or synthetic resin, but not a spar or polyurethane varnish. Add to the glaze mixture either 1 teaspoon of colors ground in oil or 1 teaspoon of Japan colors.

If the glaze does not have enough color, continue to add pigment in small increments. If the aggregate color exceeds two teaspoons, it's time to question what you are doing! The starting color for a glaze is usually burnt umber because almost all glazes are a variation of brown. Some workers prefer a mixture of raw umber (greenish brown) and burnt sienna (reddish brown). Burnt umber, however, achieves the same effect in one step. Browns are used mostly for shading, but a glaze can be any color that is appropriate for your project. Glazes used for graining will draw upon a richer variety of colors.

Some old-timers suggest that glazes be made with linseed oil instead of varnish. Glaze can be made in this manner, but there is no particular advantage to it because a much longer drying time is required. Likewise. some recipes call for a combination of oil and varnish that is no more effective than plain varnish.

Glazes can be applied with a brush or rag. I frequently apply a glaze with a pad of 0000 steel wool. Whatever method you use to apply the glaze is pretty much your own business, as long as you get it where it belongs. The usual treatment for a glaze is to brush it into an intricate area such as a cluster of carvings or the turnings on a chair or table leg. The glaze is allowed to dry for 10 to 15 minutes, but no longer than 15 minutes because it will begin to stiffen. The area is then buffed with a clean cloth. This will remove the glaze from the high spots, but leaving it in the recesses.

When glazes are used for shading, a buffing technique is not always required. For example, the front, lower stretcher of a chair receives more wear in the center where feet are placed than do either the right or left sides. In this case, the glaze can be applied with a cloth or a pad of steel wool to the left and right sides and then blended toward the center with your finger so that the evolvement of color looks natural.

The same effect can be produced by brushing the entire stretcher with the glaze and, after the requisite drying period, buffing out the center section with a piece of steel wool. Either method is acceptable. The latter method is just a reverse of the first method. In most shading work, such as the corners on table tops or the areas around molding, the glaze is rubbed on and feathered out with a finger or a small rag. Areas that would collect dirt and darken with time should be shaded.

When a glaze is to be used to cover surface imperfections of a large area the surface should first be stained. This is necessary prior to any glazing job. The stain coat, when dry, should be followed by a coat of shellac mixed 1 part shellac to 2 parts alcohol. It is necessary to seal the wood surface prior to the application of the glaze or the glaze will act as a second and stronger stain (resulting in a darker surface than you want). Allow the shellac coat to dry for three hours, rub down with steel wool, and clean.

Prepare a glaze that is darker than the original stain, brush or wipe on, and allow to dry for 10 minutes. After 10 minutes have elapsed, wipe the surface with a clean cloth, but allow the glaze to remain in the designated areas. If the glaze has stiffened to the degree that removal is very difficult, then dampen the rag with mineral spirits.

If all has gone well, the glaze will have filled the problem areas and produced a natural and harmonious effect. In the event that a few problem areas were unaffected by the glaze, such as plaster filled nail holes, then touch the areas up with colors ground in oil, Japan colors, or artist colors applied with a small brush. Allow the surface to dry at least 24 hours and shellac. It is necessary to seal the glazed surface to prevent subsequent finish coats from removing it. When rubbing down the first shellac coat, work carefully so that the glaze material is not removed. Following the sealer coat of shellac, you can continue to shellac the piece or switch to varnish.

The effects of a finish utilizing a glaze can be improved by the application of at least one coat of a *toner* (a shellac or varnish mixed with a small amount of a coloring agent). The use of a toner blends the work done and creates an overall sense of harmony and age. The toner coat is normally followed by a clear coat of the same finishing material.

The use of glazes can greatly extend the range of your finishing projects and improve the results. But like most worthwhile things, it takes a little practice and it should not be overdone.

AGING FURNITURE

A frequently heard term with regard to furniture is *distressing*. This refers to an artificial aging of furniture. In the world of mass-produced furniture, it means spattering a stained surface with flecks of paint (supposed) to indicate age. For the antique faker, distressing means whips, chains, and non-ceremonious burial at the local swamp. I prefer the term *aging* because it includes shading, glazing, and the simulation of wear. Distressing usually refers only to the simulation of wear.

Good antique fakers will go to unprecedented lengths to produce a forgery. Rough cut wood will be buried in a swamp for an aged look, then placed in an oven to promote shrinkage, or weathered for six months in the yard. Assembled furniture will be beaten with chains, painted, stripped, repainted, scorched, stripped, and refinished. Each faker has his own secret remedy but, fortunately, most of such remedies don't work well. Unfortunately, a few are highly successful.

My purpose in mentioning aging techniques is not to enduce you to set up your own lucrative business in the basement making 18th-century masterpieces for the local flea market. I especially don't want you to decide that your genuine antique does not show sufficient signs of age so that you start wacking it with chains and two-by-fours. The legitimate use of aging and distressing techniques is to make repairs appear harmonious with the remainder of the piece. If you purchase an antique table base, the replacement of a top is a simple enough project. But you don't want it to look like it came directly from the picture window of Macy's.

The basic tools for the simulation of wear are a hammer, a rasp, a knife, and an awl or an ice pick, (Fig. 9-1). The chain tool consists of three lengths of chain attached to a piece of leather and fitted with a handle. A handheld length of chain will also do. In addition to these materials, sandpaper, coloring agents, and an ounce of creativity should provide all the materials needed to age a repair. The nature of the aging game is to simulate the telltale signs of age in a non-contrived fashion. Most novices approach this work with a little too much enthusiasm and produce pieces that look as if they have been through a meat grinder.

If you give the matter of aging some thought, you will realize that it can be categorized into a few essential areas. The first aspect of aging is hard wear (loss of material by friction). This type of wear represents itself in the form of round edges such as on a table, flat spots as would be seen on finials, knobs and chair arms, or sloping concavities as seen on chair and table stretchers. The basic tool used for the removal of material is the rasp, followed by sandpaper. New edges, which should invariably lose their sharpness, have a knife or a scraper run across them. I like to use a hammer to

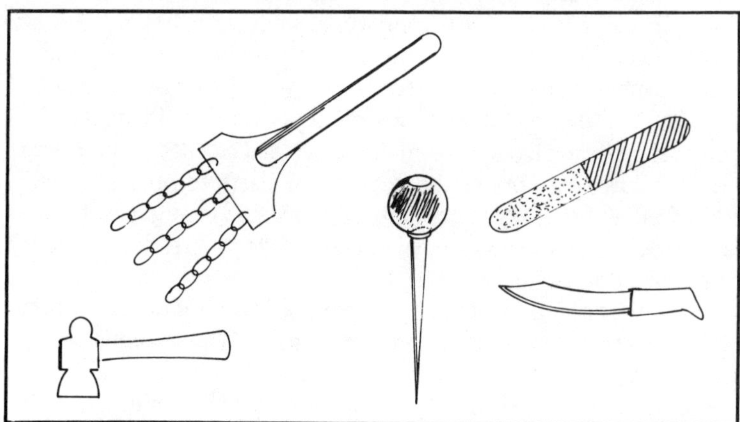

Fig. 9-1. Common tools used to distress or age a piece of furniture are a hammer, a rasp, a utility knife, an awl (ice pick), and lengths of chain attached to a handle.

247

compress the wood fiber rather than remove it. With any of this type of work, the end product should not look uniform.

Another category of aging is abrasion (nicks, dents and scratches produced by use). Abrasion marks are basically found in two areas; tops and lower extremities. The lower extremities of furniture are nicked and scratched by the rather persistent activity of feet. Tops, whether they be tables, nightstands or chests of drawers, have objects placed on them and pulled across them. Quite logically, the tops of high pieces such as tall chests and cupboards receive no wear. To produce abrasion wear, chains are hit against or pulled across a piece. The only problem with this method is that when finished, the repair piece looks like it has been hit with chains!

I think you are better advised to replicate scratches with an awl, knife or sharp nail. This work is actually harder than the removal of material because a natural effect is difficult to achieve. When replicating a scratch pattern, try to copy a pattern from another antique or old piece of furniture. It doesn't even have to be the same type of piece.

Awls and ice picks are also used to imitate worm holes. Old-timers tell of stouthearted men who loaded their shotguns with bird shot and fired away to produce worm holes. I have heard the story many times, but I have never met anyone who has done it. Worm holes can be reproduced in a random pattern with a sharp, pointed ice pick or nail and it's a lot safer than a shotgun. Worm holes can also be reproduced by dipping the tip of your paintbrush in black paint and flicking it so that a stained surface is showered by little black specks, the way mass-produced furniture is handled. What always puzzles me is why anyone would want worm holes. They are not particularly attractive or desirable. Something to keep in mind when purchasing an antique piece is that worm holes can be a sign of old age, but they can also be a sign of severe wood damage.

Repairs are also symptomatic of age and as such some restorers will purposely break and repair new parts to provide a little additional authenticity. Personally, I think this is going a little too far. If you are in the mood, have fun, but please restrict this activity to replaced parts.

Another category of the aging process is *coloration*. No antique piece has the same coloration throughout. When refinishing an antique, it is acceptable to shade and color all areas and not just the repair in order to restore the individuality of the piece and the overall appearance of age. Coloration is especially important for repair pieces if they are to look proper. Remember, when material is removed with a rasp to form a flat spot or concavity, this area must be lighter than other areas when the piece is finished because it would have worn lighter. Remember also that scratches and dents must appear darker on the finished surface than the rest of the surface as they would if naturally formed.

For an illustration of some of these points, look at the table shown in Fig. 9-2. In this drawing, the front lower stretcher is worn where feet would have been placed. The color of this stretcher would most likely pass through three evolutions.

Near each leg post the color would be darkest because of the build-up of dirt, polish, etc. As you move toward the center of the stretcher, the color would lighten and be comparable to the overall color of the piece.

As you move into the area of the concavity, the color would be the lightest as a consequence of friction. The stretcher would also have nicks and scratches produced by shoes and the like. If the stretcher were replaced, not only would the wear have to be simulated, but so would the coloration.

In this case, the new piece—once suitably worn and distressed—would receive a stain coat lighter than the overall stain used on the piece.

Following the stain coat, a glaze darker than the primary stain would be prepared and brushed on the stretcher. The glaze would be buffed off to achieve the evolution of color: dark, lighter, lightest. When the glaze had dried, a small amount of a second very dark glaze would be prepared. The second glaze would be applied, with an artist brush, to the nicks and scratches and then buffed so that the color did not stain the wood around the scratches. When the glazing was completed, a sealer coat would be applied. This would be followed by an appropriate finish coat.

The table illustrated also exhibits other types of wear such as nicks and scratches in the area of the feet and on the top of the table. Purposely, the lower stretcher on the right side of the table does not show extreme wear or abrasion. There is no Newton's first law of stretcher wear that mandates that all stretchers be badly scarred. If a table top has a long overhang, then there will be minimal stretcher wear because the distance will prohibit resting feet on the stretcher.

If you replace the table top, it will be necessary to create a random abrasion pattern for the new surface. All edges of the table top will have lost their sharpness as (Fig. 9-2). The top of the table, if a two-board top, inevitably will have separated or cracked. It is a

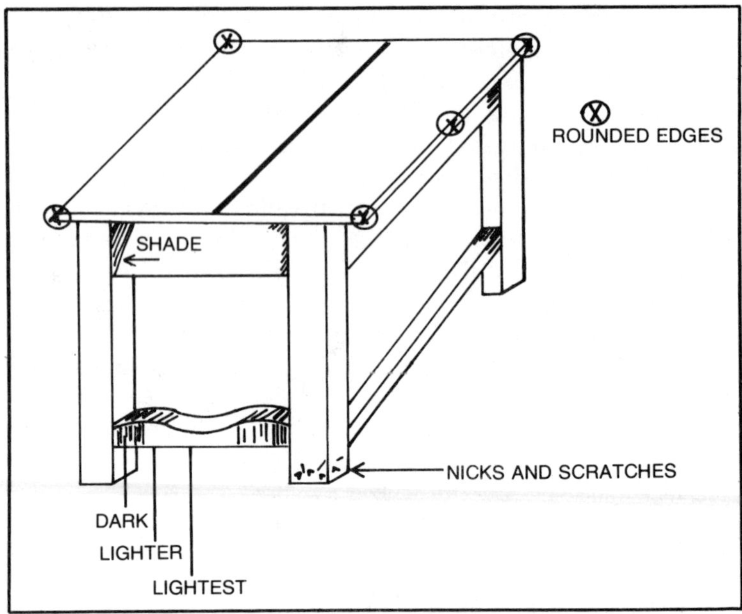

Fig. 9-2. The signs of wear and use on an antique table are: rounded edges and corners; a surface scarred by nicks, dents and scratches; and stretchers worn from foot placement. Feet are nicked, scratched and worn smooth. Dirt and old polish will have collected in nearly all joinings. These areas will be darker than the other surfaces.

simple enough proposition to make a new top, but it is not quite as simple to make it look as if it has been around for 200 years.

The best way to handle the project is to purchase old barn boards from a salvage yard. These boards will be fraught with natural wear and imperfections. Old, wide, hardwood floor boards make grand table tops. I have seen many a New England birch floor sitting atop a drop-leaf base, but that's another story. If old boards are not available, purchase some new ones and place them on the floor in the most traveled area of your home. After a few weeks on the floor, the boards will show wear that looks considerably better than the whips and chains treatment.

The aging and distressing of replacement parts, or entire reproduction pieces for that matter, is not a random act of violence with blunt instruments. It is an art. This work requires little skill, but a considerable degree of talent and creativity. The novice is best advised to study and duplicate the wear and use patterns of old furniture rather than to strike out haphazardly. Remember, in this instance a little is better than a lot.

250

FAKING A RESTORATION

In the wonderful madcap world of furniture and antiques the term *faking* implies a process by which a Volkswagen is made to look like a Rolls Royce. If this seems to be a formidable task, don't worry, it is. From time to time during the historic furniture periods, craftsmen found it necessary to make one wood look like another wood. With a few strokes of the brush and some real talent, a craftsman could instantly transform a pine chest into a richly grained mahogany chest. This transformation process has been called *graining, faking the grain,* or just plain *faking.* The craftsmen of yesteryear engaged in this practice to make an inexpensive wood look like an expensive one or because it was simply the fashion. The important question, regardless of past motivations, is under what circumstances should the novice restorer pursue faking.

When you are restoring any piece of antique furniture, the goal should be to return that furniture to a state of originality. If when you are stripping a piece of furniture you find graining, the first attempt should be to save the graining. On the other hand, if the graining is long lost, but there is evidence to suggest that it was once there, then it is perfectly acceptable to regrain the piece.

The reality of this situation is that few people will choose to paint a piece once they have spent days taking the paint off. If you purchase a piece that is already grained, but severely worn, then you have a dilemma. Purists will say leave the piece as it is, while others will say restore the worn areas.

In a situation like this, take the piece to someone who specializes in graining work. He can provide necessary direction and wisdom. In addition, the restoration of a painted, grained piece should not be undertaken by an amateur; it is highly skilled work.

Faking is the type of thing that can be done by almost anyone with a modicum of success, but it can be done well by very few. There are many fine pieces of grained furniture from the 18th century and the 19th century, but there are probably more pieces of poorly done furniture from the same period. This just indicates that is has always been a difficult proposition. Oddly enough, the art of faking seemed to reach its apogee in the late 19th century with house painters who specialized in graining simple pine moldings and door frames. Sadly, these great historic treasures are being lost to stripper, honey-toned finishes and polyurethane.

Given this healthy elaboration of why you should not do your own faking, are there any circumstances when you should attempt it? The answer is a qualified yes. When you are at your wits' end, when a piece of furniture presents a problem that can only be conquered with a paint job, then faking becomes a viable alternative. In addition, faking is always acceptable on a nonantique piece of furniture that you want to match to your collection.

Faking with a Glaze

A tenacious problem sometimes encountered with furniture is *bleed-through.* This problem occurs when a paint has deeply penetrated the wood fibers. The very process of stripping can force the paint deeper into the wood. Whatever the cause, the paint bleeds through the stain coat and creates a mottled and cloudy appearance. This problem is most often encountered with white paints.

If you are really the industrious sort, you will strip the piece a second time and start again. The only problem with this approach is that it is a waste of time because the paint will bleed through the second time as well. Even if you take the piece out for a super-caustic dip stripping, the problem is likely to occur. The most expedient solution to this problem is to grain the piece with a glaze.

Graining normally involves a base coat of a flat paint. In this case, however, the entire stain coat—that was not satisfactory itself—will serve as a base coat. Prepare a glaze (as outlined earlier in this chapter) utilizing varnish, mineral spirits, and pigment. The glaze must be darker than the original stain and it should be dark enough to provide a contrast. Once the glaze is prepared, the trick is to get it on in a manner that looks like a natural wood grain and at the same time covers the imperfections.

The glaze can be applied in a number of ways depending upon individual preference. The glaze can be applied with a stiff bristled brush, a rag, a sponge, or a special tool known as a graining comb (Fig. 9-3). You can't know which method will work best for you unless you try them all. That's not a bad approach because any practice will tend to improve upon the finished product. A brush is probably the safest approach for someone who has never done the work before.

Wood grain is essentially, but not absolutely, straight. Therefore, the glaze should be applied with a straight stroke with some minimal variation such as a waver. If you attempt to produce an exotic effect such as a flame grain, you will be doomed to failure.

As you move across the width of the piece, successive brush strokes are overlapped. The base coat should peer through the brush strokes to create the grained effect. Too much glaze will cause the piece to look painted and unattractive. If for any reason you are not satisfied with the grain effect, dip a rag in mineral spirits, wipe the glaze from the surface, and begin again. The nice part of using a glaze for graining is that mistakes are easily repairable.

When the graining has been applied in a satisfactory manner, allow the glaze to dry for a minimum of 48 hours and apply a sealer coat of shellac followed by a coat of varnish. Do not rub the piece down prior to applying the sealer. To improve the overall effect of graining, use a toner coat of varnish (varnish colored with a brown pigment). The toner coat of varnish will help meld the base coat and the grain coat and it will provide a mellow, aged look to the piece.

Allow the toner coat to dry for a minimum of 72 hours, rub down and apply a final coat of clear varnish. Allow the final coat to dry an additional 72 hours, rub down, and wax. The glaze coat plus the coats of varnish will produce a high-gloss surface. Consequently, you might have to use a coarser rubbing agent such as 00 steel wood or 220-grit paper to produce a soft luster. Care must be exercised at all times to avoid rubbing through the finish into the grain coat.

Faking with a Paint

The most prevalent method of grain faking employs the use of paints. Almost anyone who has passed through a large home center is aware of antiquing kits. The two-step antique kits are no more than commercially prepared graining kits. These kits work well enough. Nevertheless, better results can be obtained by using your own materials. One-step antiquing kits are also available. I haven't as yet, tried one of these, but I have seen the results of some who have and I have not been impressed.

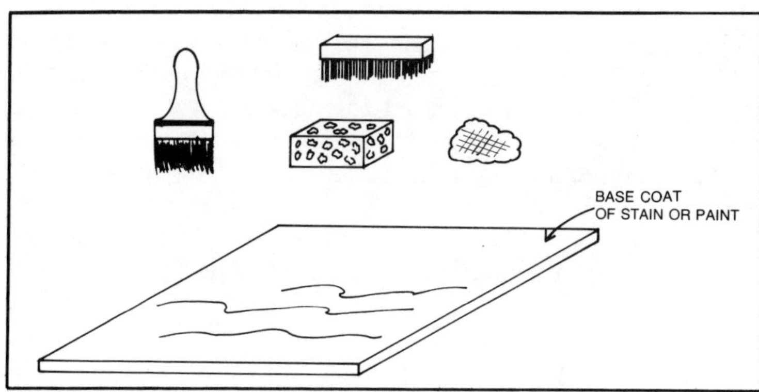

Fig. 9-3. Tools used to simulate wood grain with a glaze or paint are: a stiff brush, a special graining comb, a sponge, or a piece of steel wool.

Faking grain with a paint requires a little more skill than other forms of graining. Most people I have met have not been overly impressed with the final product of their antique kits. Doubtlessly, with a little patience and care, better results can be obtained than with an antiquing kit. The successful performance of this task requires practice, experimentation, and some artistic talent. As is recommended for graining with glazes, this work should only be undertaken if there is no other choice.

For some, the basic appeal of antiquing is the belief that the original paint does not have to be stripped away. The thought of not having to strip an old paint is appealing, but it is simply not the case. If there is to be any chance of positive results with a graining job, all coats of any previous paint should be removed and the wood surface should be thoroughly sanded.

Once the piece is stripped and sanded, it should be given a sealer coat of shellac. The shellac will provide a base so that the first coat of paint brushes on evenly and easily. Should you or some future owner want to strip the piece, the sealer coat will invariably make it an easier proposition. Allow the sealer coat to dry for three hours and then rub down with 000 steel wool.

The graining project will require a light paint and a dark paint. For example, a walnut effect will necessitate a light-to-medium brown paint and a dark brown paint. Remember, whatever colors are chosen, there must be enough variation between the base coat and the top coat to provide contrast. Flat oil base paint should be used; do not use latex base paints. You could purchase colored paints for the project, but better results will be obtained if you employ flat white paints and mix your own colors.

Colors ground in oil can be used to bring the paint up to color. Mix the paints in the same manner as you would stains. Apply the light paint, which serves as the base coat, with a brush and allow to dry. When the base coat has dried, apply a sealer coat of shellac and allow to dry for an additional three hours. After the sealer coat of shellac has dried, rub down the surface ever so lightly with 0000 steel wool.

The top coat of paint, which is the darker of the two, will be applied in the same manner as a glaze used for graining. A glaze can equally be used for a graining job over a base coat of paint. The decision to use glaze or paint for a top coat is a matter of personal preference. In any event, the graining coat can be applied with a brush, a sponge, a graining comb or a crumpled rag. Steel wood can be used to create a fine-textured grain effect.

The graining coat is applied in long, continuous, straight strokes to simulate the natural grain of wood. Some variation must be included in the stroke because wood grain is not absolutely straight. The simplest variation is produced by introducing a slight waver at various points within the stroke. Any variation that is introduced must be random so that the entire surface does not look contrived.

Other implements, such as the tip of a feather rolled against some parts of the finish, can be used to create variation as long as the end product looks natural. If you are not satisfied with the grain pattern you have created, clean the surface with turpentine and start over again. Your graining technique should be practiced on several scrap pieces prior to attempting to grain your first antique. To do otherwise is to court disaster.

Allow the graining coat of paint to dry for at least 24 hours, and somewhat longer under damp and humid conditions. At this point, you might want to prepare a glaze and use it to shade appropriate areas as you would with a stain job. In some cases, the shading will add considerable character to the piece. In other cases it might not, but this will have to be your judgment. If a glaze is used, allow an additional 24 hours for drying.

I am loath to suggest the use of a spatter pattern on a piece; Nevertheless, it often goes well with a grained piece of furniture. A spatter pattern is what commercial furniture manufacturers call a distressed finish. To produce this effect, dip your paintbrush in some flat black paint. Capture paint on the tip of the brush, but don't load it by immersing the whole brush in the paint. Point the brush at the furniture surface and flip the bristles back with your hand. Let them spring forward so that the black paint spatters in random droplets on the surface. A little spatter can add character, but please don't get carried away and produce a piece that looks like it is suffering from the pox.

When the graining coat, glaze coat, spatter coat and all such things are dry, prepare a toner coat of varnish and brush it on in the normal manner. Allow the toner coat to dry for at least 72 hours and rub it down lightly. Follow with a coat of clear varnish. Allow the final coat of varnish to dry. Rub down carefully, but make sure not to rub through the graining. Then wax the surface.

To apply a grain job in the manner discribed is obviously not an overnight job. The overall project time will be about a week and a half. This is opposed to two days when you are using a commercial graining kit. The time spent in applying the toner coat of varnish and the final coat is the difference between an amateurish effect and a professional looking job. A commercial antiquing, a varnish toner, and clear varnish can be used to greatly enhance the final product of a project.

Paints are also used for effects other than graining. Feather-painted furniture of the 18th and 19th centuries is highly desirable and sought after. Feather-painting involves the same two-step process that is employed in graining. A base coat is followed by a top coat of paint or glaze. The top coat is applied with a feather in twist, roll, or swirl patterns. Feather painting allows for a greater use of colors (especially those in the yellow family). The combination of color and pattern with feather painting can be wonderfully attractive.

Marbling is another effect achieved with a two-step paint process. With marbling, a base coat of off-white to gray-white is applied. A random streaked pattern is applied over the base in washed-out black or gray paint to create a marble effect. The paint can be applied with a feather or an artist brush. I don't consider either of these finishes appropriate for an amateur or novice to undertake because both techniques require artistic talent. If you want to attempt these techniques, use the methods outlined for graining and practice a great, great deal.

Faking with Stain

The fun part of restoring and finishing your own furniture is that there are always many surprises. Not everyone likes a surprise and some consider them downright frustrating. Keep a positive attitude about these things. It is quite possible that you might purchase a ruddy mahogany drop-leaf table, take it home, strip it and find that it is no longer mahogany. Even worse, you might find that some parts are mahogany while other parts are not.

To solve some of these problems you must return to that special magic of faking. As previously mentioned, grains can be faked with glazes over a stain base or with a two-step paint process. The glaze methods are primarily intended for surfaces that must be partially or totally obscured. An example is a surface with residual paint.

Paint techniques are employed in situations that require radical transformation such as making pine look like rosewood. The majority of faking jobs do not require elaborate paint techniques. They can be accomplished with greater simplicity and success by simple staining.

In short, one wood can be made to look like another just by changing the color. Faking with a stain is a matter of going from a light wood to a dark wood or from a dark to a light. In addition, the transition from light to dark might involve a change in color.

As a rule, light woods can be made to look like dark woods with the use of a stain. Dark woods, however, require a paint or other such opaque covering to look like light woods. In some cases, it might be possible to bleach a dark wood to obtain a desired light effect. For example, walnut can be bleached to look like butternut, but why would anyone want it to? For the most part, people want to turn light woods into darker woods, or—to be more specific—the popular types such as cherry, walnut, mahogany, and (occasionally) maple.

Cherry finishes are in vogue these days. It's a reasonable finish to duplicate. Cherry, in its natural state, runs from a pink to a tan. With age, it turns to a rich brown with a subtle reddish hue. Cherries are red, but cherry wood is not. If cherry is what you have in mind, poplar, birch, basswood, and maple can be turned into cherry just by the use of a proper stain.

Maple is quite similar to cherry. When the two are stained, it is difficult to tell them apart. Poplar and basswood are plain woods that take a stain beautifully. As such, either will make a representative cherry. Birch is adequate for the job, but its grain characteristics are different enough to cause some notice.

Of the white woods, pine presents the greatest difficulty. Turnings in pine such as legs or small areas such as drawers and side rails will take a cherry stain convincingly. Table tops or other large areas in pine will accept a cherry color very nicely, but the grain characteristics will set it apart as pine. In this case, it is best to stain these areas with the cherry color (red/brown) and accept the deviation.

The alternate choice would be to fake the grain of the top with a glaze. For most people, a more satisfactory result will be achieved by sticking with the stain. When imitating cherry with a stain, you cannot use a premixed cherry stain because it is too red. Mix your own stain that will be suitable for the job.

Pieces made of more than one wood can present some modest problems. For example, I have seen a preponderance of cherry tables with maple legs. It is a simple matter to color the maple legs to match the cherry top, but the legs should not be matched until the top has received some treatment. If the non-cherry parts are matched to the raw cherry parts prior to staining or finishing, the color relationships will be changed by the finishing. If the cherry parts are to be stained, which is rarely needed, then stain them and match the non-cherry parts to that color. If the cherry parts are to be left natural, apply one coat of the finishing material to be used, and then match the non-cherry parts to that color. Whatever finish you are working on involving two woods, always fix the color of the primary wood with a stain, wet test, or finish, prior to matching the non-primary woods.

Simulating a maple finish is a basic stain procedure. Poplar, basswood, and birch can be made to look like maple with the use of maple stain. The birch will be the least convincing. Cherry can be made to look like a very convincing red/brown maple of the darker variety. Pine will take a maple stain very well, but grain characteristics on large surfaces will be a giveaway. As with a cherry finish, you are best advised to go with the maple color and not fuss around with the large areas.

The wood effect that is most often sought after is a mahogany finish. I am not always enthusiastic about this, but it is the way of the world and I accept it. Cherry will take a mahogany stain very well and will look a great deal like mahogany without any other treatment. Maple, birch, poplar, pine and other light woods will need a graining treatment to look like mahogany, but it can be done with stains as well as glazes. To accomplish this feat, water stains are required. Therefore, it will be necessary to pre-raise the grain of the wood surface so that it will not prove to be a problem at a later time. To do this, rub the previously sanded wood surface with a wet rag. But don't give the piece a bath. Allow the wood surface to dry and sand it with a 240-grit finishing paper. Repeat the process. After the second wetdown and sanding, the piece will be ready for staining.

Prepare a light mahogany stain and a dark mahogany stain from stain powders or water-soluble aniline dyes. Apply the light stain liberally with a brush to one surface at a time. Do not remove the excess stain with a rag. While the base coat of light stain is still wet, take a rag or brush and apply a graining coat of the dark stain. The top coat of stain will bleed into the base coat. This will give a blended and natural look to the graining.

As the base coat dries, there will be less bleeding. Consequently, the top coat will appear somewhat streaky. It is best to work only one area at a time to avoid drying. If the base coat dries too quickly, brush on another coat and continue with the graining. You must attempt to replicate the natural grain pattern of the wood that you are imitating, and there must be some random variation.

This method of graining is a little tricky and it requires much practice. In the long run, it is easier and far more satisfactory than using paints because the actual grain of the wood is not obscured. The effect of this process is one of illusion as opposed to transformation.

After the graining coat of stain has been applied, allow the piece to dry for at least 24 hours. A normal finishing process would involve brushing a coat of sealer over the stain, but with this stain process a brushed-on finish is risky. The relationship of the top coat of stain to the base coat is rather fragile. A brushing could lift some of the stain and destroy the grain effect.

To remedy this problem, obtain a can of spray-on varnish that is available at most hardware stores. Spray the varnish in accordance with the directions on the can and allow it to dry for 48 to 72 hours. Do not rub down the sealer coat of varnish once it is dry.

The sealer coat is followed by a toner coat of varnish (varnish tinted with burnt umber). This will render a more natural look to the graining. When you are applying the toner coat of varnish, do not work it briskly as you normally would. Flow it on using a light touch with the brush. Allow the toner coat of varnish 72 hours to dry and rub it down ever so lightly with 0000 steel wool. Follow the toner coat with a coat of clear varnish, rub it down and then wax.

Walnut finishes are also sought after by many craftspersons. To change a light wood into a walnut, the same techniques as described above for mahogany are employed. Light browns and dark browns are substituted for the red/browns used in the mahogany finish. In general, walnut finishes look less convincing than mahogany finishes because the flamboyant figure of mahogany is easier to fake.

At best, faking in all its aspects—aging, distressing, glazing and graining—is a trial and error process. Rarely will two people agree upon the techniques involved or, for that matter, the materials to be used. The methods outlined in this chapter are meant to be a starting point and guide. By no means are they the definitive statement on the techniques. Please bear in mind that all of these techniques should be practiced on scrap pieces prior to use on your antiques or fine furniture. If during your practice you logically or instinctively think an aspect of the process should be changed, then give way to your creative urge as long as there is no risk of damage to a valuable piece.

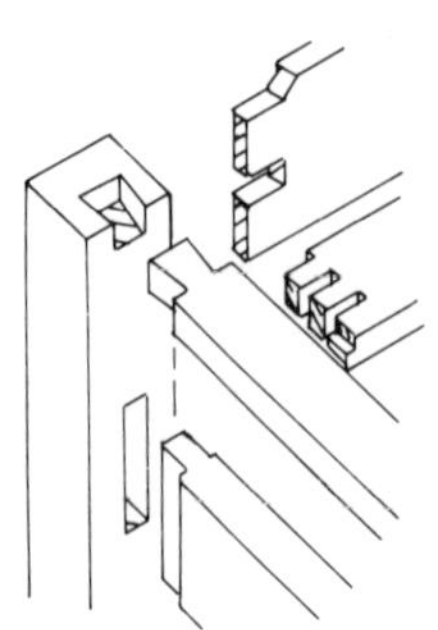

Chapter 10
Painting

Paint is the anathema of refinishers all over the world. Paint gets into the grain of the wood. It fills the pores. It is often applied in so many layers that it could not be destroyed by an atomic sledge hammer! On the other hand, paint is extremely practical and durable. A painted surface is easily applied, easily renewed, and offers more protection than most furniture finishes. With some antique furniture paint can be charming and beautiful. With other pieces, it can range from modestly interesting to ugly. I really cannot think of any one product that inspires such love and hate as does paint. Perhaps that is because paint is a personal and dynamic medium.

For the collector of country furniture and the occasional restorer of antiques, the question is where does paint fit in the general scheme of things. The simplest answer is that paint does not generally fit into the scheme of things and as usual there are a lot of "buts" and "what-ifs." If you purchase a piece of furniture with original paint, it should be left alone unless work is necessary to save it from further deterioration. Under most circumstances, a good coat of paste wax will sufice to protect paint. But even that should be approached with caution because there is some risk of removing pigment.

A good painted piece of furniture should be left alone even if it looks like a delapidated old fence post. Restorations to old paints should be done by qualified experts who specialize in antique paints. A good refinisher can repaint the piece and distress it so that it looks as old as the piece really is. An expert will not (or should not) do anything that will hurt the historical value of the piece. If you can't live with a piece of furniture with original paint in original condition, then save your money.

Now that I have established what you shouldn't do, I will discuss what you should do. Let us presume that you have purchased a simple, early 19th-century chest of drawers at an auction. The chest has the normal nine layers of decaying white paint that flakes off on you and the floor each time you move the piece.

In order to determine the original finish of the piece, you scrape an obscure spot with a knife. Nothing is observed except raw wood so you make a decision to strip the piece. With this piece, there is no way to tell what was original. All the white paint is modern. That puts it after 1860 and means it could not be original. Because there is no sign of anything under the modern paint, you might presume the piece had no finish or that the piece has since been scraped, sanded or stripped of its original finish.

There is a prevailing belief in the antique world, called Murphy's law of the unknown, which postulates that furniture with several coats of old paint must have an original finish underneath. Far be it for us to contradict one of Murphy's laws. Nevertheless, I offer Harry's First Rule of Paradox which postulates that all rules can be true and contradicted at the same time. This means that the hypothetical piece either had no original finish or that it was stripped in the 18th century, the 19th century, or the 20th century. Somebody's Great Uncle Rudy might well have stripped the original varnish or paint from the chest in 1905, and painted it with a nice, modern white paint.

All of this elaboration is to make one simple point. When you don't know and can't know, then you are free to do what you want (within reason). The hypothetical chest can be given a warm, brown stain and a varnish (most often be the case) or it can be given a rich, brownish/red, aged-milk paint finish if it suits your taste.

Either of these could have been used originally and they can now be used if there are no indications to the contrary. In the absence of the proof of an original finish, the furniture can be painted at your option as long as it is congruent with the practices of the time.

An 18th-century candlestand with a turned pedestal and snake feet would not have been painted and should not be painted. A simple country 18th-century candlestand in maple and cherry might well have been painted. A pine-top, maple-base candlestand of the early 19th century would most likely have been painted. This is what is meant by historical congruency. If you have any doubts, go to the library or a local museum and do a little research prior to starting your project.

If in the process of stripping you find paint residue, a paint-stained wood surface, or other indication of original paint surface, it means you can apply new paint. The wood surface is given a sealer coat of shellac prior to painting so that the paint does not permeate the wood and can be removed at a future date. It is perfectly acceptable to paint old or reproduction pieces to make them compatible with pieces in your collection.

APPLYING PAINT

Many people like to paint furniture because it saves them the trouble of stripping a piece. Now, in all honesty if you have a piece with five or six coats of paint on it, you can't do any harm by giving it another coat. But you will never get good results by painting over several layers of old paint. You only have to walk around any neighborhood and look at the flaking, peeling paint on some of the houses to know that coat after coat just doesn't work well.

The first rule of a good paint job is that you must have a smooth surface. In the case of furniture, this means you should strip off the old paint. If you are one of those contrary persons who refuses to do things the proper way, then remove all the flaking with a wire brush and sand the entire piece so that subsequent coats of paint will adhere. Presuming that the old paint has been removed, all dents and cracks should be stopped up with a suitable filler and be followed up with a light sanding until the surface is smooth.

After sanding, the project should be given a sealer coat of shellac. The sealer coat, overlooked by many people, is important for a number of reasons. The sealer coat prevents the paint from penetrating the wood and at the same time provides a stable base so that paint covers the surface evenly. If there is any residual paint or oils in the wood fiber, the shellac will seal it in. This will prevent bleed-through and damage of the final paint surface. This isn't a strange practice. A professional interior painter will always have a can of shellac that is used to cover stains on walls. When the shellac is dry, it is rubbed down with 000 steel wool.

Latex, water-base paints are great for the plaster walls of your home, but they are not ideal for your furniture. Water-based paints will raise the wood fiber and enter the wood deeply. This will cause problems for future strippers. Even if the sealer coat of shellac prevents the paint from entering the wood, the latex paints offer a lot of resistance to strippers.

For furniture, a flat oil base paint is the better choice. A wide variety of premixed or formula-mixed paints are available. The colors, however, tend to be a bit too bright for an antique-furniture effect. Paints can be appropriately toned down by the addition of a small amount of brown paint or a drop of burnt umber. Ideally, the paint should be applied in multiple, thin coats. That means it should be thinned slightly as it comes from the can. Add about a tablespoon of mineral spirits or turpentine to a cup of paint (oil based) and brush on vigorously—first with the grain then across the grain. Level the paint job using the tip of the brush in long, continuous, overlapping strokes in the directions of the grain.

After the paint has dried, there are two routes that you can pursue. The first route is the old and used look and the second route is the glossy, commercial furniture look. For the aged look, scuff the paint with 00 or 000 steel wool and shade the appropriate areas with a glaze. Be careful to glaze only the areas that you want shaded because the glaze could permeate the paint if applied to too large an area. If you are not satisfied with the look, tone some varnish with burnt umber and varnish the piece. When the varnish has dried, rub down the piece with 3/0 pumice and water and then clean with a fresh rag and water.

I don't think that a high-gloss paint finish is appropriate for country antique furniture, but if you are painting some new pine, or the like, then it is dynamite. When the flat-oil-based paint has dried thoroughly, two to three days later, rub it down lightly with 280- to 300-grit sandpaper. Follow the rubdown with a clear coat of varnish and allow it to dry the requisite three days. Rub down the varnish with 000 steel wool or 240-grit paper and then wax. When the piece is finished, your family will either want to know where you purchased it or where the spray gun and compressor are hidden.

OLD MILK PAINT

The most sought after of paints in the antique world is old milk paint. Milk paint was not particularly better than other types of paint, but it was more convenient. What could be easier than adding some red clay or berries to rancid milk or buttermilk. Of course, the paint smelled worse than a container of marsh gas. And if it rained within the first 48 hours, a good deal of the paint would wash away. Once the milk paint dried and cured, it served well as a protective coating. This is especially true if it was oiled occasionally. Milk paint ages well, but with 100 or so years of use it tends to powder off as opposed to flaking. Although milk paint will powder with age, it is tenacious when it comes to removing it with strippers. It almost always stains the wood the color of the paint.

Not every old paint surface encountered on furniture is a milk paint, but there is a proclivity in the trade toward describing almost everything as a milk paint. Whether the paint on an antique piece is milk paint or some other type of paint is a moot point. When it comes to making a new paint job look like it is 100 years old, then milk paint is unsurpassed. Of course, you will do nothing to hurt an original paint finish and you will only use "new old paint" for repairs and other forms of restoration.

As with any paint job, the wood surface should be sanded smooth prior to the application of the paint. Milk paint has a water base that could raise the grain of the wood. Therefore, the surface should be wetted down with a moist rag to pre-raise the grain of the wood. When the wood is dry, it is again sanded with a 240-grit finishing paper to remove the *wiskers* (raised wood fibers).

Following the sanding, the piece should be stained with a medium brown stain such as a dilute walnut stain. Staining the wood is not mandatory, but at a later point in the process when the milk paint is aged, there is a chance of rubbing through to the wood surface.

If the wood surface is white, things might look a little artificial. If a mellow brown is found under the surface, the look will be a natural one. Allow the stain to dry overnight and seal the surface with a mixture of 1 part shellac to 2 parts alcohol. When dry, rub down the shellac in the normal manner with 000 steel wool.

Milk paint can be purchased in powder form with premixed colors from catalog houses. You need only add water to the paint and you can begin your project. I have never used one of these premixed paints, but I have been told by a number of people that they are good. The reason I haven't tried on of these paints is that we mix our own paint; it's simple and a lot less expensive. To prepare your own paint, venture out to the local supermarket and purchase a box of powdered milk packets. The known brand names might taste better, but for mixing paint the house discount powdered milk will do just fine.

Milk paint must be mixed for each use because it will not keep. If you try to save some of the paint, it will crust over and generate unpleasant little life forms. For the average chair or small table, 1 cup will be more than ample. A cup and a half should do for larger pieces.

It will be necessary to add some form of pigment to the paint unless you want it to be milk white (not particularly attractive). Anything that can color water can be used to color the paint. In the old days, things such as berries, clay, roots, and blood were used.

264

The most readily available coloring agents for the modern user are dyes in the form of water stains, fabric stains, and food colors.

Dyes are good, but they are not as efficient as pigments that give body to the paint. To mix paints, I use dry colors that can be purchased at most hardware stores. Dry colors are granulated pigments normally used to color paint similar to colors ground in oil. The reds and blues available in dry colors approximate the color tones found on old pieces.

To prepare the paint, mix the powdered milk with water until a creamy consistency is obtained (but not as thick as a paint). A blender or mixer is ideal for this work, but it can be done just as well with an old-fashioned stirring stick. Allow the paint mix to stand while you mix up some of the dry pigment with water.

Add approximately one-half ounce of the dry colors to 2 ounces of water. This should produce a rich, deep color. If the color is not deep, add some more pigment. The coloring mixture should be darker than the final color that you hope to achieve because it will be reduced by the white milk base.

Add the coloring mixture to the milk paint in small increments until the preferred color is obtained. After the coloring material is mixed, a second color should be introduced to tone down the paint. New colors are bright while old paint colors are soft and mellowed. The easiest way to obtain this effect is to add a small amount of brown or black coloring. Brown is the better approach.

If you use water stains, about a quarter ounce of premixed walnut stain added to a cup of paint should do nicely. Matching stain powders or food colors can also be used. And in a real pinch so can brown water paints. Whatever color medium you opt for, use just enough of the brown to tone down the mixture, but not enough to change the color.

After the colors have been added to the paint base, it should be mixed thoroughly to distribute the pigment. Following the coloration, additional powdered milk should be added until a thick paste-like consistency is achieved. If the additional milk powder has altered the color balance significantly, the color can be brought back by the addition of a small amount of pigment. Generally, I have found that the paint needs to be mixed a little thicker than regular paint to function properly. Ideally, the milk paint should be applied in one coat. Milk paint requires a good two to three days to dry properly. During this time, the original paint that was mixed will go bad. If a second coat of paint is required, you will have to mix a new batch and it will never be the same color. The job is best done with one coat.

After the paint is mixed, apply some to a scrap piece of wood and allow it to dry for a half hour. The dry color of the milk paint will always differ somewhat from the wet color. A color test is a good precaution. This is especially true if you are matching a piece. Providing the color test has gone well, give the paint a final vigorous mix and you are ready to begin.

Any clean paintbrush can be used to apply the paint. I prefer to use a large, artist-style, white-bristle brush. I like a stiff-bristled brush because it works well with the crude nature of the paint. I am not sure that it really makes a difference. Apply the paint in straight, overlapping strokes and redo each stroke with the tip of your brush to level it out.

Homemade milk paint, or for that matter one of the prepared mixes, will not have the even consistency and sound working properties of a factory-made oil paint. Therefore, I find that it is best not to work the paint hard as you would a normal paint. The goal is to apply an even layer of paint without too many brush marks. Any method that achieves this is a good method.

Painting should be accomplished with one coat. If for some reason the first coat has not been adequate, allow the piece to dry for three or four hours and recoat with the original paint mix. The original paint will most likely have to be loosened up by the addition of some water. The application of a second coat at this point can dissolve the first coat. If it is attempted, very light strokes should be used.

Milk paint will dry to the touch in about a half hour, but it will need two to three days to fully harden before any distressing can take place. The first piece we ever painted, a bed, was ruined when we moved it out to the van on a rainy day after only an overnight drying. To our complete surprise, by the time we got the bed into the van, it was a dripping mass of red paint. Don't rush the process; allow at least three days' drying time.

A freshly painted surface will not be adequate for an antique collection. You must embark upon a program of instant aging. After the proper drying period, take some 00 steel wool and rub the paint thin in those areas where the paint would normally have worn off. This type of work should be carefully done, subtle, and limited.

Prepare a standard glaze or a simple brown glaze consisting of 1 part linseed oil, 2 parts thinner, and some burnt umber. Shade the piece with the glaze in the areas that would darken with age. Use the glaze only in selective areas and do not cover the entire surface. As paints go, milk paint is fairly porous. Any area touched with the glaze will be stained. When the shading work has been completed, use an artist brush to darken all dents, nicks, and scratches with the glazing material. Try to apply the glaze to the dent or scratch and not to the area around it. For very small scratches, use the tip of a toothpick to apply the glaze. Allow the glaze to dry overnight.

The glaze will add character to the piece, but it's not quite enough. Go out to your yard or a friend's yard and dig up a cup of dirt. It is not necessary to filter the dirt through mesh, but pick out the major rocks and boulders before using. Mix the dirt with water until a thick mud is formed and rub down the piece with a folded rag dipped generously in the mud.

The mud will act like a mild abrasive compound. Apply it only in the direction of the grain. The mud treatment will smooth out the finish slightly, tone down the color, and collect in all the crevices where debris would normally be found. Some of the pigment will be removed by this process. This is normal and acceptable. Do not rub so hard that you go through the finish.

Don't be alarmed if some small pebble or hard material in the dirt scratches the paint job because it will add a natural, aged look to the piece. Allow the mud job to dry overnight and then dust the residue off with a brush.

The combination of the simulated wear, glazing, and mud compound is going to produce an impressively aged look. There still remains a little icing to be put on the cake. Prepare a mixture of pumice and water until a paste-like consistency is achieved. Pumice is a powerful abrasive. You must be very careful not to rub the paint off. Apply the pumice with a padded rag and stroke on with the grain.

In this case, you are *applying* the pumice not rubbing the piece down. There should be only the slightest hint of pressure. Do not clean the pumice mixture off with a clean rag. Leave it deposited on the surface. Each application of a finishing step with a water base will soften the paint somewhat. Allow the surface to dry overnight after the application of the pumice. The pumice will dry as a white powder over the entire surface. Take a clean brush and dust it off. The pumice that remains on the surface and in the joints will create the illusion of a paint that is turning to powder as would an original paint.

All in all, a homemade milk paint distressed in the manner outlined will produce a very convincing instant 100-year-old paint job. Given 20 or 30 years of wear and drying, I would not envy the person who had to decide if it was an original finish.

Some persons, when seeking an aged-milk-paint effect, choose

to use two different color paints. This can be found on many originals. To achieve this effect, the first color paint is applied after the
wood is sealed and it is allowed to dry for three days. The first coat
is scuffed with 000 steel wool to provide a base for the second coat.
But it is not distressed in any manner. A second coat of a different
color milk paint such as a red over a blue is applied. When the
second coat of paint is dry, it is rubbed through in the high wear
areas to expose the paint underneath. The paint is then aged in the
manner previously described. This approach is not necessarily
better than the first approach. It merely simulates another type of
paint effect commonly found.

ANTIQUE FRENCH WHITE

In England and France during the 18th century, it was fashionable to paint high-style pieces as well as country pieces. Although
painted high-style pieces can be found across Europe, they are most
often associated with the white-painted pieces of the Louis XV style
of France. Pieces were not exclusively painted in white, but these
finishes have become the most esteemed over the years. This finish
is typified by a white background with ornamental surfaces gilded or
bronzed. The 18th-century furniture painted in this manner was
curvilinear with heavy emphasis on carving and ornamentation. A
considerable amount of gilt work was apparent. The passage of time
and the factors of wear and use have subtly shaded and distressed
these finishes in a most attractive manner.

An antique, French-white finish does not belong on any piece of
American country furniture. Nevertheless, you need only omit the
gilt or bronze step for a simple antiqued white finish that is applica-
ble to country furniture. Consistent with good practice, the piece
should be stripped and sanded lightly prior to beginning your project. If the work piece is not stripped, it must be cleaned carefully so
that all traces of dirt and wax are removed. All loose and flaking
paint should be removed with a stiff brush and the overall finish
should be scuffed with finishing paper.

New surfaces and stripped surfaces should be sealed with a
mixture of 1 part shellac to 2 parts alcohol. After drying, the sealer
coat should be rubbed with 000 steel wool. If carvings and other
decorative areas are to be gilded with bronze powders, this work
should be accomplished prior to the application of the paint. Purchase some bronze powder and bronzing liquid from a hobby shop
and mix the powder and liquid in equal parts. Apply to decorated
areas with a clean brush. If bronzing liquid is terribly expensive or

not availble, clear varnish can be substituted with equally good results. The bronze powders will dry to the touch in an hour or two, but it is best to allow them to dry overnight before going on with the rest of the project.

When the bronze powders are dry, the piece is to be painted with a flat white paint. Either latex or oil-based paints can be used. The piece should be painted in the normal fashion. Stroke with the grain, then across the grain, and with a final leveling stroke with the tip of the brush in the direction of the grain. The gilt areas are not avoided. They are painted over as if they were not there. Immediately after the piece has been painted, take a clean rag and wipe the carvings and all gilt areas.

The intention here is not to remove all the paint, but to remove enough of the paint so that it looks as if the gilt has worn off. There is no way to tell you how to do this because it involves artistic judgment. You can go to museums or furniture stores to study the effect.

Allow the paint to dry for several hours or overnight (depending upon the paint used). When the paint has dried, coat the gilt surfaces with an equal mixture of shellac and alcohol. Allow the shellac to dry for two to three hours and rub down gently with 0000 steel wool. It is necessary to seal the gilt to prevent future flaking.

When the piece has been painted and gilted, prepare a glaze of varnish and burnt umber, and rub the glaze into all carved areas. Areas around joints and edges that would normally be shaded should be treated with the glaze. Remember to wipe the glaze from the high spots after approximately 15 minutes of drying time.

If a particularly distressed look is preferred, large, flat surfaces—such as the top of a dressing table—should be scuffed with 00 steel wool. After scuffing, the top is glazed so that the glaze will flow into the fine scratches made in the paint surface by the steel wool. After a few minutes, the surface is wiped free of excess glaze. This type of effect is not difficult to achieve from a technical standpoint. Nevertheless, practice is necessary if the effect is not to look strained and artificial.

When the gilding, painting, and glazing are completed, the piece can be left as is or waxed. Some workers choose to give a piece a final toner coat of tinted varnish. A toner coat tends to give this type of finish too much gloss for an antiqued painted effect. It is an option if you are somewhat disappointed with the results.

An antique, French-painted finish, does not fall into the realm of country furniture. Nevertheless, the procedure is the same for any type of old paint look. Omit the gilt and you have an antique white paint finish. Or substitute red or blue, and so on.

GILDING

Occasionally, you might want to decorate a piece by the addition of gilt, as with an antique white paint, or you might want to restore antique picture frames and the like. Most newcomers to finishing and decorative art shy away from these processes because the techniques are presumed to be complex. Yet the methods are quite simple.

Gilt is anything that looks like gold. *Gilding* refers to the act of applying gilt or gold. Through the centuries, various methods have been used to apply gilt. The primary methods that evolved employ either powders or leaf. Both powders and leaf are used extensively today. Gold is much too expensive to use on anything but the finest of furniture. Common substitutes used for gold are bronze powders and yellow brass leaf. These products are easily obtained at hobby shops.

To apply bronze powders, a bronzing liquid is required. Varnish or shellac can be substituted for a bronzing liquid with equal results and less cost. To apply the powders, mix an equal amount of the powders and the adhesive liquid. Use a clean brush and paint the powder mixture on the surface to be decorated. No special brush stroke is required, but it is essential that the entire surface be covered. Allow the gilt powder to dry about three hours if it is shellac based or overnight if varnish based. When the gilt has dried, apply a fresh coat of dilute shellac (equal parts of shellac and alcohol) or varnish. This depends upon which product was used to apply the powders. The final shellac or varnish coat should be burnished lightly with 0000 steel wool when dry.

The alternative to using powder is gold or brass leaf. Metal leafs are thinner than paper and are packaged between sheets of tissue to prevent them from crumbling. Gold or brass leaf is applied with either a gold size or a varnish. Apply the sizing or varnish to the surface to be covered and allow it to dry for approximately 45 minutes. When the adhesive liquid is almost dry to the touch—such that there is a slight tack or adhesion when you touch your finger to the surface—then it is ready for the application of the leaf material. Break a piece of leak material to the approximate size needed and remove the cover sheet of tissue.

The leafing material is extremely fragile and should be handled gingerly. Apply the leaf to the coated area and gently pat it in place with a soft rag. The gilt material must conform to all curvatures of the surface. If a piece of the leafing breaks off during the application, you can cut a small piece and apply it to the damaged area. Allow the leafing to dry overnight and brush away any loose or excess material gently with a clean dry brush. Apply a fresh coat of clear varnish and allow it to dry for 24 to 48 hours. Rub down the final coat of varnish with 0000 steel wool when dry.

STRIPING

Striping is a type of paint decoration commonly found on 19th-century cottage furniture and modern children's furniture. This decorative technique consists of outlining a form such as the top of a dresser or the front of a drawer with a single- or double-painted line. Striping seems to conform to a basic human need of enclosing things within borders (but that is my value judgment). Striping is only found on painted furniture and then it's always darker than the base color. If you want to restore a piece of cottage furniture that has a badly damaged finish, you will need to master a striping technique.

Striping is the kind of process that makes novices tremble with fear. Actually, a little apprehension is warranted. Painting a straight line is not the simplest task in the world, but it's not the worst. If you smoke two packs of cigarettes a day and need two hands to steady the match, then striping is not for you. If you are an average person, you can do the work. Forget your apprehension; it will only make your hand shake.

The traditional method of applying a painted stripe is with a brush. This is not done with an ordinary artist brush. Use a special striping brush or a long bristled sign painter's brush. Long bristles are essential for the process. The brush must be dragged across the painted surface and not stroked.

Any flat paint can be used to paint the stripe. Japan colors thinned slightly with turpentine are ideal for the work. Some sources recommend that striping be done with glazes, but this doesn't offer any special advantages. Prior to applying a stripe, some workers prefer to lay out the stripe line with a pencil. It is not necessary to lay out the stripe if some type of guide or straightedge is used to steady the hand. If a pencil line adds to your sense of security, don't hesitate to use it. Please bear in mind that if you examine a painted stripe with your eyes 2 inches above the line, even the work of the finest professional will look irregular.

To ready your piece for striping, you must first paint it with the color of your choice. Striping looks best on light colors. It is best to study the color combinations of pieces that you have seen in shops or books rather than to come up with your own creative color combination. Select a flat paint and allow it to dry thoroughly before attempting a stripe. It will be necessary to rest your forearm on the piece while painting the stripe. If the paint is not dry, you will have a wet arm and a ruined paint job. When the paint is dry, apply a mixture of equal parts of shellac and alcohol. This will later be rubbed down with 000 steel wool.

Not everyone will seal the painted surface with a coat of shellac. It has a distinct and admirable advantage. The sealer coat of shellac will stop the striping medium from penetrating the paint. If you make a mistake while applying the stripe, you need only remove it with mineral spirits and start the process over again.

Some people have marvelously steady hands and they can follow a pencil line with a paint brush without even the slightest difficulty. Most people need some type of guide. If you are not one of those talented persons, take a piece of one by two or a straightedge and lay it on top of the piece to be striped. The straightedge should be clamped so that it will not move during the process. Position the guide to the right of your hand (if you are right-handed) approximately one hand's width away from where the stripe is to be located (See Fig. 10-1). If you are not confident about the measurement, outline the stripe with pencil. Take the striping brush in hand between your thumb and forefinger and apply it to the line. Make sure to lay your forearm on the piece. While holding the brush on the line, position the guide to the right of your hand so that it lightly touches your hand.

With the guide in place, dip the brush in the paint and draw it lightly across the lip of the container as it is removed. The brush should be loaded with paint, but not dripping. The brush is held between the thumb and forefinger and laid on the surface while resting the hand and forearm on the surface of the piece. The brush is pulled or dragged along the length of the piece while the hand is guided by the straightedge. The movement should be slow, steady and relaxed. If the brush is gripped like a life line in a storm, it will surely waiver. Ideally, the stripe is applied without removing the brush from the surface for additional paint. If the brush is removed and applied again, there is always some risk of the stripe being slightly thicker where it touched down. After the first stripe is applied, it is allowed to dry while the piece and guide are positioned for the next stripe.

If Japan colors are used to apply the stripe, the piece must be given a final coat of shellac to seal the stripe. Japan colors left unprotected are fragile. Even if Japan colors have not been used, it is generally a good practice to give the piece a final finish coat.

Striping can be mastered without too much practice, but practice is required. The person who attempts to stripe a project without developing the technique on scrap wood is plainly and simply foolish.

Striping would be a real pleasure if you could just lay down a yard stick and draw a clean line with a marker pen. This can't be done, but there is a tool on the market that makes striping almost as easy as using a pen and ruler. The fuss, muss, and nervousness associated with a brush can be avoided by the use of a *striping tool.* People who customize cars have known about striping tools for quite a while, but it has taken dyed-in-wool woodworking traditionalists a little longer to catch on. A striping tool consists of a paint container and a roller tip that can be fitted with different wheels for thin, wide, or multiple lines. The tool also has a roller support that makes it easier to hold while providing even pressure to the marking ball. A striping tool is easier, faster, and safer than a striping brush, but either can be applied with good results. You will not be able to locate a striping tool at your local department store, but they can be obtained from Albert Constantine and Son, New York. They also carry a broad line of professional finishing products for the home consumer.

HIGH-GLOSS ENAMEL FINISH

People frequently ask how they can apply an enamel finish that looks as good as the ones they see in the department stores. The

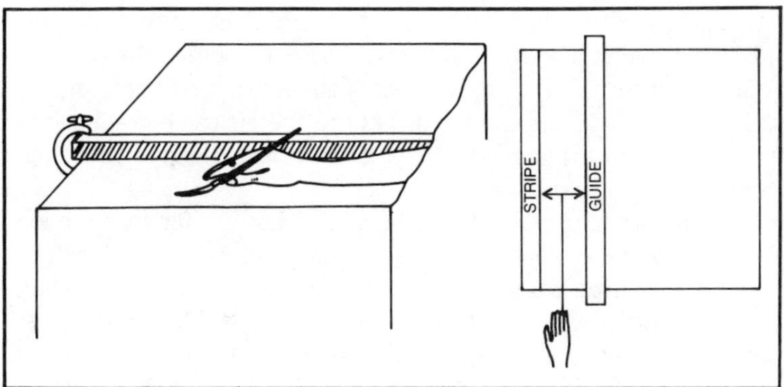

Fig. 10-1. When striping, a straightedge is clamped to the surface to provide a guide. The hand and forearm are lain on the surface. The brush is held between the thumb and forefinger and pulled across the surface.

273

answer is simple: they can't. But that's not the end of the matter. The enamel finishes seen in stores are sprayed on with very good, professional equipment under ideal conditions.

More often than not, these high-gloss finishes are alcohol-proof, pigmented lacquers and not enamels. That doesn't really matter. The enamel that you purchase for home consumption is no more than varnish with pigment added. If you have not already guessed, that is a bad combination. Not many people can brush on enamel with great success. Why try when there are alternatives? If you want your paint project to look like a Saturday-morning-rush job done by a drunken Mongolian bandit, by all means use enamel. Read the directions on the can.

The alternative to an enamel finish is to use a flat paint that is built up with several coats of clear finish. It is essential that the surface to be painted is smooth. Old paint must be removed and the wood surface sanded lightly. Prior to painting, seal the wood with a brushed-on mixture of 1 part shellac to 2 parts alcohol, and rub down with 000 steel wool. Select a flat, oil-base paint (although a latex paint can be used).

The predominant colors used for enameling effects are plain blacks and whites, but all colors can be treated in this manner. The paint is best applied in multiple thin coats. Mix about 1 tablespoon of thinner per cup of paint (oil base only) and brush on in a normal manner. Allow the first coat of paint to dry overnight and apply a second coat of paint. Do not sand or use steel wool between the first and second coats of paint. When the second coat of paint is dry after at least 24 hours, rub it down very lightly with 0000 steel wool and clean away the steel wool residue.

The use of two thin coats of paint should have omitted any signs of brush strokes. The rubdown should have smoothed the surface. Following the rubdown, apply a coat of shellac, mixed 1 part shellac to 3 parts alcohol. The ratio of alcohol to shellac can be reduced to speed up the work, but a 1-3 ratio will allow the buildup of thin, even coats.

Each coat of shellac should be allowed to dry for three to six hours. More time allowed between coats will reduce the risk of error. Apply three coats of shellac and rub down each coat (when dry) with 000 steel wool. If there is no need for the finish to be alcohol proof, continue with the shellac until a high-gloss finish is achieved. Generally, from five to eight coats of shellac will be necessary.

If you want an alcohol- and heat-resistant finish (as is normally the case with enamel), a coat of clear varnish should be applied after the third coat of shellac. Apply the varnish in the manner described for varnish finishes and allow it to dry for at least 72 hours. See the section on traditional finishes.

After the elapsed drying time, apply your thumb nail to the finish. If the finish is marked by your nail, allow additional drying time. When the varnish is dry, rub it down with 000 steel wool until it is smooth and even. Be careful not to rub through the finish.

Following the first rubdown, take a piece of 0000 steel wool, dip it in boiled linseed oil, and vigorously rub down the piece a second time. Remove as much of the linseed oil as possible, with clean rags, after the rubdown and make sure to dispose of the rags outside of the home as soon as possible. When the linseed oil has dried (the piece will no longer smell of oil), wax it with a good paste wax and buff to a high luster.

A piece of furniture painted in the manner described will not look like any brushed-on enamel you have ever seen. This will ultimately delight you. As with most things, care and patience combined with knowledge yield very satisfying results.

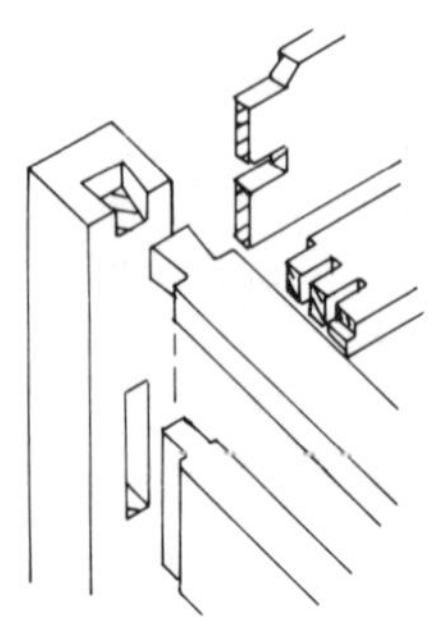

Chapter 11

Furniture Repair

The advantage of purchasing furniture in the rough is found in cost savings and the knowledge of originality. The disadvantage with this type of purchase is that the purchaser must supply labor to return the piece to good order. Not all pieces bought in the rough will need serious work, but almost all will need some work. It is a problem that must be approached head-on. For some odd reason, beginners summon the courage to strip and refinish a piece while they pale at the thought of making even the most minor repair.

Be assured that your fears are ungrounded when it comes to furniture repair. Most furniture repairs require only a modicum of patience and talent to accomplish. If you are a timid soul, I urge you to try some repair on junk-store pieces. If you can't conquer this fear, don't give up all hope of attempting a do-it-yourself project.

If a piece is purchased in the rough and needs repair, there is no reason why it cannot be sent out to a professional repair shop and then returned to the owner for refinishing. The furniture repairer might even knock down the price somewhat if he doesn't have to worry about matching the repair to the finish.

There is another line of reasoning which can be followed. Try the repair yourself and if you fail then take it to a professional. The professional might cuss a bit and say, "Who's been fooling with this?" but the work and the price will be the same. If you accept the principle that your failure does not preclude success at some point, then your whole life can change.

Some authors of do-it-yourself books contend that you don't really need any tools. Shaping can be done with a kitchen knife and nail files. Gluing can be accomplished with 16 tons of books placed over two boards, etc., etc. There is no limit to man's creativity. These things can be done. But it is still, for the most part, a lot of nonsense. A basic tool kit will be needed to accomplish simple repair tasks, but the tools involved are those generally kept around the house or those that should be in the house.

Hammers, pliers and screwdrivers are essential. Do yourself a favor and use a real hammer and screwdriver and not one of those multi-purpose things with 12 heads and a hundred bits. A regular hammer can be wrapped in heavy cloth for knocking furniture apart, but a rubber mallet will do the job much better. An electric drill with a standard set of bits will be necessary. A hand drill can be used if you like unnecessary work. Drills in three-eighth inch and one-half inch sizes turned down to a one-fourth inch shank will prove useful.

Invariably, some wood shaping will have to be done. Files and at least one good rasp will be necessary. Most householders possess a cross-cut saw, but for small repair jobs a 12-inch back saw will be necessary. These are the rectangular saws with brass ribs used in miter boxes. A dovetail saw is not absolutely necessary, but it will prove very useful. An assortment of clamps or clamping devices is essential because most repair work is no more than gluing.

You will also need wood chisels. Chisels are the bread and butter of the furniture repair diet and you need a decent set. If you are now the proud owner of a set of five-and-dime-store, Taiwanese specials, give them away and purchase a decent set of chisels such as those made by Stanley, Marples, or Buck Brothers.

Last but not least is a plane. You should have, at the minimum, a jack plane with a sharp blade. A Sears or Stanley will be fine, but a Record will be even better. Not only will you need a plane, but you will have to know how to operate it. If you don't know how to, now is the time to learn.

If all the tools required for a job are not available in the house, don't run out to the nearest hardware store and purchase them. Flea markets, found every Sunday across the United States, carry extensive lines of discounted new tools and good used tools. The nice thing about a good tool is that it can be used for a few hundred years. Our working tools span at least 200 years. Some tools were inherited, but most were picked up inexpensively at flea markets. Tools will last a very long time, but some care and attention are necessary. Screwdrivers must be reground; saws, chisels and plane irons must be kept sharp. There are few things as unsettling as a set of chisels damaged from use as pry bars, and so dull that they can't cut butter. Sharpening is not difficult, but if that's a problem local tool centers offer sharpening services at modest cost. Treat your tools well and they will treat you well.

ADHESIVES

The majority of repair work with antique furniture involves nothing more than a simple glue job. It is incumbent upon the novice worker to know a little something about glues. All glues are not the same. It isn't a difficult technical proposition to understand the working properties of four or five different products for wood repair. There are some general rules about gluing that should be understood:

☐ All glues (except contact cement) require clamping/ pressure during the initial drying period. Hot glues require pressure only during the cooling period.

☐ The set time (the period during which clamping is required) will vary from 30 minutes to 12 hours. It depends upon the product. The glue will not develop full strength until 48 to 72 hours have elapsed. This is known as the *curing period.*

☐ Gluing must be done in a warm area. Most glues require a minimum temperature of 70 degrees during the set period. Manufacturers will always indicate the necessary temperatures with packaging instructions.

☐ Glues are absorbed into the pores of the wood. Therefore, anything that inhibits penetration will produce an inadequate glue line. Sealers must not be used and old glue must be removed. Different glues are not compatible.

☐ Glues will either stain the wood around the joint or seal the wood so that stain will not penetrate. Glue is forced out from the joint by pressure and must be cleaned or removed.

☐ Moisture will cause most glues to deteriorate. Special waterproof glues are required for furniture or projects subject to exterior conditions.

The understanding of these six rules should avoid a plethora of problems, but there is also a principle of permanence and strength that should be understood. A common misconception is that the strongest possible glue should be used for a repair. In many cases that is precisely the wrong thing to do.

Presume that you have a nice ladderback chair in need of gluing. The chair is dismantled and rejoined with epoxy glue that will make a bond stronger than the wood itself. The chair is now strong and it will stay that way for another 20 years. But, alas, some careless person thrusts his body in the chair with the force of a

278

steaming locomotive. As a result, the seat rail breaks.

The replacement of the seat rail would be an easy enough task under normal conditions, but how is the chair going to be dismantled? The epoxy glue will have bonded so well that the joints will split or tear when force is applied. If a liquid hide glue had been used, the joint could have been separated by a strong blow from a mallet. Yet the glue would have been sufficient to provide years of use.

Furniture is made of pieces of wood that are meant to be permanent as well as pieces that cannot be treated as permanent. Furniture joints should be perceived as being meant to be assembled, dismantled, and reassembled. No repair should be undertaken that attempts to make a joining permanent. Glues that allow for subsequent disassembly should be used on furniture joints. Pieces that are meant to be permanent—such as a one-piece table top or the leg of a chair or table—should be glued with the strongest possible glue. In this case, the goal is a repair that never again needs work.

The most readily available glues to the weekender are common white glues such as Elmer's glue. Frequently, when I tell someone to use Elmer's glue they respond, "Are you sure?" This is definitely a case of a prophet not being recognized in his own land. White glues are excellent all-purpose wood glues. White glues provide enough strength for affecting repairs such as splits and cracks. The glue line formed by a white glue can be broken with steam or compression. It is acceptable for joint work. The set time for white glues is approximately one hour. If the repaired piece is to be under load or stress, then it should be clamped overnight.

Aliphatic resin glues, commonly known as yellow glues, are becoming increasingly popular—and for good reason. Yellow glues are much stronger than white glues and they have a shorter set time (usually 30 minutes). As with white glues, when you are using yellow glues on pieces under stress or load you should allow for five to eight hours of clamp time. Yellow glues, unlike many other glues, can be used in temperatures as low as 50 degrees. A 70-degree room temperature is still a much better proposition.

Joints assembled with this glue can be extraordinarily difficult to separate. It should be used with caution. If need be, such a joint can be separated with steam. For permanent repairs—such as for cracks, splits or patches—yellow glues far surpass white glues. The fast set time of a yellow glue can be both a help and a hindrance. If a piece such as a chest of drawers require a lengthy assembly time, then the quick setting property of this glue will cause complications.

Urea formaldehyde glues, commonly known as plastic resin glues, have long been a standard for woodworkers. These glues come in powder form and they are mixed with water when needed. The plastic glues are inexpensive, they have a long shelf life, and they are nearly indestructible.

Some restorers recommend plastic resin glues for all-around use. I do not recommend them for joint work. For permanent repairs, they are unsurpassed. The plastic-resin glues require a clamp and set time of at least 12 hours. Full strength does not develop for at least 48 hours. The low cost of these glues makes them excellent for veneer work if the requisite clamping presses are available. By way of mild warning, the formaldehyde used in plastic resin glues is a skin irritant. Appropriate precautions should be taken.

During the 18th century and the 19th century animal glues were used. Animal glues were made from hoofs and hides boiled into a gelatinous mass, allowed to cool, and subsequently broken into flake-like particles. When needed, glue flakes were added to water and heated until a thick, smelly paste was obtained. For the glue to work, the room had to be warm and so did the surfaces to be glued. The glue itself had to be heated to just the correct temperature to avoid burning and brittleness. When all of this is put together, you have a messy and tedious process which accounts for its lack of popularity.

Animal flake glue is still available and it is used today. It makes little sense to use it given the variety of modern alternatives. If you choose to work with the traditional product, you would be well advised to consider purchasing an electric glue pot. That, by the way, is a costly little item.

One of the advantages of animal glues is that the glue line fractures easily upon impact. That makes these glues ideal for joint work. The modern, easy alternative to hot animal glues is liquid hide glue. Liquid hide glues offer extreme strength in conjunction with a long set time. Given an elaborate gluing job, there will be enough time to get the job done without worry. Similar to its hot glue counterpart, hide glue is best used in a warm environment of at least 70 degrees or better. The set time or clamp time for these glues should be three hours for light duty repairs that will not be under stress. Any joint that will experience stress should be clamped for eight to 12 hours. Liquid hide glues are best applied in thin coats.

When regluing a piece such as a chair or chest, I recommend

liquid hide glues. For the permanent repair of broken parts, I suggest that you use a yellow glue.

A newcomer to the world of adhesives for the home market is hot melt glue applied with an electric glue gun. On a conceptual basis this is a great product. The gun heats in two or three minutes and the glue is applied with the mere squeeze of a trigger. No clamps are required because the pieces need only be held together with hand pressure for a brief 60 seconds. After a minute, the glue has developed 80 percent to 90 percent of its full strength.

All of these statements are true, yet the product is woefully inadequate for most repair work. To start with, you have only one minute to accomplish the gluing before the glue sets. In most cases, that precludes its use. A nice bead of glue can be made with the gun, but it is not possible to spread the glue evenly over an entire surface for a proper gluing.

Hot melt glues also have a high solids content. This makes it difficult to obtain a tight joint because the glue itself is in the way. This problem can be overcome if you can work quickly enough to clamp the piece to force the excess glue from the joint. You can't always work this fast.

I use hot melt glue on glue blocks for bracing corners and tops, but that is all I use it for. I do not recommend that you use these glues because of the problems involved.

Epoxy glue is another modern product that is extremely popular. I sometimes think the future will be dedicated to polyurethane and epoxy. And I surely don't know why. Epoxy makes a great glue, but like anything else it has its proper place. I use epoxy to repair glass, ceramics, and metal. Rarely do I use it on wood.

Epoxy is much too strong for joint work unless you want to condemn a piece to future oblivion. For permanent repairs, yellow glues and plastic resin glues work as well. Occasionally, I will use epoxy when I need a high solids content to fill gaps. An example is a split table leg that can be glued, but is lacking small pieces of wood that would create a void. More often than not, this repair can be made with an ordinary glue. If you think the void will be large, some epoxy can be mixed with sawdust and used to make the repair. The epoxy fortified with the solids from the sawdust will fill gaps and voids nicely. Only a small quantity of sawdust should be used; too much will result in a brittle joint.

Another use for epoxy and sawdust is for wood rot. Any number of old pieces, especially cupboards, will have suffered wood rot from being left in damp areas. When the piece is inverted and examined, the wood will be found to be powdery and honeycombed with cavities. The wood surface protected by paint or varnish will be intact.

A similar condition can also be caused by wood worms. To remedy this problem, mix some epoxy as indicated in the directions—1 part resin with 1 part hardener—and add a small quantity of sawdust. Force the epoxy and dust mixture into the rotten, damaged areas and allow it to dry at least 12 hours.

Another glue used for repair work is contact cement. The major advantage of contact cement is that no clamping is required. The glue is spread on both of the surfaces that are to be joined and allowed to dry for 20 or 30 minutes. When dry, the surfaces are touched to each other and there is an instant and strong bond. There is absolutely no opportunity to position the work because the bond is instant. This rules out contact cement for most repair work. Contact cement is used primarily for veneer work and inlays to avoid the purchase of costly and elaborate gluing presses. You might decide to use contact cement for a small repair where clamping is not feasible, but remember that when you fit the piece it must be perfect because there will be no second chance.

The fumes from contact cement are either inflammable and toxic, or just toxic. In either case, care should be taken to provide adequate ventilation.

As you can easily see, all glues are not the same and the selection of the proper glue will determine the final results of the repair project. Refer to Table 11-1 to jog your memory prior to making a glue selection. Please bear in mind that liquid glues have a shelf life ranging from one to two years. After that deterioration will occur. If you have had glue around the house for four or five years, discard it and don't risk ruining a repair project.

CLAMPING

The essence of any glue job is clamping. Glue simply does not work without pressure. This is a not-very-subtle point that is often missed.

Some do-it-yourself sources suggest that there is no need to invest in clamps because you can fabricate what you need from around the house. These people are correct. The principle at hand is one of pressure. Any way that you can apply pressure will work. If you are inserting a small patch in a table top and you want to load fifty pounds of lead weights on it, then why not? I know of one ingenious fellow who uses an adjustable pole lamp for this purpose by running it from the patch to the ceiling.

If you are regluing a chair, you can use a simple rope tourniquet (Fig. 11-1A). If you want something a little more elaborate, a band clamp can be made from a turnbuckle, rope, and s-hooks (Fig. 11-1B). Elastic tiedowns used for luggage racks are also excellent for this type of work. If you have a table top to be repaired, two battens can be nailed to the attic floor and used with a wedge to clamp boards (Fig. 11-2). Pressure is important. Clamping can be a function of your creativity and ingenuity. On the other hand, all of these wonderful home remedies are time consuming and on occasion a royal pain in the Achilles' heel. There is no law that states that occasional restorers must suffer pain and hardship.

Commercially made clamps are used with greater ease and frequently with better results. Clamps are not the least expensive thing in the world, but they can usually be picked up at garage sales and flea markets at less than half the retail cost.

There are several basic types of clamps that will prove useful. For large surfaces such as table tops or chests of drawers, pipe clamps are ideal (Fig. 11-3A). Pipe clamps are sold with a head and tail piece. The user supplies a piece of pipe that can be picked up at any hardware store. The nice thing about pipe clamps is that you can make them any size you want by changing the length of pipe (although three feet is a standard length). If you come across steel I-bar clamps, they serve the same function as pipe clamps. They are better made and they cost much more.

For run-of-the-mill, small clamping jobs, bar clamps, hand screws, or C-clamps shown respectively, in Fig. 11-3B, C, D, can be used. All of these clamps are used for the same purpose. Bar clamps are faster than C-clamps. Hand screws have the advantage of wooden jaws that will not mar the wood surface. Modern hand screws have threaded rods fitted through pivots. These allow the jaws to be set in non-parallel fashion for gluing irregular shapes. Old hand screws use threaded wooden dowels to form the screw. When you are purchas-

Table 11-1. A Guide to Common Wood Glues.

	White Glue	Yellow Glue	Liquid Hide Glue	Plastic Resin Glue	Hot Melt Glue	Epoxy Glue	Contact Cement
General Repair	Yes	Yes	Yes	No	No	No	No
Permanent Repair	Yes	Yes	Yes	Yes	No	Yes	No
Regluing Joints	Yes	Yes	Yes	No	No	No	No
Temperature	65°	50°	72°	70°	300°	70°	70°
Clamp Time (no stress)	60 mins.	30 mins.	3 hrs.	12 hrs.	1 min.	10 hrs.	none
Clamp Time (under stress)	8-10 hrs.	8-10 hrs.	10 hrs.	12 hrs.	1 min.	10 hrs.	none

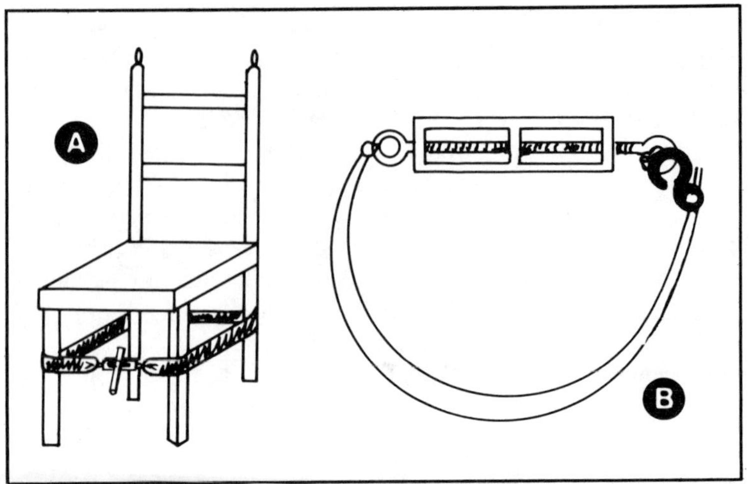

Fig. 11-1. A simple tourniquet clamp (A) using rope and a stick to provide tension. A homemade band clamp (B) made with rope, s-hooks and a turnbuckle.

ing old hand screws, make sure that the threads are not chipped away and that the screws and jaws are not mix and match. How many clamps should you buy? You can never have enough.

An extremely versatile clamp for the home workshop is a light-duty, band clamp (Fig. 11-3E). This clamp has a nylon band that is fed through a ratchet. It can be used for chairs or carcass work such as chests. This clamp can also be used on a luggage rack with much less work than rope. Heavy-duty band clamps will cost in excess of $50. Light-duty clamps can be purchased for under $10 at most hardware stores. Band clamps are extremely useful and well worth the investment.

The availability of clamps will not resolve all problems. Most clamping will be straightforward and simple, as with the broken chair piece shown in Fig. 11-4. The piece is dry fitted and clamped to determine if there are any problems. Then the clamps are removed and the piece is glued with a single clamp. Not all situations are so easy. The table top, shown in Fig. 11-5, has a tendency to buckle when clamp pressure is applied so that an even match between the two pieces is not obtained. To remedy this problem, bracing boards are clamped to each end to avoid one side rising higher than the other. The repairer must be willing to innovate and make jigs or fittings where and when necessary. Common sense is your best clamping tool.

Screws and nails are also clamping devices used when other

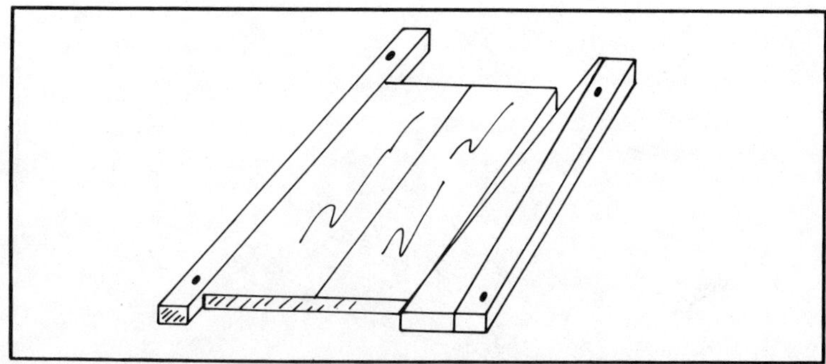

Fig. 11-2. A floor clamp made by nailing two battens to the floor. A wedge is inserted to provide tension.

forms of clamping are inadequate. Screws and nails are only used in areas where they will not be seen. Corner support blocks are frequently glued or screwed as are the arms of chairs (Fig. 11-6). Screws should never be used in a repair if they will weaken the repair to the damaged area.

Prior to commencing any glue repair, all previous glue residue must be removed from the joint. Old glue will prevent the penetration of the new glue into the wood fiber and result in a weak joint. Pieces to be glued should be fitted dry prior to gluing to determine if there are any problems. If a piece does not fit properly, it does not fit! Do not depend upon clamp pressure to force a fit; it will only result in damage.

Apply glue to both surfaces to be glued. It should be applied thickly in the case of yellow and white glues and thinly with liquid

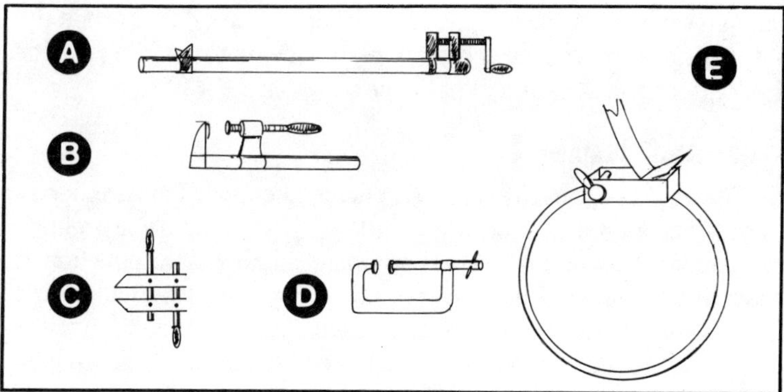

Fig. 11-3. An assortment of commercial clamping devices: (A) a pipe clamp; (B) a small bar clamp; (C) a hand screw; (D) a C-clamp; (E) an inexpensive band clamp.

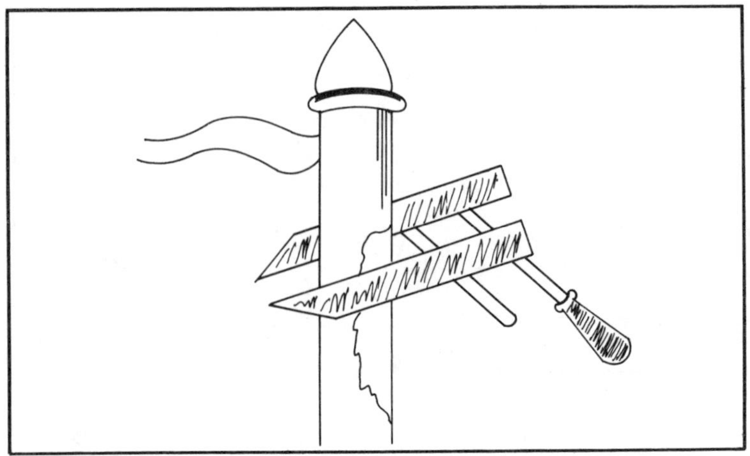

Fig. 11-4. A simple glue and clamp repair to a chair post.

hide glues and plastic resin glues. Clamp and provide enough pressure to force a small amount of glue from the glue line. Do not apply excessive pressure and starve the joint of glue. Remove excess glue completely with a rag and warm water. If the glue is not removed immediately, it can be scraped away later with a knife blade. White glues dry clear and they are difficult to see.

If repairs are being made to an area that is already finished, then mask the areas adjacent to the repair so that excess glue will flow onto the masking. When using pipe clamps, bar clamps, or C-clamps use scrap blocks of wood between the clamp and the wood surface so that the pressure does not damage the wood surface. Wood screws can be waxed so that glue forced from joints will not adhere to the clamp. Waxed paper can be used between the wood screw and the wood surface to produce the same result. Do not rush the job. For this type of work, care and patience are your best friends.

STUDY AND DISMANTLE

To reglue or not to reglue; that is the question. This is indeed a serious question. If a piece is just a little rickety, should you reglue it or should it be left as is? There is no simple answer to the question. It depends upon how you plan to use a piece. If you have a small tilt-top table that will do no more than hold a candlestick, then so what if it is rickety. If the piece in question is a kitchen table, then you are best off making the necessary repairs.

If you are hinging on the decision whether to dismantle and reglue, there are a few things you should know. As a rule, you cannot just repair one part of a piece of furniture. For example, let us suppose that you have purchased a chair that is just a little loose with the exception of one leg that is very loose.

The one bad leg could be removed and reglued. If the problem is approached in this manner, you would have a series of strong joints in the area of the repaired leg. This would unduly cause a break.

When the decision is made to glue one part, then the entire piece must be dismantled and reglued. There is one exception to this rule; some might think it runs contrary to good practice. If, during dismantling, a joint is strong and refuses to separate, then leave it alone as long as it doesn't interfere with the remainder of the dismantling. We have seen many broken chair legs caused by someone who insisted on pounding out a stretcher that was determined to stay at home.

Another thing that the restorer should be cognizant of is that a reglued piece will not return to its original shape. After 100 or 200 years of wear and shrinkage the relationships of various parts will change. A chair stretcher bowed from use will be shorter than it was originally or the side of a chest will have shrunk a quarter of an inch. If a chair leg has worn shorter than the other legs, but the chair is reglued with all four feet squarely on the floor, you will have a lopsided chair.

Changes such as these are not obvious when a piece is a little loose, but they become accentuated when reglued. During the gluing process, care should be taken to observe these variations and cor-

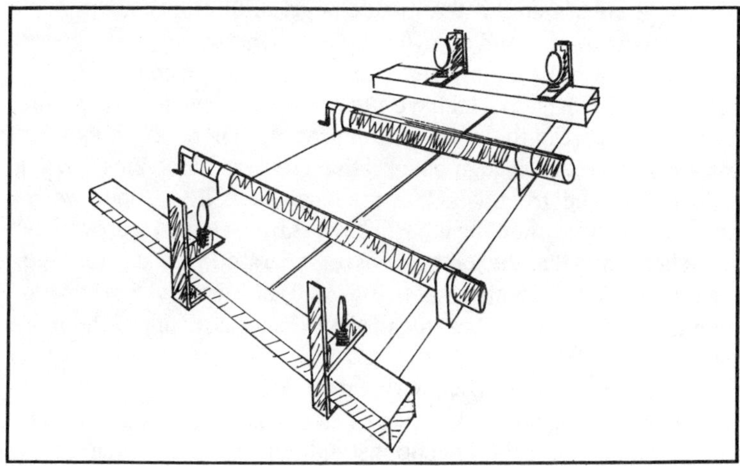

Fig. 11-5. Bracing boards are sometimes used in gluing edges to prevent the two halves from buckling under pressure.

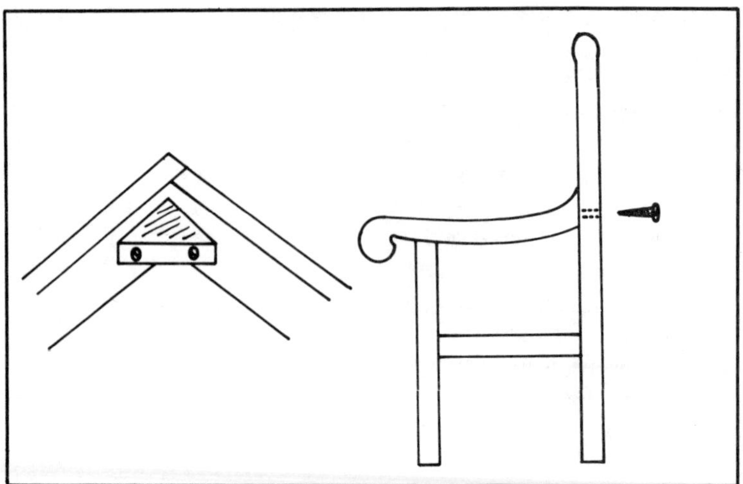

Fig. 11-6. Screws are used as clamping devices to attach an arm to a chair or to fit corner blocks..

rect them where possible. The restorer should not be dismayed by these little imperfections and problems. It is the nature of the antique beast.

The first thing to be done before attempting any dismantling job is a thorough study of the piece. The piece should be as clean as possible so that problems can be seen. Furniture construction is logical and there should be little difficulty in understanding how a piece was constructed if the matter is given a little thought.

Borrowing and studying a few books on measured drawings will prove to be of considerable benefit in understanding how pieces are put together. These books have illustrations showing the relationship of each part in the construction process. There are things that cannot be learned through observation (such as hidden joints). If a chairmaker used green wood for the legs and well-seasoned woods for the stretchers, then the leg will have shrunk so tightly around the stretcher tenon that the joint cannot be separated without breakage. If a tenon is formed with a taper (Fig. 11-7) and fitted to a green leg, then the tenon actually becomes larger than the mouth of the mortise.

A cabinetmaker might have used a hidden (foxed) wedged tenon (Fig. 11-8) that cannot be detected by examination. Hidden construction techniques are the exceptions and not the rule. When a joint refuses to separate after reasonable persuasion, then look for a reason. We have a friend from New Hampshire who lives by the

288

motto, "Use a bigger hammer." The last time he applied his philosophy, we had to come up with a new piston and cylinder for our car. Please leave the large hammer at home and find the causes of problems.

When inspecting a piece prior to dismantling, particular attention should be given to nails. More often than not, when a joint refuses to come apart, there is a nail at the root of the problem. Common round-headed nails are easy enough to see, but finishing nails can be difficult to find. Every joint on a piece must be viewed carefully for finishing nails. Remember, the nails might be countersunk and plugged. This will make discovery even harder. The technique for removing nails, which is no fun proposition, is explained in the section on chairs. Chairs are where the problem is most often encountered.

All nails that you find will not be dubious. Nails could have been used in the original construction. This is quite prevalent with 19th-century country furniture. Nails could have been used to attach tops to all types of chests and tables, and cupboards could have had their shelves nailed in place through each side. Nail holes almost always will have been filled with plaster or some other material. Some nails might have been exposed over the years.

When dismantling, locate the filled nail holes in the parts that will be involved and remove the filler material with a small chisel or a pick. If the filler material is not removed, the nail might split the wood when exiting the hole or be resistant because of the filler. Nails

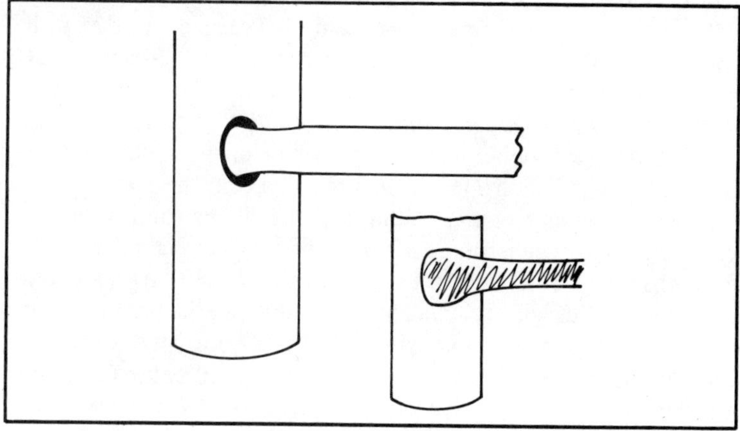

Fig. 11-7. A tapered tenon, of seasoned wood, fit to a mortise, cut into green wood, will result in an inseparable join. After shrinkage, the mouth of the mortise will be smaller than the head of the tenon.

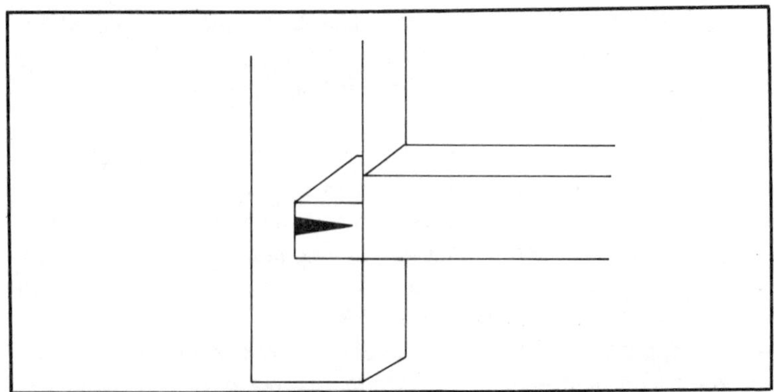

Fig. 11-8. A foxed (hidden) wedged tenon. The wedge is partially inserted in the relieved tenon and the tenon is driven into the mortise. This makes the head of the tenon larger than the mouth of the mortise. This is a hidden and inseparable join.

are not to be pried from the holes; this involves damaging the wood around the hole. When a piece is knocked apart with the mallet, the nails will come out still attached to the separated part. This only applies to nails used in the original construction. If someone has added nails to hold the piece together, and they prohibit normal disassembly, then they must be removed—pried or otherwise.

After the work piece has been cleaned and inspected, every part should be labeled prior to dismantling. Labeling systems are a matter of preference, but whatever system is employed should be logical. Alphabetical markings applied with masking tape (Fig. 11-9) will work adequately. Numbers or slash marks can be used as well. The various joints can also be marked directly with a grease pencil, but there is always the fear of accidental erasure. Whatever system is employed, mark all parts and trust nothing to memory.

A good, hard-rubber mallet or a rawhide mallet should be used for dismantling furniture joints. In a pinch, a conventional hammer wrapped in 2 inches of soft cloth can be used. Dismantling should follow the logic of construction. For example, you cannot disassemble the base of a table without first removing the top. On a good day, the rubber mallet will be sufficient to separate all the parts. This is especially true if the various pieces were loose to start with.

On occasion, the rubber mallet will be too resilient to fracture a glue line. In that case, lay a wood block across the piece to be struck and use a conventional hammer (Fig. 11-10). If it appears that the compression from the block is marring the wood surface, then wrap the block with a few layers of soft cloth.

290

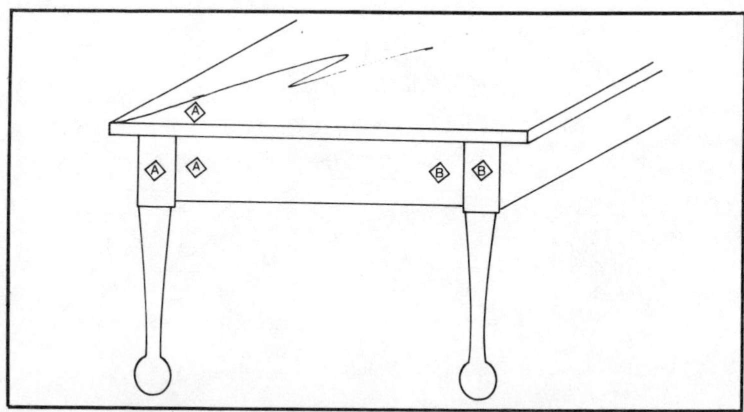

Fig. 11-9. A table is labeled with masking tape and alphabetical markings to allow for proper reassembly after gluing.

If a particular joint resists both the rubber mallet and the hammer, the only option is to steam the joint. This presumes there is no other cause of the problem such as hidden joints or nails. People frequently panic at the thought of applying steam, but there is no reason to. Very rarely does a joint need to be steamed apart. When it does, it can be done with a simple kitchen kettle. Purchase from your local auto parts store an appropriate length of rubber hose to fit snugly over the spout of your kettle. Bring the kettle water to boil and apply steam to the joint with the rubber hose (Fig. 11-11). You must use a thick kitchen mitt for holding the hose to avoid a nasty burn. The power of steam should never be underestimated. One to

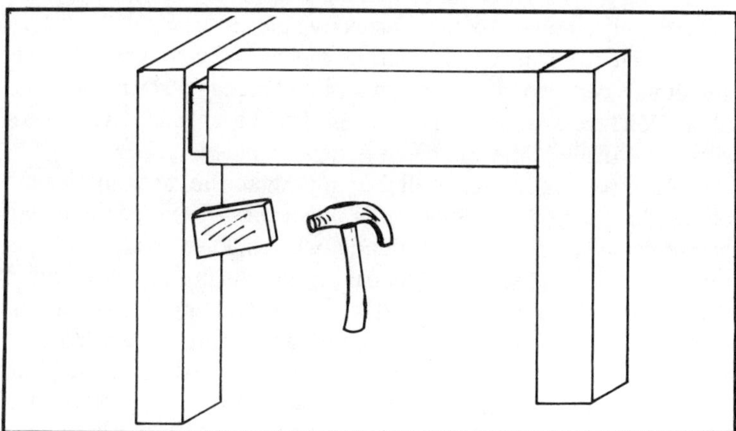

Fig. 11-10. A wood block and hammer are used to separate a glue joint that has resisted a rubber mallet.

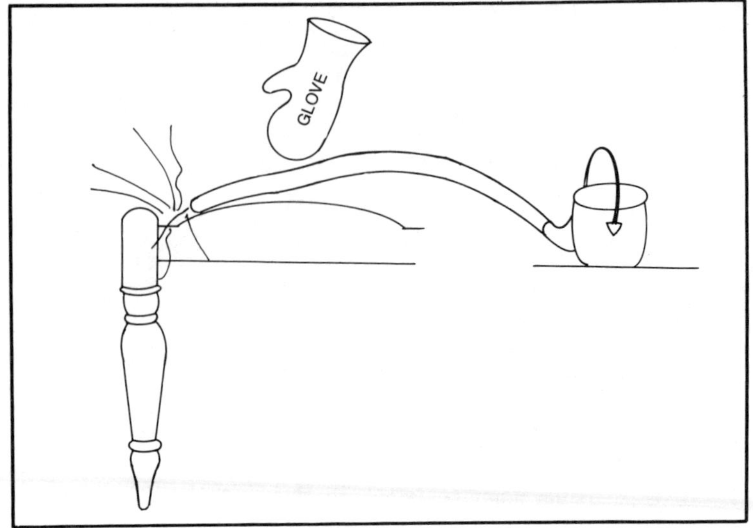

Fig. 11-11. A simple steaming device to separate glue joints can be made by attaching a rubber hose to the spout of a kettle. Gloves must be used to prevent burns.

two minutes of steam should be sufficient to soften the glue so that a mallet can be used.

If you know someone who is a coffee connoisseur, he or she might have a steamer that is used to steam milk for cappuccino. This little device makes an excellent portable steamer that can be used for furniture. There is always a risk of some splitting when you are separating a well-glued joint. In such a case, broken parts should immediately be taped to their respective pieces for gluing later on.

If you have never dismantled a piece of furniture, there is something very worrisome about a pile of pieces strewn about the floor. Don't fret. Reassembly is easier than disassembly. All repairs should be made while the piece is disassembled.

After repairs are made, all the joints should be carefully cleaned of old glue. With dowel joints, it is important to remove the dowel from both mortise holes. Frequently, when a doweled joint is separated the dowel releases from one mortise hole, but remains tight in the other. If the piece is reglued without correcting this condition, the part of the dowel not freshly glued will invariably work loose.

When disassembly, cleaning, and repairs have been completed, the piece should be reassembled dry. You might find that some joints no longer fit due to the shrinkage of one part or the other. With a tight joint, sand or trim lightly with a chisel until a snug fit is obtained.

Trimming a joint might make you feel a little insecure, but rest assured that it must be done.

Loose joints present themselves as more of a problem than tight joints because they must be built up to remedy the condition. With a mortise and tenon joint, the tenon is built up with a very thin piece of wood (usually a scrap piece of veneer as shown in Fig. 11-12A). If the joint is too tight after the buildup, it is sanded lightly. A simpler type of repair is to take a piece of muslin, saturate it in glue, and wrap it around the tenon (Fig. 11-12B). This type of repair is more adequate for the round tenon (Fig. 11-12) than it is for a conventional tenon. Building up a round tenon is an exercise in futility.

A lazy man's approach to this problem involves gluing a series of wooden matches or toothpicks to one face of the tenon (Fig. 11-13A). When the joint is driven home, the wood fiber of the matches is compressed and the joint becomes tight. This same technique can be used for round tenons (Fig. 11-13B). The mortise is saturated with glue and lined with toothpicks. The round tenon is driven home; this will break the excess from the toothpicks.

A still easier way to handle this problem is to glue the tenon and then insert the toothpicks—tapping them deeply with a small hammer. When the glue has set, the excess toothpicks are trimmed with a chisel. This might seem like a shoddy approach to the problem, but I have seen many such repairs last a very long time.

When ready, the final assembly should be accomplished in one gluing period. It is a tempting proposition—for example when gluing a table base—to glue and clamp the two sets of legs so that they can

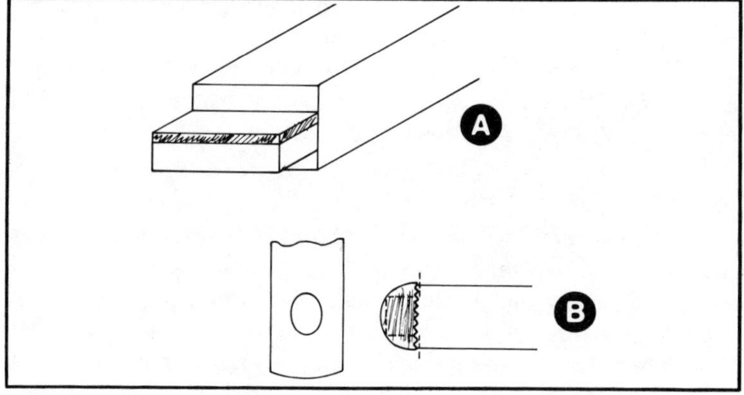

Fig. 11-12. Building up a loose tenon: (A) with a standard tenon, a piece of veneer is glued to the tenon. (B) with a round tenon, the tenon is covered with a piece of muslin saturated in glue and then inserted into the mortise.

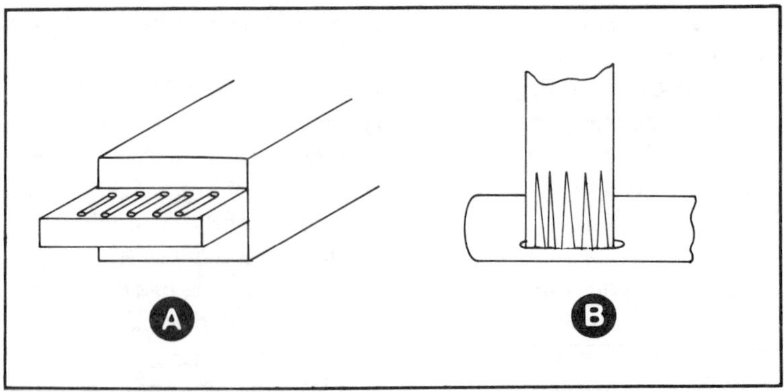

Fig. 11-13. Using toothpicks (matches) for a loose tenon: (A) toothpicks or wooden matches are aligned side by side across a tenon and glued into place. (B) with a round tenon, glue is applied and the tenon is inserted into the mortise. After assembly, the loose mortise is packed with toothpicks.

later be assembled by only the attachment of the side rails. If a piece is glued up in parts, those relationships become fixed and might cause problems with symmetry when the entire piece is assembled. Use a slow-setting glue such as liquid hide glue and assemble all parts at the same time.

When the piece is assembled, clamp lightly and look for problems and make adjustments. It is not enough for the joints just to fit. The piece itself must be returned to its original geometric shape. If the leg of the table or chair tapers inward too much, then pull it out so that it is at a right angle with the floor even if it leaves the joint somewhat askew. When all parts have been properly aligned, tighten up on the clamp pressure. Be sure to check again to see that the relationships of the pieces are not altered.

The process of disassembly, cleaning and reassembly might seem difficult when you are reading about it. Once approached, it proves to be a relatively easy task.

PATCHING

Patching refers to the repair of holes in a wood surface. Most often, patching involves no more than filling nail holes that have been uncovered during the repair process. Some surfaces might have been abused with multiple nail or screw holes as well as gouges that require more extensive repair. The usual treatment for small holes and surface imperfections is the use of a wood filler. Large damaged areas require the insertion of a plug or a new piece of wood. In the 18th century, wax or plaster were used as wood fillers. In the 19th century, plaster was used extensively. In the 20th century, we have entered the miracle age of wood putty, plastic wood, and wood dough.

Wood Fillers

Probably the best known of all fillers is Plastic Wood. Plastic Wood is a specific brand, but it has become the generic name for a range of similar products. This nifty little filler is a nitrose cellulose product. It is made by mixing wood dust with lacquer. Can you make your own by mixing sawdust with lacquer? Yes, but it will not work as well.

Plastic wood is a good product and I have no hesitation about recommending it. It does, however, have its limitations. For one thing, the filler material shrinks as it dries. This necessitates either over-filling the hole or two applications of filler. Secondly, the filler will not take a stain when dry, and it comes in a limited range of colors.

The color problem can be remedied by mixing in a small amount of pigmented oil stain prior to use. Another problem encountered is limited shelf life because the product will dry out. A special solvent is available to bring plastic wood back to life, but it is expensive. Lacquer thinner will do the same thing for less expense, but not quite as well.

When you use plastic wood make sure you fill the hole and not the wood around it because the plastic wood will stain the other wood. Any plastic wood on the surrounding wood surface must be removed or it will inhibit successive stain coats. Plastic wood as well as other wood fillers should be applied prior to any stain or finish coat because it must be sanded smooth.

A new line of latex based wood fillers has recently come on the market. The new wood fillers shrink less and have the advantage of taking a stain once dry. Unfortunately, these fillers take longer to dry than the plastic woods and when stained they take the stain lighter than the wood surface. When dry, the filled patch must be scuffed with a coarse paper and colored with a stain darker than that which will be used for the wood. It is strictly a matter of preference, but I would rather use the plastic wood than go through all of this trouble. If you decide upon a latex base product, follow the manufacturer's directions (especially with regard to drying and power sanding).

I use a powder wood filler more than any other similar product. This product is consistent with the plaster fillers used in the 18th century and the 19th century. It's simple and economical. The powdered wood is mixed with water stain that approximates the preferred color until it thickens into a putty. The filler is forced into a hole or split with a putty knife. Be careful not to get it on the surrounding wood surface because it will stain the wood. It is sometimes a good practice to mask the area around the hole to avoid potential problems. The powdered wood filler will begin to set in five to 10 minutes so only small portions are mixed at a time. The powder itself has an unlimited shelf life. Some small amount of shrinkage will occur. Holes are overfilled slightly and later trimmed flush to the surface. Small holes will dry ready to work in about an hour. Large and deep areas should be given two to three hours.

The biggest advantage with a powdered wood filler is that it can be mixed as needed to any color that is required. On the other hand, the weekend restorer who doesn't happen to have a ready mixed supply of water stains might not find this to be such a great advantage. If you want to give powdered-wood compound a try, it is available in 1-pound packages from Albert Constantine and Son, New York. Plaster of Paris can be mixed with water stains and used in the same fashion.

There is an old-timers' trick that can be used when there is a special need for the filler to be unnoticeable. Select a wood of the same type that is to be filled and sand with a very fine paper. Collect the wood dust as you go. Mix the wood dust with white glue into a paste and fill the hole with this compound. When the wood paste has dried, sand the patch with a fine paper and you should have a beautiful patch job. If the wood surface is to be stained, mix some of the stain with the wood dust prior to adding the glue. In the case of an oil stain, cut the stain in half with mineral spirits. The wood in powdered form will take the stain very dark. To get a perfect patch, you will have to experiment with the stain/thinner/wood mixture until the preferred color is achieved. This is a time-consuming practice that requires patience. If the need to camouflage is apparent, this is the route to take.

Wax and wax sticks can be used to fill nail holes and small surface imperfections. Special putty crayons sold for covering nail holes in wood paneling come in a wide range of colors and they are quite adequate for the task of small hole repair. Children's colored crayons can also be rubbed into a hole or melted to fill a hole. Remember that if wax is used, the sealer coat must be shellac because only shellac will cover wax adequately.

Shellac sticks can be used for small patching, but they are difficult to master and they result in a high-sheen patch that is inappropriate for country finishes. It is also a very laborious task to fill 20 or so nail holes in this fashion.

Plugs

Wood fillers tend to be unsightly where large areas are involved. The alternative to using filler is to use actual pieces of wood to repair holes. The easiest method involving wood is the use of the round plug. This is not necessarily the best method.

To put matters in perspective, a plug is not a dowel. A dowel has the long grain running its length while a plug has the long grain running its width (as shown in Fig. 11-14). If a dowel is used for a plug, the end grain—which is more absorbent—will appear on the surface. Consequently, it will take a stain or a finish darker and standout like the proverbial sore thumb.

Plugs are difficult to find on a commercial basis. Most woodworkers make their own plugs with a drill attachment known as a plug cutter. Plug cutters come in a range of sizes and they are generally available for under $10. The cutter is chucked in the drill and merely applied to a scrap wood surface from which the blank will be cut. It is important to draw a pencil line along the grain. This will later show on the top of the plug so that it can be aligned with the grain of the surface to be repaired (Fig. 11-15).

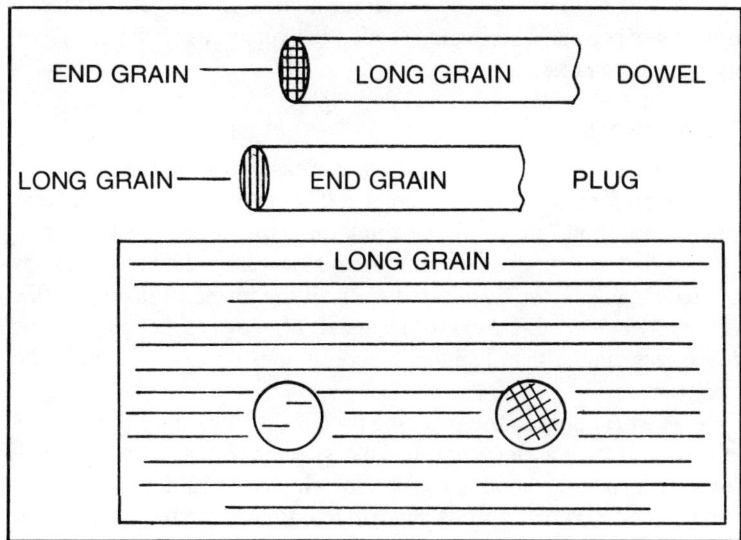

Fig. 11-14. Patching with plugs. Dowels are not used for plugs because the end grain would not conform to the long grain of the surface to be patched. Plugs must be cut from specially prepared stock as shown.

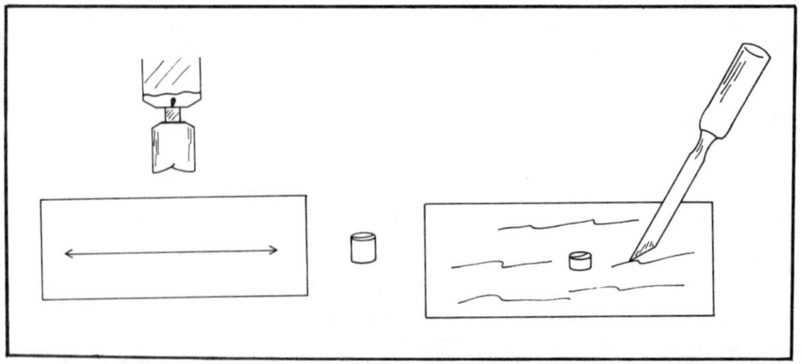

Fig. 11-15. Fitting a plug. A plug is cut with a special plug cutter fitted to a drill. A pencil mark is drawn in the direction of the grain prior to cutting so that the plug can be properly aligned. The plug is fitted and glued to a corresponding hole. When dry, the plug is trimmed with a chisel.

The damaged area is drilled to a depth of about one-fourth inch with a drill bit that corresponds to the plug cutter. A one-fourth inch cutter is made to correspond to a one-fourth inch bit, and so on. A small amount of glue is applied to the plug and it is inserted in the mating hole. Be careful to align the grain properly. The plug is allowed to protrude above the surface and it is later trimmed with a chisel.

A plug is fast and easy (even for a novice) to make, but it is a noticeable repair. When a plug is used as a repair, even the untrained eye quickly spots it.

Wood Patches

For the repair of large damaged areas, wood patches or insets are the preferred method of remedy. This is the type of repair that people "oh" and "ah" at. Some think this type of repair can only be accomplished by a master craftsperson. Actually it can be done by almost anyone. I don't want to dispell all the magic. A little practice is usually required. On the other hand, I have seen people with no more experience than hanging a screen door do it successfully the first time.

The first step in the patching process is to identify the species of wood. Locate a piece of the same species to make the repair. If locating a specific wood is a problem, which it should not be, poplar can be used to repair almost any surface. Poplar can be made to look like any wood. An old cabinetmaker's trick is to cut the patch material from an unseen surface of the piece. Consequently, the patch is always a perfect match. I do not patch in this manner because it is double the work and because I have an irrational distaste for putting more holes in a piece.

If you don't have any experience with identifying woods, purchase a veneer sample or identification kit from one of the professional supply houses. These kits come with 50 or so small veneer samples. Each is labeled with the common name and species of the wood. A few hours of study should prove to be of considerable value in identifying woods in their raw states. To take the learning step a little further, stain and finish the common wood samples so that you will know what they look like when used in furniture.

When a suitable wood is located, a patch larger than the damaged area should be cut from it. The patch should be cut to an angular, unconventional shape (Fig. 11-16). A square or a rectangular patch, like a circle, would be easily detectable. An odd-shaped patch will blend to a far better degree. You can give full vent to your imagination when you are deciding upon a patch shape. Professionals usually go with a diamond pattern due to the ease with which it can be cut and fit. The patch will be allowed to protrude above the wood surface when fitted. Therefore, it can be cut from any thickness of wood that is available. Some woodworkers choose to prepare a cardboard template for the cutting. I prefer the irregularity produced by freehand cutting.

The secret to the patch, having once been cut, is to taper the sides. Slope them toward the bottom with a chisel or a file. The

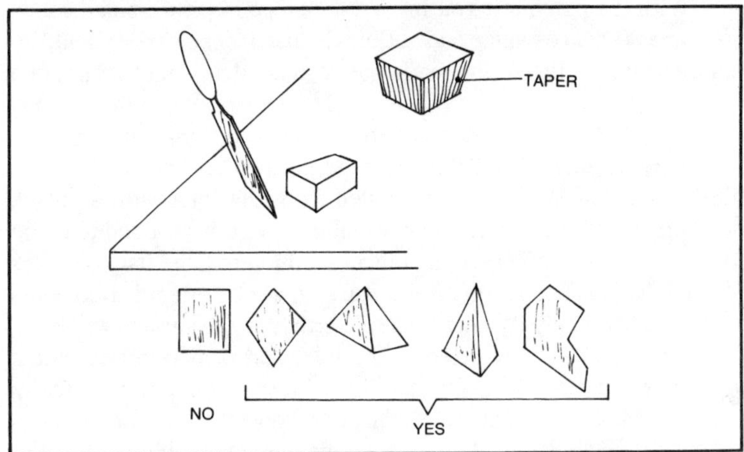

Fig. 11-16. Wood patching. A wood patch is cut to an irregular shape to make it less noticeable. Once cut, the patch piece is tapered and placed over the damaged area with the taper to the bottom. The pattern of the patch is outlined with a scribe or X-Acto knife.

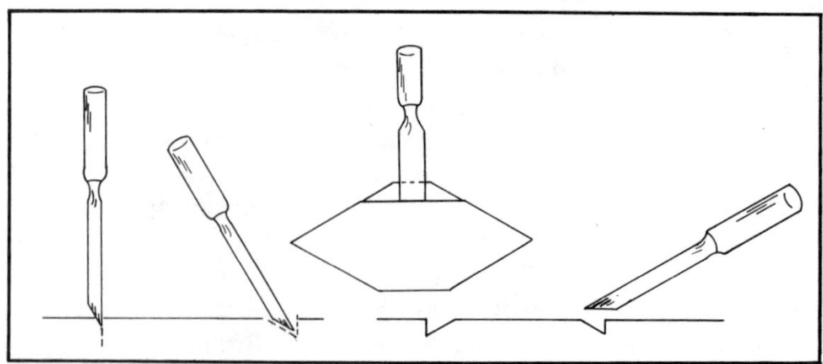

Fig. 11-17. Cutting the patch inlet. The patch inlet is outlined by placing the chisel just inside the scribe mark. The chisel is held at a 90-degree angle and pushed into the wood. When the entire inlet has been outlined, the initial chisel cuts are undercut as shown. After the undercutting, the bulk of the material is removed with the chisel.

mating inlet for the patch will be scribed from the base of the patch. Therefore, the taper will allow the patch to be driven home tightly like a wedge. Tapering the base in this manner compensates for any error that might be made in cutting the inlet and allows the novice a fair degree of success with a first attempt. When the patch has been cut and tapered, place it over the damaged area. Make sure to align the straight grain and scribe the pattern with an X-Acto knife or a scribing tool. Be as precise as possible and make sure the scribing tool follows the base of the patch.

With the patch inlet outlined, take an appropriate-sized chisel held at a 90-degree angle and outline the patch. The chisel should be on the inside of the scribe mark, but so close that you could not fit a mouse's whisker between the line and the chisel. When the patch is outlined, it should be undercut with a second and opposing stroke of the chisel (Fig. 11-17). After the undercutting has been completed, the bulk of the material is removed from the inlet with a chisel, leaving as uniform a surface as possible. There is no need to make the inlet more than one-fourth inch deep even if the damage goes deeper. This is not a structural repair, but a cosmetic repair. Therefore, you need only concern yourself with how the surface will look.

The patch is now fitted to the inlet and tapped lightly with a mallet or hammer. If the patch will not fit, trim it ever so lightly by sanding. Make sure that the sandpaper follows the lines of the taper originally established. When a basic fit is made, apply glue to the sides of the patch as well as the inlet and insert the patch. Drive the patch deeply into the inlet with a hammer or mallet, but don't pound it with the force of a crazed bull elephant or you will split the wood. It is not imperative that the patch sit on the bottom of the inlet. The patch must be level and fit tightly.

Allow the glue to dry for two to three hours and then trim the excess patch material flush with the surface. Be careful not to damage the surface of the repair piece with the chisel. When the surface is prepared, the patch should be sanded with a coarser paper than the rest of the piece because patches inevitably take a stain lighter than the rest of the surface. I can't explain this, so please accept it as one of those facts of life.

The patch will require special attention in the finishing process to assure a good match with the rest of the surface. Frequently used tricks are to run a scratch through the patch area so that it has continuity with the rest of the surface, or to have Japan colors smudged over it and feathered out so as to appear like a stain. I know of one person who uses, quite successfully at that, a pencil to grain the patch so that it matches the rest of the piece. Whatever techniques are employed, the wood patch can be easily mastered. It will allow for the resuscitation of presumed beyond-repair pieces.

CHAIR REPAIR

Probably the most frequently repaired type of furniture is the chair. There is nothing quixotic about this. There is no other type of furniture that must withstand so much use and abuse. For the most part, chairs fulfill their task admirably. As noble as chairs are, they must receive routine attention if they are to be continually used. I have seen chairs that are 150 to 200 years old that have never been disassembled and reglued. But they are rickety and I doubt that they have been in continuous use. A properly made and glued chair of the kitchen or ladderback variety should be good for 20 to 30 years before it needs attention. Padded parlor chairs that receive inter-mittant use might last a lifetime. The point is that you shouldn't feel bad if you have to reglue a chair; it is to be expected.

The majority of country chairs that you encounter will be lad-derback or stick type chairs (Fig. 11-18). For all their differences, most chairs are constructed in the same manner. Four vertical posts are connected by horizontal posts known as stretchers. The usual method of construction for chairs is one form or another of the mortise and tenon. Chairs are always connected at the top by a piece that fits over, in between, or behind the back post. Likewise, chairs will have vertical or horizontal pieces between the back posts— known as *splats* or *slats* —unless there is a series of rods that serve the same purpose.

When it comes time to repair a chair, the disassembly process should be logical and usually simple to determine. If a chair is structurally sound, every attempt should be made to make repairs without disassembling. If the need is present, there should be no hesitation about disassembling.

Nail Removal

Theoretically, there should be no nails in a chair with the exception of the top rung of a ladderback chair that will be secured in place with a nail or dowel. Wouldn't life be wonderful if such a theory held true. As reality would have it, chair owners through the centuries have insisted upon driving nails through the joints of chairs. This nefarious practice is ostensibly done to tighten the chair. I suspect that it reflects a deep hatred for those that might have to repair the chair some day! For the record, this type of repair never works in the long run. It might provide security for a few weeks or months.

Removing nails from chair joints is frustrating because it involves, under most circumstances, damage to the wood surface in and around the nail. The challenge presented by nails is not how to avoid damage, but rather how to keep it to a minimum.

If you have lived well, remembered your mother on Mother's Day, and that sort of thing, then someone will have used common nails on the problem chair. Common nails are the ones with the round heads which will protrude slightly above the surface. To remedy a common nail problem, take a screwdriver and force it under the head of the nail—rotating from right to left and vice versa—while exerting upward pressure. When the nail has been raised above the surface somewhat, use a claw hammer or other nail removal device to extract it. If there is not enough space to fit the hammer, use pliers or vice grips to pull the nail out a little further. Take care not to break the head of the nail. There is a grand tool known as a nipper and nail puller that will beat out any hammer that you have ever seen for this type of work.

More often than not, common nails are not used to secure joints because they are unsightly. Neat, almost invisible finishing nails are used. To make matters worse, finishing nails are frequently countersunk and filled with putty. If a finishing nail goes undetected, the joint will invariably be damaged when it is knocked apart.

The removal of finishing nails is neither simple nor fun. If the finishing nail extends visibly from one side of the leg post through the other side, the best approach to removal is a nail punch. Take an appropriately sized nail punch—the type with a cup center intended to fit over the head of a finishing nail—and apply it to the point (not the head) of the finishing nail (as shown in Fig. 11-19A). Strike the punch with a hammer until the head begins to exit the leg post. Use a hammer to remove the nail when a sufficient amount protrudes above the surface of the wood.

The greatest difficulty is encountered when the finishing nail is driven from one side through the tenon, but does not extend out the other side. To remove the nail, the wood fiber holding it must be relieved. Take a one-eighth-inch chisel and create a space around the head of the nail (Fig. 11-19B). Work as close to the nail as possible and create as small a space around the nail as possible.

Following the removal of the wood around the head, take a drill with a one-sixteenth inch bit or smaller and drill around the nail. Attempt to keep the bit close to and parallel with the nail (Fig. 11-19C). Run the bit through its full length. The drilling should relieve the wood around the nail so that it can be easily removed.

After the drilling, use a small pry bar or tack remover to lift the nail up so that it can be gripped with a hammer. It might be necessary to force pliers around the nail to lift it slightly if the pry bar fails. Needle-nose pliers can be used to good advantage in this situation if the nail can be grasped without slippage.

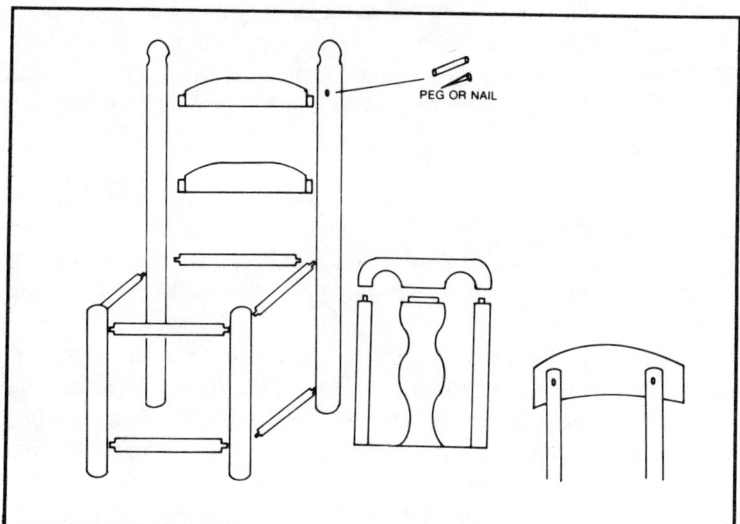

Fig. 11-18. Standard ladderback chair construction has mortise and tenon joints with a pinned top slat. Chairs other than ladderbacks will use a crest rail to secure the back posts.

303

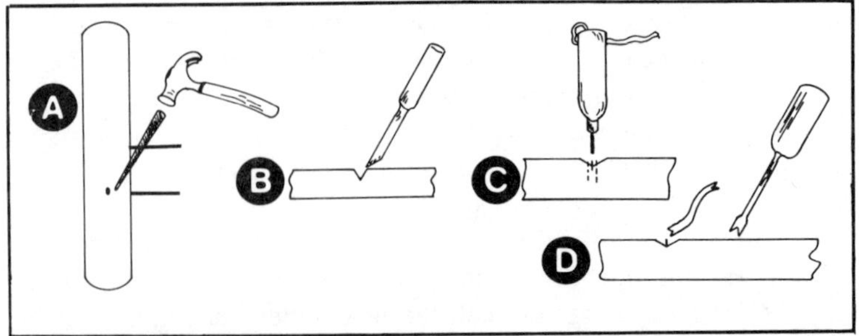

Fig. 11-19. Nail removal: When a finishing nail has been driven through a post, a nail set is applied to the point of the nail to drive it partially from the post (A). When the head of the nail exits, it is removed with a nail puller. When a nail does not extend through the leg post, the head of the nail is relieved by removing the wood fiber with a small chisel (B). The nail is further relieved by drilling around it (C) with a small drill bit (one-sixteenth inch or less). When the nail is loosened in the above fashion (D), it is pried up and removed with a puller or pliers.

In some cases, the finishing nail will have been countersunk so deeply that the method described above would be impractical due to the large amount of wood that would have to be removed. One approach to this problem is to take the nail punch and sink it deeply into the hole until it rests upon the head of the nail. When seated, the nail punch is driven so that it will force the nail through and out the other side of the tenon. Once the tenon has been freed, there is no need to attempt to force the nail through the other side of the post. Forcing a nail through a tenon should only be attempted if there is no other choice because there is a risk of splitting the tenon. When all nail removal is completed, the holes can be plugged or filled.

Stretcher Replacement and Repair

Damage, quite logically, occurs to those parts of chairs that receive the most wear and stress. Back posts, seat rails, and lower stretchers suffer stress damage. Leg post bottoms and feet receive the most wear. The greatest damage will usually be found on stretchers.

Seat rails and stretchers are either rectangular or round. Rectangular forms are mostly a product of the 18th century and the late 19th century. Rectangular stretchers and rails (Fig. 11-20A) use either mortise and tenon construction or dowel construction. There is little need to discuss the repair of dowel stretchers because it is obvious; replace the dowels.

A rectangular stretcher breaks infrequently, but when it does, repair can be made in a number of ways. Three methods of repair are shown in Fig. 11-20B. The first method involves a new tenon piece that is attached to the original stretcher with a lap joint reinforced with a dowel. This joint is strong, easy to make, and reasonably unsightly. With the second method shown, a new tenon and front piece are added with a butt joint reinforced by dowels. This approach is the simplest and is as effective as an original doweled joint. It is not however, as secure or as sightly as a lap joint. The third method illustrated is a scarf joint reinforced with dowels. This joint is strong and the most sightly. It is difficult to accomplish withput a power saw or some familiarity with hand tools.

When a rectangular stretcher or rail breaks, it is not, as a rule, the main body that breaks, but the tenon itself which is the weakest part of the stretcher. If you have a great deal of skill and patience, you could cut the tenon flush to the shoulder.

A new tenon could be put into place by chiseling a mortise to receive it. If you are a slave to work, attempt this method. If not, use one of the simple methods shown in Fig. 11-20C. With the first method shown, the remainder of the damaged tenon is drilled to

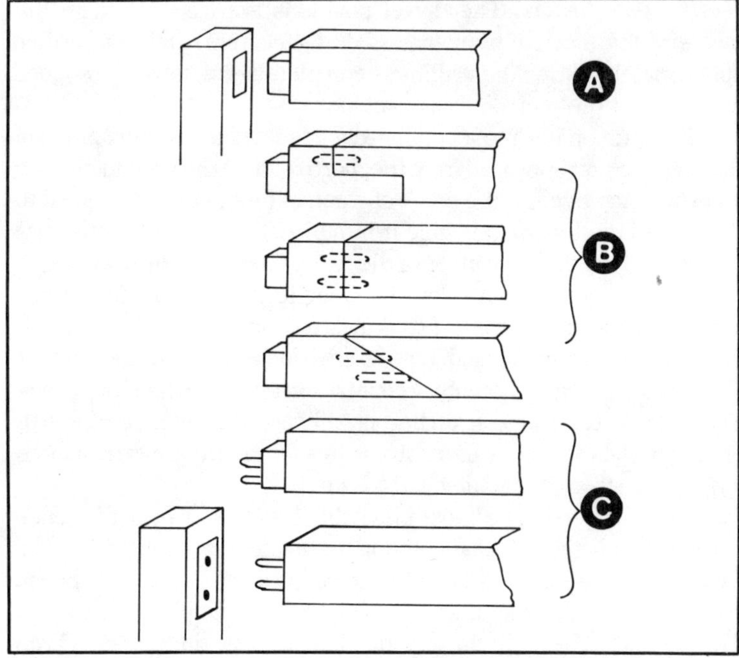

Fig. 11-20. Repair of rectangular rails and stretchers: (A) standard mortise and tenon stretcher; (B) repair using a lap joint and dowel, and repair utilizing a scarf joint and two dowels; (C) a tenon repaired with the use of dowels only (the mortise is plugged and the tenon is trimmed and fitted with dowels).

305

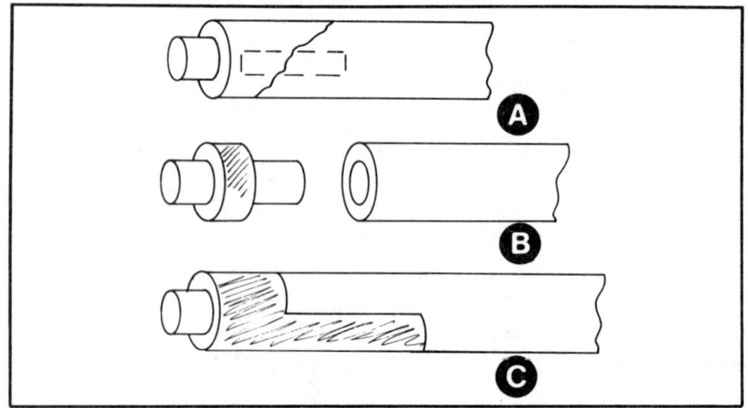

Fig. 11-21. Repairs to a round tenon stretcher: Regluing broken parts, but reinforced with a dowel (A). A new piece is cut from dowel stock matched to the stretcher (B). A hole is drilled through the repair piece and into the stretcher. The repair piece is attached with a dowel the same size as the tenon. A new piece (C) is added with a lap joint. The tenon is formed after the repair is made.

receive two dowels. The dowel positions are transferred to the inside of the mortise by means of dowel centers, and then drilled appropriately. When the drilling is completed, the dowels are glued in place and the piece is reassembled.

If the tenon is almost completely gone and the mating piece of the tenon has disappeared from the mortise, then the second method shown is employed. Cut a piece of wood to fill the mortise (equal to the size of the tenon), and glue it into place. When the mortise has been filled, cut the remainder of the tenon flush with the shoulder of the stretcher and fit with dowels. Complete the repair by drilling corresponding holes in the fitted mortise, and glue.

Round stretchers and rails, found in ladderback and similar chairs dominating 19th-century country furniture, are far more prone to breakage. The round stretcher, usually no more than three-fourth or seven-eighths inch, suffers stress to a far greater degree than its larger and stronger rectangular cousin.

Round stretchers almost inevitably break at or near the tenon because that is the weakest point on the stretcher. When a stretcher has a center break, you can almost be sure that some 420-pound cretin attempted to use it as a stepladder. The simple regluing of a damaged stretcher will not be sufficient to bear the stress. Three methods of repair for this type of problem are shown in Fig. 11-21.

If the stretcher exhibits a clean break, it can be reinforced with a dowel and reglued as shown. The fitting and mating of the dowel for this type of repair is not simple due to the angular nature of the break. An alternative to this method is to glue the stretcher without reinforcement. When the glue has set, the tenon is trimmed flush to the shoulder and the stretcher is bored for a new tenon that will extend through the repaired area.

This alternative method is essentially the same as the second method of repair shown. The second method is used when the broken stretcher cannot be reglued or when the mating piece has been lost. A piece of dowel or other stock is cut to the same size as the stretcher and equal to the piece lost or being replaced. The new piece of stretcher and the stretcher are drilled to receive a new tenon that joins the new pieces when fitted.

The third method of stretcher and tenon repair shown involves fitting a new piece to the stretcher with a lap joint. In this case, it is easier to make the new piece out of square stock that is oversized and shaped to the stretcher after gluing. The third method of repair is less visible than the second and if done properly it is stronger.

If a stretcher is damaged beyond repair or if it is missing, a new one can be made with relative ease. For a chair with maple stretchers, new pieces can be made from common dowel stock of maple or birch. Some mail-order houses offer dowel stock made up from cherry, walnut, oak, etc. If the appropriate wood (often hickory) is not available in dowels, you will have to make your own from square stock. This task is not as hard as it might sound. Square stock can be brought into round with a drawknife in a few minutes. If a drawknife is not available, the stock can be formed into an octagon by running a plane over the edges. Once the piece has been roughed out with a plane, it can be trued up with a rasp and sandpaper. If you have access to a lathe, avoid all this mess and turn the piece.

Most difficulty encountered in making a new stretcher is found in the cutting of the tenons. Ideally, the tenon should be turned on a lathe. I cut them by hand; it's much faster and easier than setting up the lathe. To prepare a tenon, mark off the length of the tenon on the stock and remember that the stretcher must be equal to the distance between the two leg posts, plus double the length of one tenon. The tenon length can be marked off with a marking gauge by rotating it around the stock. When the tenon length has been marked off, take a small saw—preferably a bead saw—and cut the shoulder of the tenon. The depth of cut is nominal because it can later be trued. It should not be so deep that it will undercut the tenon.

Find the center on the end of the dowel and, using a compass or divider, form the radius of the tenon (Fig. 11-22). When the tenon has

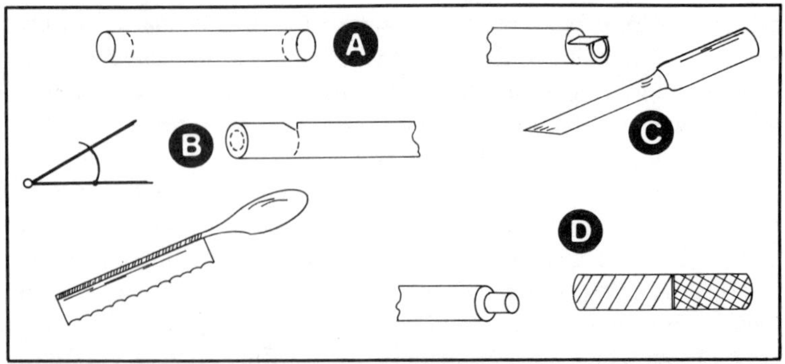

Fig. 11-22. Cutting a tenon: (A) the stretcher is measured and marked for the tenons; (B) the diameter of the tenon is scribed in the end grain with a divider or compass while an initial depth cut is made with a small saw; (C) excess material is cut away with a chisel; (D) the tenon is brought into round with a rasp.

been marked off, use a chisel to form a square. Work the outside of the scribe line. Tap the chisel lightly and it should move to the previously cut shoulder with ease.

After the tenon has been cut square, pare the corners with the chisel to form an octagon or general round shape. Finish shaping the tenon with a rasp or file. When fitting the tenon, use sandpaper to make final adjustments. When the tenon is complete, taper the forward part of the tenon slightly and round the edges to make a good fit. The entire process of forming the tenon can be accomplished with just a rasp or file, but it will not be as accurate or as simple as the method just described.

The replacement of a seat rail or upper stretcher usually necessitates the dismantling of the chair (at least in part). The replacement of a lower stretcher can often be accomplished by spreading the leg post and forcing in the new stretcher. It is not always necessary to destroy a rush seat to replace a seat rail. If a chair has been fitted with a real rush seat in the traditional manner—which means the starting strands of the rush are tied to the rear seat rail—then the old seat rail (left, right and center)can be slipped out and be replaced with a new one.

If the chair has been re-rushed in modern times, the starting strands of rush have probably been tacked to the left and right seat rails. This means only the front and rear rails can be replaced without destroying the seat. Repairs should only be made in this manner if the remainder of the chair is structurally sound. Should the chair be loose, it makes more sense to dismantle and reglue it.

Another likely candidate for breakage is a back post. As can well be expected, back posts break in the area where the two seat rails meet because this receives the most stress and is the weakest area of the post. On an armchair, the back post might break where the arm is connected to the post. It depends upon the manner in which the arm was fitted to the post. Front posts rarely break, but when they do it is in the area of one of the rails or stretchers.

Four methods of repair for a back post are illustrated in Fig. 11-23. There are many more approaches to the problem.

Figure 11-23A illustrates a post that has split in the area of the seat rail. If the split is clean and if the surfaces can be realigned, then the leg can be glued. But it is unlikely that the post will accept the stress without breaking again.

Figure 11-23B shows a better approach that involves fitting the two broken halves with a dowel to provide resistance to stress. The only problem with this approach is that it can be very difficult to fit and align a dowel within the two broken halves of the post.

Another, and easier, approach to the problem is shown in Fig. 11-23C. The two halves of the post are glued with yellow glue or plastic resin glue, clamped, and allowed to set and cure for 48 hours. After the elapsed drying time, a recess is cut, with a saw and chisel, into the rear of the post.

It is imperative that the floor or bottom of the recess be perfectly flat and level so that a good glue bond can be made with the

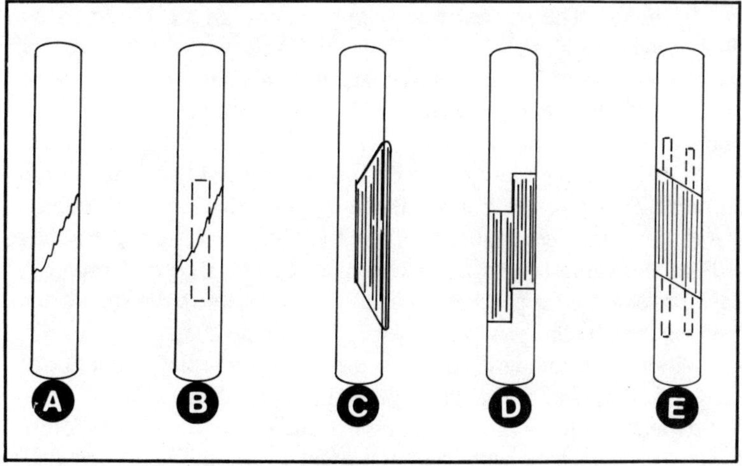

Fig. 11-23. Methods of chair post repair: (A) glue alone (weak); (B) glue reinforced with a dowel (difficult); (C) gluing followed by inletting a patch (good); (D) double-lap joint used to replace lost or damaged material (good); (E) doweled scarf joint used to replace lost or damaged material (good but difficult).

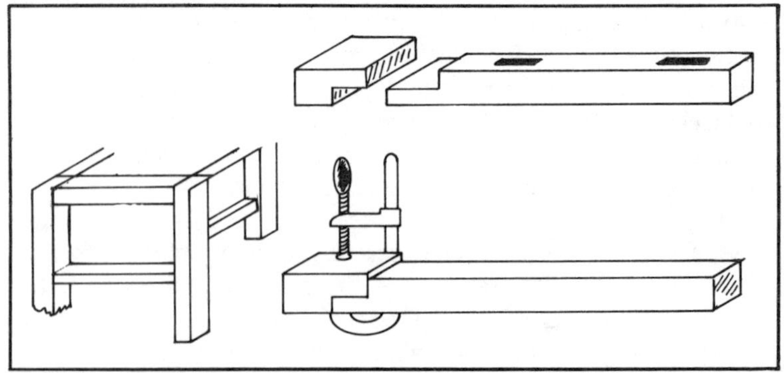

Fig. 11-24. Chair leg repair (rectangular). New stock is fitted oversized with a lap joint. After clamping, the repair piece is trimmed to size.

patch piece. The recess is fitted and glued with an oversized patch of appropriate wood. Do not make a small patch for aesthetic reasons. The greater the glue surface, the stronger the repair will be.

After the patch has been fitted and glued, it can be brought to shape with a rasp and sandpaper. In cases where you anticipate that the chair will receive heavy use, leave the patch thicker in the rear than the chair was originally. A little additional material in the rear is hardly noticeable and it might add considerable strength to the chair.

If a back post cannot be glued due to the loss or damage of material in the area of the break, then a different type of repair must be attempted. The easiest way to approach this type of repair is a double lap joint as shown in Fig. 11-23D. The two broken halves of the leg post are trimmed and each is cut with a lap half the diameter of the post. For maximum strength, the laps or recesses are on opposite sides of the post (see Fig. 11-23).

Care must be taken in the cutting and assembly so that all rail and stretcher mortise holes will be in the same line after gluing. Careful measurement must be made to assure that the repaired leg will be the same length as the original leg. This type of repair is easier to affect if the patch material is cut oversized in the square and later shaped to the post with rasps, files, and sandpaper.

Another method of repair that requires the replacement of lost material is shown in Fig. 11-23E. With this method, the back posts are trimmed with a bias cut or angular cut known as a *scarf*. A new piece of appropriate wood is cut to mate with the scarf and then doweled into place. The proper fitting of this joint requires at least two dowels in each end of the replacement part. This method of repair is as strong, if not stronger, than the double lap type of repair (while being far less noticeable). On the other hand, a scarf-joint repair requires more skill than the double lap.

Square or rectangular leg posts are repaired in the same manner as round posts. As shown in Fig. 11-24, a broken foot is repaired with a lap joint as would be used with a round post. As in the case of a round post, a patch is cut oversized and later trimmed. The result is a greater degree of success. The lap joint is frequently the easiest type of repair. Nevertheless, any of the methods illustrated in Fig. 11-23 can be used.

A very common problem encountered with country chairs is wear or damage to one or more of the feet. More often than not, the rear legs have been worn by a hundred years of chair tippers. Unfortunately, some people choose to handle this problem by cutting all of the chair legs until they are even. This is an unsavory and unnecessary practice because it is a simple matter to build up a foot. The simplest approach to this problem is to select a piece of dowel equal in diameter to the leg. Cut the dowel to the appropriate size and glue and screw it to the bottom of the post (Fig. 11-25). It is best to countersink the screw so that the repair piece can be trimmed if necessary. Sand and color the repair piece. That's all there is to it.

DRAWERS

Drawers represent the ultimate in functional construction as a box within a box. They are lightweight, strong, and throughout a lifetime they can withstand tremendous use. I am constantly amazed at how often I find drawers that have been in continuous service for 150 years and in need of no attention. Frequently, the only problem

Fig. 11-25. Building up a leg. The chair leg is matched with dowel stock. A repair piece is cut and attached with glue and a screw. The screw hole is countersunk to allow for subsequent trimming of the repair.

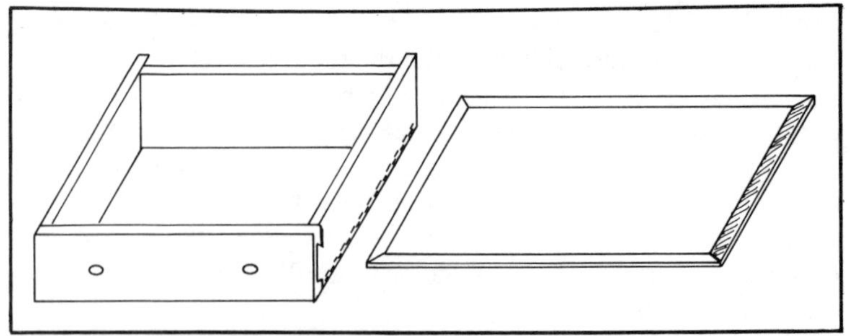

Fig. 11-26. Typical 19th-century drawer construction.

encountered with a drawer is one of wobbliness. To remedy this problem, knock the side piece out a little so that glue can be applied around the dovetail. Do the same to the rear where the side rail connects with the backboard. Then clamp the piece and allow it to dry.

Many drawers from the late 18th century and the 19th century have the chamfered bottom boards nailed to the backboard. Nailing the board in this manner makes it stationary. Consequently, when the drawer bottom shrinks, it pulls loose from its mortise in the drawer front. If the drawer bottom has been glued in the mortise or restrained in some other manner, it will have split under the tension. The proper remedy to this problem would require that the drawer bottom have new material added to make up for the wood lost in shrinkage. More often than not, I merely remove the nails that hold the bottom board to the backboard and return the board to the front mortise. This leaves a small gap in the rear.

The area that receives the most wear on a drawer is the runner. Quite logically, if a drawer is opened 10 times a day and thousands of times in a lifetime, it should show wear on the bearing surface (the runner). This type of repair tends to frighten people off, but it's one of those jobs that looks harder than it really is.

To begin the repair, the drawer must be dismantled by first knocking off the side pieces. Figure 11-26 illustrates a typical method of drawer construction that can be used as a guide. Once apart, each runner, which is no more than the bottom of the side, is trued up with a plane and fitted with a new piece as shown in Fig. 11-27A. This type of repair is very common. It might be necessary to cut a new groove for the drawer bottom. The face as well as both sides of a drawer will have a channel to hold the drawer bottom. When the drawer runners wear, they break at the weakest point (the channels).

To make repairs, you might have to trim the side above the channel. This requires that a new channel be cut later on. The easiest way to cut a new channel is with a plough plane or a multi-plane. Unfortunately, the average homeowner does not possess them. The job can be done equally well with a table saw, a radial arm saw or a router. If you don't have any of these tools, making this repair is going to be a difficult proposition at best. Nevertheless, it can be done with a chisel.

Lay out the channel accurately, and preferably with a marking gauge if you have one. Take some small pieces of wood that are true on at least two adjacent sides and clamp them to the outside of the channel markings to act as guides for your chisel (Fig. 11-27B).

If the area does not lend itself to clamping, the guides can be fastened with rubber cement applied to one wood surface only. A channel can be cut without clamping a guide. But if you do not have access to any of the tools mentioned, it is not likely that you will have the skill to use a chisel without assistance.

Having cut a new channel, some woodworkers like to provide more protection with the addition of a glue block (Fig. 11-27C). The degree to which this might help is questionable.

If you have done a fine job regluing a drawer and replacing the worn runners, but you still find that the drawer does not work easily, check the drawer guides on the inside of the piece. Drawer guides are easily lost over the years and infrequently replaced because the drawer will work without them (albeit poorly). This is a straightfor-

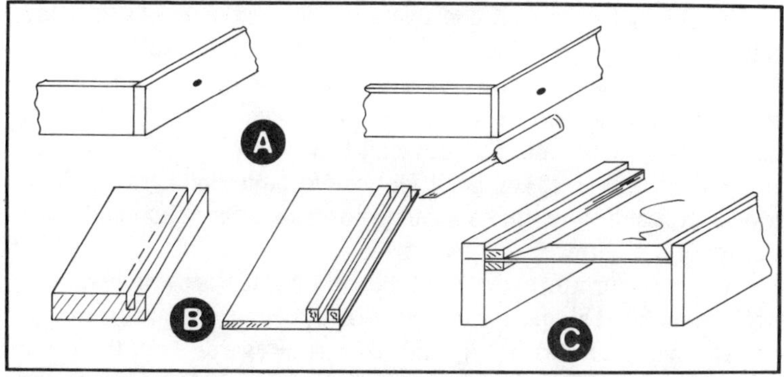

Fig. 11-27. Drawer repair. Drawer runners (A) are repaired by truing the worn area with a plane and adding a new piece. If a repair to a runner makes cutting a new channel (B) necessary, it is best accomplished with a plough plane, table saw or router. If you do not have the proper tool, wooden strips can be clamped to the side to outline the channel, and the channel can subsequently be cut with a chisel. Glue blocks (C) are sometimes used to reinforce a damaged channel.

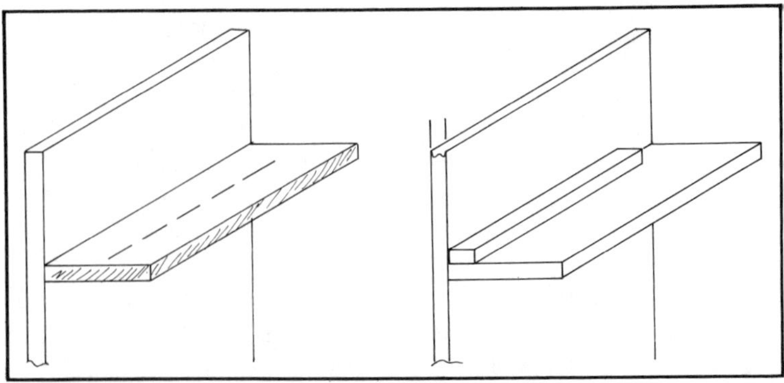

Fig. 11-28. Drawer guides are often lost from the insides of chests. Replacement is a simple matter of cutting and gluing a new piece.

ward and simple repair. Just size a new block and glue it in place (Fig. 11-28).

When purchasing antiques in the rough, you might find that drawers are missing. The absence of a drawer hurts the value of a piece, but it does not mean that the piece should be avoided. If a drawer is missing, you have no choice but to make a new one. A drawer is one of those things that it takes a master to make properly. Yet almost anyone can make one that will work.

The drawer shown in Fig. 11-26 is typical of the construction used for drawers in the late 18th century and early 19th century. It can be used as a model for a new drawer. With this drawer, the side pieces extend beyond the rear piece and they are nailed (as opposed to dovetailed) for ease of construction. The extension of the side rails allows the trimming and easier fitting of the drawer. The bottom of the drawer is one piece, chamfered, and fitted to a channel that is cut into the face piece and the side pieces. The drawer shown has one large dovetail. The dovetail can be omitted and the side rebated and nailed. If you don't feel comfortable enough to make a drawer yourself, then find a local restorer or repair shop and commission a new drawer.

Country furniture of the 19th century is rarely found with original knobs. This puts it ahead of 18th-century furniture that is almost never found with original hardware. Regardless of the roots of the problem, you will find it necessary to replace the wooden knobs. Knobs are attached to furniture in a number of different ways. On 18th-century and some 19th-century pieces, the wooden knobs were turned with a dowel shank that was fitted to a mating hole in the drawer front.

314

Another treatment involved fitting the knob with a piece of threaded dowel and likewise boring and threading a mating hole in the drawer front. The most prevalent method for the attachment of a knob to a drawer involved using a simple screw fitted from the inside of the drawer front. This last type of knob can be replaced without difficulty because it is the same attachment mode as is used on modern wooden knobs.

The replacement of threaded knobs is somewhat of a problem because the threading boxes used by different makers were not uniform. If the knobs are missing, but the threaded stock remains in the hole, then consider the threaded dowel as a plug. Bore a pilot hole in the plug for the screw and attach the knob in a conventional manner. You may also simply drill the knob and shank and attach it with a dowel.

Where both the knob and threaded shank have been lost, leaving a pair of large holes in the drawer front, there are two methods of approach. For the first method, cut a piece of dowel stock just a hair larger than the hole to be plugged. Apply glue and force the plug into place. The fit should be tight enough so that the glue is only an extra precaution. When the glue has dried, the plug is drilled for a conventional screw and knob attachment. A simpler, but somewhat less sightly, approach to this problem is to leave the hole as is and attach a new wooden knob with a screw and washer (Fig. 11-29). The knob will cover the hole on the face side of the drawer while the washer

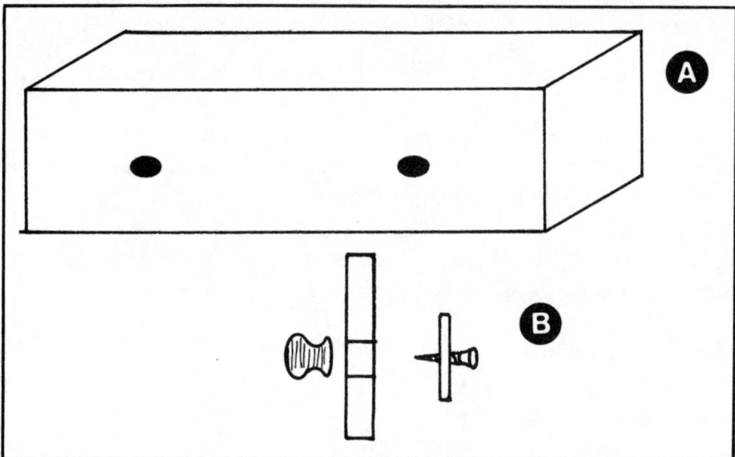

Fig. 11-29. Knob replacement: (A) plugging an oversized hole with a dowel; (B) attaching a new knob with a screw and washer. The washer is used to compensate for the oversized hole.

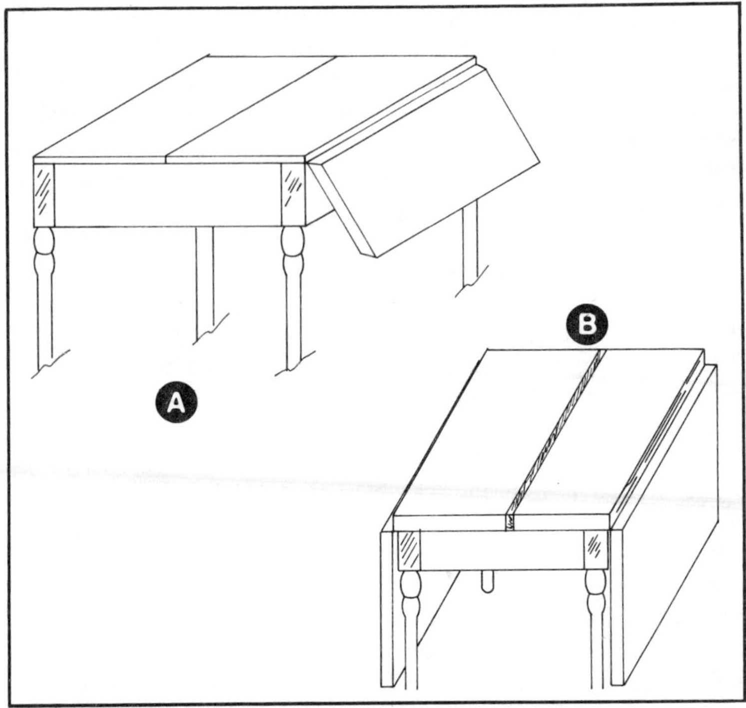

Fig. 11-30. Drop leaf, table-top repair: (A) regluing a split table top (the result of shrinkage) on a dropleaf table, the result of which is the raising of the leaf like a wing; (B) the proper method of repair calls for adding a new piece between the split halves to make up for lost material.

will cover it on the inside. This will provide enough tension to keep both the knob and washer in place.

When a knob with a round shank is required, a conventional wooden mushroom-shaped knob can be drilled and fitted with an appropriate-size dowel. Some Shaker-style wooden knobs with round shanks are available at craft houses, but they are difficult to locate. If you have access to a lathe, you can learn to make any variety of knobs with only a modicum of practice.

TABLES

Tables cause trouble. Table bases are rarely a problem, but table tops are almost always a problem. If you will recall the discussion of shrinkage in the early part of the book, then you will understand why table tops are a problem. Any plain-sawn board that is fixed at opposing points must, in time, split or pull loose. That's all there is to that.

Table tops as well as other types of tops that do not support leaves can be repaired by removing the top and regluing it. The split area must be cleaned carefully prior to gluing because it will have collected the dirt and debris of many years. If the two split halves cannot be rejoined tightly, it might be necessary to plane the surfaces true prior to gluing. When the top is replaced on the base, the original points of attachment, whether they are screw or nail, will no longer line up because the top is actually smaller than it was originally. The shrinkage loss might range from one-fourth to one-half inch, but it should not prove to be unsightly.

With drop-leaf tables, shrinkage splits are more of a problem. If the top is just removed and reglued, it pulls the leaves in too tightly. This would lift them into a winged effect (Fig. 11-30A). Sometimes there will be enough overhang on a drop-leaf table so that this is not a problem, but more often than not it is a problem. To remedy it, each side of the split must be trued up with a plane. Then a new piece of wood, equal to the shrinkage loss, must be fitted and the top must be reglued (Fig. 11-30B). This is the proper way as well as the only way to handle this problem. If you are concerned with the aesthetics of the piece, you must learn to live with it as is or repair it in this fashion.

If you have never used a hand plane to true surfaces for edge gluing, you are most certainly not going to do it properly the first time. Hand planing is a basic skill in woodworking that is being replaced by machinery that produces perfect results the first time. I

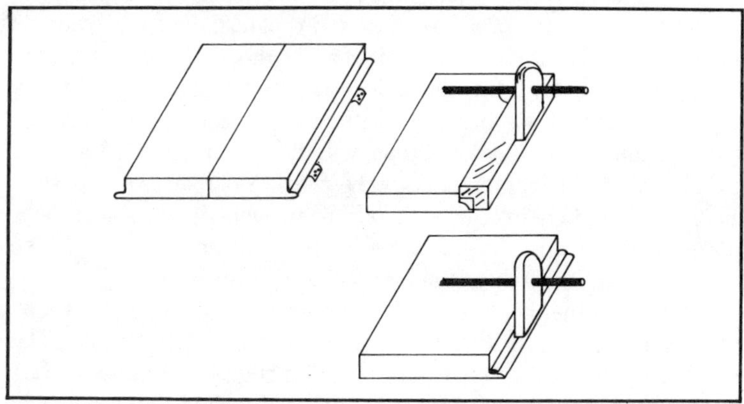

Fig. 11-31. Gluing a top with a half-rule joint. To avoid damaging the rule joint during gluing, a length of scrap stock is rebated and fit over the molding. Alternatively, a dowel can be used to prevent the clamp from damaging the molding. Tape the dowel in place.

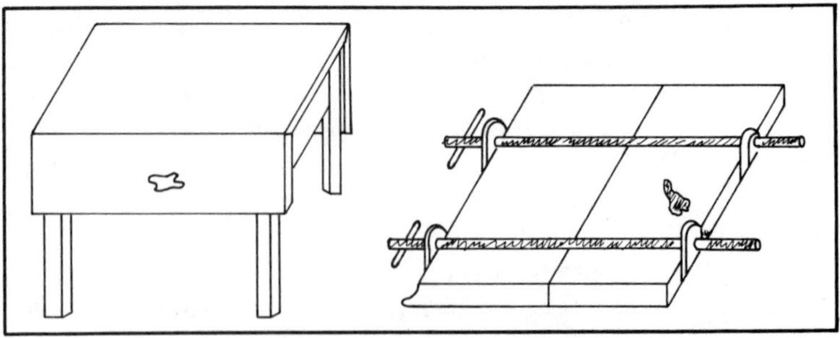

Fig. 11-32. A badly damaged table leaf can be repaired by cutting the leaf into two parts. The damaged member is inverted and the leaf is reglued.

am not being anti-modern or knocking the machines. It's just a matter of a homeowner not being able to afford some of the machines. To remedy this problem, find someone who knows how to use a hand plane and who can show you. Chances are there is someone in your family or a friend of a friend who knows how. If all else fails, find a good carpenter and pay him to show you. If you are the type of person who likes to learn on your own, then obtain a copy of *Planecraft: Hand Planing by Modern Methods* by C. and S. Hampton. This very worthwhile book can be purchased from the Woodcraft Supply Corp., Woburn, Massachusetts.

Clamping a drop-leaf table can be a problem when a half-rule joint is involved (which is most of the time). If a clamp is applied directly to the joint, there is an excellent chance of breaking the joint. This is especially true on an antique piece. To remedy this problem, prepare two lengths of scrap stock and rebate them to fit over the joint (Fig. 11-31). If you are in a bit of a lazy mood, the same task can be accomplished by fitting the half-rule joint with an appropriate-size dowel. Tape the dowel into place with masking tape and then clamp.

Genuine antique table tops will have a variety of surface problems—from dents to holes and gouges. Most surface imperfections are handled by the methods previously discussed: fillers, plugs, and patches. On occasion, damage to an area can be so extensive that a patch would be unsightly (Fig. 11-32).

The treatment of this problem requires that the table top (or as shown in this illustration the leaf) be cut into two pieces. The damaged piece is reversed and the leaf is reglued. If the work has been properly done and the entire table refinished, the repair will hardly be noticeable. I cannot say that this repair does not hurt the value and originality of a piece, but I presume a table with this type of damage was purchased at a reasonable price.

318

Round table tops lend themselves to being repaired in the same manner as square or rectangular tops, but they present one heck of a problem when it comes to clamping if you don't know how to do it. No matter how ingenious you are, some type of special jig must be made to glue a round table.

The simplest approach to the problem is to trace the radius of the circle into some plywood or scrap stock. Make two jigs in this fashion as shown in **Fig. 11-33A** and you are ready to glue the top. The only problem with this solution is that the jig is made to order for only one table top. And given the price of wood today, this can be an expensive proposition.

A better approach to the problem involves making a gluing jig such as the one shown in **Fig. 11-33B.** The jig is made up of 1-by-3-inch pine or plywood about 28 inches long. Inserted between the two 1 by 3's is a piece of three-fourths inch stock approximately 3 inches square and trimmed to a 45-degree angle. A pair of sleeves made in this fashion will accommodate a variety of different-size round table tops.

Once prepared, the sleeves are fit over the top and secured with pipe clamps pulling the joint together along the full line of fracture. If a heavy-duty band clamp is available, an attempt can be made to use it for a round top. More often than not, the two halves buckle at the joint.

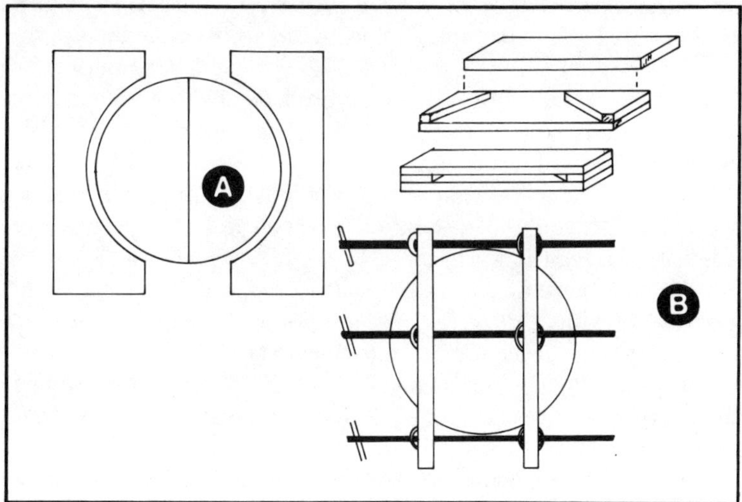

Fig. 11-33. Regluing a round top: (A) gluing forms cut to the radius of the top and prepared from scrap wood; (B) special gluing sleeves are prepared and fitted to each side of the top, and then the assembly is clamped.

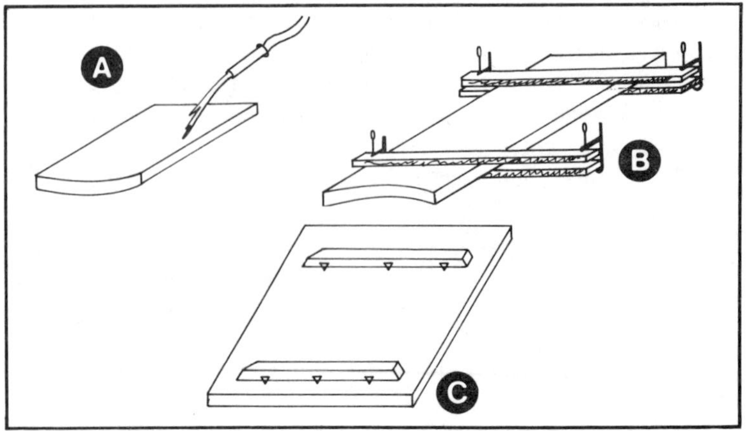

Fig. 11-34. Removing a warp. The concave side of the warp (A) is soaked with water (all finish has been removed). The board is brought outdoors to dry in direct sunlight. The convex side toward the sun and the wet side is on the bottom (B). Pressure is applied to the warp by clamping wood braces. The clamps are tightened as the board returns to shape. The braces are kept in place for several days after the warp has been removed and the board has been brought indoors. Battens are attached to the board (C) to prevent it from returning to its previously warped shape.

Warps

Warped table tops are the potholes of woodworking. If you think that means I don't like them, you are 100 percent correct. Table tops have a nasty habit of warping. Actually, the proper term is *cupping*, but that does not change the nature of the problem. One reason for this problem is that our great and revered woodworking ancestors, when putting a finish on a table, only finished the top surfaces. This looked all fine and dandy, but a finish on one surface inhibits the absorption of moisture while the lack of finish on the other surface allows for a great deal of absorption. The end product of this type of unequal treatment is warpage.

If you acquire a table with a warped top, my best advice is to learn to live with it. If you find that it is not possible to live with the warped top, my second piece of advice is to farm the job out to a pro so that you can sleep peacefully at night. If you are a fearless and adventurous soul who welcomes a challenge, then you can attempt the job yourself.

Remove the offending member of the table top (usually one of the leaves). Soak the concave side of the warped board with water; soak *only* the concave side. After the water has been soaked up by the wood, wet the surface again and apply a double set of battens drawn together with clamps (Fig. 11-34). Bring the project out to your yard or driveway on a warm, sunny day and place the wet side (concave) down. Allow the convex side to face the sun.

The board should start to warp again, but opposite to the original warp. As the sun dries out the board, adjust the clamp pressure until the board is level. Surprisingly, a warped board can be returned to normal in this fashion almost like magic. When the board is dry, it can be sanded and finished on both sides and reattached to the table.

Odds are that in time the board will return to the shape of the original warp. One way to cope with this problem is to attach battens with screws to the underside of the table when the top is dried. The battens should provide sufficient rigidity to prevent the top from returning to the original warp condition. Battens do not look particularly attractive on the underside of a drop leaf. That is why we advise that you live with a warp if at all possible. A better approach to the battens would be to cut a dovetail channel across the width of the leaf with the insertion of a dovetailed batten. In this case, the batten would move with the top and avoid any risk of splitting created by the use of a batten screwed into place.

The soundest approach to a warped leaf, from a technical point of view, is perhaps the least acceptable from an antique point of view. With this method, the warped leaf would be sawn into several boards approximately 3 inches wide. The table leaf would then be reglued as in Fig. 11-35. Alternate the growth rings of each board so that future stress would neutralize itself. When the leaf has been reglued, it is planed level. This will remove any trace of the warp.

Usually, a small piece of new wood has to be added because some material will have been lost in the warpage and the cutting process. Once the board has been planed, it will be thinner than the

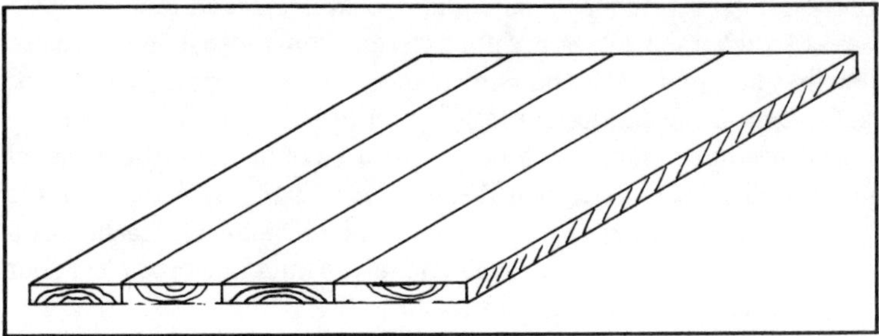

Fig. 11-35. Removing a warp. The warp piece is cut into 3-inch or 4-inch sections and reglued, alternating the growth rings. After drying, the board is planed to a true surface.

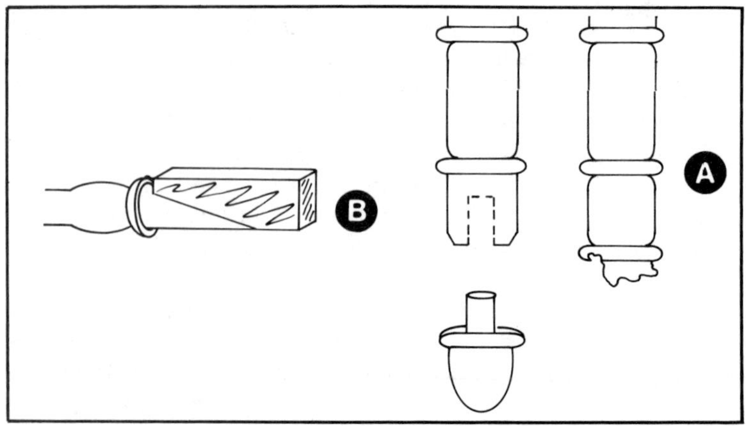

Fig. 11-36. Repair to a table leg. The damaged leg (A) is trimmed at natural breakpoint (visual) or below a ring turning. A new piece is shaped and fitted with a tenon or dowel. The damaged area is trimmed (B) with a scarf cut made on a table saw. New stock is glued and the piece is re-turned on a lathe.

other top boards. It should not be terribly perceptible. This method does damage the originality of the piece. It's also a lot of work. But it does offer a permanent solution to the problem of warpage.

If you have not already realized it, the existing finish on the warped piece must be removed in its entirety prior to treating. The wetting process will, in all likelihood, raise the grain of the wood. This can be easily remedied with a light sanding. Please remember that once you have taken the effort to remove a warp, both the top and bottom surfaces of a table must receive equal amounts of finish.

Table Bases

Table bases do not lend themselves to the same multitude of damages as do table tops. Problems that will be encountered include broken legs, stretchers, leaf supports, and damaged feet.

Stretchers on tables are not different from those found on chairs and they are repaired in the same manner. A table leg can be repaired in the same fashion as a chair leg (Fig. 11-35). Unlike chair legs, table legs break infrequently and then in the area of the feet (the weakest point of the leg). Repairing the foot of a chair involves a simple procedure of building up the foot with a piece of dowel attached by a screw. Repairing the foot of a table involves the same procedure, but with a slight bit more elaboration.

As shown in Fig. 11-36A, the foot has been damaged and lost from the point of the last ring turning. To prepare for a new piece, the leg is trimmed immediately above the ring turning. As long as

322

repairs are contained to natural visual breaks in the turnings, they will not be noticeable. If the break had occurred at a middle point between the next to last ring turning and the last ring turning, then the leg would be trimmed flush immediately below the next to last ring turning.

When the leg has been trimmed, a new piece is copied from one of the remaining legs and attached with a dowel or a tenon formed as an integral part of the repair piece. Repairing any sort of turned work is easier if you have access to a lathe, but it is not essential. A new foot can be made just as well with a rasp and file as it can be by a lathe, but surely not as quickly. If you take care in examining and measuring the other feet on the table, you will find that no two are alike. Consequently, there is room for a little deviation in the making of the new foot. It is best to oversize the foot somewhat when making it by hand so that final shaping will occur while the foot is in place. A replacement made on a lathe should be turned to its final dimensions.

The usual professional treatment for a broken foot or lower leg section is to make a scarf cut (Fig. 11-36B). Glue up a new piece of stock and re-turn the entire leg on the lathe.

The pivots or leaf supports on a drop-leaf table have to withstand a great deal of use and stress. Given the task at hand, leaf supports—which always appear undersized—perform admirably, but nonetheless break with some degree of frequency. This is another one of those repairs that appear to be difficult, but turn out to be a simple task when you get down to it.

The most difficult part of this task will be the removal of the table top. If the top has been screwed in, which is common with

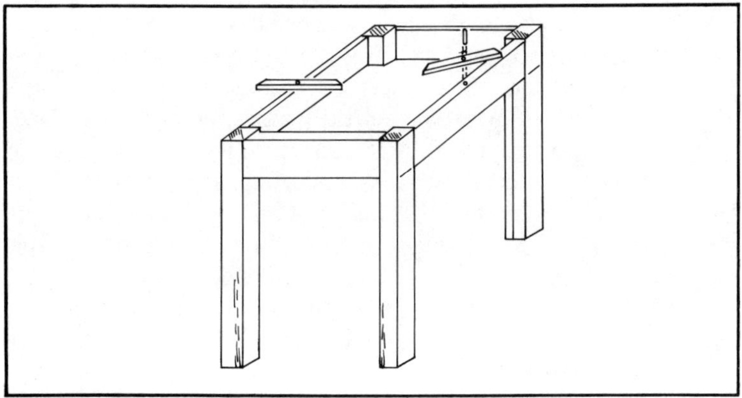

Fig. 11-37. Single arm supports for a drop-leaf table have a wooden pivot pin or a metal pivot pin.

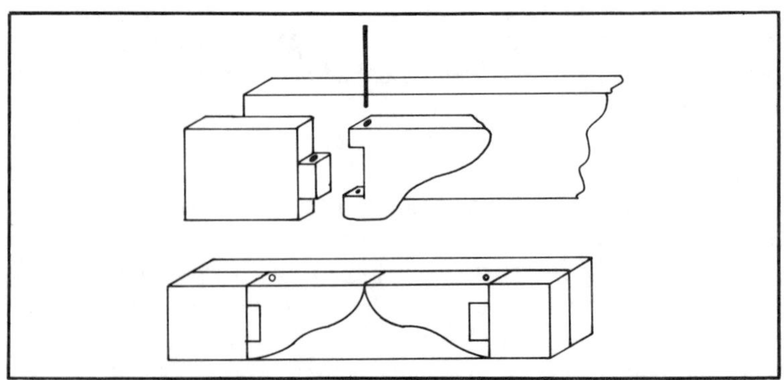

Fig. 11-38. A wooden knuckle joint with a metal pin used to support the leaf of a drop-leaf table.

19th-century tables, then dismantling requires only removal of the screws. Make a reference point on the underside of the table and the top so that the top is replaced in the same manner that it was removed.

Care should also be taken to mark all the screws so that they are returned to the same holes from which they have been removed.

Nailed table tops present more of a problem than screwed on tops. To remove the top, lay the table on end so that the floor supports both leaves and the center piece. Strike the underside of the top with a rubber mallet; work the four corners where the top has been nailed. If all goes well, the top will lift off with all the nails intact. Some nails might remain in the base and break loose from the top. In that case, they will have to be replaced. The worst that can be expected, if your luck has turned sour, is a split in the area around a resistant nail. Similar to a top that is screwed on, a nailed top should be given a reference marking. Tops should be removed with the leaves intact, but care should be taken not to stress the assembly.

Once the table top is removed, the majority of the work is done. Remove the undamaged leaf support and trace its shape on paper or trace it in place if it is difficult to remove. Transfer the pattern to a piece of cardboard and cut it out slightly oversized. Fit the pattern to the recess left by the missing support and trim appropriately. The two leaf supports will be similar, but they are not always identical. Do not just replicate the remaining support. Cut a new support from a piece of maple or cherry and pin it to the table base similar to the support shown in Fig. 11-37.

After the table is reassembled, one or both of the leaves might be found to droop as the result of years of wear. To remedy a drooping problem, glue small pieces of veneer to the tops of the leaf supports.

Better-made drop-leaf tables will have leaf supports with a wooden knuckle joint such as the one shown in Fig. 11-38. The repair of this type of support is more difficult than the single-arm support previously described. On the positive side, this joint does not break all that often. A loose or sloping support can be drilled and fitted with a larger pin. If one knuckle of the support is broken, the piece can be trimmed and fitted with a new piece. It is just as easy to make a new support. If you find it necessary to make a new support, the knuckles must be rounded for the smooth operation of the hinge. Check the operation of a repaired hinge carefully prior to reassembling the table.

Pedestal Bases

Pedestal base tables present a different kind of problem. A pedestal can be repaired with dowels in the manner of a table leg or chair post, but pedestals rarely break. An assortment of problems related to chipped ring decorations or age splits will be encountered, but these are cosmetic problems that can be treated with patches and filler materials.

As with any piece of furniture, problems with pedestal base tables can be expected at the weakest point (in the area of the feet). The scrolled Victorian feet or gently sloping Queen Anne feet found

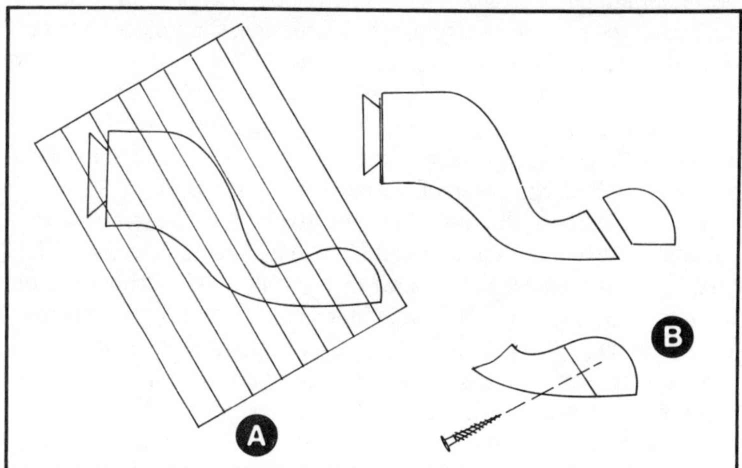

Fig. 11-39. Legs for a pedestal table: (A) a leg must be laid out to maximize the strength of the wood grain; (B) breaks that occur at the ankle (the weakest point) can be repaired with glue and a recessed screw.

325

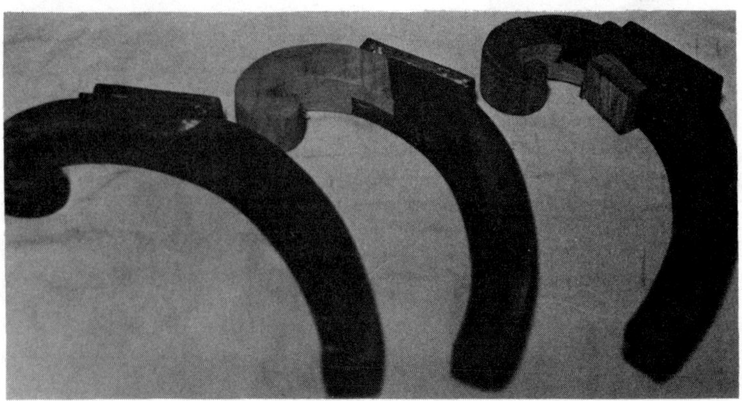

Fig. 11-40. Three pedestal table legs. The first leg is original and intact. The second leg has a new scroll added with a lap and scarf joint. The third leg has a replaced scroll as well as wood patch inlet to repair a large gouge.

on pedestal bases do not lend themselves to principles of sound design. To begin with, the leg must be laid out and cut in a manner that emphasizes the strength of the wood grain (Fig. 11-39A).

If you find it necessary to replace a piece of a leg or an entire leg, keep this grain relationship in mind. Although this manner of layout provides the greatest strength, the leg is still very weak at the ankle where breaks usually occur (Fig. 11-39B). To repair this type of damage, the broken piece is glued and reinforced with a screw from the underside of the foot (see Fig. 11-39). The use of a screw eliminates the need for a clamp in this situation. Care must be taken when drilling the pilot hole for the screw.

Three damaged table feet are shown in Fig. 11-40. The first foot had a clean split and was simply glued. The entire scroll of the second foot was missing. The scroll was copied from the unbroken leg and attached with a combination scarf and lap joint. See Fig. 11-40. The scarf cut did not add to the strength of the joint but the diagonal nature of the cut allowed for a less detectable repair. The third foot was repaired in the same manner. A wood patch was inset to repair a large gouge. The remainder of the table (Fig. 11-41) was stripped of multiple coats of brown paint. Repairs were made to the dovetail mortises. The top was reglued and battens from a previous repair were removed. The finished table is shown in Fig. 11-42.

Damage sometimes occurs to the dovetail mortise cut in the pedestal base. This is especially true if someone has tried to knock it apart like a doweled joint. To take care of this dilemma, the damaged area must be leveled with a chisel, as shown in Fig. 11-43, and fitted with a new piece of wood. The repair piece is fitted oversized and shaped to the curvature of the pedestal prior to laying out the mortise. The dovetail on the leg is used as a template to scribe the shape of the mortise on the repair piece. It must carefully be aligned with the original remaining mortise. When the mortise is marked out, the waste material is carefully and slowly removed with a chisel. As the mortise is cut, the dovetailed leg should be fitted every inch or so to gauge the progress of the work.

This type of repair is no problem for someone experienced with hand tools. It can be quite a problem for the novice. If you are a novice and you don't perceive yourself as particularly skillful with tools, then you would be best advised to commission this work.

Just gluing the feet on a pedestal base table can be a problem. The foot, whether dovetailed or doweled, should be dry-fitted prior to gluing. If the foot is a good fit, it might be possible to pull it together with a band clamp. In the event that the band clamp does not work, a jig will have to be made that follows the contours of the leg. The jig is notched to accept a clamp and each leg is glued individually (Fig. 11-44).

WASHSTANDS

Two types of country washstands are often encountered; both types were popular. One style of stand is rectangular with doors and

Fig. 11-41. A pedestal table base after the removal of multiple coats of brown paint.

Fig. 11-42. The repaired and finished pedestal table. A shellac finish was used over the natural wood. The repaired parts were colored to match the mellow cherry tone of the rest of the piece (courtesy of Wainscot Antiques).

a drawer and is no more than a small cupboard. The other style washstand is lighter in proportion; it has four turned legs, a drawer, and a shelf. Neither style washstand is particularly susceptible to breakage. The turned-leg washstands experience some foot problems similar to tables and they are treated in the same way. Rectangular stands are repaired in the same manner as cupboards.

Both styles of washstand exhibit problems with tops split as a result of shrinkage. To remedy this problem, the top is removed and reglued. If it is necessary to plane the joint prior to gluing or if a great deal of material has been lost due to shrinkage, it can be added to the rear edge of the top.

In the case of a drop-leaf table, new material would be added between the split halves. But with a top such as this, it is easier and more aesthetically pleasing to make up the material in the rear. Washstands favored light tops ranging from three-eighths to one-half inch; three-fourth inch tops can be found. The tops were put into place with nails and the extensive use of glue blocks on the underside to provide rigidity and inhibit warping. When you are regluing and refitting a top it is wise to return all the glue blocks to their original positions.

The most prevalent problem with regard to washstands is the absence of a splashguard. I would venture to speculate that at least one-half of all the washstands that I have ever seen are lacking an original splashguard. To determine whether or not the piece originally had a splashguard, look at the relationships between the top and the backboards. If the top is flush with the backboards, that is, if the backboards fit under the top, then you can presume the piece never had a splashguard. If the rear of the top falls short of the backboards, you can presume it originally had a splashguard. To confirm your suspicions, look for nail holes or screw holes in the rear edge of the top that would have been used to attach the splashguard. The purpose of this exercise is to determine whether or not you should replace the splashguard.

The common woods for washstand tops are maple, birch, pine, and poplar. Splashguards are usually, but not exclusively, made of the same wood. If there is any doubt about what wood to use for a replacement piece, poplar is a good choice. Poplar has a fairly inconspicuous grain and it takes a color very nicely. Splashguards are mostly cut from three-eighths inch stock and on occasion from one-half inch stock, but rarely do they exceed one-half inch.

A simple pattern, such as the one shown in Fig. 11-45, can be used, but it is best to find a similar washstand in a book on antiques and copy the splashguard from the piece illustrated. Once the splashguard is copied and colored, it is put in place with glue and nails. If at all possible, reuse the original nail holes.

CUPBOARDS

A veritable plethora of country cupboards known by a great number of names is available to the collector. There are hutch, dutch, step, pewter, jam, jelly, pie, corner, chimney, hanging, etc.,

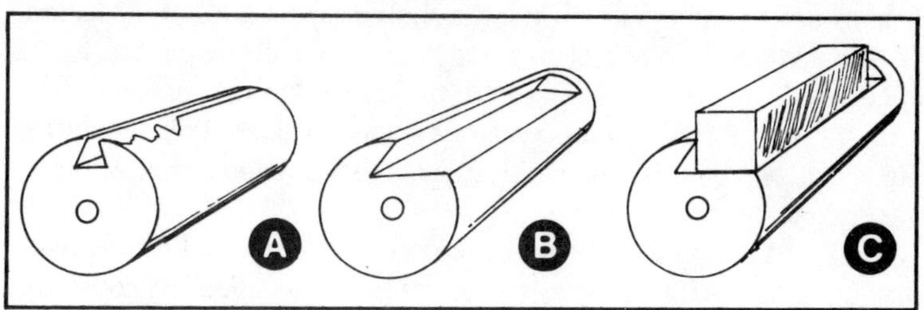

Fig. 11-43. Repair details for dovetail mortise; (A) a damaged mortise; (B) the damaged area is removed and the surface is trimmed and prepared for a new piece; (C) new stock is glued into place oversized. The repair piece is shaped to the base and marked for a new mortise. The new mortise is cut with saw and chisel using the sliding dovetail on the leg as a guide.

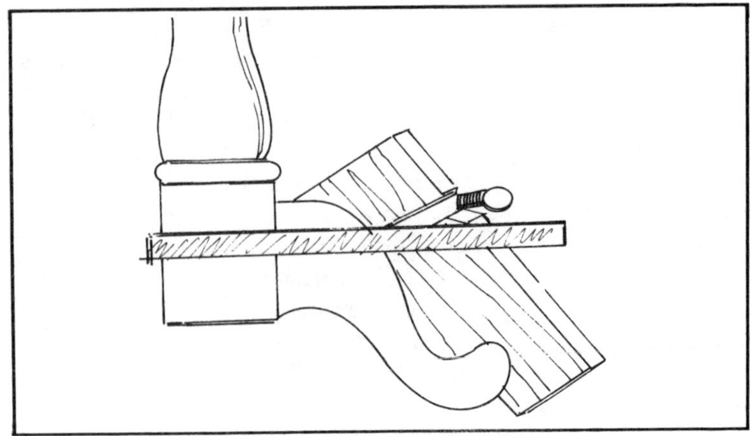

Fig. 11-44. Gluing the leg of a pedestal table, whether dovetailed or doweled, requires the preparation of a special gluing jig.

Each name describes a different type of cupboard. No matter how many types are labeled, they are all no more than a box. Cupboards are boxes with doors, drawers, and shelves in various combinations. A jelly cupboard is a closed box with at least one drawer and one door. A pewter cupboard is a half-open and half-closed box with doors and/or drawers. A step-back cupboard is an open box upon a closed box, and so on. Cupboards are boxes, and the good thing about that is boxes are simple and strong. Most country cupboards you are likely to encounter will have withstood the test of time well. They should need little repair.

Shaky Cupboards

Country cupboards do not tend to employ elaborate joining techniques for the main carcass or case construction. The case is usually nailed and rebated while the shelves are mortised and nailed. Given a hundred years of use and shrinkage, the cupboard might become a little (or for that matter a whole lot) shaky. On occasion the structural integrity of a piece can be so jeopardized that the entire piece will have to be dismantled and reassembled. This is rarely necessary.

To put a shaky cupboard back on the road to health, you must first square it up if it is listing desperately to one side. The cupboard can be squared with band clamps or by placing one side against a wall and having a friend hold it in place. When the cupboard is positioned, take a nail set and countersink every nail used to put the backboards in place. Once the backboards have been tightened, repeat the

330

procedure for the nails on each side used to secure the shelves, and then the nails securing the top. If the nail holes on the sides and top have been filled with plaster, the plaster must be removed first. By driving each nail home just a little, a piece can be made as sound as a rock in 10 to 15 minutes.

Feet

The feet are the most likely aspect of a cupboard to be damaged. This is understandably so because they receive the most wear. Broken feet look worrisome and difficult to repair. Actually, the task is usually uncomplicated. Figure 11-46 illustrates a simple cupboard with a damaged rear foot that might have rotted, broken, or been cut away.

Not only does time exact its toll on furniture, but there are all kinds of damages perpetuated on furniture by destructive people who will cut it up to make it fit just where they want. I have seen half the back cut off a cupboard so that it could be placed over a radiator. At any rate, the foot in the illustration is a bracket type foot that is formed by cutting into the plank side of the cupboard. To repair the foot, the break or damage must first be trimmed flush.

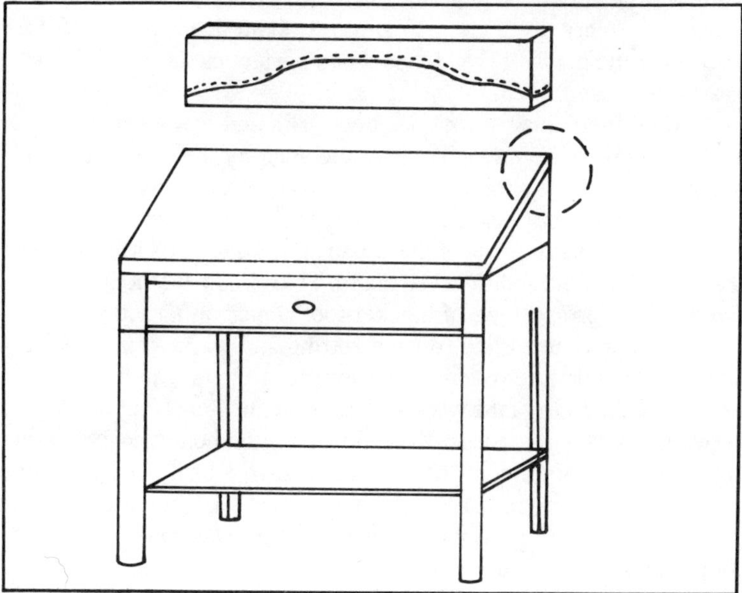

Fig. 11-45. A washstand with a replaced splashguard. Note the shoulder between the top and backboards. This indicates the piece originally had a splashguard.

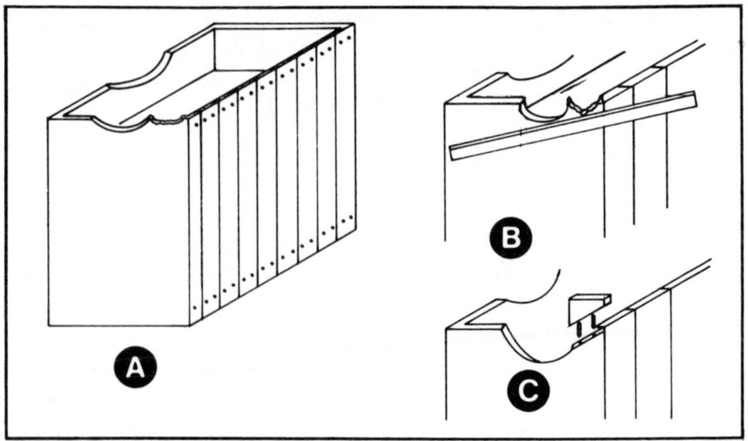

Fig. 11-46. Repairs to a damaged foot: (A) a damaged cupboard foot as the result of rot; (B) a straightedge or board used to outline a cut and to guide the saw; (C) a new foot fitted with dowels. The angle of the cut is transferred with a sliding bevel or template.

A straight cut could be used to trim the foot, but a cut on the bias will provide for a better and more aesthetically pleasing glue bond. To make the cut, lay a length of square board across the side of the cupboard to mark the angle. Clamp the straightedge in place and use it to guide the blade of the saw so that a perfect cut is made. A back saw is best used for this type of work.

When the damaged foot has been trimmed, cut a repair piece from an appropriate wood. Transfer the angle of the scarf cut to the repair piece with a sliding level or by making a cardboard pattern. Glue alone will not be sufficient to secure the new foot; it must be doweled. To further secure the repair, put a glue block into place (Fig. 11-47) to lend additional strength. This simple method of repair can be used for any type of bracket-foot repair on a case piece.

Cupboards are prone to have rotting and water-damaged feet because of the damp environments they are often relegated to. When examined, the faces of the wood will appear to be intact, but the wood between the face surfaces will be powdery and honeycombed with holes. It might not always be possble to save a badly deteriorated area, but every attempt should be made to do so. The outer face of the problem area normally remains undamaged because of paint or some other finishing treatment.

It might be possible to lift the face surface of a damaged area like a veneer as (Fig. 11-48). If this maneuver is possible, lift the surface, apply glue, and resecure the surface with pins or masking tape.

With rotted wood, clamp pressure might crumble the wood. Therefore, alternative clamping measures such as taping should be used. After the face piece has dried, take some white glue and cut it one-third with water, and saturate the rotted area. If a glue injector is available, use the fine point to penetrate as deeply as possible into the damaged area.

Following the glue saturation of the damaged area, mix some 2-part epoxy glue with sawdust. A mixture of 4 parts glue to 1 part sawdust should work well. Apply the epoxy/sawdust mixture to the rotted area, filling in all the gaps and crevices. When these measures have been completed, further reinforcement of the damaged area should be made with the addition of a glue block (Fig. 11-47). In this case, the glue block should rise just a fraction of an inch above the damaged foot area so that the glue block, not the damaged foot, will support the weight of the piece.

Doors

The case, or basic box, of a cupboard uses simple methods of joinery; the doors and drawers utilize sophisticated methods. To be sure, some cupboards will be encountered with simple plank doors, but most will have mortised and tenoned, paneled doors.

On 18th-century pieces, mortise and tenon paneled doors were pinned rather than glued. The predominant mode of construction in the 19th century was glue. The net difference between these two techniques is that the pinned doors remain snug and tight, while the glued doors frequently come unglued.

If you purchase a piece with sloping doors—doors with some side to side movement—my best advice is to leave it that way. Should the movement in the door disturb you deeply, then it must be disassembled, cleaned and reglued. Disassembly and reassembly is

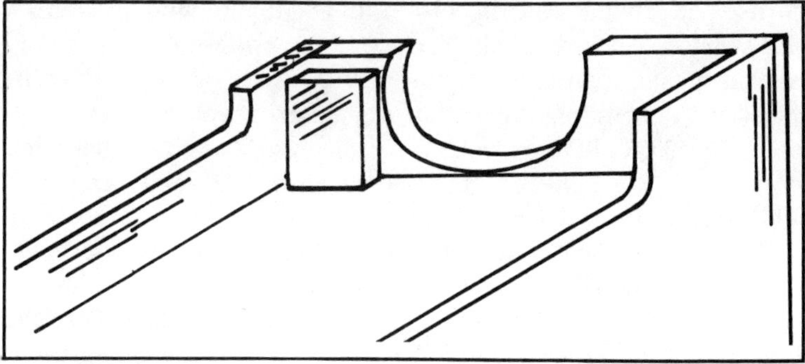

Fig. 11-47. A damaged foot is reinforced with a glue block.

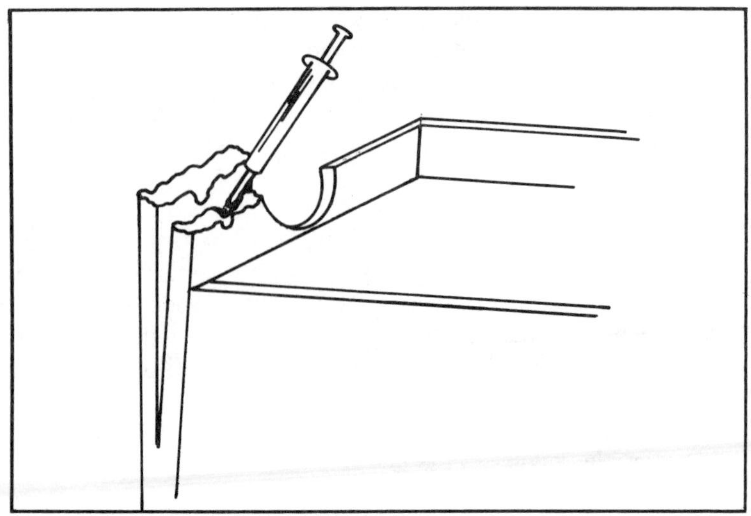

Fig. 11-**48**. With a badly rotted foot, the face surface is separated like a veneer and the area is saturated with glue. Clamping is usually accomplished with pins or tape to avoid damage.

not a difficult job, but prior to dismantling take care to locate and remove any hidden nails that might have been put through the joint.

Before the door is reglued, the pieces should be dry fitted and the door should be moved into place. When the cupboard was new, the finely made rectangular door would doubtlessly have fitted an equally rectangular opening. The passing of time might have changed these relationships. Adjustments must be made in the gluing of the door to allow for dimensional changes that have occurred. This type of adjustment is not always a simple task. I suggest you leave doors as they are if the problem is not severe.

When paneled doors break, they do so in the area of one of the mortise and tenon joins (Fig. 11-49). In addition to joint problems, split panels are a fairly common occurrance. The whole purpose of paneled construction is to avoid shrinkage splits. Consequently, a reasonable person might question why so many splits are encountered. The secret to this mystery is paint. Over the years, multiple coats of paint can collect around the panel mortises and lock them tight as if they had been glued. The end product of this is splitting.

To repair a split panel, you must disassemble the door and reglue the panel. The panel should be dry fitted into the door frame before gluing to determine how much material has been lost to shrinkage. If the panel will not fit into both the right and left mortises, then a strip of new wood must be added.

Damage to the joint areas on a door frame usually occurs to the mortised pieces and not the tenoned cross members. If the frame material is cut from seven-eighth inch stock, which is common, the mortise is cut for a three-eighth inch tenon. This will leave only one-fourth inch of wood on each side of the mortise. These joints hold up very well given the somewhat meager proportions.

To repair a joint, the damaged member is trimmed with a scarf cut (Fig. 11-49B). The depth of cut is one-half the thickness of the piece. The bulk of the waste material is removed with a chisel. The final surface is trued up with a small plane. A repair piece is cut to fit, glued, and clamped.

Following the requisite drying period, a new mortise must be cut into the repair. Actually, only half of the mortise will have to be cut because the part of the original mortise will remain (as shown in Fig. 11-49). After the mortise has been cut, the channel for the panel will have to be extended into the repaired area. This work is best done with a plough or multi-plane. It can also be done with a chisel if you work carefully.

Should both the mortise piece and the tenon piece be broken, an easier method of repair can be employed. Repair the mortise

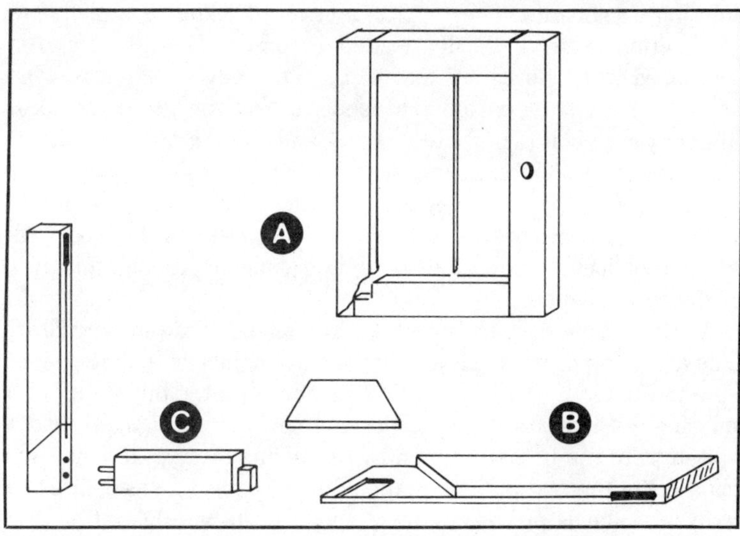

Fig. 11-49. Mortise and tenon door repair. With frame and panel doors, damage usually occurs to one of the stile mortises (A). Repair is affected by making a scarf cut one-half the diameter of the piece (B). The cut is cleaned up with a plane and new stock glued. The mortise is recut after patching. An alternate method of repair involves repairing and plugging the mortise (C). The tenon is cut away and the cross member is fitted with dowels.

piece—which will always be one of the upright members of the frame—in the manner described, but instead of cutting a new mortise, fill the mortise with new stock. Trim the broken tenon flush with the shoulder of the cross member and dowel into place (Fig. 11-49C). If only a tenon is broken, it can be repaired simply with dowels.

A cupboard purchased in the rough at an auction or junk store might lack one piece to a door or the entirety of a door. If you possess some woodworking skills, the making of a new door should present a worthwhile challenge. On the other hand, if you do not possess the skills to make part or all of a door, don't give up on a worthwhile cupboard. A new door can be commissioned at a local restoration shop. If the damaged cupboard was priced appropriately, you might still come out well ahead. As much as I like totally original pieces, there is a wonderful feeling in seeing an old, damaged piece returned to new life and use.

Backboards and Sundry Things

Backboards do not normally fall off of cupboards, and they are not readily damaged. Nevertheless, you will encounter a lot of missing backboards. The replacement of a backboard is a simple proposition even for the least skilled worker. The new board is measured, cut, and nailed into place. The only question is what should be used to replace a backboard. You can go to the local lumber yard, obtain a new piece of pine and give it a dark stain. But it just doesn't look right. I suggest that you find a salvage yard (they are often listed in the telephone directory) and obtain some old floorboards or barn boards. There is no reason why the barn board is any better than the new pine board; it is just an irrational, romantic preference of mine.

Many cupboards described as jelly cupboards had splashguards. These cupboards were often used as bedroom pieces and they never saw the likes of a jelly jar. But that doesn't alter the status of a missing splashguard. Whether or not the piece originally had a splashguard can be determined by examining the top. If a space is apparent at the rear of the top, then the piece has a splashguard. As with washstands previously mentioned, locate an illustration of a cupboard in an antique book and replicate the splashguard.

The doors on cupboards receive much use. Consequently, a great deal of wear is placed on the hinges. With the passage of time, stress can damage the wood around the screws causing a loose hinge. To remedy this situation, take some toothpicks and cut them

336

to the depth of the screw hole. Apply white glue to the hole, insert the toothpicks, position the hinge, and insert the screw. As the screw goes in, it will make a gooey mess, but it will hold.

Some owners in their zeal to tighten a loose hinge might have substituted a gargantuan screw; the end product is a split-hinge mortise. In such a case, use a glue syringe to force glue into the crack and then clamp. Make sure to wipe away any excess glue that runs onto the face surface of the wood. Leave the clamp in place and allow to dry for at least 48 hours. Stuff the screw hole with tooth-picks an glue in the manner described above. Then select an appropriate-sized screw. If possible, keep the clamp in place when inserting the new screw to provide additional strength.

CHESTS

Chests encompass a range of case pieces used for storage of clothing or bedding. There are tall chests, bachelor's chests, blanket chests, seamen's chests, etc. Similar to a cupboard, a chest is basically a box fitted with a set of drawers or a lift top. Cupboards tend toward simple nailed-rebate construction. Chests range from simple nailed construction to sophisticated dovetailed construction. A well-made 18th-century chest will have plank sides with dovetailed dustboards and a dovetailed top with molding. Even the bracket feet might be dovetailed. A simple 19th-century cottage chest might have glued drawer guides and rails and a nailed top. Whether employing sophisticated or simple joinery, chests are, for the most part, sturdy survivors of time.

One problem commonly encountered with chests is looseness or side sway. There is, unfortunately, no simple solution to this problem as there is with a cupboard. The backboards have an integral role in the structural integrity of a chest. Therefore, they should first be tightened with a hammer and nail set. If tightening the backboards in this manner works, then all is well. If it does not work, there are no other shortcuts and the chest must be reglued.

Prior to dismantling a chest, study its construction carefully. All chests can be logically disassembled, but not all are disassembled in the same way. As with other types of furniture, the examination should include a search for hidden nails in joints.

After dismantling, all joints should be cleaned and repairs should be made. When ready for reassembly, the entire chest should be glued at the same time with a slow-setting glue such as liquid hide glue.

Clamp the chest with light pressure, and then put the drawers in place to assist in bringing the chest to its proper geometric relationship. With the drawers in place, tighten the clamp pressure, but check to see that the chest does not distort in the process. When the chest is square and tight, the backboards can be nailed into place.

A number of 19th-century chests of drawers had splashguards consistent with the fashion of the time. As with other forms of furniture they are frequently lost. The replacement of a splashguard on a chest should be treated in the same manner as a cupboard or a washstand. Whether or not a chest originally had a splashguard can be detected by an examination of the top.

Foot damage is common to chests. They do not experience as much water damage and rot because they are not relegated to as many damp, wet places. Bracket feet are predominant on chests. Ball and turned feet will also be encountered. For the repair of turned feet, follow the same procedures as when repairing a table leg or foot. The repair of a bracket foot, when the foot is formed by a cutout, can be treated in the same manner as a cupboard foot. When bracket feet are originally made from separate pieces of wood, they can be repaired by removing or replacing with a new piece. All bracket foot repairs should be additionally supported by glue blocks. It is generally good practice to replace any glue blocks that have been lost with time.

Chests of drawers will develop top splits and side splits. Top splits are by far the easier of the two problems to handle. If the split extends through only part of the top, then the entire top must be removed in order to glue. Remove all dirt and debris from the damage area. Then glue and clamp.

If the top is less than three-fourths of an inch thick, it might buckle when clamped. Precautions should be taken. With a split that extends through the top (Fig. 11-50), the rear section of the split can be removed while the forward section remains in place. Glue is applied to the split and the top is clamped. It might be necessary to add new wood to the top if shrinkage has removed more than one-eighth inch of wood.

This repair does not require that the new wood be placed between the split as with a drop-leaf table. Instead the new wood is added to the rear of the top as shown in Fig. 11-50. Adding new stock to the rear is easier and less noticeable in the long run. The rear half of the top is nailed in place after gluing and clamping has been completed.

Side splits on a chest constitute far more serious problems. Sides are secured to the top, bottom, front, and back in addition to being bound by drawer runners and guides. All of these attachments prevent the side panel from natural contraction which results in shrinkage splits.

A side split is illustrated in Fig. 11-51. To repair this split, the top must be removed and the sides disconnected from the drawer nails or other structural members that hold the sides to the main body of the case. At least one backboard immediately adjacent to the damaged side will have to be removed. When the damaged side is free from the rest of the structure, the drawer guides and runners must be removed because they will inhibit the two split halves from being joined. After the side is freed from obstructions, it is glued and clamped in the normal manner. If a good fit cannot be obtained between the two split halves, then the two mating surfaces will have to be trued up with a plane.

It will be necessary to add a strip of new material to the damaged side piece (see Fig. 11-51). Otherwise, the drawer runners will project beyond the side once returned to their proper position. The runners and guides should have been marked carefully prior to removal and their positions marked on the side in pencil. If at all possible, the runners and guides should be replaced while the side is still off the chest. This will allow room for clamping. If the structure of the chest requires that the runners be installed after assembly, then they can be attached with glue and nails or screws.

All in all, the repair to a side split is not a difficult task, but neither is it a fast and easy task. Some people will attempt to shortcut this work by filling the crack. This is a wasted effort; it must fail in the long run. The damage side piece will continue to

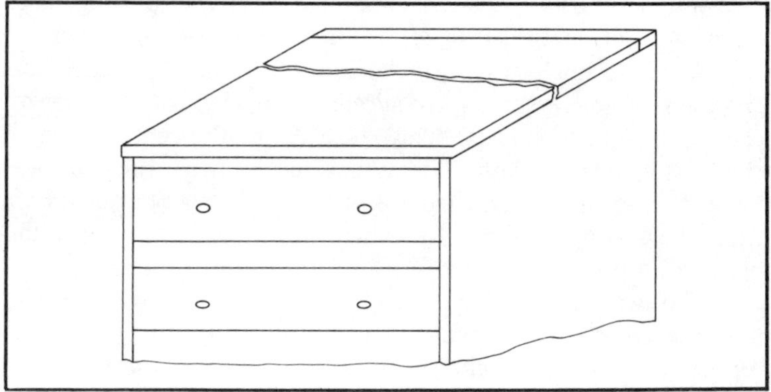

Fig. 11-50. With a damaged chest top, the rear piece of the break is removed and reglued to the forward piece (which remains stationary). Material that is lost as a result of shrinkage is made up by the addition of a new piece positioned to the rear.

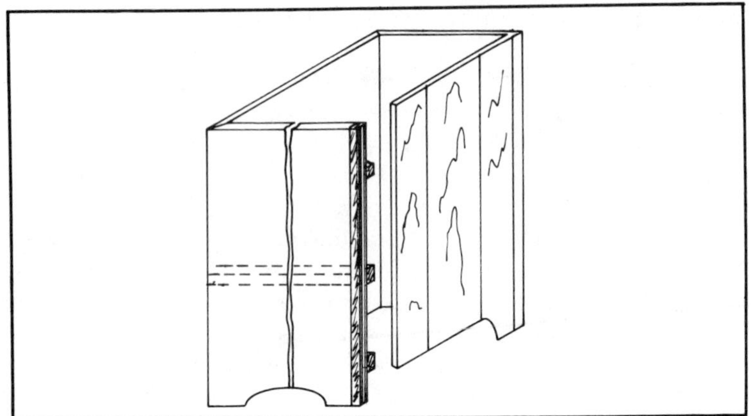

Fig. 11-51. To repair a side split on a chest, the top, drawer rails, drawer guides and runners, and at least 1 backboard must be removed. The split is glued and clamped. New material must be added. Otherwise, the runners and guides will protrude beyond the rear of the chest.

contract with changes in moisture. The movement of the side will, in time, result in the filler material falling out. In this case, the good way is the more difficult way.

Seamen's chests and blanket chests are less complicated forms of a chest of drawers. The really nice thing about these chests is that very few problems are ever encountered. When chests are dovetailed on all sides, the dovetails allow for the necessary movement of the wood. Split problems are not usually encountered. The tops or lids of these chests develop more problems than the tops of conventional chests. Tops often warp and split. The splitting, more often than not, is the result of the chest being used for a seat.

A good example of some of the things that can happen to a chest and the restorative services required can be seen with the blanket chest shown in Fig. 11-52. This chest is an 18th-century blanket chest in old red paint with a lift top and single drawer. The chest was found in a barn in Vermont and was probably of New England origin. From the outside, the chest looks fine. When examined closely, the problems are easily noticed.

The two drawings shown in Fig. 11-53 give cut-away views of how the chest should (and did) look. Drawing A of Fig. 11-53 represents how the chest looked when found. A separation board had originally fit into now-empty mortise slots (marked X and Y), but they had subsequently been moved to the bottom. The drawer is no more than a facade nailed to the front through the sides. Modern round nails were used to secure the false front (drawing A of Fig.

340

11-53) suggesting that the modification had occurred some time after 1875. The color of the drawer front closely matches the rest of the chest, but it is not the original drawer front. Resting on the remnants of the drawer runners at the bottom of the chest is a new bottom that had not previously existed in that place. The lid to the chest is original; at some point the top had been screwed into place. The lid is connected to the chest by badly deteriorated snipe hinges. The various crevices of the chest are filled with grain. This suggests that the chest's most recent use was that of a grain bin.

In drawing B of Fig. 11-53, the chest is shown as it should be. A dustboard mortised at points X and Y separates the top compartment. A drawer with linings is set upon two single runners. The runners alone support the drawer because there is no evidence of a bottom board. The dovetails on the drawers are a reasonable presumption, but they are not supported by any evidence supplied by the chest.

No one can know exactly what happened to this chest, but it seems likely that at some point the original drawer was lost or damaged. A subsequent owner chose to make a false drawer front rather than make a new drawer. Once the drawer was sealed off, the dustboard was cut away and reused as a bottom board so that the full depth of the chest could be available. Whatever happened to the chest in the past, our task was to return it to its original function. Surprisingly, it was not all that difficult.

Fig. 11-52. A blanket chest of pine (painted red). It is from the first half of the 18th century (courtesy of Wainscot Antiques).

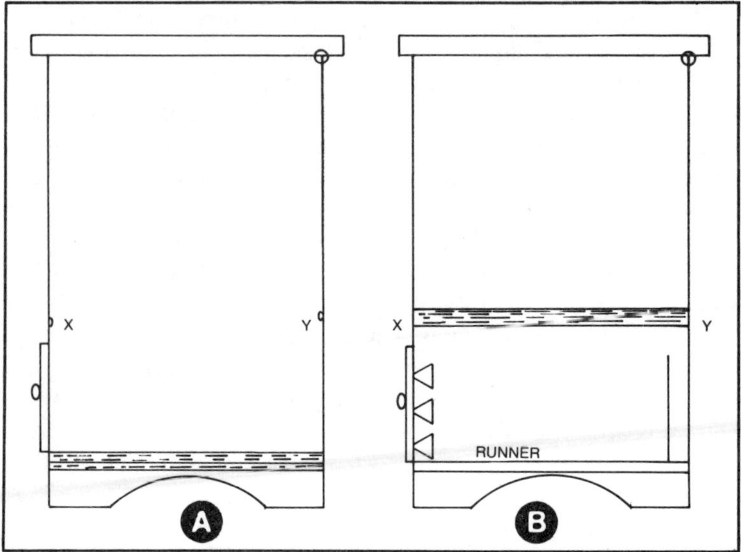

Fig. 11-53. Blanket chest. The condition of the blanket chest as found (A). Note the absence of a dustboard (points X to Y), the false drawer front, and the addition of a bottom board. The blanket chest (B) as it was originally constructed (including the dustboard and drawer).

Figure 11-54 shows the false drawer cut away from the piece. The drawer front had been nailed in place from the side of the chest. That could have involved some ugly gouging for us to remove the nails. To avoid this problem, we inserted a hacksaw blade between the drawer front and the side so that the nail could be cut away. This is tedious and unfriendly work. When all the nails were severed, we removed the front and drove the nails out from the inside of the chest with a nail set. We saved the drawer front to make the new drawer. It was already cut to order and painted.

In Fig. 11-55, the backboards of the chest are shown. The lower backboard had to be removed in order to return the bottom board to its original position (separating the two compartments). The backboard was tapped lightly from the inside of the chest with a rubber mallet. When the board separated slightly from the rear, it was gently pryed away with a small pry bar. We taped the old nails to their respective holes to await reassembly. We found that the backboards had originally been attached with hand-forged blacksmith nails, but machine-cut nails and modern wire nails also appeared at various locations.

Figure 11-56 displays what remains of the original drawer

Fig. 11-54. The false drawer (nailed from the sides) is removed by inserting a hacksaw blade between the drawer and side. The nails were cut away.

runner. Using a hacksaw blade to cut away the nails in the same manner that the drawer front was cut away, we removed the dustboard that had improperly been positioned on the drawer runners. When the dustboard had first been moved from its original mortise to be used as the bottom board, it had been shortened to fit between the sides. To return it to its original position we added three-eighths of an inch wooden strips to each end to make up for the shortening. We made a new piece of drawer runner to match the old

Fig. 11-55. The lower backboard is labeled and removed in order to return the dustboard to its original position.

Fig. 11-56. The remains of the original drawer runners are found and saved. Note the bottom board set upon the runners. This was a later modification.

one and attached it so that the runner now extends from side to side (Fig. 11-57). We used old nails to attach the new piece and later touched them up with paint to match the old piece.

The chest had suffered a shrinkage crack in one side. To remedy the problem, we injected glue into the crack with a syringe and clamped the side (Fig. 11-58). No supports or runners were restricting the side. Therefore, clamping was a simple procedure. One foot showed signs of rot and was treated with a mixture of epoxy glue and sawdust.

While the sides of the chest were drying, we turned the false drawer front into a real drawer with the addition of sides and a bottom (Fig. 11-59). We dovetailed the new drawer for the piece. Someone lacking experience in making dovetails could have used simple nailed rebate construction. A nailed and rebated drawer is not as good as a dovetailed one, but I have seen sturdy drawers made in that fashion that are over 200 years old.

Figure 11-60 shows problematic screw holes in the lid of the chest being filled in. The chest lid had, for some unknown reason, been screwed shut at one time. We filled the holes with plaster mixed with red dry colors and brown water stain to match the paint color of the chest. To achieve the proper color, more than one mixing was required. We masked the areas around the holes to avoid damaging the paint. The color match turned out very well and the holes are virtually unnoticeable.

When all the repair work on the chest was completed, we replaced the backboard and fit the drawer. We made new snipe

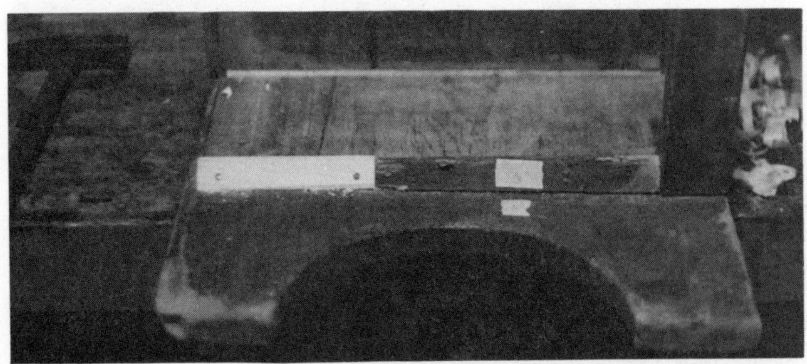

Fig. 11-57. Repair pieces are copied from the original runners and glued and nailed in place. Note that the bottom board has been removed and returned to its original position as a dustboard.

hinges by heating cotter pins with a torch and reworking them hammer-and-anvil-fashion for the proper smith-made look. The hinges were subsequently rusted and installed. The completed chest is shown in Fig. 11-61. The finished chest hardly looks any different from when it was purchased, but now it stands proudly as it did in the 18th century. The red paint on the chest, that appears to be a very old milk paint, was cleaned, but not otherwise touched.

SEAT RUSHING

All too frequently, a restoration project calls for the replacement of a seat. This would not be difficult if seat work were

Fig. 11-58. While other work is ongoing, age splits in the side of the chest are glued and clamped.

Fig. 11-59. The false drawer front is cut for dovetails and fitted with linings. The use of dovetails in this case is a presumption, but a reasonable one.

inexpensive—but it is not. A new seat can, in some instances, cost more than the chair itself. The weekend craftsperson should master at least one seat-replacement technique.

Most 18th-century and 19th-century country chairs that did not have plank seats were rushed or splinted. To be sure, other seating materials were used. Examples are the tape seats of the Shakers or the hide seats found in the Southwest. Nevertheless, rush and splint were the predominant seat materials. Of the two materials, rush is the easier to apply and it is appropriate for any country chair.

Similar to many other aspects of finishing and repair, people tend to overestimate the skills necessary to weave a seat. The average person can weave a good seat, not necessarily a great seat, with his very first attempt. Second and third attempts at rushing usually result in near-professional results. The seat shown in **Fig. 11-62** represents the absolute worst first attempt at rushing that the author has ever seen, but it is still a usable seat. Most first attempts achieve vastly superior results when compared to the chair in the photo.

Rush and Fiber Rush

The traditional material used to weave a rush seat is natural rush. This may sound a little redundant, but it's not really because most modern seats are woven with fiber rush. Real rush is vastly superior to fiber rush when it comes to longevity, but it is also more work. Natural rush must be harvested from the local swamp in late summer and brought home to dry and cure. After curing and prior to use, the rush must be soaked in water for five to 10 hours and then paired and twisted into strands—somewhat like making rope. Even

346

Fig. 11-60. Screw holes (of unknown purpose) in the lid of the chest are filled with plaster mixed with pigment to match the paint. Note that masking tape has been used to protect the paint surface around the holes.

if natural rush is available from a craft house, it must still be soaked and twisted. This is tedious and aggravating work that requires skill and practice. I do not recommend that beginners attempt a natural-rush seat.

A natural-rush seat might last 50 years. A fiber-rush seat will last an average of 15 to 20 years, I have seen them last up to 40 years. Considering the ease with which a fiber-rush seat can be woven, I don't think that 15 to 20 years is a bad life span. Fiber rush is nothing more than strands of heavy brown paper twisted together. The fiber rush looks identical to natural rush and has the advantage of being readily available in rolls of continuous length. Fiber rush can be obtained from craft houses and it is available in a range of sizes (3/32, 4/32, 5/32, 6/32 of an inch). I usually recommend the 6/32-inch

Fig. 11-61. The completed blanket chest does not look very different from the way it was found. It has been returned to its proper historical function (courtesy of Wainscot Antiques).

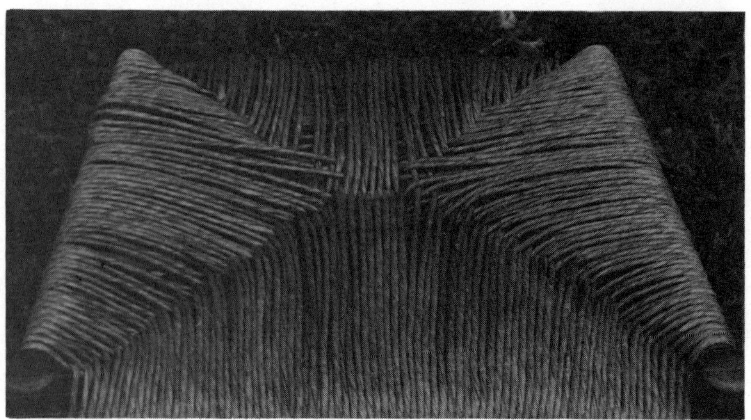

Fig. 11-62. A poor first attempt at seat rushing (courtesy of Mr. Stuart Sammis).

diameter rush because the wider strand requires less weaving. A small rush will look better on a demure chair.

Weaving

Three types of seat will be encountered when rushing: square, rectangular, and trapezoidal. Perfectly square seats are rarely found. Even where they appear to be square, they turn out to be rectangular. Rectangular seats are found on occasion, but the majority of seats encountered are trapezoidal. A trapezoidal seat has a front that is larger than the back and it has non-parallel sides that taper to the rear. In short, a standard chair shape. The weaving technique is the same for all chairs, but the method for starting a trapezoidal seat is different.

If you have never attempted to rush a seat, it would be a good idea to practice the weaving technique with a ball of twine. It doesn't take more than a few minutes to master the weaving technique. Practice with the twine could stave off some frustrating moments.

When you are ready to begin your project, cut a workable length of rush. I like manageable lengths of about 5 yards, but you must determine what is a comfortable length. Cut several lengths of the rush so as to avoid constant stopping and cutting.

Some sources suggest that fiber rush be soaked for a few minutes prior to use to make it manageable. I have found that this leads to an unraveling of the cord. As an alternative approach to this problem, I recommend the use of a sponge to wet the rush. Place a large sponge in a water basin positioned near you. When you are ready to work a strand of rush, pull it through the wet sponge. This method should impart enough moisture to make the rush pliable, but not be enough to damage it.

Take the starting strand of rush and tack one end to the inside of the left seat rail. The traditional method for starting a strand involves tieing it to the rear seat rail with a piece of wire or string. It is much less work to tack it in place.

Once fastened, take the strand over the front rail, under the rail, and then over the left rail (see point A in Fig. 11-63). The strand is then taken under the left rail, and across to and over the right rail. Next, the strand is brought under the right rail and over the front rail (see point B in Fig. 11-63). The strand is brought to the rear and over the back rail, under the rail, and then over and under the right rail (see point C in Fig. 11-63). The strand is moved to the left side and over the rail, under the rail and then over and under the rear rail (see point D in Fig. 11-63). Having completed the fourth corner at point D of Fig. 11-63, the strand is brought forward to point A and the entire process is repeated. See Fig. 11-64. The weaving technique might appear to be a little confusing in written form. A few minutes of study given to the diagram (Fig. 11-64) should simplify the task.

As the strands of rush are woven into their proper places, they should be pulled snugly. The operative words here are "snug" and "tight," but not stretched or distorted. If your hands and wrists start

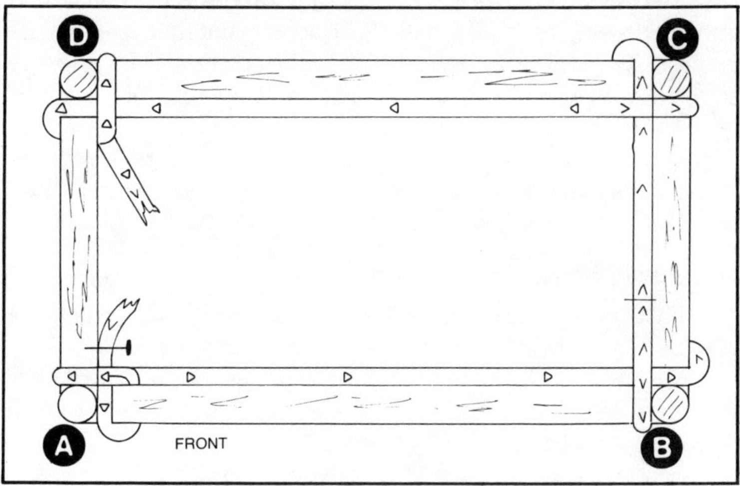

Fig. 11-63. Fiber rush is started at the front left corner and follows the formula of: (A) Over and under the front rail, then over and under the side rail; (B) Over and under the side rail, then over and under the front rail; (C) Over and under the rear rail, then over and under the side rail; (D) Over and under the side rail, then over and under the rear rail. Start at point A and begin again.

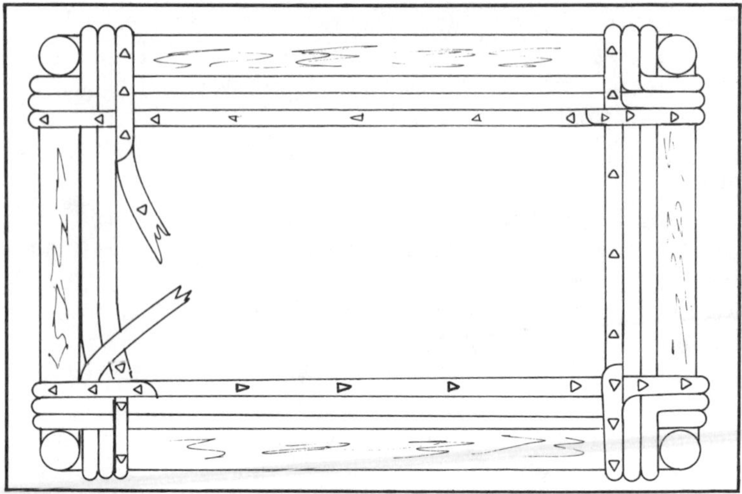

Fig. 11-64. The same weaving procedure as shown in Fig. 11-63; however, three strands are shown.

to hurt within a few minutes, you are probably pulling the rush too hard. As well as being snug, each strand on the front and rear rails should be at a right angle with its corresponding member on the side rail.

The maintenance of this relationship will result in a fine seat. If the relationship is lost, trouble will be encountered later in the process. As an aid to the maintenance of the proper angular relationship, place a pencil next to the corner post (see Fig. 11-65). The pencil will prevent the rush fiber from compressing and generally help with the alignment of the strands. As you progress with the weaving, use a hammer and wooden block to push the strands close together so that the proper angle and alignment is maintained.

Tieing and Padding

It will be necessary to connect new lengths of rush as others are used up. To attach one length of rush to another, you can align them side by side and wrap them tightly with a piece of wire. Wire makes for a very neat way to join the rush but it is time consuming and it often pulls apart if not done properly.

A simple knot can be used effectively as an alternative to wire. You can use any knot that you are comfortable with, but I recommend the use of a square knot. It is simple, strong, and unobtrusive. For how to tie a square knot, see Fig. 11-66. A square knot is one of the all-time great knots and is worth knowing.

All joining should be done on the underside of the chair and at least 2 or 3 inches away from any rail. If you come to the end of a run and find yourself on top of the seat, merely backtrack in your weaving until you have the strand at a suitable point for joining. When the rushing is completed, the final strand can be tied to one of the other strands.

As the chair weaving proceeds, it will be necessary to pad the seat because voids will be created between the upper and lower strands of the rush. I have seen a number of seats that have not been padded, but they do not look good and they wear through prematurely. With natural rush seats, odds and ends of the fibers are used to pad the seats.

Fiber rush cannot be used to pad a seat successfully. Therefore, I recommend the use of a stiff cardboard. Heavy brown paper such as that used for supermarket bags can be applied as padding, but it is not as adequate as cardboard. As pockets are created in each corner of a chair (Fig. 11-67), cardboard triangles should be cut and fitted. Each triangle can be cut to size for its respective place, but it should extend from corner post to corner post. If additional stuffing is required in the pockets, it can be added by way of folded heavy brown paper. It is imperative that the padding material be brown and in the same general range of color as the rush. When the seat is finished, some of the padding will be visible through the rush fibers.

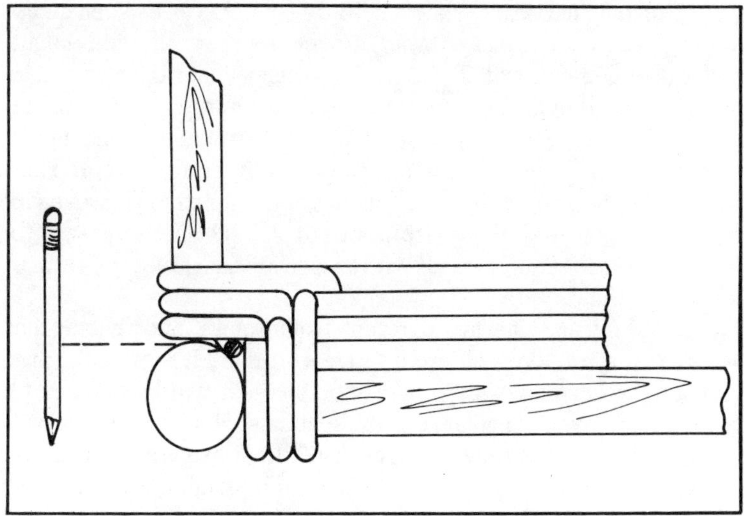

Fig. 11-65. A good rushing job requires that the front strands be at right angles with the side strands. To make this alignment easier, insert a pencil at the corner post. This will help to keep things square.

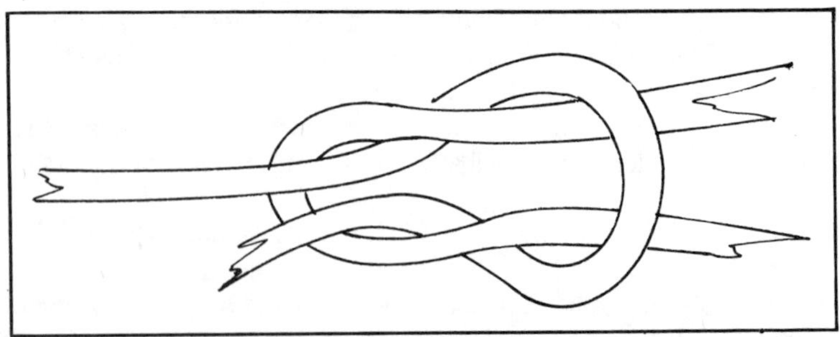

Fig. 11-66. New strands of rush are wired or tied to old strands. The most effective knot for tieing is the square knot. Knots are made on the underside of the chair at least 2 inches from each post.

Rectangular and Trapezoidal Seats

With a square seat, the weaving will continue in the manner described until all sides are filled. At this point, all strands will have met perfectly at the center of the chair and no problem will be encountered. A square seat is rarely ever square. Some empty space is usually encountered in the center of the chair when all sides have been filled. This is the problem encountered with rectangular seats. They always have open spaces after the sides have been filled. This is not really a problem at all because the resolve only requires a simple in and out weaving of the rush.

A rectangular seat is shown in Fig. 11-68. As can be seen in the drawing, the lead strand is brought over the rear rail and brought under the middle strand. The strand continues under the seat and is brought up and over the front rail, and then returned to the middle strand. The lead strand again goes under the middle strand and is brought up and over the rear rail (replicating the first step). This weave is nothing more than a simple figure 8. The strand is woven in this manner until all the space is fitted. It might be necessary to compress these center strands with a wood block in order to fit a final length of strand.

Trapezoidal seats are different from square and rectangular seats and they require a different setup procedure. It is essential that this step be accomplished properly or the seat will be doomed to failure. To weave an angular seat, the seat must first be made square. A trapezoidal seat is shown in Fig. 11-69. In drawing A, a square is used to align the rear post with the front rail (establishing a square within the trapezoid). When the seat is marked off in this fashion, the line represented by points W and X will be equal to and parallel to the line represented in points Y and Z. The squaring of the seat will

352

result in the formation of two triangular areas outside of the square. The triangular areas must first be filled in so that you can proceed with the normal weaving of the chair.

Cut several strands of fiber approximately 5 feet long. Take a strand of rush and tack it to the inside of the left side rail. Take the strand over and under the front rail and then over the left side rail in the manner of a normal weave. Continue the strand across the chair and over and under the right rail, and then over and under the front rail again in the manner of a normal weave.

At this point, the lead strand is tacked to the inside of the right rail (as shown in Fig. 11-69B). Excess rush material beyond the point of the tack is trimmed away. When this has been completed, another strand is tacked just behind the first strand on the left rail and processed in the same manner. Tack its end just behind the strand at the right rail. This step is repeated until the triangular sections are filled. This creates a square or rectangle within their perimeters.

Once the seat has been squared in this manner, a new strand is attached to the left side rail and the seat is woven in the normal manner. The seat is padded as shown in Fig. 11-67. When all sides of the chair have been fitted with rush, the remaining space is woven in the same figure 8 manner as a rectangular seat (see Fig. 11-68).

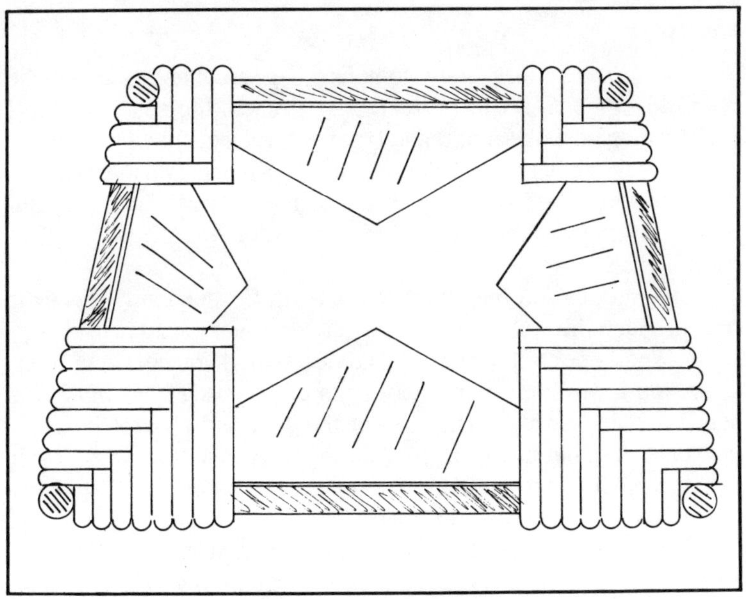

Fig. 11-67. As a seat is woven, it is necessary to stuff the pockets with cardboard. Cut the cardboard in triangles and pack as needed.

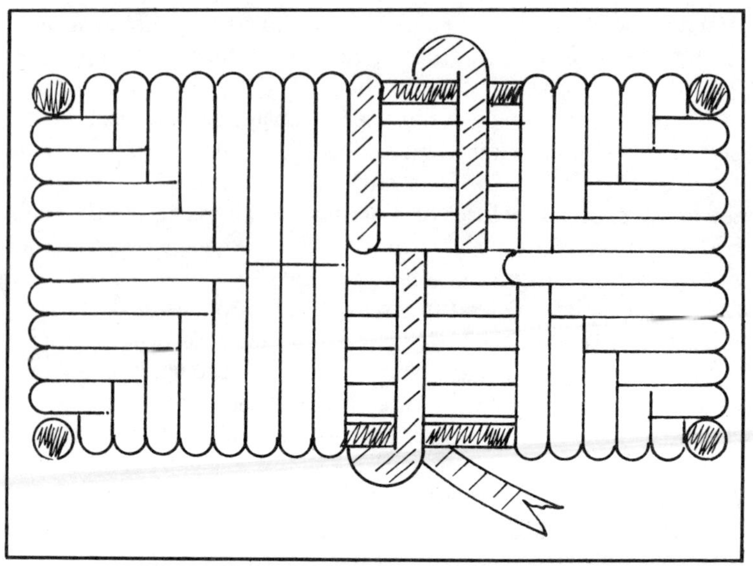

Fig. 11-68. With a rectangular seat, open space will be encountered at the center of the seat when all sides have been filled. Weave the center by taking the strand under the center strand, under the seat, over the front rail and then under the center strand. Continue to weave in this figure 8 motion until complete.

Finishing

When a seat has been completed, a suitable finish will be required. If a seat is not protected by a finish, the soft fibers will easily rub against one another and the seat will wear quickly whether natural rush or fiber rush. Prior to applying a finish, you must decide whether or not the seat should be stained. Fiber rush comes in plain brown and variegated which replicate color variations found in natural rush.

In either case, I find the rush too light. Consequently, I stain it to reproduce the softer and deeper brown tones found on old rush seats. Whether or not to stain is your decision. If you decide to stain, use an oil-base stain and preferably an oil-base sealer stain. Water stains will loosen the rush fiber of the seat and absorb the stain unevenly. A sealer stain will provide an even consistent color. If you decide to omit the stain, the finishing process will nevertheless darken the rush fibers somewhat.

When you are ready to proceed to a finish, prepare a mixture of 1 part shellac to 1 part alcohol and brush on liberally to both the top side and the under side. Give extra attention to the turns around the seat rails. Be careful not to splatter the shellac on the finish of the

354

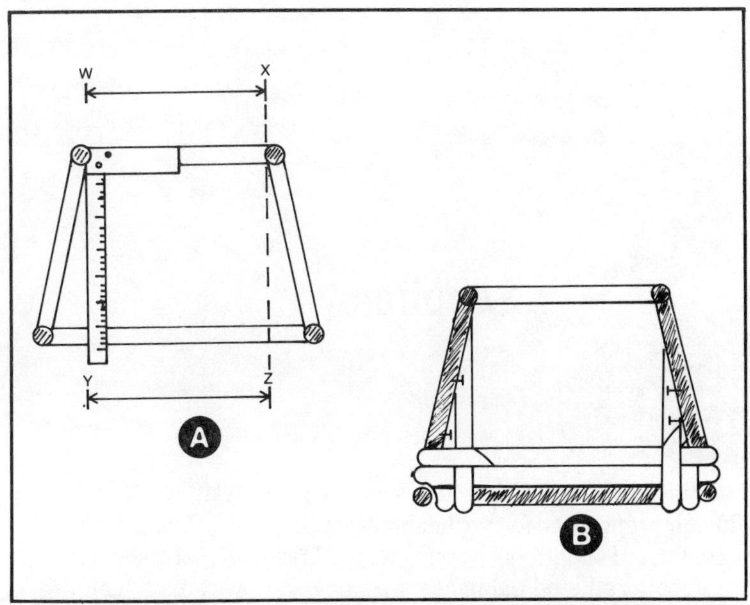

Fig. 11-69. With an irregular seat (trapezoid), special measures must be taken. The seat (A) must be squared using a carpenter's square or straightedge. The distance between points Y and Z must be the same as points W and X. Point Y must be at a right angle to point W. All points taken together form a square. When squared, the front posts (only) are woven until the square is made (B). This is accomplished one strand at a time. The strand is tacked to the inside of the left seat rail and then to the inside of the right rail when the two posts have been woven.

chair. Allow the sealer coat of shellac to dry for three hours or longer, recoat with undiluted shellac, and allow to dry overnight. A final coat of varnish can be used over the sealer coat of shellac, but it is just a matter of prerogative. If a chair is to be exposed to outdoor conditions such as on a screened porch, then a varnish finish is advised.

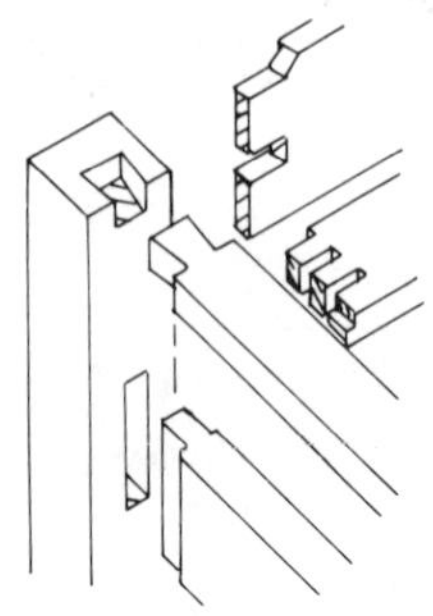

Suppliers

Locating sources of supplies necessary for craft work can be a difficult proposition for the beginning craftsperson. I have included a partial list of suppliers covering a broad range of materials. Each of the suppliers listed publishes a catalog and operates a mail-order business. The cost of catalogs varies with each supplier. It is best to call or write to determine the current catalog price.

Ball and Ball
463 West Lincoln Highway
Exton, PA 19341

Extensive line of quality reproduction brasses and hardware. Restoration and duplication service available for original brasses.

Barap Specialties
835 Bellows Avenue
Frankfurt, MI 49635

Assorted tools, hardware, lamp parts, and limited finishing supplies.

Cohasset Colonials
Cohasset, MA 02025

Reproductions of country antique furniture available in kit form. Limited brass, knob, and nail reproductions.

Conover Woodcraft Specialties Inc.
18125 Madison Road
Parkman, OH 44080

Limited line of quality woodworking tools. Full range of wood thread boxes and tops. Thread boxes available in kit form.

Constantine's
2050 Eastchester Road
Bronx, NY 10461

Extensive line of professional finishing products for the home consumer. Hardwoods in small or large quantities. Veneers, tools, clockworks, hardware, and craft items.

Craftsman
2727 South Mary Street
Chicago, IL 60608

Hardwoods in small and large quantities. Tools, clockworks, finishing supplies, and craft items.

Frog Tool Co. Ltd.
700 West Jackson Boulevard
Chicago, IL 60606

Quality hand woodworking tools. Finishing supplies. An extensive line of craft books and antique books.

Garret Wade
161 Avenue of the Americas
New York, NY 10013

Quality hand woodworking tools. Professional finishing supplies for the consumer.

Horton Brasses
P.O. Box 95
Nooks Hill Road
Cromwell, CT 06416

An extensive line of quality reproduction brasses and hardware.

Industrial Abrasives Company
642 North 8th Street
Reading, PA 19603

An extensive line of paper abrasives and cloth abrasives.

John Harra
Wood and Supply Co.
39 West 19th Street
New York, NY 10011

An extensive line of hardwoods (small and large quantities). Woodworking tools and finishing supplies.

Mason and Sullivan Co.
39 Blossom Avenue
Osterville, MA 02655

Clock movements, kits and music box movements.

Merritt's Antiques
R.D. 2
Douglassville PA 19518

Clock movements (antique and new). Reproduction clocks. An extensive line of clock repair parts and tools.

Peerless Rattan
45 Indian Lane-East
P.O. Box 8
Towaco, NJ 07082

Rush, cane, splint, and seating materials in single chair lots or large quantities. Craft books.

The Renovators Supply
Millers Falls, MA 01349

Assorted line of reproduction architectural hardware.

Tremont Nail Co.
P.O. Box 111
Wareham, MA 02511

An extensive line of square shank machine cut nails, hardware, and reproduction items.

Woodcraft
313 Montvale Avenue
Woburn, MA 01888

Extensive line of quality hand woodworking tools. Finishing supplies. Craft Items.

Woodworker's Supply Inc.
5604 Alameda, N.E.
Albuquerque, NM 87113

A quality line of hand woodworking tools. Finishing supplies.

Index

Edited by Steven Bolt